Business Record Keeping

third edition

David Cox
Michael Fardon
Douglas Portsmouth

Published by Osborne Books Limited
Unit 1B Everoak Estate
Bromyard Road
Worcester WR2 5HN

www.osbornebooks.co.uk

Printed by The Bath Press, Bath

A CIP catalogue record for this book is available from the British Library

ISBN 1 872962 33 5

introduction

aims

Business Record Keeping has been written to provide a practical study text for students taking courses based on the NCVQ Level 2 Accounting competences, and book-keeping courses offered by RSA and other awarding bodies.

contents

Business Record Keeping is an essentially practical text and contains progressive sections covering:

- documents used when buying and selling and returning goods
- cash and banking procedures
- double-entry book-keeping
- computer accounting
- stock control
- payment of wages
- the background to business – contract and communications

Each chapter is a unit in itself, containing fully worked examples of the topics covered, and followed by student activities covering the competences developed. In addition there are self-contained assignments which may be used in student competence assessment.

appendices

Appendix 1 contains blank documents which may be photocopied for use in student activities at the end of each chapter. Most assignments include the necessary blank documents, but the contents of Appendix 1 may be photocopied when required.

Appendix 2 contains the catalogue, price list, and customer discount list of Wyvern (Office Products) Limited and extracts from the catalogues of other fictitious stationery suppliers. A number of student activities and assignments involve reference to catalogues so that students can obtain competitive quotations and place orders.

note to the third edition

This third edition has retained much of the tried and tested structure of the earlier editions but has updated the chapters on payments to reflect changes in banking practice. The payroll section has also been amended to reflect recent budget changes. The tax tables incorporated as an Appendix in earlier editions have not been included, largely because up-to-date tax tables are now readily available from local tax offices.

David Cox, Michael Fardon, Douglas Portsmouth

Worcester

Spring 1998

acknowledgements

The authors wish to thank the following for their help with the reading and production of the book: Christopher Cormack, Jean Cox, Peter Fardon and Roger Petheram. Thanks are also due to the following for permission to reproduce material: the Association of Accounting Technicians and the Controller of Her Majesty's Stationery Office. The authors are also indebted to Sage plc for allowing their software to be used in the computer accounting exercises, and to the staff and students at Worcester College of Technology who tried and tested the exercises.

authors

David Cox has more than twenty years' experience teaching management and accountancy students over a wide range of levels. Formerly with the Management and Professional Studies Department at Worcester College of Technology, he now lectures on a freelance basis and carries out educational consultancy work in accountancy studies. He is author and joint author of a number of textbooks in the areas of accounting, finance and banking.

Michael Fardon has extensive teaching experience of a wide range of business and accountancy courses at Worcester College of Technology. He is now a writer and educational consultant in the area of business and finance.

Douglas Portsmouth has had over twenty years' experience in the engineering industry. He currently lectures at Worcester College of Technology where he has taught students over a wide range of levels. His present commitments include Industrial Management courses and the teaching of finance and accounting.

contents

assignments and computer exercises

assignments

Assignment work forms an important part of the teaching of business competences. In order to assist lecturers, trainers and students, eight fully-developed assignments have been included in the text. These assignments are ready for use, and for the most part incorporate all the blank forms that will be necessary. Lecturers and trainers may prefer to circulate photocopies of blank forms for student use. These are available in Appendix 1.

computer exercises

Nowadays many small businesses and almost all large businesses use computers to handle their business record keeping. In order to reflect fully current business practice, two fully developed computer exercises have been written, and thoroughly tested by lecturers and students:

- *Chapter 19 "Computer accounting"* which follows through a number of book-keeping transactions for a new business (supplemented by Assignment 7, which provides further computer accounting practice)

- *Chapter 23 "Computer payroll"* which sets up the payroll for a small business and then processes the payroll for a tax year

While these exercises have been written for use with Sage software, they can be amended easily so as to be suitable for users of other software. Furthermore, they have been written for a number of versions of the Sage software and, in the case of payroll, for the tax codes and allowances of any recent tax year.

Provision has also been made for the use of computer spreadsheets in the petty cash assignment (page 223). Many other student activities can be adapted for the use of spreadsheets: day books (Chapters 4 and 6), cash books (Chapter 15), and petty cash books (Chapter 16).

The authors would welcome comments from lecturers, trainers, and students on the use of these computer exercises.

NCVQ Level 2 Accounting competences

NVQ Unit	element	chapters
1	**recording and accounting for cash transactions**	
	1.1 record and bank monies received	12,13
	1.2 make and record payments	12,13,14
	1.3 maintain petty cash records	16
	1.4 account for cash and bank transactions	15,17
2	**recording and accounting for credit transactions**	
	2.1 process documents relating to goods and services supplied on credit	1,2,3
	2.2 process documents relating to goods and services received on credit	1,2,3
	2.3 Account for goods and services supplied on credit	4 to 11,19
	2.4 Account for goods and services received on credit	4 to 11,19
3	**recording and accounting for payroll transactions**	
	3.1 operate and maintain a payroll accounting system	22,23
	3.2 make authorised payments to employees	20 to 23
	3.3 make authorised payments, claims and returns to external agencies	20 to 23

1 Business organisations and record keeping

This book aims to explain and illustrate the recording of business financial transactions. These transactions, which are normally carried out by the *accounting* staff in a business, involve the procedures for:

- buying and selling goods and services
- making and receiving payments
- dealing with the bank
- paying wages

We will deal with these specific financial transactions later in the book. In this chapter we will examine the context in which they operate by looking at:

- the different types of business organisation
- the way in which the accounting staff fit into the structure of a business organisation

different types of organisation

If you are working for an organisation or applying for a job, it is important to realise the type of organisation with which you are dealing. The first distinction to be drawn is that between the *public sector* organisation and the *private sector* business organisation.

Public sector organisations are government owned or government controlled, and include large public corporations such as the Post Office, bodies such as the Civil Service and more local organisations such as the local Council.

Private sector business organisations, on the other hand, are not owned by the government but either directly or indirectly by private individuals. They include one-person businesses, partnerships and companies. Examples range from well-known names such as Marks and Spencer, J Sainsbury and Barclays Bank, to the local dentist, builder and corner shop.

The distinction between these forms of organisation will be explained in the next section. The important point to remember is that they all need to record financial transactions accurately and with proper documentation: whether it is Sainsbury's purchasing ten thousand frozen chickens or the corner-shop buying fifty packets of fish fingers, the principles of business record keeping remain exactly the same.

business organisations:
sole trader, partnership, limited company

sole trader

A sole trader is an individual trading in his or her name, or under a trading name.

This is the simplest way to set up in business. Your local plumber will most likely be a sole trader; if you look at his business card it will either state just his name, eg 'Stan Taylor' or give a trading name, eg 'Henwick Plumbing Services' plus his name and address.

The advantages of being a sole trader are simplicity and cheapness of operation, freedom (you are your own boss) and control. But it is also the most risky form of business (if the enterprise becomes bankrupt, so do you) and one of the most time-consuming (long hours, few holidays). As a sole trader you will be personally responsible for keeping accurate financial records.

partnership

If the sole trader plumber sees a big market in shower installation and wants to go into business with an electrician, they may form a *partnership* of two.

A partnership is a group of individuals working together in business, aiming to make a profit.

The advantages of forming a partnership are added expertise in the business (an electrician in this case), often more money available to run the business, and relief for holidays. The disadvantages include the tendency for partners to fall out with each other (a very common situation!) and the fact that if the business goes bankrupt so do *all* the partners. Common examples of partnerships include dentists, doctors, solicitors and accountants. Normally there are between two and twenty partners in a partnership. A partnership, like a sole trader, needs to keep accurate financial records. Because of the more elaborate nature of the business, these will usually be more complex than for a sole trader.

limited company

The largest business organisations are usually limited companies. A limited company is quite different from a sole trader and a partnership in that it exists as a business in its own right, separately from its owners, the shareholders, who have only limited liability for the company's debts.

A limited company is a separate legal body, owned by shareholders and managed by directors.

There are two types of limited company: a *private limited company* and a *public limited company*.

Private limited companies, which have 'limited' (abbreviated to 'ltd') in the name, are usually small or medium-sized businesses. They raise their finance from shareholders in return for *shares* which are held in private hands, and are *not* for sale through the Stock Exchange. Often the shares in private limited companies are held by the directors who run the company.

Public limited companies, which have 'plc' in their name (eg J Sainsbury plc) are larger limited companies whose shares may be traded through the Stock Exchange. A member of the public can buy shares in J Sainsbury plc, whereas the same private investor cannot usually buy the shares of a *private* limited company, such as the local garage. There is no significant difference between private and public limited companies, apart from that of size and availability of shares. The major advantage of a *limited* company is that if the company goes bankrupt (insolvent) the shareholders – the owners – do not also become bankrupt. The most they can lose is their money investment in that company.

business record keeping

The purpose of this book is to explain in detail the financial records kept by a business, whether that business is a sole trader, a partnership or a limited company If you consider all the business activities undertaken during a working day, you will see that there are many different transactions taking place, all of which need recording accurately.   The following example examines the transactions of two businesses:

* *Stan Taylor,* a sole trader plumber, who carries out jobbing work and employs two assistants
* *Osborne Electronics Limited,* a computer and office machine company, which supplies businesses in the area and employs eight people

STAN TAYLOR
(sole trader)

sales of goods and services
* installation of lavatory for Fred Lush, £250 paid in cash, receipt given by Stan
* repair of burst pipe at City Architect's office, invoice for £95.50 issued to City Council, payment to be made in 30 days' time (normally a cheque will be posted to Stan)

purchases and payment of expenses
* pay for jacuzzi bath, a special order from the manufacturer, a £750 cheque issued by Stan
* settle account with builders merchant, a £1,750 cheque issued by Stan for items bought over the last six weeks
* buy petrol for van, pay £12 in cash at local garage

visit the local branch of the National Bank plc
* pay in cheques totalling £1,753.95
* cash a cheque, £250, for wages for employees
* query charges on the bank statement

pay wages
* complete documentation, including wage slips, and pay employees £250 for work carried out for the business

OSBORNE ELECTRONICS LTD
(limited company)

sales of goods and services
* sale of fax machine to Merton Textiles, cost £750, cheque received with order, receipted invoice sent in the post
* installation of photocopier for Mereford Tourist Office, cost £2,450, invoice issued to City Council,   payment to be made in 30 days' time (normally a cheque will be posted to Osborne Electronics)

purchases and payment of expenses
* pay for colour laser printer, a special order from the manufacturer, a £2,750 cheque issued by Osborne Electronics
* settle account with Nippon Importers for computer software, a £5,675 cheque issued by Osborne Electronics for goods bought over the previous two months
* issue cheque for £3,500 to Wessex Insurance Brokers for comprehensive insurance of premises, stock and other risks

visit the local branch of the National Bank plc
* pay in cheques totalling £10,645.50, money received from customers
* cash a cheque, £2,500, for the week's wages
* query charges on the bank statement

pay wages
* complete documentation, including wage slips, make up pay packets, totalling £2,500

reasons for business record keeping
As you will see from the very varied items in the illustrations above, recording financial transactions is a complex business, not just measuring money in and money out, but involving a number of complications:

timing of payments	you have to keep track of • who owes you what, and when the payment is due • amounts that you owe, and when the payment is due
banking money	you have to record what you pay into the bank and what you draw out, and know what you have in your account
wages	you need to record what work has been done for you and the amounts paid in wages
stock	you need to know what items you have in stock, eg for Stan, the stock will consist of plumbing items

We will not at this stage explore in any detail *how* these transactions are recorded – such areas will be covered later in the book – but it is worth noting that if these transactions are not recorded accurately, the owner of the business and other interested parties will not know how the business is progressing!

other parties interested in the financial records

The owner of a business is not the only person who has to consult the financial records; they are needed for other people interested in how a business is progressing.

The bank manager – to assess lending propositions

The tax authorities – the Inland Revenue and HM Customs and Excise (the 'VAT man') – can inspect the records in order to make sure the owner is not avoiding payment of tax!

The accountant, in the case of a limited company business, will need to see the financial records for the annual audit which is required by law. Partnerships and sole traders may also employ an accountant to advise about and oversee the accounts, although this is not required by law.

accounting functions within the organisation

Whereas a sole trader is likely to carry out all the financial transactions himself (or herself), an organisation such a limited company will be structured into different levels of authority, each with its own responsibilities and duties. The diagram below shows an accounts department.

position	**role and duties**
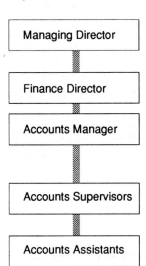 Managing Director	directs all company policy, including financial policy
Finance Director	responsible for financial policy: buying, selling, raising money, controlling costs
Accounts Manager	responsible for the running of the Accounts Department, liaises with the Finance Director and other Departmental Managers
Accounts Supervisors	in charge of the day-to-day running of the Accounts Department, working alongside the Accounts Assistants
Accounts Assistants	processing the day-to-day financial transactions of the company: dealing with documents,banking transactions, writing up the books, paying wages

You should note the following points from the structure chart:

- the routine transactions are carried out at the 'Accounts Assistants' level – this is the area covered by this book
- the middle levels – Supervisors and Managers – are concerned more with day-to-day decision making
- the higher levels – the Directors – are mostly involved with policy making

It must be stressed that the chart represents a limited company structure. Other forms of business may divide the functions areas of transactions, decision-making and policy making differently. A sole trader is likely to carry out all three!

You will appreciate when looking at the structure chart that communication between the different parts of the business is of great importance. Equally important is the ability of the business to communicate with its customers.

business communications

Communicating with your colleagues and your customers is an essential part of your job, if you are in employment. If you are studying, you are likely to be required to draw up the basic forms of written communication as part of your course work.

The communication process involves a number of stages

- formulating your message
- choosing the means of sending it
- composing and sending it
- confirming that it has been received
- dealing with any queries and carrying out any follow-up actions

In business organisations there are likely to be many set procedures for communicating: for example there will be standard letters on word processor file for giving price quotations, for chasing up bad payers, and so on. There will be situations, however, when you may be required to compose one of the following forms of communication:

internal communications	*external communications*
a memorandum	a letter
a note	a fax message

In Chapter 25 "Business communications" we set out in detail the format of these written communications. You will be required to produce them as part of the Student Activities and Assignments in this book, so refer to Chapter 25 whenever necessary.

business contracts

Part of your course may require you to understand the legal background to business dealings. The cornerstone of business law is the *contract*. A contract is a legally binding agreement between two individuals, and occurs, for example when

- goods are bought or sold – the contract of sale
- an employer employs an employee – the contract of employment

If one of the individuals breaks the agreement, the wronged person can take that person to court.

The theory of contract requires a full explanation, and this is set out in Chapter 24 "Business contracts" to which you should refer as and when you need.

chapter summary

❑ There are three main types of business organisation: sole trader, partnership and limited company.

❑ Business organisations need to record business transactions for:
- the sale of goods and services
- purchases of stock and other items
- payment of expenses
- operating the bank account
- paying wages
- maintaining stock

❑ The records are kept for the benefit of the management of the business, and outside bodies such as the bank, the tax authorities and the accountant.

❑ The role of accounting staff within a business will vary according to the level of seniority within the organisation. This book deals with the day-to-day financial administration of a business carried out at the clerical level.

❑ Written communications – both internal and external – are essential to the efficient running of a business. Important forms of written communication include
- the letter
- the memorandum
- the fax
- the note

In the next chapter we look at the documents involved when a business orders goods from a supplier.

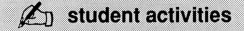 **student activities**

1.1 Make a list of all the organisations with which you have dealings during a typical working or studying day. These organisations should include any that provide you with goods or services (eg corner shop, bus service). State whether they are
(a) public sector or private sector organisations, and if they are private sector
(b) whether they are sole trader, partnership or limited company businesses

1.2 You work as an assistant in a firm of accountants, Granby and Granby of 3, The Bullring, Mereford Green, MR7 6FT. You are asked to draft a letter for the signature of your Manager Mr H Edwards to explain to Mr T Henderson of 7 Hillview Gardens, Mereford MR2 5CV the difference between a sole trader, a partnership, and a limited company. Mr Henderson has written in asking for advice for setting up a new business (letter dated five days before today's date).Your Manager says "Do not go into too much detail, but do stress to what extent the owner is liable for business debts."

1.3 Explain why business transactions need to be recorded. What sort of people are interested in them?

2 Business documents: ordering goods

Business documents form the paperwork involved in the buying and selling of goods or services. The businesses concerned may be selling to each other, or to members of the public. The amount of documentation involved will vary depending upon what is being purchased or sold, and by whom. A private purchase in a shop by you or me may not necessarily involve any documentation unless perhaps we are given, or ask for, a receipt, but a business purchase involving quotations and delivery will require a number of different documents to satisfy the business' operating procedures.

The flow chart below summarises the basic flow of business documents between buyer and seller, assuming that the business' operating procedure requires all of these. It must be appreciated that not all business transactions will require all of these documents. For example, the enquiry and quotation stages may be carried out over the telephone, if the order is a small one, or if the goods have been ordered before. It is also possible that the seller may issue a catalogue, price list and pre-printed order form, in which case an order may be posted or faxed to the supplier. The flow chart therefore shows the full and formal procedure for ordering and paying for goods.

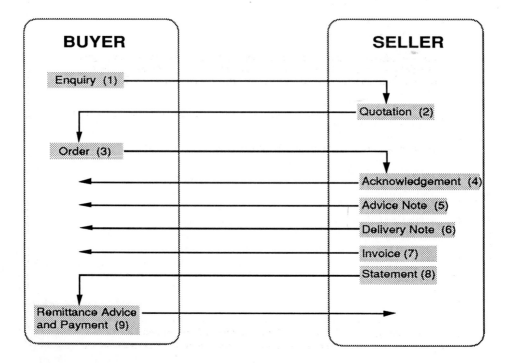

The following pages illustrate and explain the format of each of the business documents. The format is a guidance layout and may not be followed to the last detail by every business; many businesses have their own blank documents printed to suit their own purpose, or they may produce them on a computer. The documents follow a Mereford based company, Camtec Ltd., purchasing tables and chairs, from Wyvern (Office Products) Ltd., for use in its works canteen.

letter of enquiry (1)

A person wishing to buy goods will try to find out information about those products. He or she will send a letter of enquiry to a seller (or many sellers), requesting such information as:

- specifications (details of the goods)
- prices
- delivery period

The enquiry may be a letter or it may be a standard printed form on which the information required is filled in as required. The illustration below shows a letter signed by Don Shaw, the Chief Buyer.

CAMTEC Ltd
18 Forth Street
Mereford MR2 5FT

Tel: (0605) 44672   Fax: (0605) 14121   VAT Reg No 910 729097

---

1 September 19-9

Wyvern (Office Products) Ltd
12 Lower Hyde Street
MEREFORD MR1 2JF

Dear Sirs

We would be pleased to receive, as soon as possible, your quotation for the supply of the following items. Your quotation should include delivery period and inclusive price.

4 x Steel framed stackable canteen tables approx. 1 metre square

16 x Stacking chairs with one piece moulded seat

Yours faithfully

D. Shaw

D Shaw
Head Buyer

Registered office: 18 Forth Street, Mereford, MR2 5FT. Registered Number 21487612

quotation (2)

Having received the enquiry, the seller will send a quotation giving details of what can be offered. This can take many forms: a price list which gives a description and price, or an illustrated leaflet or catalogue with prices indicated, or a letter headed 'Quotation' giving the required details. Appendix 3 in this book sets out the sales catalogue of Wyvern (Office Products) Ltd. and extracts from other catalogues.

In the example of a letter below, note how the seller uses a separate catalogue reference number to identify each item offered; this helps to avoid confusion where two particular descriptions are so similar that a mistake can be made. The abbreviation 'Cat' is commonly used (as here) to refer to a catalogue number.

The quotation also states that the goods are 'VAT exclusive'. This means that the price does not include VAT (Value Added Tax). VAT is a tax charged by the government on the sale of most goods and services, and will, in this case, be added to the price quoted at a later stage.

QUOTATION

Wyvern (Office Products) Ltd.
12 Lower Hyde Street
MEREFORD   MR1 2JF

Tel: (0605) 24185
Fax: (0605) 11461
VAT Reg No 841 116011

4 September 19-9

Mr D Shaw
Head Buyer
Camtec Ltd
18 Forth Street
MEREFORD MR2 5FT

Dear Mr Shaw

Thank you for your letter of enquiry dated 1 September. We are pleased to offer the following quotation. Please note that prices and delivery periods are those current at the time of writing and are only valid for a period of three months from the date of this letter, after which time a new quotation should be requested.

   4 Canteen tables, Cat No F1034 @ £47.75 each, VAT
     exclusive (tables are stain, heat and scratch resistant,
     welded steel frame, stackable, sized 90 cm x 90 cm and
     available in light oak or teak finish)

  16 Stacking chairs, Cat No C1025 @ £8.75 each, VAT
     exclusive (chairs have one piece polypropylene seat
     available in grey, orange, charcoal or brown; frames are
     welded steel)

Delivery is carriage paid, 10 days from receipt of order.

Yours sincerely

J. Lock

J LOCK
Sales Manager

Registered Office: 12 Lower Hyde Street, Mereford, MR1 2JF. Registered Number: 8214612

purchase order (3)

If the buyer finds the quotation satisfactory, he or she will send the seller an official purchase order which sets out details of:

- the goods that are required (with catalogue number)
- the place for delivery (this may be a separate warehouse address)
- the date delivery is required
- the agreed price (this may be an item price, as shown below, or an estimated total price)
- the quality or specification required

Note in the example below that the order has a number in the top right-hand corner: this number reference makes it easy to refer to a particular order and easier to find the order in a filing system.

PURCHASE ORDER

Order No: 13448

CAMTEC Ltd
18 Forth Street
Mereford MR2 5FT

Tel: (0605) 44672   Fax: (0605) 14121   VAT Reg No 910 729097

10 September 19-9

Wyvern (Office Products) Ltd
12 Lower Hyde Street
MEREFORD   MR1 2JF

Quantity	Cat. No.	Description	Price £ p
4	F1034	90 cm x 90 cm Canteen table (teak finish)	47.75 each
16	C1025	Stacking chairs (colour charcoal)	8.75 each

Delivery to:
Factory 'A' Stores, CAMTEC Ltd,
Ford Road Industrial Estate, Mereford, MR7 0BE.

Delivery 10 days from date of order. Carriage paid.

D. Shaw
D SHAW
Head Buyer

Registered office: 18 Forth Street, Mereford, MR2 5FT. Registered Number 21487612

acknowledgement of order (4)

Having received the order from the customer, the seller will often send an acknowledgement stating:

• that the order has been received
• that the goods required can be supplied
• when delivery is expected to be made

The acknowledgement may be in the form of a letter or a printed form and repeats the information set out on the order. When the buyer receives the acknowledgement, he or she will check it thoroughly to see that it agrees with the order.

ACKNOWLEDGEMENT

Wyvern (Office Products) Ltd.
12 Lower Hyde Street
MEREFORD   MR1 2JF

Tel: (0605) 24185
Fax: (0605) 11461
VAT Reg No 841 116011

12 September 19-9

Mr D Shaw
Head Buyer
Camtec Ltd
18 Forth Street
MEREFORD   MR2 5FT

Dear Mr Shaw

Order No. 13448

We thank you for your recent order dated 10 September and confirm that we can comply fully with your instructions.

Your order:

 4 x Canteen tables, teak finish, Cat. No. F1034 @ £47.75 each
16 x Stacking chairs, charcoal, Cat. No. C1025 @ £8.75 each

We confirm delivery will be 10 days from order date at your Factory 'A' Stores, Ford Road Industrial Estate, Mereford, MR7 0BE.

Yours sincerely

J. Lock

J Lock
Sales Manager

Registered Office: 12 Lower Hyde Street, Mereford, MR1 2JF.   Registered Number: 8214612

advice note (5)

The advice note is sent ahead of the goods to the buyer's office, to advise the buyer that the goods are on the way and their arrival can be expected. If the goods do not arrive within a reasonable period of time (depending upon how far the goods must travel), then the buyer will notify the seller so that enquiries can be made with the carrier of the goods.

ADVICE NOTE   **No:** 143721

Wyvern (Office Products) Ltd.   Tel: (0605) 24185
12 Lower Hyde Street   Fax: (0605) 11461
MEREFORD   MR1 2JF   VAT Reg No 841 116011

19 September 19-9

Mr D Shaw
Head Buyer
Camtec Ltd
18 Forth Street
MEREFORD   MR2 5FT

Order No. 13448
Despatch details: road 8 packages

Quantity	Cat. No.	Description	Price £ p
4	F1034	90 cm x 90 cm Canteen table (teak finish)	47.75 each
16	C1025	Stacking chairs (colour charcoal)	8.75 each

Delivery to:
Factory 'A' Stores, CAMTEC Ltd,
Ford Road Industrial Estate, Mereford, MR7 0BE.

J. Lock

J LOCK
Sales Manager

Registered Office: 12 Lower Hyde Street, Mereford, MR1 2JF. Registered Number: 8214612

delivery note (6)

The delivery note is usually packed in with the goods and when the buyer unpacks the parcels a check can be made that the items stated on the delivery note have been received.

Where a company uses its own vehicles to deliver goods the driver will be given a copy of the delivery note which he or she will get the receiver of the goods to sign in order to confirm receipt.

If the goods are delivered by transport other than the seller's own, then a document, very much the same as the delivery note but called a consignment note, is given to the carrier, to obtain a signature.

DELIVERY NOTE   No. 145712

Wyvern (Office Products) Ltd.
12 Lower Hyde Street
MEREFORD   MR1 2JF

Tel: (0605) 24185
Fax: (0605) 11461
VAT Reg No 841 116011

20 September 19-9

Mr D Shaw
Head Buyer
Camtec Ltd
18 Forth Street
MEREFORD MR2 5FT

Order No. 13448
Despatch details: road 8 packages

Quantity	Cat. No.	Description
4	F1034	Canteen tables
16	C1025	Stacking chairs

Deliver to Factory 'A' Stores,
Camtec Ltd., Ford Road Industrial Estate, Mereford, MR7 0BE.

J. Lock

J LOCK
Sales Manager

Received 8 packages

signed ....

on behalf of ....

Registered Office: 12 Lower Hyde Street, Mereford, MR1 2JF. Registered Number: 8214612

invoice (7)

This is one of the most important and probably the most well known of trading documents. It is sent from the seller to the buyer to advise how much is owed to the seller for a particular delivery of goods. The invoice states:

- the quantity of goods supplied
- the individual prices
- the VAT charged
- the total amount owed

It need not necessarily be regarded as an immediate demand for payment because many invoices may be sent by a seller to a buyer, and it may be that the buyer will pay for all the invoices in one payment at the end of the month.

Where the buyer's office is separate from the warehouse or factory, the invoice is sent to the office. The invoice may either be typed manually or produced on the business' computer system. The example shown on the next page has been typed on the firm's printed stationery.

Note that the invoice shows:

- The individual invoice number and the buyer's order number. This helps the buyer know to which order the invoice refers.

- Date/tax point: this shows the date for Value Added Tax purposes (the tax point), on which the sale was made.

- VAT is calculated at 17.5% (the current rate) of the total selling price of £331.00 = £57.92. The total amount due to be paid is therefore £331.00 + £57.92 = £388.92. What happens to the VAT is explained in full at the end of this chapter.

statement of account (8)

Rather than expecting a customer to pay for each individual invoice that has been sent (which could mean that he would have to write out several cheques during the month), the seller will send a statement of account at the end of the month to sum up all the business that has taken place during the month. This statement may be typed out manually or it may be produced on the business' computer.

The statement of account (illustrated on page 19) will show:

- any amounts outstanding and unpaid from previous statements shown normally by the words 'previous balance' or 'balance brought forward' in a 'Balance' column on the right

- amounts which increase the debt the buyer owes to the seller, i.e. invoices sent, in a 'Debit' column on the left

- amounts which decrease the debt, i.e. credit notes (dealt with in the next chapter) issued, and any payments made, in a 'Credit' column

- the amount due at the end of the month at the bottom of the 'Balance' column

You will see on the statement illustrated on page 19 the invoice no. 10452 for the tables and chairs entered on 25 September, the date of issue. At the end of the month Camtec Ltd. owes £547.89.

INVOICE

No. 10452

Wyvern (Office Products) Ltd.
12 Lower Hyde Street
MEREFORD   MR1 2JF

Tel: (0605) 24185
Fax: (0605) 11461
VAT Reg No 841 116011

Date/Tax Point:
25 September 19-9

Accounts Dept
Camtec Ltd
18 Forth Street
MEREFORD   MR2 5FT

Order No. 13448

Quantity	Description	Catalogue Number	Unit Price £ p	Total Amount £ p
4	Canteen tables	F1034	47 75	191 00
16	Stacking chairs	C1025	8 75	140 00
			Total excluding VAT	331 00
			VAT	57 92
			Total due	388 92

Registered Office: 12 Lower Hyde Street, Mereford, MR1 2JF. Registered Number: 8214612

STATEMENT OF ACCOUNT

Wyvern (Office Products) Ltd.
12 Lower Hyde Street
MEREFORD   MR1 2JF

Tel: (0605) 24185
Fax: (0605) 11461
VAT Reg No 841 116011

Accounts Dept
Camtec Ltd
18 Forth Street
MEREFORD   MR2 5FT

Date	Reference	Debit £ p	Credit £ p	Balance £ p
19-9				
30 Aug.	previous balance			200 00
2 Sep.	Invoice no. 10381	120 60		320 60
10 Sep.	Payment		150 50	170 10
25 Sep.	Credit note no. 11461		11 13	158 97
25 Sep.	Invoice no. 10452	388 92		547 89
	Amount now due			547 89

Registered Office: 12 Lower Hyde Street, Mereford, MR1 2JF.   Registered Number: 8214612

remittance advice and payment (9)

A buyer making payment to a seller may not wish to pay all the amounts outstanding on the statement of account, but will wish to indicate to the seller which invoices are being paid. This is shown by sending a *remittance advice* and a cheque. The advice shows the amount of the payment and the invoices to which it relates. It may either be a typed form or a computer produced advice. Some computer produced remittance advices have the cheque attached, in which case the computer will print the details on the cheque.

Note that the remittance advice below:

- pays invoice 10381 (see the statement on page 19)
- takes into account a cheque payment made on 6 September
- takes into account the refund from credit note 11461
- shows a 'C' against the credit note and the cheque payment
- ignores invoice 10452 which has just been received (this will be paid in November)

REMITTANCE ADVICE   No. 146

CAMTEC Ltd
18 Forth Street
Mereford MR2 5FT

Tel: (0605) 44672   Fax: (0605) 14121   VAT Reg No 910 729097

---

6 October 19-9

Wyvern (Office Products) Ltd
12 Lower Hyde Street
MEREFORD   MR1 2JF

Cheque reference no: 252147

Date	Description	Reference No.	Amount Payable £ p	Balance £ p
19-9				
30 Aug.	Previous balance	Statement	200 00	200 00
2 Sep.	Invoice	No.10381	120 60	320 60
6 Sep.	Payment	Chq.291703	150 50C	170 10
25 Sep.	Credit note	No.11461	11 13C	158 97
		Total cheque enclosed		158 97

Registered office: 18 Forth Street, Mereford, MR2 5FT. Registered Number 21487612

prime documents

Some of the documents looked at in the chapter will be used by the business' accounts department to update the accounting records. These documents are known as *prime documents*. Examples of prime documents illustrated so far in this chapter include:

- invoices (issued and received)
- credit notes (issued and received)

We shall be looking at how these prime documents are recorded in the accounting system in later chapters.

VAT (Value Added Tax)

VAT (Value Added Tax) is a government tax on the selling price charged to buyers at every level of sales, from the first supplier to the final consumer.

As we have seen on some of the business documents illustrated in this chapter, VAT is added to the purchase price of items sold. On this and the next page we look in further detail at the workings of this tax, and how it affects businesses and other organisations.

registering for VAT

In Britain most businesses with a sales turnover (i.e. the total amount of sales in a given period) over a certain limit must be registered for VAT. This turnover figure (£50,000 in 1998/99) is increased from time-to-time as a part of the Chancellor of the Exchequer's budget proposals.

Once registered, a business is issued with a VAT registration number which must be quoted on all invoices and on other business documents. It charges VAT at the standard rate (currently 17.5 per cent) on all taxable supplies, i.e. whenever it sells goods, or supplies a service. From the supplier's viewpoint the tax so charged is known as *output tax*. A number of items are *zero-rated* and no tax is charged when they are supplied: for example, food and children's clothing are zero-rated.

Businesses registered for VAT must pay to the VAT authorities (H M Customs and Excise Department):

- the amount of VAT collected (output tax)
- *less* the amount of VAT charged to them (input tax) on all taxable supplies bought in

If the amount of input tax is larger than the output tax, the business claims a refund of the difference from H M Customs and Excise.

Every three months a form known as a VAT return (Form VAT 100) has to be completed, although some smaller businesses submit a VAT return on an annual basis. Payment of VAT due (if the business is not claiming a refund) is made with the VAT return.

exempt supplies

A few types of goods and services are neither standard-rated nor zero-rated for VAT: instead they are *exempt*. The effect of this is that the supplier of such goods cannot charge VAT on outputs (as is the case with zero-rated goods). However, unlike the supplier of zero-rated goods, the supplier of exempt goods cannot claim back all the tax which has been paid on inputs. Examples of exempt supplies include postal services, loans of money, sales or lettings of land or some property, and certain types of education and health care.

a tax on the final consumer

VAT is a tax which is paid by the final consumer of the goods. If we take, for example, a member of the public buying a computer for £705, the amount paid includes VAT of £105 (i.e. 17.5% of £600). The buyer stands the cost of the VAT, but the VAT is actually *paid* to H M Customs and Excise by all those involved in the manufacturing and selling process. This procedure is illustrated by the flow chart shown in fig. 2.1 below. You will see that the right-hand column shows the amount of VAT paid to the Customs and Excise at each stage of the process.

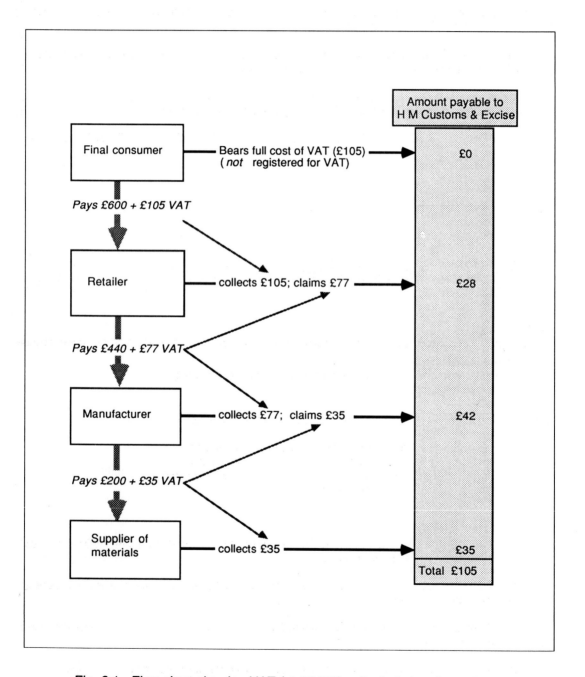

Fig. 2.1   Flow chart showing VAT (at 17.5%) collected at various stages

chapter summary

❏ In order that businesses may record their buying and selling transactions accurately, it is necessary that correct documentation is forwarded and received.

❏ There are a number of documents involved, although not all businesses will use all of them. The two most important ones are the purchase order and the invoice.

❏ The purchase order is the document which states the requirements of the buyer and the invoice states the value of the sales and the amount payable by the buyer.

❏ In order to obtain payment, the seller must normally send regular statements of account so that the buyer can forward payment with a remittance advice.

❏ VAT (Value Added Tax) is a government tax on the selling price charged to buyers of most goods and services, and must be included where appropriate on invoices.

student activities

Notes:
* *Some of the Student Activities require blank forms.   The forms in Appendix 1 of this book may be photocopied as required.*
* *VAT amounts calculated are normally rounded down to the nearest penny.*

2.1   Using the following words, complete the sentences listed below.

List of words to be used to complete the sentences:

advice note	*delivery note*
invoice	*remittance advice*
statement of account	

(a) An .... advises the buyer that the goods have been despatched and their arrival can be expected soon.

(b) A .... is forwarded to a buyer to advise the total amount due at the end of the month.

(c) When a buyer is making payment to a seller, a .... may be forwarded with the cheque.

(d) A .... advises the buyer what goods have been received.

(e) An .... advises the buyer of how much is owed to the seller for a particular order.

2.2 (a) Obtain from your work placement or place of work one each of the following documents:
* order form
* delivery note
* invoice
* statement of account (not bank statement)

(b) Explain the purpose of each of the documents.

(c) List and explain the details that need to be completed on each document (but not the preprinted details).

2.3 Calculate the total price, VAT amount (at a rate of 17.5%), and the total invoice price on the following orders received by Wyvern (Office Products) Ltd.:

	Quantity	Cat No	Description	Unit Price
Order no. 101	1	C1040	Chair	£142.50
Order no. 102	2	C1033	Chair	£63.25
Order no. 103	2	C1010	Chair	£52.95
Order no. 104	3	C1021	Chair	£48.95

2.4 Write out the purchase orders to Wyvern (Office Products) Ltd. from Martin Westdale, 24 Thornbrook Grove, Spalding, SP2 8AK, for the following items (which appear in the catalogue in Appendix 3):

Order No. 111   1 x Fisley Series 39 Multidrawer 15 cabinet,
colour goose grey

Order No. 112   1 x Fisley two drawer filing cabinet, colour coffee and cream
2 x Fisley four drawer filing cabinet, colour coffee and cream

Order No. 113   6 x Wyvern office table 180 cm x 60 cm, teak finish
6 x Wyvern office table 120 cm x 60 cm, teak finish
12 x Wyvern metal framed chairs (no arms), charcoal finish

2.5 You are a clerk at Wyvern (Office Products) Ltd. Complete the invoices for each of the above purchase orders.

2.6 H. Willis of 24 High Street, Mereford, MR1 2AJ, has an account with Wyvern (Office Products) Ltd. At the beginning of April 19-1, the outstanding balance of this account was £113.00 owing. During the month, the following invoices were sent by Wyvern (Office Products) Ltd.:

6 April	£140.25	(invoice no. 21073)
12 April	£84.75	(invoice no. 21391)
24 April	£91.37	(invoice no. 21723)
28 April	£52.84	(invoice no. 21895)

(a) Complete the statement of account as sent out by Wyvern (Office Products) Ltd. on 1 May 19-1.

(b) It is H. Willis' policy to pay only invoices that are over two weeks old. Complete the remittance advice that H. Willis will forward to Wyvern (Office Products) Ltd. on 5 May 19-1.

(c) In May 19-1 Wyvern (Office Products) Ltd. send a further two invoices (No. 22001, 6 May, £100.75; No. 22089, 12 May, £179.32) to H. Willis. Complete the statement of account sent by Wyvern (Office Products) Ltd. on 1 June 19-1.

ASSIGNMENT 1

Ordering stationery: Wellan, Wellan and Smart

SITUATION 1

You are Joan (or John) Brown. You are in charge of the stationery store at the local Estate Agents, Wellan, Wellan & Smart, 18 London Road, Mereford, MR6 2JK.

The stock of the following items are running low:

- bond white 85 gsm paper
- copier white 80 gsm paper
- plain white envelopes, size 220 x 110 mm

STUDENT TASKS

1. Write letters of enquiry requesting a quotation for 20 reams of each type of paper and 2000 envelopes (note: 1 ream = 500 sheets). The letters, which you can sign, should be sent to:

    - Wyvern (Office Products) Ltd.,12 Lower Hyde Street, Mereford, MR1 2JF.
    - Pen & Ink Ltd., 12 Haven Road, Mereford, MR1 8ST.
    - Quality Quill, 215 West Street, Mereford, MR2 6PQ.

    If you wish, you can prepare the letters on a word processor.

2. In reply to your letters of enquiry, you receive catalogues from each of the stationery supply companies (relevant extracts from these catalogues can be found in Appendix 3).

    You are to work out the cost of your requirements from each of the three companies and forward a purchase order (see next page) to the company offering the cheapest quotation. (The order is No. 52670, dated 10 September 19-1 and signed by Mr. J. Wellan.)

PURCHASE ORDER

Order No:

Wellan, Wellan & Smart
Estate Agents
18 London Road
Mereford   MR6 2JK
Telephone (0605) 29173   Fax (0605) 29029

Quantity	Cat. No.	Description	Price £ p

J. Wellan, S. Wellan & R. Smart.   *VAT Reg No 207 710652*

SITUATION 2

You are now to assume the role of Jackie (or Jack, if you prefer) Smith, who works in the accounting department of the company which receives the purchase order prepared in Situation 1.

STUDENT TASKS

1. Assuming the goods have been ordered and despatched to Wellan, Wellan & Smart, complete the invoice for the transaction. Date the invoice 20 September 19-1 and number it 526214.

INVOICE   No.

Date/Tax Point:

Order No.

Quantity	Description	Catalogue Number	Unit Price £ p	Total Amount £ p

		Total excluding VAT	
		VAT	
		Total due	

2.   The business procedure for the stationery company is to forward statements of account at the end of each month. You are to prepare the statement of account which will be sent to Wellan, Wellan & Smart on 30 September 19-1.

The balance outstanding was £101.50 on 1 September 19-1.

Other transactions were:
2 September 19-1, invoice no. 526001   £84.00
5 September 19-1, payment made by cheque   £101.50

STATEMENT OF ACCOUNT

Date	Reference	Debit £ p	Credit £ p	Balance £ p
			Amount now due	

SITUATION 3

You are now to return to your original role of Joan (or John Brown) and undertake this final task.

STUDENT TASK

Assuming Wellan, Wellan & Smart pay all their outstanding debt to the stationery company, complete the remittance advice on 5 October 19-1.

REMITTANCE ADVICE		**No.**		

Wellan, Wellan & Smart
Estate Agents
18 London Road
Mereford   MR6 2JK
Telephone (0605) 29173   Fax (0605) 29029

Date	Description	Reference No.	Amount Payable £ p	Balance £ p
	Total cheque enclosed			

J. Wellan, S. Wellan & R. Smart.   *VAT Reg No 207 710652*

3 Terms of business

In Chapter 2 we looked at the basic documents required when goods are bought and sold. This chapter looks in more detail at the terms and conditions of the sale, and also at the documents involved when faulty or unwanted goods are returned to the supplier. The chapter concludes with an examination of the procedure for checking incoming documents and for authorising payment of invoices.

invoice terms

Look at the invoice on the next page (fig. 3.1). You will see that there are a number of additions and numerical differences from the invoice shown in the previous chapter (page 18):

The *additional terms* found on this invoice are:

• terms 2.5% 30 days, otherwise net (i.e. a 2.5% discount offered for early settlement)
• carriage paid
• E & OE

The *totals* of the invoice differ because of the discount offered:

• the VAT total is lower
• the total amount due is lower

We will now look in more detail at these terms and conditions often found on invoices.

E & OE
You will see these letters shown in the bottom left-hand corner of the invoice on the opposite page. They stand for the words *Errors and Omissions Excepted*. Here the seller is telling the buyer that he reserves the right to correct any errors made on the invoice at some later date. For example, the invoice total reads £387.47 but, had the keyboard operator entered £287.47 by mistake, the seller has the right to correct the error when it is discovered. The buyer will not get away with the £100!

carriage paid
The invoice price includes delivery of the goods to the buyer's premises.

INVOICE

No. 10452

**Wyvern (Office Products) Ltd.
12 Lower Hyde Street
MEREFORD   MR1 2JF**

Tel: (0605) 24185
Fax: (0605) 11461
VAT Reg No 841 116011

Date/Tax Point:
25 September 19-9

Accounts Dept
Camtec Ltd
18 Forth Street
MEREFORD   MR2 5FT

Order No. 13448

Quantity	Description	Catalogue Number	Unit Price £ p	Total Amount £ p
4	Canteen tables	F1034	47 75	191 00
16	Stacking chairs	C1025	8 75	140 00
			Total excluding VAT	331 00
			VAT	56 47
			Total due	387 47

Terms 2.5% 30 days, otherwise net
Carriage paid
E & O E

Registered Office: 12 Lower Hyde Street, Mereford, MR1 2JF. Registered Number: 8214612

Fig. 3.1   Invoice, with terms and conditions

Terms 2.5% 30 days, otherwise net

This wording, as it appears in the invoice on page 31, refers to a *cash discount* which the seller offers in order to encourage the buyer to pay the debt quickly. This term means that if the buyer takes less than 30 days to pay, then the seller will allow 2.5% off the invoice price. Where the buyer takes more than 30 days to pay, the terms are *net*; in other words, no cash discount will be allowed.

If you compare the invoices on pages 18 and 31, you will see that the VAT total is different when cash discount terms are offered. The reason for this is that *VAT is chargeable only on the discounted total*, although the total (before VAT) without discount is recorded on the invoice. Cash discounts are allowed only on the amount of the invoice before VAT is added.

Consider invoice no. 10452 issued by Wyvern (Office Products) Ltd. on page 31:

- the total exclusive of VAT is £331.00

- the terms are 2.5% cash discount

- the discounted total = £331.00 - (£331.00 x $^{2.5}/_{100}$) = £331.00 - £8.28 = £322.72

- VAT on discounted total = £322.72 x 17.5% = £56.47
  (in VAT calculations, fractions of a penny are ignored)

- the VAT quoted on the invoice = £56.47

- the invoice total = £331.00 + £56.47 = £387.47

If the invoice is paid within 30 days, the discount allowed = £331.00 x $^{2.5}/_{100}$ = £8.28
i.e. the buyer will pay £387.47 – £8.28 = £379.19.

If the invoice is paid after 30 days, then no discount is allowed, i.e. the buyer will pay the full invoice price of £387.47.

The following terms (not shown on fig 3.1) may also be found on invoices: ✓

ex works

The price quoted is from the supplier's premises, and does not include delivery; the purchaser must arrange and pay for transport and delivery.

cash on delivery

The buyer will have to pay for the goods when they are delivered.

further discount terms

In addition to the *cash discount* for early settlement just considered, there are three other types of discount that need to be dealt with.

trade discount

A trade discount is normally given when the buyer and the seller are in the same trade. For example, a small shop purchasing stationery for resale from a major stationery supplier, might be given a trade discount of, say, 30%.

quantity discount

Some companies offer discount when an order exceeds a certain figure. For example, Wyvern (Office Products) Ltd. might advertise that all orders received which amount to more than £200 will be allowed a 5% quantity discount.

customer discount

To encourage customers to purchase goods regularly from them, businesses will sometimes offer a discount on all their purchases. For example, Wyvern (Office Products) Ltd. offer Enock Ltd., as a valued customer, a discount of 10% on all their purchases; they also offer Mereford College 15% discount. In Appendix 3 is set out a list of Wyvern (Office Products) Ltd's customer discounts.

Customer discounts entered on the invoice are deducted from the invoice price *before* VAT is added on. VAT is calculated on the *discounted* price.

Case Study: Customer discount

Situation

Enock Ltd. orders (order no. 6214) from Wyvern (Office Products) Ltd. two medium duty hole punches. Wyvern allows Enock Ltd. a 10% customer discount, but no cash discount.

The order details received on 5 October 19-9 are:

Hole punch, catalogue no. H1012, price £7.95 each.

Calculate the invoice amount, and prepare invoice no. 10572 dated 5 October 19-9.

Solution

The steps involved in calculating the total invoice price are as follows:

Step one: Calculate the total price before discount
2 x £7.95 = £15.90

Step two: Calculate the discount
£15.90 x $^{10}/_{100}$ = £1.59

Step three: Calculate the price before VAT
£15.90 - £1.59 = £14.31

Step four: Calculate the VAT
£14.31 x 17.5% = £2.50

Step five: Calculate the total invoice price
£14.31 + £2.50 = £16.81

The invoice will be prepared as shown in fig. 3.2 on page 34.

The additional terms and conditions found on this invoice are:

- E & OE
- Carriage Paid
- Terms 30 days, net (i.e. no cash discount)

INVOICE

No. 10572

Wyvern (Office Products) Ltd.
12 Lower Hyde Street
MEREFORD   MR1 2JF

Tel: (0605) 24185
Fax: (0605) 11461
VAT Reg No 841 116011

Date/Tax Point:
5 October 19-9

Accounts Dept
Enock Ltd
84 Shire Way
BRINTON   BT5 6RS

Order No. 6214

Quantity	Description	Catalogue Number	Unit Price £ p	Total Amount £ p
2	Hole Punch Less 10% customer discount	H1012	7 95	15 90 1 59
		Total excluding VAT VAT		14 31 2 50
		Total due		16 81

Terms: 30 days net
Carriage paid
E & O E

Registered Office: 12 Lower Hyde Street, Mereford, MR1 2JF. Registered Number: 8214612

Fig. 3.2 Invoice, with customer discount

CREDIT NOTE

No. 1643

**Wyvern (Office Products) Ltd.
12 Lower Hyde Street
MEREFORD   MR1 2JF**

Tel: (0605) 24185
Fax: (0605) 11461
VAT Reg No 841 116011

Date/Tax Point:
7 October 19-9

Accounts Dept
Camtec Ltd
18 Forth Street
MEREFORD   MR2 5FT

Quantity	Description	Catalogue Number	Unit Price £ p	Total Amount £ p
2	Stacking chairs	C1025	8 75	17 50
			Total excluding VAT	17 50
			VAT	3 06
		Total credit		20 56

Reason for credit:

Two chairs damaged (purchase order 13448, our invoice no. 10452)

Registered Office: 12 Lower Hyde Street, Mereford, MR1 2JF. Registered Number: 8214612

Fig 3.3   Credit note

credit note

It might happen that a customer is sent an invoice but, before the invoice is paid, it is discovered that the customer is entitled to a reduction in the amount charged. The document which shows the reduction is called the *credit note*. It is prepared by the seller and sent to the buyer, often in response to a document – a *debit note* – prepared by the buyer.

There are many reasons why the customer may be entitled to a reduction on the invoice value:

• the price charged on the invoice may be too high
• some of the goods sent may have been faulty
• not all the goods invoiced may have been delivered
• the seller has agreed to accept back an unwanted order, or part of an order

Whatever the reason, the credit note has the effect of reducing the debt that the buyer owes to the seller. The credit note is often printed in red and will show:

• the reason why the credit note is issued
• the goods involved, their price and VAT chargeable (if goods are returned)
• the description 'overcharge', the amount and VAT chargeable (if the invoice is incorrect)
• the reference number of the original invoice involved in the sale

Consider the example shown in the last chapter, i.e. the purchase by Camtec Ltd. of 4 canteen tables and 16 stacking chairs from Wyvern (Office Products) Ltd. Assume that, after unpacking the delivery packages, Camtec discover that two of the stacking chairs are damaged and have to be returned. Their head buyer informs Wyvern's Sales Department of the problem and they agree to forward a credit note to remedy the matter.

The credit note issued by Wyvern (Office Products) Ltd. is shown in fig. 3.3 on page 35.

checks and controls: purchases

When an organisation purchases goods, it is important that the process includes checks and controls to ensure that:

• the correct goods have been received in an acceptable condition
• the correct terms and price have been applied
• the goods are only paid for once (paying for goods twice is more common than might be supposed!)

The three documents involved in the checking process are

• the purchase order
• the delivery note or advice note
• the invoice

You should note that some organisations use an internal document known as a *goods received note* on which the buyer records the receipt of the goods and the details set out on the delivery note or advice note sent by the supplier. This may be used in the checking process instead of the delivery note or advice note. In this chapter, however, we will refer to the *delivery note* as the record of goods received.

The checks to be carried out are set out on the next four pages.

checking the invoice, delivery note and purchase order

The checking process involves two separate procedures carried out in the Accounts Department:
- checking the three documents – the invoice, delivery note and purchase order – with each other
- checking the calculations on the invoice

We will deal with these in separate stages, starting with the checking of the three documents:

check 1 – goods received and delivery note

When the goods are received they should be checked against the delivery note - the quantities should be counted and the condition of the goods checked. Any discrepancies or damage should be notified immediately to the supplier, usually on a *discrepancy note*, so that repacements can be sent or the buyer credited with the value of the missing or damaged goods (i.e. the bill reduced by the issue of a *credit note*).

check 2 – delivery note and purchase order

The delivery note should then be checked in the Accounts Department against the original purchase order. The illustration on the next page shows the details that should be checked:

- *catalogue number* (i.e. the supplier's catalogue) – has the right type of goods been delivered?
- *quantity* - has the right number been delivered?
- *specifications* – are the goods delivered to the same specifications as those ordered
- *purchase order reference number* – do the goods relate to the purchase order being cxamined?

If all is in order, the delivery note will be filed with the purchase order under the purchase order reference number, ready for checking against the invoice when it arrives.

check 3 – invoice, delivery note and purchase order

When the invoice arrives from the supplier, it should be checked against the delivery note and the purchase order (which should be filed together). The specific points to look at are:

- *invoice and delivery note*
  Are the details of the goods on the invoice and on the delivery note the same? The product code, description and quantity of the goods should agree.

- *invoice and purchase order*
  Has the correct price been charged? The unit price quoted by the supplier or obtained from the supplier's catalogue will be stated on the purchase order, and should agree with the unit price stated on the invoice. If there is a difference, it should be queried with the supplier. The difference could be a mistake on the supplier's part, or it could be the buyer using an out-of-date catalogue, in which case the invoice price would hold.

student task

Look at the invoice and the purchase order and delivery note on the following pages. Can you spot any discrepancies?

The answers are set out below the invoice.

PURCHASE ORDER
MARTLEY MACHINE RENTAL LTD
67 Broadgreen Road
Martley MR6 7TR
Tel 090655 6576 Fax 090655 6342

Stourford Office Supplies
Unit 12
Avon Industrial Estate
Stourford SF5 6TD

No
Date   13 March 19-9
Delivery   to above address

47700

catalogue	quantity	description	price
3564749	15 reams	100gsm white Supalaser paper	£4.00 per ream

authorised   signature... *C J Farmer* ....   date...13 March 19-9

catalogue number   quantity   specifications   purchase order reference number

◼ DELIVERY NOTE ◼

Stourford Office Supplies
Unit 12, Avon Industrial Estate, Stourford SF5 6TD
Tel 0807 765434 Fax 0807 765123

Martley Machine Rental Ltd
67 Broadgreen Road
Martley
MR6 7TR

Delivery Note No   26754
Date   26 March 19-9
Order No   47700
Delivery   Van Delivery

product code	quantity	description
3564749	15 reams	100 gsm white Supalaser paper

received
signature... *G Hughes* ...print name (capitals)... *G HUGHES* ...
date... *30 March 19-9* ...

Fig. 3.4 Details to check on the purchase order and delivery note

■ INVOICE ■

Stourford Office Supplies
Unit 12, Avon Industrial Estate, Stourford SF5 6TD
Tel 0807 765434 Fax 0807 765123
VAT Reg 0745 4672 76

invoice to

Martley Machine Rental Ltd 67 Broadgreen Road Martley MR6 7TR	Invoice No 652771 Account MAR435 Date/tax point 30 March 19-9 Your Reference 47780

deliver to

as above

product code	description	quantity	price	unit	total	disc %	net
3564748	80 gsm white Supalaser	15	3.50	ream	52.00	0	52.00

Terms
Net monthly
Carriage paid
E & OE

GOODS TOTAL	52.00
CASH DISCOUNT	00.00
SUBTOTAL	52.00
VAT	9.01
TOTAL	42.99

answer to student task

The purchase order and delivery note agree, but the invoice has a number of discrepancies:

- the order reference differs (47700 and 47780)
- the product code differs (3564749 and 3564748)
- the product description differs (100 gsm and 80 gsm)
- the price differs (£4.00 and £3.50 per ream)

checking the calculations on the invoice

Another important step is for the Accounts Department to check the calculations on the invoice. If any *one* of these calculations is incorrect, the final total will be wrong, and the invoice will have to be queried with the supplier, so accurate checking is essential.   The checks to be made are:

quantity x unit price   The quantity of the items multiplied by the unit price must be correct. The result – the *total price* or *price extension* – is used for the calculation of any trade discount applicable.

trade discount   Any trade discount – an allowance given to approved customers - must be *deducted* from the total price worked out.   Trade discount is calculated as a percentage of the total price, e.g. a trade discount of 20% on a total price of £150 is calculated

$$£150 \times \frac{20}{100} = £30$$

The net price charged (before VAT) is therefore

$$£150 - £30 = £120 = \text{net total}$$

cash discount   Any cash discount - an allowance sometimes given for immediate payment - is *deducted* from the net total *before* VAT is calculated. In the invoice illustrated this calculation would be shown in the box at the bottom right of the document.

VAT   Value Added Tax is charged at the rate of 17.5%. To calculate VAT, the total *after* the deduction of any cash discount is treated as follows

$$\text{Total} \times \frac{17.5}{100} = \text{VAT amount}$$

If you are using a calculator, all you need to do is to multiply the total by 0.175 to give the VAT, which is then added to the total.

Remember that any fractions of a penny are ignored. For example if the total price is £55.75, the VAT will be

$$£55.75 \times 0.175 = £9.75625$$

£9.75625 then loses the last three digits – the fraction of a penny – to become £9.75. The figure is *not* rounded up to £9.76, although you may find some computer invoices produced do round up!

For the purpose of your studies you must assume that the calculations on all invoices must be checked.   In practice, computer produced invoices perform the calculations automatically, and in principle should be correct.

Now check the calculations on the invoice on the previous page. You should be able to detect a large number of errors - one can only assume that the person who prepared the invoice must have had a bad day! The errors are:
- *quantity x unit price should be £52.50, not £52.00*
- *the VAT is wrongly calculated £52.00 x 0.175 = £9.10, not £9.01 (it would be £9.18 on £52.50)*
- *the VAT has been deducted instead of added: the total should be £52.50 + £9.18 = £61.68*

authorising the invoice for payment

In most organisations checked invoices are passed to the person in the Accounts Department who deals with making payments to suppliers. First, however, an invoice will have to be *authorised* for payment. It will then be paid after the statement arrives and the due date for payment is reached. Clearly only correct invoices can be passed forward for payment. Invoices with errors will need to be queried with the seller.

authorising correct invoices

When an invoice is checked and found to be correct, the person carrying out the check will usually mark the document and authorise it for payment. This authorisation can take a number of forms:

- the checker can initial and date the invoice, and tick it or write 'pay' as an authorisation
- the organisation may have a special rubber stamp which can be used in the autorisation process – see the illustration below

This procedure of authorisation obviously helps the efficiency of the organisation:

- only authorised invoices will be passed forward in the Accounts Department for payment
- the checker's initials will be there in case of any future query on the invoice, e.g. an undetected error

```
┌──────────────────────────────────────────┐
│  invoice check                            │
│                                           │
│  supplier...............   date............│
│                                           │
│  goods..................   date............│
│                                           │
│  prices.................   date............│
│                                           │
│  input by..........batch no..............date.............│
│                                           │
│  authorised.........................................│
└──────────────────────────────────────────┘
```

the person authorising the payment of the invoice will sign here

this is the initial of the computer operator who input the invoice into the accounting system (a batch is a group of documents input together)

the various checks are initialled and dated here – the identity of the supplier, the goods supplied and the price calculations

Fig. 3.5 Authorisation stamp placed on an invoice received for checking

goods received notes (GRNs)

As mentioned earlier in the chapter *some* businesses use a document known as a *goods received note (GRN)*. This is essentially a checklist on which is recorded the name of the supplier and details of the goods ordered. As the goods are received and are checked in, the GRN is ticked and initialled to indicate that the right quantity and description of goods have been received. The GRN forms part of the payment authorisation process: only when a completed and correct GRN is received by the Accounts Department can the relevant invoice be paid. As you will see, the GRN fulfills the same checking function as the entries on the invoice authorisation stamp in fig 3.5 above.

chapter summary

❑ Terms and conditions are often stated on invoices. The most common terms and conditions refer to cash discounts and delivery charges, for example:

• Terms 2.5% 30 days,	If payment is made within 30 days of invoice date, a 2.5% cash discount is allowed. If payment is made after 30 days, no cash discount is allowed.
• Ex works	The price quoted is from the supplier's premises, and does not include delivery
• Carriage paid	Invoice price includes delivery.

❑ Additional discounts might be offered, for example:

• Trade discount	Discount offered when buyer and seller are in the same trade.
• Quantity discount	Discount offered when order exceeds a certain figure.
• Customer discount	Discount offered to valued customers, clubs and associations, to encourage sales.

❑ The document which shows that a customer is entitled to a reduction in the amount charged is a credit note. A credit note will be forwarded by the seller to the buyer if:

  • some of the goods delivered were faulty
  • not all the invoiced goods were delivered
  • the price charged on the invoice was too high

❑ When an organisation orders goods it is essential that the documentation is carefully checked:
  • purchase order and delivery note
  • delivery note and invoice
  • invoice calculations

❑ When an invoice has been found to be in order it will marked to that effect, authorised and passed for payment on the due date.

✍ student activities

Note: Blank documents, which are needed in some of these activities, are to be found in Appendix 1. These may be photocopied.

3.1   Using the following words, complete the sentences listed on the next page.

List of words to be used to complete the sentences:

cash on delivery	*carriage paid*
cash discount	*errors and omissions excepted*
trade discount	*terms net*
value added tax	*ex works*

(a) .... is a deduction made in the price if the purchaser pays within a stated time.

(b) When a customer is in the same trade as the seller, the discount is called ....

(c) .... means no cash discount or settlement discount is allowed.

(d) When goods have to be paid for at the time they are delivered this is called ....

(e) A Government tax added to an invoice is called ....

(f) The price quoted, including delivery to the customer's door, is called ....

(g) The price at the supplier's premises (not including delivery) is called ....

(h) If a mistake of undercharging is found on an invoice and the words .... appear on the invoice it is quite in order for the supplier to forward the customer a demand for the balance to make the invoice total up to the correct level.

3.2 Calculate the invoice price exclusive of VAT, the VAT chargeable, and the total due for the order below, assuming the three following sets of terms apply (note: three separate amounts due are to be calculated, as they will appear on the invoice):

- Terms net
- Terms 2.5% 30 days
- Terms 5% 30 days

Order details:
One Wyvern Secretarial Unit desk, light oak finish, Wyvern (Office Products) Ltd. Catalogue no. F1010, price £175.00.

3.3 Greenhouse Supplies of 101 Mall Street, London, WX12 5PQ, ordered three Fisley two-drawer all steel filing cabinets (goose grey finish) from Wyvern (Office Products) Ltd. Complete the invoice after checking if a discount is allowed to Greenhouse Supplies. (A list of customer discounts is given at the end of Wyvern's catalogue in Appendix 3.)

3.4   Mereford College, Bishops Road, Mereford MR1 2JF, ordered the following from Wyvern (Office Products) Ltd.:

> 6 boxes of HB general office pencils
> 4 boxes of Banmate 2000 blue fine point ballpoint pens
> 2 boxes of Banmate 2000 red medium point ballpoint pens

Check to see if a discount is given to Mereford College (in Appendix 3) and complete an invoice.

3.5   The office manager of P. Woodhouse Ltd. of 18 York Road, Leeds, LS2 5PX, has written to three office equipment suppliers for quotations on the following items:
>   2 long arm staplers
>   8 medium duty, two-hole punches
>   10 junior staplers

She receives catalogues from three companies who offer the following trade discounts:

> Wyvern (Office Products) Ltd.   10% discount
> Pen & Ink Ltd.   15% discount
> Quality Quill   5% discount

Using the catalogues as they appear in Appendix 3, calculate which supplier offers the cheapest quotation. Prepare the purchase order to be sent to this supplier.

3.6   Champson & Sons (16 High Street, Mereford, MR1 6ST) ordered on 12 December (order number 2050) from Wyvern (Office Products) Ltd. ten reams of Sherman, light blue, 100 gsm wove paper. The goods were received together with the invoice. (Note: 500 sheets = 1 ream)

On unpacking the goods Champson & Sons discover that one ream of paper is water damaged. They refer to Wyvern (Office Products) Ltd. and Wyvern agree to forward a credit note.

Complete the credit note sent by Wyvern to Champson & Sons.

3.7   You work as a clerical assistant in the office of Wyvern (Office Products) Ltd. Part of your job is to check that invoices are correct before you send them to your customers. Check the invoices shown on the next three pages, and if mistakes are found, draw up fresh invoices. Note that you will need to check if:

- the discount offered is correct (see the customer discount list in Appendix 3)

- the price agrees with current catalogue prices (see Appendix 3)

- the arithmetic is correct

- other details are correct

INVOICE

No. 10623

Wyvern (Office Products) Ltd.
12 Lower Hyde Street
MEREFORD   MR1 2JF

Tel: (0605) 24185
Fax: (0605) 11461
VAT Reg No 841 116011

Date/Tax Point:
18 November 19-9

Accounts Dept
A H Shatterford
16 Boyton Road
HIRMINGTON   HR5 6PQ

Order No. 1004

Quantity	Description	Catalogue Number	Unit Price £ p	Total Amount £ p
2	Bookcase, open front	F1051	39 95	79 90
2	Bookcase, glass front	F1060	9 95	191 90
	Total before discount			271 80
	Less 10% customer discount			27 18
	Total excluding VAT			244 62
	VAT			42 80
	Total due			287 42

Terms: 30 days net
Carriage paid
E & O E

Registered Office: 12 Lower Hyde Street, Mereford, MR1 2JF. Registered Number: 8214612

INVOICE

No. 10624

**Wyvern (Office Products) Ltd.
12 Lower Hyde Street
MEREFORD   MR1 2JF**

Tel: (0605) 24185
Fax: (0605) 11461
VAT Reg No 841 116011

Date/Tax Point:
18 November 19-9

Accounts Dept
J Smith & Son Ltd
101 High Street
MEREFORD MR6 5ZY

Order No. 2541

Quantity	Description	Catalogue Number	Unit Price £ p		Total Amount £ p	
4	Fisley Filing Cabinets (two drawer)	S1010	99	95	399	80
2	Fisley Filing Cabinets (four drawer)	S1012	94	95	189	90
	Total before discount Less 5% customer discount				589	70
					29	49
		Total excluding VAT VAT			619	19
					108	35
		Total due			727	54

Terms: 30 days net
Carriage paid
E & O E

Registered Office: 12 Lower Hyde Street, Mereford, MR1 2JF.   Registered Number: 8214612

INVOICE

No. 10626

**Wyvern (Office Products) Ltd.
12 Lower Hyde Street
MEREFORD   MR1 2JF**

Tel: (0605) 24185
Fax: (0605) 11461
VAT Reg No 841 116011

Date/Tax Point:

```
Accounts Dept
Carpminster College
Knot Road
CARPMINSTER  CP5 2IF
```

Order No. 6218

Quantity	Description	Catalogue Number	Unit Price £ p	Total Amount £ p
3	Roll storage unit	F1090	41 95	215 85
1	Flat storage unit	F1080	114 95	114 95
	Total before discount Less 15% customer discount			240 80
				36 12
	Total before VAT VAT			276 92
				84 46
	Total due			361 38

Terms: 30 days net
Carriage paid
E & O E

Registered Office: 12 Lower Hyde Street, Mereford, MR1 2JF. Registered Number: 8214612

ASSIGNMENT

2 Ordering goods: Mereford City Council

SITUATION ONE

Paul Atkins works as a clerical assistant in the housing department of Mereford City Council. His responsibilities include issuing purchase orders, and checking invoices received from suppliers. Paul receives a memorandum (see below) from the Administration Manager, Mr Harry Leek, requesting him to order some office equipment and stationery. Mereford City Council uses a local wholesaler, Wyvern (Office Products) Ltd, which sells a wide range of furniture, equipment and stationery. Paul has their current catalogue and price list (see Appendix 3).

MEMORANDUM

To: Paul Atkins   **Ref:**   HL/JEC

From: H Leek, Admin Manager   **Date:**   5 November 19-9

Please order from Wyvern (Office Products) Ltd:

1.   two reams of high quality, A4, 80 gsm wove white paper and 1000 envelopes to match

2.   two long-arm staplers (colour red, if possible) and six boxes of staples to suit

H. Leek

STUDENT TASKS

You are to assume the role of Paul Atkins (or Pauline Atkins if you prefer) and undertake the following tasks:

1.   Using Wyvern's catalogue (see Appendix 3), complete the following purchase order form for the items required by your administration manager. Allocate purchase order number 64125 to the document. The purchase order will be returned, with a covering memorandum, to Harry Leek for his signature. He will check it for accuracy, and if there are any inaccuracies, it will be returned to you for correction. Your tutor may act in the role of Harry Leek.

PURCHASE ORDER　　　　　　　**MEREFORD CITY COUNCIL**
　　　　　　　　　　　　　　　　　　　　Guildhall
　　　　　　　　　　　　　　　　　　　　Avon Road
　　　　　　　　　　　　　　MEREFORD MR6 1AT
　　　　　　　　　　　　　　　　Tel: (0605) 84192

To:　　　　　　　　　　　　　　　　Order No. ....

　　　　　　　　　　　　　　　　　　Date ....

Dear Sirs,

Please supply and deliver the following goods to the above address on or before
.... (state date).

Quantity	Cat. No.	Description	Price £ p

Yours faithfully

for and on behalf of Mereford City Council

....

2. A week later you receive invoice no. 10752 from Wyvern (Office Products) Ltd.

You are to:

- Check that the invoice reflects your initial order and that the arithmetic is correct.
- If errors are found in the invoice, write a letter to the Accounts Department, Wyvern (Office Products) Ltd pointing out the errors. The letter should be for the signature of Harry Leek.

INVOICE

No. 10752

Wyvern (Office Products) Ltd.
12 Lower Hyde Street
MEREFORD   MR1 2JF

Tel: (0605) 24185
Fax: (0605) 11461
VAT Reg No 841 116011

Date/Tax Point:

12 November 19-9

```
Housing Dept
Mereford City Council
Guildhall
Avon Road
MEREFORD   MR6 1AT
```

Order No. 64125

Quantity	Description	Catalogue Number	Unit Price £ p		Total Amount £ p	
2	stapler	M1013	20	65	41	30
6 boxes	staples	M1091	0	90	5	40
2 reams	white wove paper	P1010	12	60	25	20
2 boxes	white wove envelopes	E1010	29	95	59	90
			Total excluding VAT		131	80
			VAT		23	06
			Total due		154	86

Terms: 30 days net
Carriage paid
E & O E

Registered Office: 12 Lower Hyde Street, Mereford, MR1 2JF. Registered Number: 8214612

SITUATION TWO

You are now to assume the role of John (or Jane) Harris, a clerical assistant in the office of Wyvern (Office Products) Ltd. You receive a message from your boss, the office manager, asking you to deal with the letter (written in Situation One, Task 2) received from Mereford City Council Housing Department. You are to carry out the following tasks:

1. Complete credit note no.1709 as at 20 November 19-9 to correct the invoice sent to Mereford City Council.

CREDIT NOTE

No. 1709

Wyvern (Office Products) Ltd.
12 Lower Hyde Street
MEREFORD   MR1 2JF

Tel: (0605) 24185
Fax: (0605) 11461
VAT Reg No 841 116011

Date/Tax Point:

Quantity	Description	Catalogue Number	Unit Price £ p	Total Amount £ p

Total excluding VAT	
VAT	
Total credit	

Reason for credit:

Registered Office: 12 Lower Hyde Street, Mereford, MR1 2JF.   Registered Number: 8214612

2.   On 21 November 19-9 a further purchase order is received from Mereford City Council. The details of the order are:

Purchase Order No. 64147   *Date :* 20 November 19-9

Quantity	Cat. No.	Description	Price £
2	F1003	Executive double pedestal desk with drawers both sides. Teak finish	124.95
2	C1044	Executive black leather chair, high back, swivel base.	169.50

Check that the prices and details are correct and complete invoice no. 10817 for this order.

INVOICE   **No.**

Wyvern (Office Products) Ltd.   Tel: (0605) 24185
12 Lower Hyde Street   Fax: (0605) 11461
MEREFORD   MR1 2JF   VAT Reg No 841 116011

Date/Tax Point:

                                        Order   No.

Quantity	Description	Catalogue Number	Unit Price £ p	Total Amount £ p
			Total excluding VAT	
			VAT	
			Total due	

Registered Office: 12 Lower Hyde Street, Mereford, MR1 2JF. Registered Number: 8214612

3.   Complete the statement as at 30 November 19-9 for sending to Mereford City Council, to cover these transactions.

STATEMENT OF ACCOUNT

Wyvern (Office Products) Ltd.
12 Lower Hyde Street
MEREFORD   MR1 2JF

Tel: (0605) 24185
Fax: (0605) 11461
VAT Reg No 841 116011

Date	Reference	Debit £ p	Credit £ p	Balance £ p
			Amount now due	

Registered Office: 12 Lower Hyde Street, Mereford, MR1 2JF.   Registered Number: 8214612

4 Financial records – day books

In the previous two chapters we saw how documents are used by businesses for the purchase and sale of goods. These documents are then used as a means of recording transactions in the accounting system.

The two most common types of accounting transactions are:
- *the purchase of goods* with the intention that they should be resold at a profit, eg a plumbers' merchant buying bath taps from the manufacturer
- the *sale of goods* in which the business trades, eg a plumbers' merchant selling bath taps to plumbers and other customers

With both purchases and sales of goods, the transaction might be conducted on a *cash* or *credit* basis. For example, a plumbers' merchant will sell some of its goods for cash, but regular customers will buy on credit and will settle their accounts at intervals.

In this chapter we will examine how credit transactions are recorded in the accounting system of the business in *day books*. As these books are the first books in which the transactions are recorded, they are also known as *books of prime entry* or *books of original entry*.

purchases day book

The purchases day book is a collection point for accounting information on the credit purchases of a business and it takes the following form (with sample entries shown):

Purchases Day Book

Date	Details	Invoice No	Folio	Net	VAT*	Gross
19-1				£	£	£
2 Jan.	P Bond Ltd	1234	PL 125	80.00	14.00	94.00
11 Jan.	D Webster	A373	PL 730	120.00	21.00	141.00
16 Jan.	P Bond Ltd	1247	PL 125	40.00	7.00	47.00
20 Jan.	Sanders & Sons	5691	PL 495	160.00	28.00	188.00
31 Jan.	Totals for month			400.00	70.00	470.00

* VAT = 17½ per cent

Notes:
- The purchases day book is prepared from invoices received from suppliers.
- It is totalled at appropriate intervals – daily, weekly or monthly – and the total of the *net* column will tell the business the amount of purchases for the period.
- The *gross* column records the amount of each invoice, ie after VAT has been included.
- We will see in Chapter 5 how the amounts from the day book are recorded in the business' book-keeping system.
- The *folio* column is used for cross-referencing to the book-keeping system: 'PL' refers to Purchases Ledger, followed by the account number – see Chapter 5.
- When control accounts (see Chapter 10) are in use, the total of the gross column from the purchases day book is entered into the purchases ledger control account.

sales day book

The sales day book works in the same way as the purchases day book but, as its name suggests, it lists the sales made by a business. In its simplest form the total sales recorded by a shop till for the day, week or month acts as a sales day 'book'. For a business that sells on credit terms, with the issue of an invoice for each transaction, the sales day book, which is prepared from the invoices, takes the following form (with sample entries shown):

Sales Day Book

Date	Details	Invoice No	Folio	Net	VAT	Gross
19-1				£	£	£
3 Jan.	Doyle & Co Ltd	901	SL 58	120.00	21.00	141.00
8 Jan.	Sparkes & Sons Ltd	902	SL 127	160.00	28.00	188.00
12 Jan.	T Young	903	SL 179	80.00	14.00	94.00
15 Jan.	A-Z Supplies Ltd	904	SL 3	200.00	35.00	235.00
18 Jan.	Sparkes & Sons	905	SL 127	120.00	21.00	141.00
31 Jan.	Totals for month			680.00	119.00	799.00

Notes:
- The sales day book is prepared from invoices issued to customers.
- The total of the net column of the day book tells the business the amount of sales for the period.
- The gross column includes VAT.
- In Chapter 5 we will see how the amounts from the day book are recorded in the book-keeping system; the folio column refers to 'SL', ie Sales Ledger, followed by the account number – see Chapter 5.
- When control accounts (see Chapter 10) are in use, the total of the gross column from the sales day book is entered into the sales ledger control account.

Case Study: Mr I Lewis

Situation

Mr I Lewis runs an engineering business, which is registered for VAT. All his purchases and sales are on credit terms. He employs a clerk on a part-time basis to keep his accounting data up-to-date. Unfortunately the clerk was taken ill last week and Mr Lewis, knowing nothing about finance, asks if you can help. On investigation you find an 'in-tray' with last week's invoices received from suppliers of goods, together with copies of invoices sent out to customers by Mr Lewis' secretary. The list is as follows:

19-1

8 Dec. Invoice no 1234 received from MPF Metals for £108.75 + VAT* of £19.03

8 Dec. Invoice no A 340 sent to Johnson Bros for £220.00 + VAT of £38.50

9 Dec. Invoice no X 678 received from A Osborne for £85.50 +VAT of £14.96

9 Dec. Invoice no A 341 sent to McGee's Metals for £180.25 + VAT of £31.54

10 Dec. Invoice no A 342 sent to Wilson Trading Co for £112.40 + VAT of £19.67

10 Dec. Invoice no P 41 received from Murray Ltd for £115.00 + VAT of £20.12

11 Dec. Invoice no 1256 received from MPF Metals for £111.50 + VAT of £19.51

12 Dec. Invoice no A 343 sent to Johnson Bros for £121.00 + VAT of £21.17

* VAT = 17½ per cent (note that fractions of a penny are ignored, ie VAT is rounded down to the nearest penny)

You are asked to enter these transactions in the appropriate day books (leave the folio column blank).

Solution

Purchases Day Book

Date	Details	Invoice No	Folio	Net	VAT	Gross
19-1				£	£	£
8 Dec.	MPF Metals Ltd	1234		108.75	19.03	127.78
9 Dec.	A Osborne	X678		85.50	14.96	100.46
10 Dec.	Murray Ltd	P41		115.00	20.12	135.12
11 Dec.	MPF Metals Ltd	1256		111.50	19.51	131.01
12 Dec.	Totals for week			420.75	73.62	494.37

Sales Day Book

Date	Details	Invoice No	Folio	Net	VAT	Gross
19-1				£	£	£
8 Dec.	Johnson Bros Ltd	A340		220.00	38.50	258.50
9 Dec.	McGee's Metals	A341		180.25	31.54	211.79
10 Dec.	Wilson Trading Co Ltd	A342		112.40	19.67	132.07
12 Dec.	Johnson Bros Ltd	A343		121.00	21.17	142.17
12 Dec.	Totals for week			633.65	110.88	744.53

day books and Value Added Tax

Many businesses and other organisations are registered for Value Added Tax (VAT). This means that:

• VAT is charged on invoices issued to customers

• VAT charged on invoices received from VAT-registered suppliers can be either reclaimed from HM Customs and Excise (the VAT authority), or set off against VAT charged on invoices issued

When writing up day books you should always check to see if VAT should be charged on invoices issued to suppliers, or has been charged on invoices received from suppliers; if so, the amount is entered in the VAT column of the day book, with the total amount of the invoice in the gross column, and the amount of the invoice before VAT in the net column.

When a business is not registered for VAT, it cannot charge VAT on invoices issued and it cannot reclaim VAT charged on invoices received from suppliers. In such circumstances the total amount of the invoice is recorded in both the net and gross columns; a dash may be inserted in the VAT column. In Chapter 5 we shall see how the VAT columns from the day books are entered into the book-keeping system.

analysed day books

An analysed day book is used whenever a business needs to analyse its purchases, sales and returns (see Chapter 6) between different departments, or between different categories of products. For example, a paint and wallpaper shop may decide to write up its purchases day book (invoice and folio columns not shown) as follows:

Purchases Day Book

Date	Details	Net	VAT	Gross	Paint	Wallpaper
19-1		£	£	£	£	£
8 Aug.	DIY Sales Ltd	200.00	35.00	235.00	75.00	125.00
12 Aug.	Luxor Paints	120.00	21.00	141.00	120.00	–
16 Aug.	Colours Ltd	280.00	49.00	329.00	180.00	100.00
22 Aug.	Southern Traders	160.00	28.00	188.00	60.00	100.00
31 Aug.	Totals for month	760.00	133.00	893.00	435.00	325.00

Note that the analysis columns show the amounts of purchases net of VAT.

An analysed day book can also be used to list all credit purchases, not only of goods for resale but also for expenses and other items. An example of this is shown in fig 4.1 where the analysis columns are for goods for resale, telephones, advertising, other expenditure.

In using analysed day books, a business can adapt the accounting records to suit its own particular requirements for information. There is no one standard way in which to present accounting records – the needs of the user of the information are paramount.

Purchases Day Book

Date	Details	Invoice No	Folio	Net £	VAT £	Gross £	Goods for resale £	Telephone £	Advertising £	Other expenditure £
19-1										
2 Sep.	Fashions Ltd	1478	PL 87	110.00	19.25	129.25	110.00			
4 Sep.	Eastern Communications	Z479	GL 234	149.50	26.16	175.66		149.50		
7 Sep.	Mercian Models	9799	PL 102	256.80	44.94	301.74	256.80			
12 Sep.	Grant, Wadley	202	GL 84	450.00	78.75	528.75			450.00	
15 Sep.	Style Ltd	4621	PL 379	368.40	64.47	432.87	368.40			
20 Sep.	Wyvern Motors	A284	GL 80	127.50	22.31	149.81				127.50
26 Sep.	Denim Traders	K312	PL 45	274.35	48.01	322.36	274.35			
30 Sep.	Totals for month			1,736.55	303.89	2,040.44	1,009.55	149.50	450.00	127.50

Fig 4.1 Analysed purchases day book, including goods for resale and other expenses

Notes:
• The analysis columns show the amount of purchases net of VAT.
• The references in the folio column are to 'PL' Purchases Ledger, and 'GL' General Ledger – see also Chapter 5.

chapter summary

❑ Day books are used as listing devices for credit transactions such as purchases and sales.

❑ The *purchases day book* is prepared from invoices received from suppliers.

❑ The *sales day book* is prepared from invoices sent to customers.

❑ Day books are *books of prime entry* because transactions are recorded in them as the first part of the accounting system.

❑ Analysed day books are used when a business needs to analyse its purchases and sales between different categories of products (including expenses), or between different departments.

In the next chapter we shall look at how information from the purchases and sales day books is recorded in the double-entry book-keeping system.

Student Activities

- *In these activities, the rate of Value Added Tax is to be calculated at the current rate (17½% at the time of writing). When calculating VAT amounts, you should ignore fractions of a penny, ie round down to a whole penny.*
- *Leave the folio column blank, unless otherwise stated.*

4.1 You are working for Wyvern Wholesalers and are required to enter up the purchases day book from the following details:

19-1
2 Apr. Bought goods from Severn Supplies £250 + VAT, their invoice no. 6789
4 Apr. Bought goods from I Johnstone £210 + VAT, her invoice no. A241
10 Apr. Bought goods from L Murphy £185 + VAT, his invoice no. 2456
12 Apr. Bought goods from Mercia Manufacturing £180 + VAT, their invoice no. X457
18 Apr. Bought goods from AMC Enterprises £345 + VAT, their invoice no. AMC 456
24 Apr. Bought goods from S Green £395 + VAT, her invoice no. 2846

After entering the above, total the purchases day book at 30 April.

4.2   The following details are to be entered in the sales day book of Wyvern Wholesalers:

19-1
  2 Apr.   Sold goods to Malvern Stores £55 + VAT, invoice no. 4578
  4 Apr.   Sold goods to Pershore Retailers £65 + VAT, invoice no. 4579
  7 Apr.   Sold goods to E Grainger £28 + VAT, invoice no. 4580
 10 Apr.   Sold goods to P Wilson £58 + VAT, invoice no. 4581
 12 Apr.   Sold goods to M Kershaw £76 + VAT, invoice no. 4582
 14 Apr.   Sold goods to D Lloyd £66 + VAT, invoice no. 4583
 18 Apr.   Sold goods to A Cox £33 + VAT, invoice no. 4584
 22 Apr.   Sold goods to Dines Stores £102 + VAT, invoice no. 4585
 24 Apr.   Sold goods to Malvern Stores £47 + VAT, invoice no. 4586
 27 Apr.   Sold goods to P Wilson £35 + VAT, invoice no. 4587
 29 Apr.   Sold goods to A Cox £82 + VAT, invoice no. 4588

After entering the above, total the sales day book at 30 April.

4.3   Jason Smythe owns a business selling furniture and carpets. During April 19-4 he received the following invoices from his suppliers:

19-4
  2 Apr.   Invoice no. 2790 for furniture from T Table Ltd for £1,247.50 + VAT
  6 Apr.   Invoice no. 8461 for carpets from Eastern Imports for £796.80 + VAT
 10 Apr.   Invoice no. A2431 for carpets from Minster Carpets Ltd for £1,875.24 + VAT
 12 Apr.   Invoice no. 27998 for furniture from Pegasus Ltd for £498.13 + VAT
 16 Apr.   Invoice no. 98421 for carpets from United Carpets Ltd for £476.22 + VAT
 20 Apr.   Invoice no. 47921 for furniture from Gerrard Furniture for £831.49 + VAT
 23 Apr.   Invoice no. 2934 for furniture from T Table Ltd for £648.90 + VAT
 27 Apr.   Invoice no. 8991 for carpets from Eastern Imports for £1,297.31 + VAT

You are to:
• enter the above transactions into an analysed purchases day book
• total the day book at 30 April 19-4

4.4   The Oasis Trading Company records its credit purchases in an analysed day book with the following headings: goods for resale, photocopying, telephone, other expenditure. The transactions for March 19-3 are as follows:

19-3
  2 Mar.   Bought goods for resale from Severn Valley Traders £255.50 + VAT, invoice no. X1247
  4 Mar.   Bought goods for resale from Mercian Suppliers £356.25 + VAT, invoice no. 7977
  6 Mar.   Received invoice no. Z495 for £136.95 + VAT from Copy Services Ltd for photocopying
 10 Mar.   Bought goods for resale from D James Ltd £368.21 + VAT, invoice no. 2461
 14 Mar.   Received invoice no. 769431 for £218.25 + VAT from British Telecom for telephone costs
 16 Mar.   Received invoice no. A419 for £45.40 + VAT from Wyvern Garage for vehicle repairs
 19 Mar.   Bought goods for resale from A-Z Traders £496.84 + VAT, invoice no. AZ7231
 21 Mar.   Received invoice no. 561742 for £154.65 + VAT from Saturn Communications for telephone costs
 23 Mar.   Received invoice no. 2761 for £151.20 + VAT from A J Knowles for decorating work
 25 Mar.   Bought goods for resale from Severn Valley Traders £357.24 + VAT, invoice no. X1299
 30 Mar.   Received invoice no. 597234 for £121.47 + VAT from Total Communications plc for telephone costs
 31 Mar.   Received invoice no. Z610 for £117.25 from Copy Services Ltd for photocopying

You are to:
• enter the above transactions into an analysed purchases day book
• total the day book at 31 March 19-3

5 Double-entry book-keeping – an introduction

Having looked at the different business documents (Chapters 2 and 3) and the way in which these documents are recorded in purchases and sales day books (Chapter 4), we now turn our attention to the further recording of financial transactions in the accounting system by means of *double-entry book-keeping*. Firstly, though, we will take an overview of the accounting system to see how the various parts fit together.

the accounting system

The accounting system can be summarised as follows:

documents
processing of documents relating to financial transactions, eg invoices, cheques

books of prime entry
initial recording of financial transactions in *summary* books (books of prime entry)

double-entry accounts system
regular transfer of figures from the books of prime entry into the double-entry book-keeping system of accounts contained in 'the ledger'

trial balance
extraction of figures (often monthly) from the double-entry accounts in the ledger to check their accuracy in the form of a list of figures known as the trial balance

final accounts
production from the double-entry accounts of a profit statement, and a balance sheet – the 'final accounts' – normally monthly or annually

We have already looked at the first two areas. The next two areas – double-entry accounts and the trial balance – are looked at in this and the next three chapters. Financial statements – the profit statement and balance sheet – are the end result of the accounting system; they are outside the scope of this book but, if you continue your studies in accounting, you are certain to be involved in their preparation and interpretation.

the use of accounts

The accounting system is organised on the basis of a number of *accounts* which record the money amounts of financial transactions: collectively these accounts are known as 'the ledger'.

Accounts are maintained in the names of customers and of suppliers of the business, and also for other transactions such as the receipt and payment of money for various purposes. Accounts can be kept in the form of:

- handwritten records
- computer records

In a handwritten system, accounts are maintained either in a bound book or a series of separate sheets of paper or card – each account occupying a separate page. The business can set up its own manual system, or can buy one ready-made from a business supplies shop.

In a computerised system each account is held as data in a computer file. Whether a handwritten or computerised system is being used, the principles remain the same. We shall see how a business can use a computer to keep its accounts up-to-date in Chapter 19. The theory of keeping accounts is the same whether a handwritten system or a computer system is in use. For the time being we will concentrate on handwritten accounts.

A handwritten system can either use specially ruled accounting paper – known as ledger paper – which can be purchased from a business supplies shop, or a suitable layout can be ruled as follows:

Debit				**Name of Account, eg Purchases Account**		Credit	
Date	Details	£	p	Date	Details	£	p
↑ of trans- action	↑ name of other account	↑ amount of trans- action					

Note the following points about the layout of this account:

- the name of the account is written at the top
- the account is divided into two identical halves, separated by a central double vertical line
- the left-hand side is called the 'debit' side ('debit' is abbreviated to 'Dr.' – short for <u>D</u>ebito<u>R</u>)
- the right-hand side is called the 'credit' (or 'Cr.') side
- the date, details and amount of the transaction are entered in the account
- in the 'details' column is entered the name of the other account involved in the book-keeping transaction

In practice, each account would occupy a whole page in a handwritten book-keeping system but, to save space when doing exercises, it is usual to put several accounts on a page. In future, in this book, the account layout will be simplified to give more clarity as follows:

Dr.		**Purchases Account**		Cr.
19-1	£	19-1		£

This layout is often known in accounting jargon as a 'T' account; it is used to illustrate accounts because it separates in a simple way the two sides – debit and credit – of the account. An alternative style of account has three money columns: debit, credit and balance. This type of account is commonly used for bank statements, building society passbooks and computer accounting statements. Because the balance of the account is calculated after every transaction, it is known as a *running balance account* (see page 95).

debits and credits

The principle of double-entry book-keeping is that for every financial transaction two entries are made, usually in different accounts:

- one account is debited, and
- one account is credited

The principle is often known as the *dual aspect* of book-keeping, ie each transaction has a dual effect on the accounts – one account gains, while another account gives value by recording a payment or a liability.

Debit entries are on the left-hand side of the appropriate account, while credit entries are on the right. The rules for debits and credits are:

- *debit entry* – the account which gains value, or records an asset, or an expense
- *credit entry* – the account which gives value, or records a liability, or an income item

This is illustrated as follows:

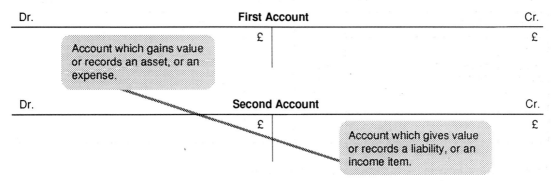

Dr.	First Account	Cr.
£		£
Account which gains value or records an asset, or an expense.		

Dr.	Second Account	Cr.
£		£
	Account which gives value or records a liability, or an income item.	

When one entry has been identified as a debit or credit, the other entry will be on the *opposite* side of the other account.

division of the ledger

Accounts, as mentioned above, are normally written on separate pages of a book known as 'the ledger'. In practice, several separate ledgers are kept, each containing different classes of accounts:

- *sales ledger*, containing the accounts of the firm's debtors (customers)
- *purchases ledger*, containing the accounts of the firm's creditors (suppliers)
- *cash book*, containing the bank account and cash account records of the business
- *general ledger* (often known as *nominal ledger*) containing all other accounts, such as income, expenses, fixed assets, owner's capital, etc.

purchases and sales

In book-keeping the terms purchases and sales have specific meanings:

- *purchases* – the purchase of goods with the intention that they should be resold at a profit
- *sales* – the sale of goods in which the business or organisation trades

Thus an office stationery supplies business buying goods from a manufacturer records the transaction in *purchases account*. When office supplies are sold to customers, the transactions are recorded in *sales account*. Other items purchased in connection with the running of the busines – eg buildings, equipment, vehicles – are recorded in suitably named accounts, ie buildings account, equipment account, vehicles account, etc.

The following ledgers and accounts are used in connection with purchases and sales:

GENERAL (OR NOMINAL) LEDGER

- *purchases account* – to record the purchase of goods, whether bought on credit or for cash
- *sales account* – to record the sale of goods, whether sold on credit or for cash
- *Value Added Tax account* – to record the VAT amount of purchases and sales

SALES LEDGER

- separate accounts for each *debtor*, ie customers who owe money to the business

PURCHASES LEDGER

- separate accounts for each *creditor*, ie suppliers to whom the business owes money

double-entry book-keeping for purchases

Invoices received from suppliers form the prime documents for the preparation of the purchases day book (see Chapter 4). After the day book, the double-entry book-keeping accounts are written up.

The example purchases day book (already seen on page 54) is reproduced for reference:

Purchases Day Book

Date	Details	Invoice No	Folio	Net	VAT*	Gross
19-1				£	£	£
2 Jan.	P Bond Ltd	1234	PL 125	80.00	14.00	94.00
11 Jan.	D Webster	A373	PL 730	120.00	21.00	141.00
16 Jan.	P Bond Ltd	1247	PL 125	40.00	7.00	47.00
20 Jan.	Sanders & Sons	5691	PL 495	160.00	28.00	188.00
31 Jan.	Totals for month			400.00	70.00	470.00

* VAT = 17½ per cent

The accounts in the purchases ledger and general ledger to record the above transactions are:

PURCHASES LEDGER

Dr.		**P Bond** (account no 125)		Cr.
19-1	£	19-1		£
		2 Jan. Purchases		94
		16 Jan. Purchases		47

Dr.		**Sanders & Sons** (account no 495)		Cr.
19-1	£	19-1		£
		20 Jan. Purchases		188

Dr.		**D Webster** (account no 730)		Cr.
19-1	£	19-1		£
		11 Jan. Purchases		141

GENERAL LEDGER

Dr.		**Purchases Account**		Cr.
19-1	£	19-1		£
31 Jan. Purchases Day Book	400			

Dr.		**Value Added Tax Account**		Cr.
19-1	£	19-1		£
31 Jan. Purchases Day Book	70			

Note that from the purchases day book:

- the total of the net column, £400, has been debited to purchases account (ie the account which has gained value)
- the total of the VAT column, £70, has been debited to VAT account (which has gained value)
- the amounts from the gross column *for each separate purchase* have been credited to the accounts of the suppliers, ie the business owes to each creditor the amounts shown
- the purchases day book incorporates a folio column which cross-references each transaction to the personal account of each creditor in the purchases ledger (PL); this enables a particular transaction to be traced from prime document (invoice received), through the book of prime entry (purchases day book), to the creditor's ledger account

summary

The accounting system for purchases fits together in the following way:

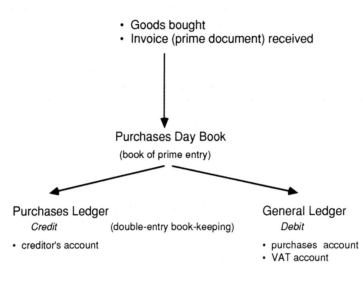

double-entry book-keeping for sales

Invoices issued by a business form the prime documents used in the preparation of the sales day book (see Chapter 4). After the day book, the double-entry book-keeping accounts are written up.

The example sales day book (see also page 55) is shown below:

Sales Day Book

Date	Details	Invoice No	Folio	Net	VAT	Gross
19-1				£	£	£
3 Jan.	Doyle & Co Ltd	901	SL 58	120.00	21.00	141.00
8 Jan.	Sparkes & Sons Ltd	902	SL 127	160.00	28.00	188.00
12 Jan.	T Young	903	SL 179	80.00	14.00	94.00
15 Jan.	A-Z Supplies Ltd	904	SL 3	200.00	35.00	235.00
18 Jan.	Sparkes & Sons	905	SL 127	120.00	21.00	141.00
31 Jan.	Totals for month			680.00	119.00	799.00

The accounts in the sales ledger and general ledger to record the above transactions are:

SALES LEDGER

Dr.		A-Z Supplies Ltd (account no 3)			Cr.
19-1		£	19-1		£
15 Jan.	Sales	235			

Dr.		Doyle & Co Ltd (account no 58)			Cr.
19-1		£	19-1		£
3 Jan.	Sales	141			

Dr.		Sparkes & Sons Ltd (account no 127)			Cr.
19-1		£	19-1		£
8 Jan.	Sales	188			
18 Jan.	Sales	141			

Dr.		T Young (account no 179)			Cr.
19-1		£	19-1		£
12 Jan.	Sales	94			

GENERAL LEDGER

Dr.	Sales Account			Cr.
19-1	£	19-1		£
		31 Jan.	Sales Day Book	680

Dr.		Value Added Tax Account			Cr.
19-1		£	19-1		£
31 Jan.	Purchases Day Book	70*	31 Jan.	Sales Day Book	119

* Amount already entered from purchases day book.

Note that from the sales day book:
- the total of the net column, £680, has been credited to sales account (ie the account which has given value)
- the total of the VAT column, £119, has been credited to VAT account (which has given value)
- the amounts from the gross column *for each separate sale* have been debited to the accounts of the customers, ie the business has a debtor for the amounts shown
- the folio column gives a cross-reference to the debtors' accounts in the sales ledger (SL)

summary

The accounting system for sales fits together in the following way:

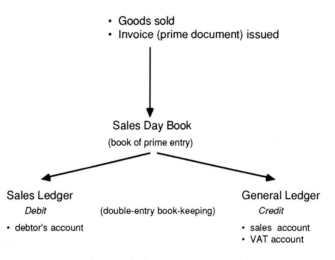

recording credit transactions: a summary

* Purchases: invoice received from supplier
  - *debit* purchases account with the amount of the invoice before VAT is added
  - *debit* VAT account with amount of VAT on invoice
  - *credit* creditor's account with total amount of invoice, including VAT
* Sales: invoice issued to customer
  - *debit* debtor's account with total amount of invoice, including VAT
  - *credit* sales account with the amount of the invoice before VAT is added
  - *credit* VAT account with amount of VAT on invoice

recording payments

When payment is received from customers or made to suppliers, the method of payment is usually either by cheque or in cash. While separate accounts are kept for bank (ie cheque) transactions and for cash transactions, most organisations bring these two accounts together in a division of the ledger called *cash book*. We shall be looking at the use of cash book in detail in Chapter 15.

payment received from debtors (customers)

When debtors pay for goods that have been sold to them, the double-entry book-keeping entries are:

* payment received by cheque
  - *debit* bank account
  - *credit* debtor's account

* payment received in cash
  - *debit* cash account
  - *credit* debtor's account

payment made to creditors (suppliers)

Payment for purchases is recorded by the following double-entry book-keeping entries:

* payment made by cheque
  - *debit* creditor's account
  - *credit* bank account

* payment made in cash
  - *debit* creditor's account
  - *credit* cash account

cash sales and cash purchases

If sales or purchases are made with immediate payment at the time of the transaction (called a 'cash sale' or 'cash purchase' – when payment is made in cash *and* by cheque), debtors' and creditors' accounts are not used. Instead the book-keeping transactions are:

* Cash sales
  - *debit* bank account (cheque), or cash account (cash) with total amount, including VAT
  - *credit* sales account with amount of invoice before VAT is added
  - *credit* VAT account with amount of VAT on invoice

* Cash purchases
  - *debit* purchases account with amount of invoice before VAT is added
  - *debit* VAT account with amount of VAT on invoice
  - *credit* bank account (cheque), or cash account (cash) with total amount, including VAT

sales and purchases using credit cards

The principle of credit cards (see Chapter 12) is that the cardholder is able to obtain goods and services immediately, but will pay the credit card company at a later date. The cardholder signs a credit card voucher at the seller's premises or, in the case of mail order or telephone sales, quotes his or her card number to the seller.

As we will see in Chapter 13 the seller pays in the credit card vouchers to the bank using a normal paying-in slip. The bank credits the seller's account, and then forwards the vouchers to the credit card company, which reimburses the bank. At a later date, the credit card company will make a charge for the percentage commission on the sales – this is settled by means of a direct debit (see page 184) to the seller's account.

Both the company selling the goods and the customer buying the goods with a credit card will treat the transaction as being a 'cash transaction', although no cash or cheque has changed hands. The seller will not open a debtor's account in the customer's name in its records.

recording credit card sales

The process of recording credit card sales from the seller's viewpoint, together with the double-entry book-keeping is:

Stage	Book-keeping
Credit card sale	– *debit* bank account
	– *credit* sales account (or credit card sales account)
Commission charged by credit card company	– *debit* expenses account (eg credit card commission paid account)
	– *credit* bank account

Thus the credit card sale is treated as a cash transaction, with the cash book (and not the sales day book) being the book of prime entry. A business which has a lot of credit card sales may adapt the accounting system and use a subsidiary day book for such sales, transferring the total at the end of each day to sales account (or a separate credit card sales account) and cash book.

From time-to-time credit card transactions will be returned by the card company; the reasons will include:
• stolen cards
• errors in completion of the voucher
• no authorisation code, where the transaction is above the seller's limit

Where the seller is at fault, the card company will debit the seller by direct debit to the bank account. In the seller's accounts this is recorded as:
– *debit* sundry customers' account*
– *credit* bank account

* The sundry customers' account is a temporary account used while the seller tries to trace the customer and recover the amount of the sale. If the customer cannot be found, then the amount will have to be written off as a bad debt (see Chapter 9).

recording credit card purchases
A less common transaction is where a business buys goods using a credit card – the majority of credit cards are held by individuals rather than businesses. Recording a purchase is a two-stage process:

Stage	Book-keeping
Credit card purchase	– *debit* purchases account
	– *credit* credit card company
Payment to credit card company	– *debit* credit card company
	– *credit* bank account

With credit card purchases, it is appropriate to open an account in the name of the credit card company in the purchases ledger. The account will be cleared when payment is made (generally on a monthly basis) to the card company. As a purchases ledger account is used, credit card purchases will be recorded in the purchases day book as the book of prime entry – this differs from the accounting treatment of credit card sales, which are considered to be 'cash' sales.

methods of coding in accounting systems

In a very small business there is no need for the accounting system to incorporate a complex method of coding, or cross-referencing, of transactions. As a business grows larger, more formal methods of coding need to be used. We will relate this to the different stages in the accounting system, ie
• documents
• books of prime entry (day books)
• double-entry accounts system
• trial balance
• financial statements

Although not all of these stages have been covered so far in your studies, we have reached the point where you have an appreciation of the accounting system as a whole. Uses of coding in the stages of the accounting system are:

- **Documents**
  - each document, eg invoice, credit note, is numbered
  - goods listed on invoices have reference numbers, eg catalogue number, which, if a computer accounting system is used, will enable the business to analyse sales by product

- **Books of prime entry**
  - the number of the document, eg invoice, credit note (see next chapter) is recorded
  - the number of the debtors or creditors account is recorded in the folio column, eg 'PL' for purchases ledger, or 'SL' for sales ledger, followed by the account number (or short name – see below)

- **Double-entry accounts system**
  - the accounts system is divided into sections, the division of the ledger (see page 63): sales ledger, purchases ledger, cash book, and general ledger
  - each account is numbered (or some accounting systems use an abbreviated name, or short name, for debtors and creditors, eg the account of Peterhead Trading Company might be coded as 'PETER')
  - general (or nominal ledger) accounts are numbered and are often arranged in a particular order, eg

0001 – 1299	Assets
2100 – 2399	Liabilities
3000 – 3099	Capital
4000 – 4999	Sales
5000 – 5299	Purchases
6000 – 8299	Expenses

    Note: the above account numbers are taken from the general (or nominal) ledger used in the computer accounting program (see Chapter 19).

- **Trial balance**

  We shall see in Chapter 8 how the trial balance consists of a list of the balances of all the accounts within the accounting system. As well as the name of each account, it is quite usual to show the account number listed in a separate 'folio' column. We shall see this in the computer accounting trial balances in Chapter 19.

- **Financial statements**
  - the accounts from the various division of the ledger can be arranged in numerical order to produce the profit statement and balance sheet.

The coding or cross-referencing system used by a business is tailored to suit the particular needs of the business. For example, if the general ledger account numbers for sales are 4000 – 4999, this can be further sub-divided:

4000 – 4099	UK and European Community sales
4100 – 4199	export sales
4900 – 4999	miscellaneous sales

Developing the coding system further, account number 4000 could be for UK sales of product A, 4001 for product B, etc; account number 4100 could be for export sales of product A, 4101 for product B, etc. In this way, the four digit number can be broken down: the first digit, 4, tells us that the item is sales, the next digit, for example, 1, tells us that it is export, the last two digits, for example, 01, indicate that it is product B.

In a similar way, expenses can be coded. For example, if the general ledger account numbers for heat, light and power are 7200 – 7299, this can be further sub-divided:

7200 – 7209	electricity
7210 – 7219	gas
7220 – 7229	oil
7230 – 7239	other heating costs

The costs for each department within the business can be further coded, for example:

7200	electricity, department 1
7201	electricity, department 2
7210	gas, department 1
7211	gas, department 2

The main reason for using coding systems is to ensure that accounting transactions are recorded against the correct heading, and also to enable sales to be analysed by product. A feature of all coding systems is that not all numbers are used initially. For example, in the sales codes above there are 100 account numbers in each major category of sales, leaving room for new products to be added later on as the business develops.

chapter summary

❏ The accounting system comprises a number of specific stages of recording and presenting financial transactions:
  • documents
  • books of prime entry
  • double-entry book-keeping
  • trial balance
  • final accounts

❏ Financial transactions are recorded in accounts using double-entry principles.

❏ The rules for debit and credit entries in accounts are:
  • *debit entries* – the account which gains value
  • *credit entries* – the account which gives value

❏ Division of the ledger divides the accounts contained in the accounting system between four sections:
  • *sales ledger* – containing the accounts of debtors
  • *purchases ledger* – containing the accounts of creditors
  • *cash book* – containing the bank account and cash account
  • *general (or nominal) ledger* – containing all other accounts

❏ Within an accounting system, use is made of coding to identify and cross-reference transactions and products.

In the next chapter we shall look at recording returns transactions – where a credit note has been issued.

✍ Student Activities

- *In these activities, the rate of Value Added Tax is to be calculated at the current rate (17½% at the time of writing). When calculating VAT amounts, you should ignore fractions of a penny, ie round down to a whole penny.*
- *Leave the folio column blank, unless otherwise stated.*

5.1   J Lewis started in business in November 19-1 as a supplier of office carpets and office furniture. During the first month of trading, the following credit transactions took place:

19-1

1 Nov.	Bought carpets for resale and received invoice no. 5681 from Carpminster Manufacturing Ltd, £250.00 + VAT
2 Nov.	Bought office furniture for resale and received invoice no. 2938 from Wyvern (Office Products) Ltd, £450.00 + VAT
5 Nov.	Sold carpet and forwarded invoice no. 1001 to Mereford City Council, £320.00 + VAT
6 Nov.	Sold carpet and forwarded invoice no. 1002 to Carpminster College, £180.00 + VAT
10 Nov.	Sold office furniture and forwarded invoice no. 1003 to Mereford City Council, £520.00 + VAT
12 Nov.	Bought carpets for resale and received invoice no. 5702 from Carpminster Manufacturing Ltd, £350.00 + VAT
20 Nov.	Bought office furniture for resale and received invoice no. 3012 from Wyvern (Office Products) Ltd, £600.00 + VAT

You are to:

(a)   enter the above transactions in J Lewis' purchases day book and sales day book

(b)   record the accounting entries of J Lewis' purchases ledger, sales ledger and general ledger

5.2   James Scriven started in business as a furniture wholesaler on 1 February 19-2. He has registered for Value Added Tax. During the first month of business, the following credit transactions took place:

19-2

1 Feb.	Bought furniture for resale and received invoice no. 961 from Softseat Ltd, £320 + VAT
2 Feb.	Bought furniture for resale and received invoice no. 068 from PRK Ltd, £80 + VAT
8 Feb.	Sold furniture and issued invoice no. 001 to High Street Stores, £440 + VAT
14 Feb.	Sold furniture and issued invoice no. 002 to Peter Lounds Ltd, £120 + VAT
15 Feb.	Bought furniture for resale and received invoice no. 529 from Quality Furnishings, £160 + VAT
18 Feb.	Sold furniture and issued invoice no. 003 to Carpminster College, £320 + VAT
19 Feb.	Bought furniture for resale and received invoice no. 984 from Softseat Ltd, £160 + VAT
25 Feb.	Sold furniture and issued invoice no. 004 to High Street Stores, £200 + VAT

You are to:

(a)   enter the above transactions in James Scriven's purchases day book and sales day book

(b)   record the accounting entries in James Scriven's purchases ledger, sales ledger and general ledger

6 Recording returns

A credit note is a document that is issued by a business when it makes a refund to a customer who has bought goods on credit. A credit note reduces the amount owed by the debtor. There are two situations for recording credit notes in the accounting system:

- *purchases returns*, when goods purchased on credit by the business are now being returned to the suppliers
- *sales returns*, when goods previously sold on credit are now being returned to the business by its customers

In this chapter we look at the recording of returns in the accounting records.

accounting procedures

As with recording purchases and sales, the accounting procedures for returns are:

documents

⇓

initial recording of transactions: books of prime entry (day books)

⇓

double-entry accounts system

The *documents* are either credit notes received (for purchases returns), or credit notes issued (for sales returns).

The *day books* are:
- purchases returns day book, for credit notes received
- sales returns day book, for credit notes issued

The *ledgers* and *accounts* used are:

GENERAL LEDGER
- *purchases returns account* – to record the amount of credit notes received
- *sales returns account* – to record the amount of credit notes issued
- *Value Added Tax account* – to record the VAT amount of purchases returns and sales returns

SALES LEDGER
- separate accounts for each *debtor*

PURCHASES LEDGER
- separate accounts for each *creditor*

purchases returns day book

The purchases returns day book uses almost the same layout as the purchases day book and sales day book that we have seen in Chapter 5. It operates in a similar way, storing up information about purchases returns until such time as a transfer is made into the double-entry accounts system. The prime documents for purchases returns day book are credit notes received.

example transactions

19-1
20 Jan.   Returned goods, £40 + VAT to D Webster, credit note no 123 received
27 Jan.   Returned goods, £80 + VAT to Sanders & Sons, credit note no 406 received

The purchases returns day book is written up as follows:

Purchases Returns Day Book

Date	Details	Credit Note No	Folio	Net	VAT	Gross
19-1				£	£	£
20 Jan.	D Webster	123	PL 730	40.00	7.00	47.00
27 Jan.	Sanders & Sons	406	PL495	80.00	14.00	94.00
31 Jan.	Totals for month			120.00	21.00	141.00

Notes:

- The purchases returns day book is totalled at appropriate intervals – weekly or monthly.
- The total of the *net* column tells the business the amount of purchases returns for the period. This amount is transferred to the credit of purchases returns account in the general ledger (see below).
- The total of the *VAT* column is transferred to the credit of the VAT account in the general ledger.
- The VAT-inclusive amounts are debited to the creditors' personal amounts in the purchases ledger.
- The *gross* column records the amount of each credit note received, ie after VAT has been included. When control accounts (see Chapter 10) are in use, the total of the gross column is entered into the purchases ledger control account.

The accounts to record the above transactions (including any other transactions already recorded on these accounts – see Chapter 5) are:

PURCHASES LEDGER

Dr.			**Sanders & Sons** (account no 495)		Cr.
19-1		£	19-1		£
27 Jan.	Purchases Returns	94	20 Jan. Purchases		188

Dr.			**D Webster** (account no 730)		Cr.
19-1		£	19-1		£
20 Jan.	Purchases Returns	47	11 Jan. Purchases		141

GENERAL LEDGER

Dr.	Purchases Returns Account			Cr.
19-1	£	19-1		£
		31 Jan. Purchases Returns Day Book		120

Dr.	Value Added Tax Account			Cr.
19-1		£	19-1	£
31 Jan. Purchases Day Book		70	31 Jan. Sales Day Book	119
			31 Jan. Purchases Returns Day Book	21

summary

The purchases returns day book fits into the accounting system as follows:

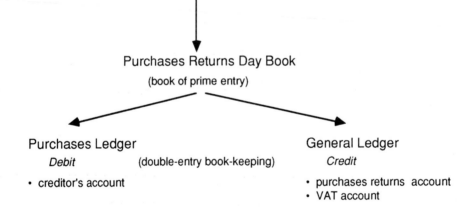

- Goods returned to the supplier
- Credit note (prime document) received from supplier

Purchases Returns Day Book

(book of prime entry)

Purchases Ledger	General Ledger
Debit (double-entry book-keeping)	*Credit*
• creditor's account	• purchases returns account
	• VAT account

sales returns day book

The sales returns day book uses the same layout and operates in a similar way to the purchases returns day book. The prime documents for the sales returns day book are credit notes issued.

example transactions

19-1
15 Jan.   T Young returns goods, £40 + VAT, credit note no CN702 issued
25 Jan.   A-Z Supplies Ltd. returns goods, £120 + VAT, credit note no CN703 issued

The sales returns day book is written up as shown on the next page:

Sales Returns Day Book

Date	Details	Credit Note No	Folio	Net	VAT	Gross
19-1				£	£	£
15 Jan.	T Young	CN702	SL 179	40.00	7.00	47.00
25 Jan.	A-Z Supplies Ltd	CN703	SL 3	120.00	21.00	141.00
31 Jan.	Totals for month			160.00	28.00	188.00

Notes:

- The sales returns day book is totalled at appropriate intervals – weekly or monthly.
- The total of the *net* column tells the business the amount of sales returns for the period. This amount is transferred to the debit of sales returns account in the general ledger (see below).
- The total of the *VAT* column is transferred to the debit of the VAT account in the general ledger.
- The VAT-inclusive amounts are credited to the debtors' personal amounts in the sales ledger.
- The *gross* column records the amount of each credit note issued, ie after VAT has been included. When control accounts (see Chapter 10) are in use, the total of the gross column is entered into the sales ledger control account.

The accounts to record the above transactions (including any other transactions already recorded on these accounts) are:

SALES LEDGER

Dr.		A-Z Supplies Ltd (account no 3)		Cr.
19-1		£	19-1	£
15 Jan. Sales		235	25 Jan. Sales Returns	141

Dr.		T Young (account no 179)		Cr.
19-1		£	19-1	£
12 Jan. Sales		94	15 Jan. Sales Returns	47

GENERAL LEDGER

Dr.		Sales Returns Account		Cr.
19-1		£	19-1	£
31 Jan. Sales Returns Day Book		160		

Dr.		Value Added Tax Account		Cr.
19-1		£	19-1	£
31 Jan. Purchases Day Book		70	31 Jan. Sales Day Book	119
31 Jan. Sales Returns Day Book		28	31 Jan. Purchases Returns Day Book	21

summary

The sales returns day book fits into the accounting system as follows:

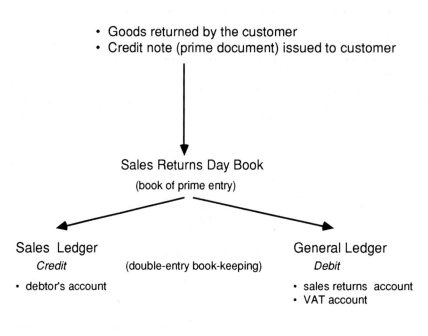

- Goods returned by the customer
- Credit note (prime document) issued to customer

Sales Returns Day Book

(book of prime entry)

Sales Ledger		General Ledger
Credit	(double-entry book-keeping)	*Debit*
• debtor's account		• sales returns account
		• VAT account

worked example: credit transactions and returns

To bring together the material covered in this chapter and Chapters 4 and 5, we will look at a comprehensive worked example. This makes use of purchases day book, sales day book, purchases returns day book, and sales returns day book.

The credit transactions are:

19-1

1 Apr.	Bought goods from Midland Supplies, £120.00 + VAT, their invoice no 12486
2 Apr.	Sold goods to P Woodhouse, £200.00 + VAT, invoice no 2416
9 Apr.	Returned goods to Midland Supplies, £20.00 + VAT, credit note no 104 received
10 Apr.	P Woodhouse returns goods, £60.00 + VAT, we issue credit note no CN12
13 Apr.	Bought goods from National Stationery, £60.00 + VAT, their invoice no A184
13 Apr.	Sold goods to Blackheath Ltd, £80.00 + VAT, invoice no 2417
20 Apr.	Blackheath Ltd returns goods, £10.00 + VAT, we issue credit note no CN13
25 Apr.	Sold goods to Butterworth Ltd, £160.00 + VAT, invoice no 2418
26 Apr.	Bought goods from Swan Equipment, £160.00 + VAT, their invoice no P102
30 Apr.	Returned goods to Swan Equipment, £40.00 + VAT, credit note no X102 received

The day books and accounts are illustrated on the next four pages: arrows indicate the transfers from the day books to the individual accounts. Note that some accounts have been repeated on different pages in order to show, on the same page, the accounts relating to a particular day book: in practice a business would keep all the transactions relating to an account together in one account.

Purchases Day Book

Date	Details	Invoice Number	Folio	Net £ p	VAT £ p	Gross £ p
19-1						
1 Apr.	Midland Supplies	12486	PL45	120 00	21 00	141 00
13 Apr.	National Stationery	A184	PL67	60 00	10 50	70 50
26 Apr.	Swan Equipment	P102	PL112	160 00	28 00	188 00
30 Apr.	Totals for month			340 00	59 50	399 50

PURCHASES LEDGER

Swan Equipment   (account no 112)

Debit / Credit

Date	Details	£ p	Date	Details	£ p
			19-1 26 Apr.	Purchases	188 00

National Stationery   (account no 67)

Debit / Credit

Date	Details	£ p	Date	Details	£ p
			19-1 13 Apr.	Purchases	70 50

Midland Supplies   (account no 45)

Debit / Credit

Date	Details	£ p	Date	Details	£ p
			19-1 1 Apr.	Purchases	141 00

GENERAL LEDGER

Value Added Tax Account

Debit / Credit

Date	Details	£ p	Date	Details	£ p
19-1 30 Apr.	Purchases Day Book	59 50			

Purchases Account

Debit / Credit

Date	Details	£ p	Date	Details	£ p
19-1 30 Apr.	Purchases Day Book	340 00			

Sales Day Book

Date	Details	Invoice Number	Folio	Net		VAT		Gross	
19-1				£	p	£	p	£	p
2 Apr.	P Woodhouse	2416	SL248	200	00	35	00	235	00
13 Apr.	Blackheath Ltd	2417	SL27	80	00	14	00	94	00
25 Apr.	Butterworth Ltd	2418	SL35	160	00	28	00	188	00
30 Apr.	Totals for month			440	00	77	00	517	00

SALES LEDGER

Butterworth Ltd (account no 35)

Debit					Credit		
Date	Details	£	p	Date	Details	£	p
19-1 25 Apr.	Sales	188	00				

Blackheath Ltd (account no 27)

Debit					Credit		
Date	Details	£	p	Date	Details	£	p
19-1 13 Apr.	Sales	94	00				

P. Woodhouse (account no 248)

Debit					Credit		
Date	Details	£	p	Date	Details	£	p
19-1 2 Apr.	Sales	235	00				

GENERAL LEDGER

Value Added Tax Account

Debit					Credit		
Date	Details	£	p	Date	Details	£	p
19-1 30 Apr.	Purchases Day Book*	59	50	19-1 30 Apr.	Sales Day Book	77	00

Sales Account

Debit					Credit		
Date	Details	£	p	Date	Details	£	p
				19-1 30 Apr.	Sales Day Book	440	00

* transaction entered previously

Purchases Returns Day Book

Date	Details	Credit Note No	Folio	Net		VAT		Gross	
19-1				£	p	£	p	£	p
9 Apr.	Midland Supplies	104	PL45	20	00	3	50	23	50
30 Apr.	Swan Equipment	X102	PL112	40	00	7	00	47	00
30 Apr.	Totals for month			60	00	10	50	70	50

PURCHASES LEDGER

Debit   **Swan Equipment**   (account no 112)   Credit

Date	Details	£	p	Date	Details	£	p
19-1				19-1			
30 Apr.	Purchases Returns	47	00	26 Apr.	Purchases	188	00*

Debit   **Midland Supplies**   (account no 45)   Credit

Date	Details	£	p	Date	Details	£	p
19-1				19-1			
9 Apr.	Purchases Returns	23	50	1 Apr.	Purchases	141	00*

GENERAL LEDGER

Debit   **Value Added Tax Account**   Credit

Date	Details	£	p	Date	Details	£	p
19-1				19-1			
30 Apr.	Purchases Day Book	59	50*	30 Apr.	Sales Day Book	77	00*
				30 Apr.	Purchases Returns Day Book	10	50

Debit   **Purchases Returns Account**   Credit

Date	Details	£	p	Date	Details	£	p
				19-1			
				30 Apr.	Purchases Returns Day Book	60	00

* transactions entered previously

Sales Returns Day Book

Date	Details	Credit Note No	Folio	Net		VAT		Gross	
19-1				£	p	£	p	£	p
10 Apr.	P Woodhouse	CN12	SL248	60	00	10	50	70	50
20 Apr.	Blackheath Ltd	CN13	SL27	10	00	1	75	11	75
30 Apr.	Totals for month			70	00	12	25	82	25

SALES LEDGER

Debit   **Blackheath Ltd**   (account no 27)   Credit

Date	Details	£	p	Date	Details	£	p
19-1				19-1			
13 Apr.	Sales	94	00*	20 Apr.	Sales Returns	11	75

Debit   **P Woodhouse**   (account no 248)   Credit

Date	Details	£	p	Date	Details	£	p
19-1				19-1			
2 Apr.	Sales	235	00*	10 Apr.	Sales Returns	70	50

GENERAL LEDGER

Debit   **Value Added Tax Account**   Credit

Date	Details	£	p	Date	Details	£	p
19-1				19-1			
30 Apr.	Purchases Day Book	59	50*	30 Apr.	Sales Day Book	77	00*
30 Apr.	Sales Returns Day Book	12	25	30 Apr.	Purchases Returns Day Book	10	50*

Debit   **Sales Returns Account**   Credit

Date	Details	£	p	Date	Details	£	p
19-1							
30 Apr.	Sales Returns Day Book	70	00				

* transactions entered previously

recording credit transactions and returns: summary

The diagram below (fig. 6.1) summarises the material that we have studied in both this and the previous two chapters. It shows the procedures for recording transactions in the accounting system for

- purchases and purchases returns
- sales and sales returns

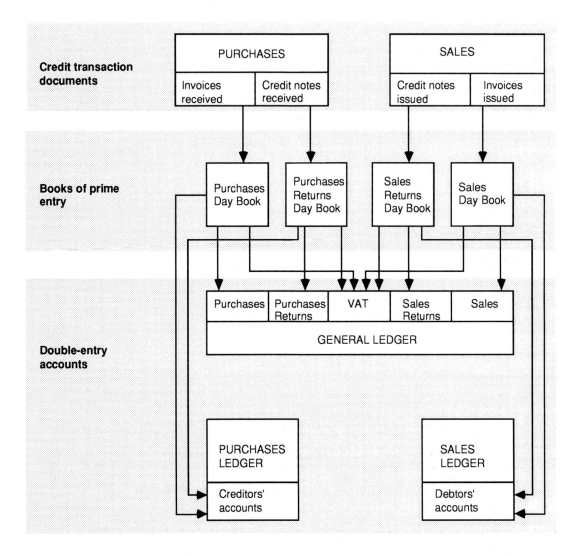

Fig. 6.1 *The accounting system for credit purchases, sales, returns*

chapter summary

❑ *Purchases returns* are when goods purchased on credit by the business are now being returned to the suppliers.

❑ *Sales returns* are when goods previously sold on credit are now being returned to the business by its customers.

❑ The prime document for returned goods is a credit note, which is issued by the business making the refund to the customer.

❑ *Purchases returns day book* is used to record credit notes received.

❑ *Sales returns day book* is used to record credit notes issued.

❑ Money amounts are transferred from the returns day books into the double-entry accounts system – the purchases ledger, sales ledger and general ledger.

In the next chapter we look at further aspects of the double-entry accounts system.

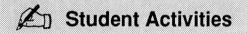 **Student Activities**

- *In these activities, the rate of Value Added Tax is to be calculated at the current rate (17½% at the time of writing). When calculating VAT amounts, you should ignore fractions of a penny, ie round down to a whole penny.*
- *Leave the folio column blank, unless otherwise stated.*

6.1   You are working for Wyvern Wholesalers and are required to enter up the purchases returns day book from the following details:

19-1
6 Apr.   Returned goods to Severn Supplies £50 + VAT, credit note no. CN225 received
14 Apr.   Returned goods to L Murphy £80 + VAT, credit note no. X456 received
21 Apr.   Returned goods to AMC Enterprises £125 + VAT, credit note no. C3921 received
29 Apr.   Returned goods to S Green £68 + VAT, credit note no. CN/SG247 received

After entering the above, total the purchases returns day book at 30 April.

6.2   The following details are to be entered in the sales returns day book of Wyvern Wholesalers:

19-1
8 Apr.   Pershore Retailers returns goods £20 + VAT, we issue credit note no. CN572
10 Apr.   E Grainger returns goods £28 + VAT, we issue credit note no. CN573
16 Apr.   D Lloyd returns goods £33 + VAT, we issue credit note no. CN574
26 Apr.   Malvern Stores returns goods £20 + VAT, we issue credit note no. CN575
30 Apr.   A Cox returns goods £40 + VAT, we issue credit note no. CN576

After entering the above, total the sales returns day book at 30 April.

6.3 The following are the credit transactions of Eveshore Engineering Suppliers for the month of August:

19-8

1 Aug. Bought goods from Steel Suppliers £250 + VAT, their invoice no. A83
3 Aug. Bought goods from Howard Engineering £110 + VAT, their invoice no. 2014
5 Aug. Sold goods to Green Bros. £95 + VAT, invoice no. 5678
6 Aug. Returned goods to Steel Suppliers £50 + VAT; credit note no. 412 received
7 Aug. Sold goods to G Gregory £105 + VAT, invoice no. 5679
10 Aug. Green Bros return goods £20 + VAT, we issue credit note no. CN771
12 Aug. Bought goods from Howard Engineering £125 + VAT, their invoice no. 2907
14 Aug. Sold goods to Mereford Manufacturing £220 + VAT, invoice no. 5680
17 Aug. Bought goods from Birmingham Foundry £355 + VAT, their invoice no. BM2841
20 Aug. Mereford Manufacturing returns goods £25 + VAT, we issue credit note no. CN772
21 Aug. Sold goods to Green Bros £250 + VAT, invoice no. 5681
24 Aug. Returned goods to Birmingham Foundry £75 + VAT; credit note no. CN/BM 330 received
26 Aug. Bought goods from Steel Suppliers £125 + VAT, their invoice no. A107
28 Aug. Sold goods to G Gregory £158 + VAT, invoice no. 5682

You are to:
(a) enter the above transactions in the *appropriate* day books of Eveshore Engineering Suppliers
(b) enter the transactions in the accounts in Eveshore Engineering Suppliers' purchases ledger, sales ledger and general ledger

6.4 Anne Green owns a shop selling paint and decorating materials; she is registered for Value Added Tax. She has two suppliers, Wyper Ltd (account no 301) and M Roper & Sons (account no 302). During the month of May 19-2 Anne received the following business documents from her suppliers:

19-2

2 May Invoice no. 562 from M Roper & Sons for £190 + VAT
4 May Invoice no. 82 from Wyper Ltd for £200 + VAT
10 May Invoice no. 86 from Wyper Ltd for £210 + VAT
18 May Invoice no. 580 from M Roper & Sons for £180 + VAT
18 May Credit note no. 82 from M Roper & Sons for £30 + VAT
21 May Invoice no. 91 from Wyper Ltd for £240 + VAT
23 May Credit note no. 6 from Wyper Ltd for £40 + VAT
25 May Invoice no. 589 from M Roper & Sons for £98 + VAT
28 May Credit note no. 84 from M Roper & Sons for £38 + VAT

You are to:
(a) enter the above transactions in the *appropriate* day books (to include a folio column) which are to be totalled at the end of May
(b) enter the transactions in the accounts in Anne Green's ledgers

7 Further aspects of double-entry accounts

In the previous two chapters we have seen how financial transactions for purchases, sales and returns are entered in the double-entry accounts. In this chapter we will look at:

- division of the ledger
- double-entry accounts for
  - capital
  - fixed assets
  - expenses
  - income
  - drawings
  - loans

division of the ledger

In the previous two chapters we have already made some use of the division of the ledger, whereby separate ledgers are kept, each containing different classes of account. The ledger of a business is usually divided into four sections:

- *sales ledger*, containing the accounts of the firm's debtors (customers)
- *purchases ledger*, containing the accounts of the firm's creditors (suppliers)
- *cash book*, containing bank account and cash account records of the business
- *general ledger* (often known as *nominal ledger*) containing all other accounts

When computers are used for accounting, the physical ledger books do not exist. However, the principles of manual and computerised accounting are the same, and the term 'ledgers' is used in computer accounting systems. Accounting software is available for each of the ledgers mentioned above, usually combined into one integrated computer program. We shall be using a computerised book-keeping system in Chapter 19.

The four divisions of the ledger are illustrated in full in fig. 7.1 on the next page.

SALES LEDGER	Sales ledger contains the accounts of debtors, and records: • sales made on credit to customers of the business • sales returns by customer • payments received from debtors • cash discount allowed (see Chapter 9) for prompt settlement Sales ledger does *not* record cash sales. Sales ledger contains an account for each debtor and records the transactions with that debtor. The total of the sales ledger account balances is the debtors figure which appears in the trial balance (see Chapter 8).
PURCHASES LEDGER	Purchases ledger contains the accounts of creditors, and records: • purchases made on credit from suppliers of the business • purchases returns made by the business • payments made to creditors • cash discount received (see Chapter 9) for prompt settlement Purchases ledger does *not* record cash purchases. Purchases ledger contains an account for each creditor and records the transactions with that creditor. The total of the purchases ledger account balances is the creditors figure which appears in the trial balance (see Chapter 8).

CASH BOOKS	The cash books comprise:
	• *Cash Book* (see Chapter 15)
	  – records all transactions for bank account and cash account
	  – cash book is also often used for listing the amounts of cash discount received and allowed and Value Added Tax
	
	• *Petty Cash Book* (see Chapter 16)
	  – records low value cash payments too small to be entered in the main cash book

GENERAL (NOMINAL) LEDGER	The general (or nominal) ledger contains the other accounts of the business:
	• *Nominal Accounts*
	  – sales account (cash *and* credit sales)
	  – purchases account (cash *and* credit purchases)
	  – sales returns, purchases returns
	  – expenses and income
	  – loan
	  – capital, drawings
	  – Value Added Tax (where the business is VAT-registered)
	
	• *Real Accounts*
	  – fixed assets, eg premises, computers, motor vehicles

Fig. 7.1 Division of the ledger

types of accounts

Within a book-keeping system there are different types of accounts: a distinction is made between *personal* and *impersonal* accounts. Personal accounts are in the names of people or businesses, eg the accounts for debtors and creditors. Impersonal accounts are the other accounts; these are usually divided between *real accounts,* which represent things such as cash, bank, computers, motor vehicles, machinery, etc, and *nominal accounts,* which record income and expenses such as sales, purchases, wages, etc.

Fig. 7.2 distinguishes between the different types of accounts.

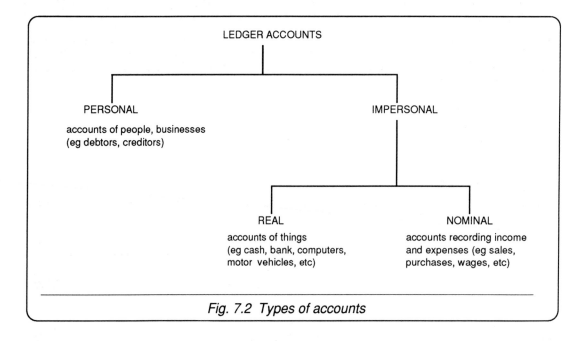

Fig. 7.2 Types of accounts

double-entry accounts

In the previous two chapters we have used accounts to record transactions for purchases, sales, and returns. In order to see how accounts are used to record other types of transactions, we will look at a new business which has just been set up by Natasha Wilson:

19-1
1 Sep.	Started in business with capital of £5,000, a cheque from Natasha Wilson paid into the bank account of the business
7 Sep.	Bought office equipment for £2,500, paying by cheque
12 Sep.	Paid rent for her office £500, by cheque
15 Sep.	Received commission of £100, in cash
20 Sep.	Withdrew £50 in cash for her own use (drawings)
26 Sep.	Received a loan of £1,000 from James Herbertson by cheque

Note: the business is <u>not</u> registered for Value Added Tax

All of these transactions involve the firm's bank account or cash account. The rules of debit and credit for bank account and cash account transactions are:

- *money in* is recorded on the debit side
- *money out* is recorded on the credit side

We will build up the entries in bank account and cash account by studying the transactions of Natasha Wilson's business listed above.

capital account

Capital is the amount of money invested in the business by the owner (or owners). The amount is *owed* by the business to the owner, although it is unlikely to be repaid immediately as then the business would be unable to operate. A *capital account* is used to record the amount(s) paid into the business; the book-keeping entries are:

- **capital introduced**
  - *debit* bank account or cash account
  - *credit* capital account

example transaction

1 Sep 19-1   Started in business with capital of £5,000, a cheque from the owner paid into the bank account of the business.

Dr.		Capital Account		Cr.
19-1	£	19-1		£
		1 Sep. Bank		5,000

Dr.		Bank Account		Cr.
19-1	£	19-1		£
1 Sep. Capital	5,000			

The dual aspect (see page 63) of this transaction is that bank account has gained value and has been debited; capital account records a liability (to the owner) and is credited. Notice that book-keeping entries look at transactions from the point of view of the business or organisation.

The introduction of capital into a business is often the very first transaction to be entered into the accounts.

fixed assets

Fixed assets are items purchased by a business for use on a permanent or semi-permanent basis. Examples are buildings, machinery, motor vehicles and office equipment. All of these are bought by a business with the intention that they will be used for some time in the business. Without fixed assets, it would be difficult to continue in business, eg without machinery it would prove difficult to run a factory; without delivery vans and lorries it would be difficult to transport the firm's products to its customers.

When a business buys fixed assets, the expenditure is referred to as *capital expenditure*. This means that items have been bought for use in the business for some years to come. By contrast, *revenue expenditure* is where the items bought will be used by the business quite quickly. For example, the purchase of a car is capital expenditure, while the cost of petrol for the car is revenue expenditure.

fixed assets and double-entry book-keeping

When fixed assets are bought, a separate account for each type of fixed asset is used, eg buildings account, machinery account, motor vehicles account, etc. The book-keeping entries are:

- **purchase of a fixed asset**
    - *debit* fixed asset account (using the appropriate account)
    - *credit* bank account or cash account

example transaction

7 Sep 19-1   Natasha Wilson bought office equipment for £2,500, paying by cheque.

Dr.		Office Equipment Account			Cr.
19-1		£	19-1		£
7 Sep.	Bank	2,500			

Dr.		Bank Account			Cr.
19-1		£	19-1		£
1 Sep.	Capital	5,000	7 Sep.	Office equipment	2,500

Note: we have debited the account which has gained value – office equipment account. The account which has given value – bank – has been credited.

expenses

Businesses and other organisations pay various running expenses, such as rent, wages, electricity, telephone, vehicle running expenses, etc. These day-to-day expenses are *revenue expenditure*. A separate account is used in the accounting system for each main class of revenue expenditure, eg rent account, wages account, etc.

The book-keeping entries are:

- **payment of an expense**
    - *debit* expense account (using the appropriate account)
    - *credit* bank account (or cash account)

example transaction

12 Sep. 19-1   Natasha Wilson pays rent for her office £500, by cheque.

Dr.		Rent Paid Account			Cr.
19-1		£	19-1		£
12 Sep. Bank		500			

Dr.		Bank Account			Cr.
19-1		£	19-1		£
1 Sep. Capital		5,000	7 Sep. Office equipment		2,500
			12 Sep. Rent paid		500

Note: The accounting rules followed are that we have debited the account which has gained value (rent paid – the business has had the use of the office for a certain time). The account which has given value (bank) has been credited.

income

From time-to-time a business or organisation may receive amounts of income apart from its normal sales income, eg rent received, commission received, or fees received. These are recorded in separate accounts for each category of income, eg rent received account, commission received account. The book-keeping entries are:

* **receipt of income**
  - *debit* bank account or cash account
  - *credit* income account (using the appropriate account)

example transaction

15 Sep. 19-1   Natasha Wilson received commission of £100, in cash.

Dr.		Cash Account			Cr.
19-1		£	19-1		£
15 Sep. Commission received		100			

Dr.		Commission Received Account			Cr.
19-1		£	19-1		£
			15 Sep. Cash		100

Note: We have debited the account which has gained value, ie cash, and credited the account which has given value, ie commission received.

owner's drawings

Drawings is the term used when the owner takes money, in cash or by cheque (or sometimes goods), from the business for personal use. A *drawings account* is used to record such amounts; the book-keeping entries for withdrawal of money are:

- **owner's drawings**
    - *debit* drawings account
    - *credit* bank account or cash account

example transaction
20 Sep. 19-1   Natasha Wilson withdrew £50 in cash for her own use.

Dr.		Drawings Account		Cr.
19-1	£	19-1		£
20 Sep. Cash	50			

Dr.		Cash Account		Cr.
19-1	£	19-1		£
15 Sep. Commission received	100	20 Sep. Drawings		50

loans

When a business or organisation receives a loan, eg from a relative or the bank, it is the cash account or bank account which gains value, while a loan account (in the name of the lender) records the liability.

- **loan received**
    - *debit* bank account or cash account
    - *credit* loan account (in name of the lender)

example transaction
26 Sep. 19-1   Natasha Wilson received a loan of £1,000 from James Herbertson by cheque

Dr.		Bank Account		Cr.
19-1	£	19-1		£
1 Sep. Capital	5,000	7 Sep. Office equipment		2,500
26 Sep. J Herbertson: loan	1,000	12 Sep. Rent paid		500

Dr.		James Herbertson: Loan Account		Cr.
19-1	£	19-1		£
		26 Sep. Bank		1,000

further transactions

Using the accounts which we have seen already, here are some further transactions:

- **loan repayment**
  - *debit* loan account
  - *credit* bank account

- **sale of a fixed asset, or return of an unsuitable fixed asset**
  - *debit* bank account
  - *credit* fixed asset account

- **withdrawal of cash from the bank for use in the business**
  - *debit* cash account
  - *credit* bank account

- **payment of cash into the bank**
  - *debit* bank account
  - *credit* cash account

VAT and double-entry accounts

When a business is registered for Value Added Tax it is able to claim back VAT paid on purchases of goods, fixed assets, and expenses. At the same time it must charge VAT whenever it supplies goods and services (except for zero-rated and exempt goods and services).

We have already seen in the previous two chapters how VAT is dealt with for purchases, sales and returns. When a business buys, for example, fixed assets it will enter the amount of VAT direct to the debit side of VAT account.

example transaction

On 16 April 19-1, XYZ Supplies Ltd, a company which is registered for Value Added Tax, buys a new computer at a cost of £600 + VAT (at 17½%) of £105, paying by cheque. This is recorded in the double-entry accounts as:

GENERAL LEDGER

Dr.		Computer Account			Cr.
19-1		£	19-1		£
16 Apr.	Bank	600			

Dr.		Value Added Tax Account			Cr.
19-1		£	19-1		£
16 Apr.	Bank	105			

CASH BOOK

Dr.		Bank Account		Cr.

19-1	£	19-1		£
		16 Apr. Computer (including VAT)		705

The payment for expenses, where VAT is charged, will be recorded in the accounts following the above principle. Also, when a VAT-registered business sells a fixed asset, it must charge VAT on the selling price.

Value Added Tax account

The Value Added Tax account in the general ledger will record:

Value Added Tax Account

Debits (input tax)	*Credits* (output tax)
• VAT on purchases	• VAT on sales and/or services
• VAT on purchases of fixed assets (except cars)	• VAT on the sale of fixed assets
• VAT on expenses	• VAT on purchases returns
• VAT on sales returns	

Note: Not all goods and services purchased can be assumed to include VAT: as well as zero-rated and exempt goods, the supplier might be a business which is not registered for VAT.

VAT calculations

It is easy to calculate the VAT amount when the price of goods before the addition of VAT is known; eg using a rate of VAT of 17½ per cent, goods costing £100 plus VAT of £17.50 gives a total cost of £117.50.

When the total cost *including* VAT is known, the amount of VAT is found by multiplying the amount by 17.5 and dividing by 117.5. For example:

Total cost	=	£117.50
Amount of VAT is $^{17.5}/_{117.5}$ of £117.50	=	£ 17.50
VAT-exclusive cost	=	£100.00

The VAT-exclusive price can be found by dividing the amount by 1.175. For example:

$$\frac{£117.50}{1.175} = \text{VAT-exclusive cost of } £100$$

Note that the divisor of 1.175 applies only with a rate of VAT of 17½%. With a rate of 10%, for example, the divisor is 1.10.

When calculating VAT amounts, fractions of a penny are ignored, ie the tax is rounded down to a whole penny.

business and organisations not registered for VAT
Where businesses and other organisations are not registered for Value Added Tax, they cannot reclaim VAT paid on purchases, fixed assets and expenses, nor can they charge VAT when they supply goods and services.

Thus the business not registered and buying the computer (see above) for £600 + VAT of £105 will record the purchase in the double-entry accounts as:

GENERAL LEDGER

Dr.		Computer Account			Cr.
19-1		£	19-1		£
16 Apr.	Bank	705			

CASH BOOK

Dr.		Bank Account			Cr.
19-1		£	19-1		£
			16 Apr.	Computer	705

Likewise, for a non-registered business, expenses which include VAT are entered in the accounts at the full invoice value.

running balance accounts

The layout of accounts that we have used has a debit side and a credit side. Whilst this layout is very useful when learning the principles of book-keeping, it is not always appropriate for practical business use. Most 'real-life' accounts have three money columns: debit transactions, credit transactions, and balance. A familiar example of this type of account is a bank statement. With a three-column account, the balance is calculated after each transaction has been entered – hence the name *running balance* accounts. For handwritten accounts, it can be rather tedious to calculate the balance after each transaction (and a potential source of errors) but, using computer accounting, the calculation is carried out automatically.

The following is the bank account used earlier in this chapter, set out in 'traditional' format:

Dr.		Bank Account			Cr.
19-1		£	19-1		£
1 Sep.	Capital	5,000	7 Sep.	Office equipment	2,500
16 Sep.	J Herbertson: loan	1,000	12 Sep.	Rent paid	500

The account does not show the balance, and would need to be balanced (see next chapter).

In 'running balance' layout, the account appears as:

Bank Account

19-1		Debit £	Credit £	Balance £
1 Sep.	Capital	5,000		5,000 Dr.
7 Sep.	Office equipment		2,500	2,500 Dr.
12 Sep.	Rent paid		500	2,000 Dr.
16 Sep.	J Herbertson: loan	1,000		3,000 Dr.

With a running balance account, it is necessary to state after each transaction whether the balance is debit (Dr.) or credit (Cr.). Note that the bank account in the books of this business has a *debit* balance, ie there is money in the bank – an asset of Natasha Wilson's business.

When looking at a bank account, do not get confused as to the meaning of the balance. In the example, above, the debit balance of £3,000 shows that *from the business' point of view* the business has an asset, ie there is £3,000 in the bank. However, the bank statement – which is *from the bank's point of view* will show a *credit* balance of £3,000, ie the bank owes the money back to the customer. To summarise:

* **money in the bank**
  – *debit* balance in firm's own accounts, ie an asset of the business
  – *credit* balance on bank statement, ie a liability of the bank

* **overdraft at the bank**
  – *credit* balance in firm's own accounts, ie a liability of the business
  – *debit* balance on bank statement, ie an asset of the bank

the use of posting sheets

In a large business or organisation, the various aspects of the accounting function will be allocated to a number of staff. For example, to look more closely at the recording and payment of credit purchases:

* one person may be involved in checking invoices received
* another person may prepare the purchases day book
* another person may pass invoices or statements received for payment
* another person may prepare remittance advices and cheques for sending to creditors
* another person may keep the double-entry accounts up-to-date

The above job allocations are given as an example only – as always, it is for the business to organise its accounting function to suit its needs. The essential point, though, is that in a larger business several people may be involved in just one area of record keeping, such as purchases, sales, etc. (In a small business, all of these tasks and more would, most likely, be carried out by just one person.)

One feature of a large business is that use may be made of a *posting sheet*. This lists transactions that are to be entered (or posted) into the double-entry accounts and will be prepared by a member of the accounts department. For example, a simple posting sheet for the transactions of Natasha Wilson in this chapter would be prepared as follows:

Posting Sheet

Account	Folio	Debit	Credit
		£	£
Bank	CB	5,000	
Capital	GL		5,000
Office equipment	GL	2,500	
Bank	CB		2,500
Rent paid	GL	500	
Bank	CB		500
Cash	CB	100	
Commission received	GL		100
Drawings	GL	50	
Cash	CB		50
Bank	CB	1,000	
J. Herbertson: loan	GL		1,000
TOTALS		9,150	9,150

Prepared by ___*J. Jarvis*___   Date ___*26 Sep 19-1*___

Checked by ___*N. Wilson*___   Date ___*26 Sep 19-1*___

Posted by ___*S. Short*___   Date ___*26 Sep 19-1*___

Notes:

- The posting sheet can be designed in any format to suit the needs of the business.

- It can be used for one day's transactions, or for longer periods such as a week or a month – much depends on the number of transactions to be recorded.

- Essential information includes:

  - name of account

  - folio, usually together with the account number, eg PL 253

  - amount of debit entry

  - amount of credit entry

- The posting sheet is totalled – this shows that the money amounts of debit entries are equal to credit entries.

- The name of the person preparing the posting sheet is stated with the date, together with the person checking it and the date.

- The name of the person posting the transactions to the firm's double-entry accounts, together with the date, is given.

batched data entry

A variation on the posting sheet is often used – particularly with computer accounting programs. Here it is usual to *batch* a series of transactions, eg to deal with a number of sales ledger transactions, or purchases ledger transactions. By batching, there is less need to keep changing from one area of the program to another. Before entering a batch of transactions, it is usual to *pre-list* them on a separate form such as that shown below for a batch of sales invoices:

Sales Invoice Batch

Customer		Invoice		Net	VAT	Gross
Account No	Name	Date	No	£	£	£
		Check list totals				

The sales invoice batch form will be completed from invoices which have been prepared separately. The transactions will then be entered from the invoices into the computer. The computer screen will show the total money amount of invoices and this is compared with the check list total from the sales invoice batch form; if there is a discrepancy, the error must be located and corrected.

chapter summary

❑ Accounts are kept in 'the ledger'. This is often divided up into several separate ledgers:
   – *sales ledger*, containing debtors' accounts
   – *purchases ledger*, containing creditors' accounts
   – *cash book*, containing bank account and cash account
   – *general ledger* (or *nominal ledger*), containing all other accounts

❑ Entries in the bank account and cash account are:
   – *debit* money in
   – *credit* money out

❑ Capital is the amount of money invested in the business by the owner.

❑ Fixed assets are items purchased by a business for use on a semi-permanent basis, eg premises, motor vehicles, machinery and office equipment. The purchase of such items is called *capital expenditure*.

❑ Running expenses of a business, such as rent, wages, electricity, etc are called *revenue expenditure*.

❑ Drawings is where the owner takes money (or goods) from the business for personal use.

In the next chapter we will see how accounts are balanced, and a trial balance is extracted.

✏️ Student Activities

7.1   James Anderson has kept his bank account up-to-date, but has not got around to the other double-entry book-keeping entries. Rule up the other accounts for him, and make the appropriate entries.

Dr.			Bank Account		Cr.
19-1		£	19-1		£
1 Feb.	Capital	7,500	6 Feb.	Computer	2,000
14 Feb.	Bank loan	2,500	8 Feb.	Rent paid	750
20 Feb.	Commission received	145	12 Feb.	Wages	425
			23 Feb.	Drawings	200
			25 Feb.	Wages	380
			28 Feb.	Van	6,000

Note: James Anderson is not registered for Value Added Tax.

7.2   The following are the business transactions of Tony Long for the month of May 19-2:

19-2
1 May	Started a business with capital of £6,000 in the bank
4 May	Bought a machine for £3,500, paying by cheque
6 May	Bought office equipment for £2,000, paying by cheque
10 May	Paid rent £350, by cheque
12 May	Obtained a loan of £1,000 from a friend, Lucy Warner, and paid her cheque into the bank
15 May	Paid wages £250, by cheque
17 May	Commission received £150, by cheque
20 May	Drawings £85, by cheque
25 May	Paid wages £135, by cheque

You are to:

(a)   Write up Tony Long's bank account

(b)   Complete the double-entry book-keeping transactions

Note: Tony Long is not registered for Value Added Tax.

7.3   Enter the following transactions into the double-entry book-keeping accounts of Jean Lacey, who is registered for Value Added Tax:

19-5
1 Aug.	Started in business with capital of £5,000 in the bank
3 Aug.	Bought a computer for £1,800 + VAT, paying by cheque
7 Aug.	Paid rent £100, by cheque
10 Aug.	Received commission £200 + VAT, *in cash*
12 Aug.	Bought office fittings £2,000 + VAT, paying by cheque
15 Aug.	Received a loan, £1,000 by cheque, from a friend, Sally Orton
17 Aug.	Drawings £100, *in cash*
20 Aug.	Returned some of the office fittings (unsuitable) and received a refund cheque of £240 + VAT
25 Aug.	Received commission £160 + VAT, by cheque
27 Aug.	Made a loan repayment to Sally Orton of £150, by cheque

Note: use the current rate of Value Added Tax (17½% at the time of writing)

8 Balancing accounts; the trial balance

With the 'traditional' form of account (a 'T' account) that we have used in Chapters 5, 6 and 7, it is necessary to calculate the balance of each account from time-to-time, according to the needs of the business, and at the end of each financial year. The balance of an account is the total of that account to date, eg the amount of wages paid, the amount of sales made. In this chapter we shall see how this *balancing of accounts* is carried out.

We shall then use the balances from each account in order to check the double-entry book-keeping by extracting a *trial balance,* which is a list of the balances of ledger accounts.

balancing the accounts

At regular intervals, often at the end of each month, accounts are balanced in order to show the amounts, for example:
- owing to each creditor
- owing by each debtor
- of sales
- of purchases
- of sales returns (returns in)
- of purchases returns (returns out)
- of expenses incurred by the business
- of fixed assets, eg premises, machinery, etc owned by the business
- of capital and drawings of the owner of the business
- of other liabilities, eg loans

We have already noted earlier that, where running balance accounts (see page 95) are used, there is no need to balance each account, because the balance is already calculated – either manually or by computer – after each transaction.

method of balancing accounts

On the next page is an example of an account which has been balanced at the month-end:

Dr.		Bank Account					Cr.
19-1			£	19-1			£
1 Sep.	Capital		5,000	2 Sep.	Computer		1,800
5 Sep.	J Jackson: loan		2,500	6 Sep.	Purchases		500
10 Sep.	Sales		750	12 Sep.	Drawings		100
				15 Sep.	Wages		200
				30 Sep.	Balance c/d		5,650
			8,250				8,250
1 Oct.	Balance b/d		5,650				

The steps involved in balancing accounts are:

Step 1
The entries in the debit and credit money columns are totalled; these totals are not recorded in ink on the account at this stage, but can be recorded either as sub-totals in pencil on the account, or noted on a separate piece of paper. In the example above, the debit side totals £8,250, while the credit side is £2,600.

Step 2
The difference between the two totals is the balance of the account and this is entered on the account:
• on the side of the smaller total
• on the next available line
• with the date of balancing (often the last day of the month)
• with the description 'balance c/d', or 'balance carried down'

In the bank account above, the balance carried down is £8,260 – £2,600 = £5,650, entered in the credit column.

Step 3
Both sides of the account are now totalled, including the balance which has just been entered, and the totals (the same on both sides) are entered *on the same line* in the appropriate column, and double underlined. The double underline indicates that the account has been balanced at this point using the figures above the total: the figures above the underline should not be added in to anything below the underline.

In the bank account above, the totals on each side of the account are £8,250.

Step 4
As we are using double-entry book-keeping, there must be an opposite entry to the 'balance c/d' calculated in Step 2. The same money amount is entered on the *other side of the account* below the double-underlined totals entered in Step 3. We have now completed both the debit and credit entry. The date is usually recorded as the next day after 'balance c/d', ie often the first day of the following month, and the description can be 'balance b/d' or 'balance brought down'.

In the example above, the balance brought down on the bank account on 1 October 19-1 is £5,650 debit; this means that, according to the firm's accounting records, there is £5,650 in the bank.

A practical point
When balancing accounts, use a pen and not a pencil (except for Step 1). If any errors are made, cross them through neatly with a single line, and write the corrected version on the line below. Do *not* use correcting fluid: at best it conceals errors, at worst it conceals fraudulent transactions.

further examples of balancing accounts

Dr.		Wages Account		Cr.
19-1		£	19-1	£
9 Apr.	Bank	750	30 Apr. Balance c/d	2,250
16 Apr.	Bank	800		
23 Apr.	Bank	700		
		2,250		2,250
1 May	Balance b/d	2,250		

The above wages account has transactions on one side only, but is still balanced in the same way. This account shows that the total amount paid for wages is £2,250.

Dr.		B Lewis Ltd		Cr.
19-1		£	19-1	£
10 Apr.	Purchases Returns	30	7 Apr. Purchases	280
26 Apr.	Bank	250		
		280		280

This account in the name of a creditor has a 'nil' balance after the transactions for April have taken place. The two sides of the account are totalled and, as both debit and credit side are the same amount, there is nothing further to do, apart from entering the double-underlined total.

Dr.		A Holmes		Cr.
19-1		£	19-1	£
1 Apr.	Balance b/d	105	10 Apr. Bank	105
11 Apr.	Sales	125	11 Apr. Sales Returns	25
			30 Apr. Balance c/d	100
		230		230
1 May	Balance b/d	100		

This is the account of a debtor and, at the start of the month, there was a debit balance of £105 brought down from March. After the various transactions for April, there remains a debit balance of £100 owing at 1 May.

Dr.		Office Equipment Account		Cr.
19-1		£	19-1	£
12 Apr.	Bank	2,000		

This account has just the one transaction and, in practice, there is no need to balance it. It should be clear that the account has a debit balance of £2,000, which is represented by the asset of office equipment.

Dr.		Malvern Manufacturing Co		Cr.
19-1	£	19-1		£
29 Apr. Bank	250	18 Apr. Purchases		250

This creditor's account has a 'nil' balance, with just one transaction on each side. All that is needed here is to double underline the amount on both sides.

extracting a trial balance

The book-keeper extracts a trial balance from the accounting records in order to check the arithmetical accuracy of the double-entry book-keeping, ie that the debit entries equal the credit entries.

A trial balance is a list of the balances of every account forming the ledger, distinguishing between those accounts which have debit balances and those which have credit balances.

A trial balance is extracted at regular intervals – often at the end of each month.

example of a trial balance

Trial balance of A-Z Suppliers as at 31 January 19-1

Name of account	Dr. £	Cr. £
Purchases	750	
Sales		1,600
Sales returns	25	
Purchases returns		50
J Brown (debtor)	155	
T Sweet (creditor)		110
Rent paid	100	
Wages	150	
Heating and lighting	125	
Office equipment	500	
Machinery	1,000	
Cash	50	
Bank	455	
J Williams – loan		800
Capital		1,000
Drawings	250	
	3,560	3,560

Notes:

- The debit and credit columns have been totalled and are the same amount. Thus the trial balance proves that the accounting records are arithmetically correct. (A trial balance does *not* prove the *complete* accuracy of the accounting records – see below.)
- The heading for a trial balance gives the name of the business whose accounts have been listed and the date it was extracted, ie the end of the accounting period.

- The balance for each account listed in the trial balance is the figure brought down after the accounts have been balanced.
- As well as the name of each account, it is quite usual to show in the trial balance the account number. Most accounting systems give numbers to accounts and these can be listed in a separate 'folio' or 'reference' column.

debit and credit balances – guidelines

Certain accounts always have a debit balance, while others always have a credit balance. You should already know these, but the lists set out below will act as a revision guide, and will also help in your understanding of trial balances.

Debit balances include:
- cash account
- purchases account
- sales returns account (returns in)
- fixed asset accounts, eg premises, motor vehicles, machinery, office equipment, etc
- expenses accounts, eg wages, telephone, rent paid, etc
- drawings account
- debtors' accounts (many businesses use a *sales ledger control account* – see Chapter 10 – the balance of which gives the total of debtors: this balance is entered in the trial balance as 'debtors')

Credit balances include:
- sales account
- purchases returns account (returns out)
- income accounts, eg rent received, commission received, fees received, etc
- capital account
- loan account
- creditors' accounts (many businesses use a *purchases ledger control account* – see Chapter 10 – the balance of which gives the total of creditors: this balance is entered in the trial balance as 'creditors')

Note: bank account can be either debit or credit – it will be debit when the business has money in the bank, and credit when it is overdrawn.

if the trial balance doesn't balance . . .

If the trial balance fails to balance, ie the two totals are different, there is an error (or errors):
- *either* in the addition of the trial balance
- *and/or* in the double-entry book-keeping

The procedure for finding the error(s) is as follows:
- check the addition of the trial balance
- check that the balance of each account has been correctly entered in the trial balance, and under the correct heading, ie debit or credit
- check that the balance of every account in the ledger has been included in the trial balance
- check the calculation of the balance on each account

- calculate the amount that the trial balance is wrong, and then look in the accounts for a transaction for this amount: if one is found, check that the double-entry book-keeping has been carried out correctly

- halve the amount by which the trial balance is wrong, and look for a transaction for this amount: if it is found, check the double-entry book-keeping

- if the amount by which the trial balance is wrong is divisible by nine, then the error may be a reversal of figures, eg £65 entered as £56, or £45 entered as £54

- if the trial balance is wrong by a round amount, eg £10, £100, £1,000, the error is likely to be in the calculation of the account balances

- if the error(s) is still not found, it is necessary to check the book-keeping transactions since the date of the last trial balance, by going back to the prime documents and books of prime entry

errors not shown by a trial balance

As mentioned earlier, a trial balance does not prove the complete accuracy of the accounting records. There are six types of errors that are not shown by a trial balance.

1. Error of omission

Here a business transaction has been completely omitted from the accounting records, ie both the debit and credit entries have not been made.

2. Reversal of entries

With this error, the debit and credit entries have been made in the accounts but *on the wrong side* of the two accounts concerned. For example, a cash sale has been entered wrongly as debit sales account, credit cash account. (This should have been entered as a debit to cash account, and a credit to sales account.)

3. Mispost/error of commission

Here, a transaction is entered to the wrong person's account. For example, a sale of goods on credit to A T Hughes has been entered as debit A J Hughes' account, credit sales account. Here, double-entry book-keeping has been completed but, when A J Hughes receives a statement of account, he or she will soon complain about being debited with goods not ordered or received.

4. Error of principle

This is when a transaction has been entered in the wrong type of account. For example, the cost of petrol for vehicles has been entered as debit motor vehicles account, credit bank account. The error is that motor vehicles account represents fixed assets, and the transaction should have been debited to the expense account for motor vehicle running expenses.

5. Error of original entry (or transcription)

Here, the correct accounts have been used, and the correct sides: what is wrong is that the amount has been entered incorrectly in *both* accounts. This could be caused by a 'bad figure' on an invoice or a cheque, or it could be caused by a 'reversal of figures', eg an amount of £45 being entered in both accounts as £54. Note that both debit and credit entries need to be made incorrectly for the trial balance still to balance; if one entry has been made incorrectly and the other is correct, then the error will be shown.

6. Compensating error

This is where two errors cancel each other out. For example, if the balance of purchases account is calculated wrongly at £10 too much, and a similar error has occurred in calculating the balance of sales account, then the two errors will compensate each other, and the trial balance will not show the errors.

Correction of errors is covered fully in Chapter 11.

importance of the trial balance

A business will extract a trial balance on a regular basis to check the arithmetic accuracy of the book-keeping. However, the trial balance is also used as the starting point in the production of the *final accounts* of a business. These final accounts, which are produced once a year (often more frequently) comprise:

- trading account
- profit and loss account
- balance sheet

The final accounts show the owner(s) how profitable the business has been, what the business owns, and how the business is financed. The preparation of final accounts is an important aspect of accountancy and will form a part of your further studies in the subject. For the moment, we can say that extraction of a trial balance is an important exercise in the business accounts process: it proves the book-keeper's accuracy, and also lists the account balances which form the basis for the final accounts of a business.

chapter summary

❑ The traditional 'T' account needs to be balanced at regular intervals – often at the month-end.

❑ When balancing accounts, the book-keeper must adhere strictly to the rules of double-entry book-keeping.

❑ When each account in the ledger has been balanced, a trial balance can be extracted.

❑ A trial balance is a list of the balances of every account forming the ledger, distinguishing between those accounts which have debit balances and those which have credit balances.

❑ A trial balance does not prove the complete accuracy of the accounting records; errors not shown by a trial balance are:
  – error of omission
  – reversal of entries
  – mispost/error of commission
  – error of principle
  – error of original entry
  – compensating error

❑ The trial balance is used as the starting point for the preparation of a business' final accounts.

In the next chapter we will consider some further aspects of debtors and creditors.

Student Activities

8.1 Andrew Jarvis started in business on 1 April 19-2, paying £1,000 into his business bank account as opening capital.

During the month he had the following transactions:

19-2
2 Apr.   Bought goods for resale, paying by cheque, £255
4 Apr.   Paid for advertising by cheque, £60
7 Apr.   Sold goods, £195, a cheque being received
8 Apr.   Paid rent by cheque, £125
10 Apr. Sold goods, £248, a cheque being received
11 Apr. Drawings £100 by cheque
14 Apr. Bought goods for resale, paying by cheque, £240
16 Apr. Received a loan from J Couchman, £1,000 by cheque
18 Apr. Sold goods, £220, a cheque being received
20 Apr. Bought shop fittings, £1,250, paying by cheque
23 Apr. Bought goods for resale, paying by cheque, £180
24 Apr. Paid for advertising by cheque, £90
26 Apr. Sold goods, £312, a cheque being received
28 Apr. Paid rent by cheque, £125
30 Apr. Drawings £125 by cheque

You are to:

(a) Record the transactions in his bank account
(b) Record the transactions in his other double-entry accounts
(c) Balance each account at 30 April 19-2
(d) Draw up a trial balance at 30 April 19-2

Notes:
• day books are not required
• Andrew Jarvis is not registered for VAT

8.2 Produce the trial balance of Jane Greenwell as at 28 February 19-1. She has omitted to open a capital account.

	£
Bank overdraft	1,250
Purchases	850
Cash	48
Sales	730
Purchases returns	144
Creditors	1,442
Equipment	2,704
Van	3,200
Sales returns	90
Debtors	1,174
Wages	1,500
Capital	?

8.3 The following are the business transactions of Robert Jefferson, a bookshop owner, for the months of January and February 19-1:

Transactions for January
19-1
1 Jan. Started in business with capital of £5,000 in the bank
2 Jan. Paid rent on premises £200, by cheque
4 Jan. Bought shop fittings £2,000, by cheque
5 Jan. Bought stock of books £2,500, on credit from Northam Publishers
8 Jan. Book sales £1,200, paid into bank
9 Jan. Book sales £1,000, paid into bank
12 Jan. Bought books £5,000, on credit from Broadheath Books
15 Jan. Book sales £1,500 to Teme School, a cheque being received
17 Jan. Book sales, £1,250, paid into bank
19 Jan. Bought books from Financial Publications £2,500, by cheque
23 Jan. Teme School returned unsuitable books £580, cheque refund sent
30 Jan. Sold books on credit to Wyvern College, £1,095

Transactions for February
19-1
3 Feb. Book sales £2,510, paid into bank
5 Feb. Paid rent on premises £200, by cheque
7 Feb. Bought shop fittings £1,385, by cheque
10 Feb. Book sales £3,875, paid into bank
11 Feb. Sent cheque, £2,500, to Northam Publishers
13 Feb. Bought books £1,290, on credit from Northam Publishers
14 Feb. Sent cheque, £5,000, to Broadheath Books
17 Feb. Book sales £1,745, paid into bank
18 Feb. Wyvern College returned books, £250
21 Feb. Book sales £1,435, paid into bank
24 Feb. Bought books £1,250, on credit from Associated Publishers
28 Feb. Book sales £3,900, paid into bank

You are to:

(a) Record the January transactions in his double-entry accounts. Each account is to be balanced at 31 January 19-1

(b) Draw up a trial balance at 31 January 19-1

(c) Record the February transactions in his double-entry accounts. Each account is to be balanced at 28 February 19-1

(d) Draw up a trial balance at 28 February 19-1

Notes:
• day books are not required
• Robert Jefferson is not registered for VAT

8.4 A friend, who is just beginning her studies of book-keeping comments:

• "if the trial balance totals agree it is proof that the book-keeping entries are 100 per cent correct"

• "I wouldn't know where to start looking if the trial balance totals did not agree"

Reply to your friend.

ASSIGNMENT
3

Day books and ledger accounts:
Turner & Sons Ltd

SITUATION

Kevin Kemp works in the accounts department of a manufacturing company that produces components for the car industry. The company, Turner & Sons Ltd, Unit 10, Valley Road Industrial Estate, Mereford, MR1 5PQ, has just computerised its accounting system.

The accountant, Mr T Worth, has instructed Kevin that for the first few months, while the accounts are being produced by computer, he is to keep separate manual records of the company's transactions. (*Note to students:* it is good practice to keep manual records in the first months of computerisation – Chapter 19 deals with computer accounting in more detail.) Kevin's instructions are to record only the documents issued and received; the accountant will record manually cash and bank transactions.

The computer accounting system was introduced on 1 March 19-1. At that date, Turner & Sons Ltd had the following accounts in the purchases and sales ledgers:

Purchases ledger

Ace Forgings Ltd, balance	£550.00
Round Tubes Ltd, balance	£610.00
Bright Metal Company Ltd, balance	£120.00

Sales ledger

Vord Motors plc, balance	£870.00
Portland Vehicles Ltd, balance	£940.00
Boxhall Vehicles plc, balance	£340.00

Turner & Sons Ltd also had the following account balances in the general ledger on 1 March 19-1:

• purchases	£4,050.00
• sales	£9,600.00
• Value Added Tax (credit balance, ie VAT owing)	£832.50

During the first month that the computer was operational (March 19-1), Kevin recorded the invoices issued and received shown on pages 110 to 112.

Invoice No. 1011

INVOICE   No. 1011

TURNER & SONS LTD
Unit 10
Valley Road Industrial Estate
MEREFORD
MR1 5PQ

Tel/Fax: 0605 732491
VAT Reg No 407 8693 82

To:		
Vord Motors plc	Date/Tax Point	1 Mar 19-1
Mondeo Way	Customer Order No.	5871/91
AINTREE	Customer Account No.	V 0141
Essex		
AN4 7JH		

Quantity	Description	Unit Price £ p	Total Amount £ p
20	Mouldings: type ABC123	10 00	200 00
	Total Goods		200 00
	Value Added Tax		35 00
	Total Due		235 00

Terms: Net Monthly
E & OE

Invoice No. 1012

INVOICE   No. 1012

TURNER & SONS LTD
Unit 10
Valley Road Industrial Estate
MEREFORD
MR1 5PQ

Tel/Fax: 0605 732491
VAT Reg No 407 8693 82

To:		
Boxhall Vehicles plc	Date/Tax Point	2 Mar 19-1
Cavalier House	Customer Order No.	27469/01
140-144 Corsa Way	Customer Account No.	B 0103
BLUTON		
Bedfordshire		
BL2 8AH		

Quantity	Description	Unit Price £ p	Total Amount £ p
250	Mouldings: type BV861	2 00	500 00
	Total Goods		500 00
	Value Added Tax		87 50
	Total Due		587 50

Terms: Net Monthly
E & OE

Ace Forgings Ltd — Invoice 87

INVOICE

Ace Forgings Ltd
Ace Works Tipton Way
PUDLEY PY3 8TD
Tel/Fax: 0681 234966
VAT Reg No 684 9143 21

Invoice to		
TURNER & SONS LTD	Invoice no:	87
Unit 10	Account:	428
Valley Road Industrial Estate	Date/tax point:	6 Mar 19-1
MEREFORD MR1 5PQ	Order no:	TS 6851

Quantity	Description	Unit Price £ p	Total Amount £ p
200 metres	Steel section: type 457	4 00	800 00
	Total Goods		800 00
	Value Added Tax		140 00
	Total Due		940 00

TERMS

NET MONTHLY

CARRIAGE PAID

E & OE

Round Tubes Ltd — Invoice 101

INVOICE

Round Tubes Ltd
The Tube Works
Terry Hill Industrial Estate
BARLASTON PY3 1AJ
Tel/Fax: 0681 794238
VAT Reg No 986 3217 64

Invoice to		
TURNER & SONS LTD	Invoice no:	101
Unit 10	Account:	TU 317
Valley Road Industrial Estate	Date/tax point:	7 Mar 19-1
MEREFORD MR1 5PQ	Order no:	TS 6852

Quantity	Description	Unit Price £ p	Total Amount £ p
100 lengths	Plate steel tube: type OJ/157	3 00	300 00
	Total Goods		300 00
	Value Added Tax		52 50
	Total Due		352 50

TERMS

NET MONTHLY

CARRIAGE PAID

E & OE

INVOICE

No. 1013

TURNER & SONS LTD
Unit 10
Valley Road Industrial Estate
MEREFORD
MR1 5PQ

Tel/Fax: 0605 732491
VAT Reg No 407 8693 82

To:		
Boxhall Vehicles plc	Date/Tax Point	10 Mar 19-1
Cavalier House	Customer Order No.	27521/01
140-144 Corsa Way	Customer Account No.	B 0103
BLUTON		
Bedfordshire		
BL2 8AH		

Quantity	Description	Unit Price £ p	Total Amount £ p
50	Gear units: type 747/21	20 00	1,000 00
	Total Goods		1,000 00
	Value Added Tax		175 00
	Total Due		1,175 00

Terms: Net Monthly
E & OE

Invoice no. 58

BRIGHT METAL COMPANY LTD
Unit 91, Cotheridge Industrial Estate
CARPMINSTER   CA3 4JT

Tel/Fax: 0724 683910
VAT Reg No: 226 4932 71

Invoice to		
TURNER & SONS LTD	Account:	4271
Unit 10	Date/tax point:	15 Mar 19-1
Valley Road Industrial Estate	Order no:	TS 6853
MEREFORD MR1 5PQ		

Quantity	Description	Unit Price £ p	Total Amount £ p
200	Plated pressings: type 6/09	3 00	600 00
	Total Goods		600 00
	Value Added Tax		105 00
	Total Due		705 00

TERMS
NET MONTHLY
CARRIAGE PAID
E & OE

INVOICE

No. 1014

TURNER & SONS LTD
Unit 10
Valley Road Industrial Estate
MEREFORD
MR1 5PQ

Tel/Fax: 0605 732491
VAT Reg No 407 8693 82

To:		
Portland Vehicles Ltd	Date/Tax Point	18 Mar 19-1
Metro Works	Customer Order No.	386/17
TONGBRIDGE	Customer Account No.	P 0170
West Midlands		
TG4 1AP		

Quantity	Description	Unit Price £ p	Total Amount £ p
75	Gear units: type 747/25	20 00	1,500 00
	Total Goods		1,500 00
	Value Added Tax		262 50
	Total Due		1,762 50

Terms: Net Monthly
E & OE

INVOICE

No. 1015

TURNER & SONS LTD
Unit 10
Valley Road Industrial Estate
MEREFORD
MR1 5PQ

Tel/Fax: 0605 732491
VAT Reg No 407 8693 82

To:		
Vord Motors plc	Date/Tax Point	25 Mar 19-1
Mondeo Way	Customer Order No.	6010/91
AINTREE	Customer Account No.	V 0141
Essex		
AN4 7JH		

Quantity	Description	Unit Price £ p	Total Amount £ p
120	Mouldings: type ABC123	10 00	1,200 00
	Total Goods		1,200 00
	Value Added Tax		210 00
	Total Due		1,410 00

Terms: Net Monthly
E & OE

INVOICE

Ace Forgings Ltd
Ace Works Tipton Way
PUDLEY PY3 8TD
Tel/Fax: 0681 234966
VAT Reg No 684 9143 21

Invoice to		
TURNER & SONS LTD Unit 10 Valley Road Industrial Estate MEREFORD MR1 5PQ		

Invoice no:	96
Account:	428
Date/tax point:	25 Mar 19-1
Order no:	TS 6854

Quantity	Description	Unit Price £ p	Total Amount £ p
100 metres	Steel section: type 457	4 00	400 00
	Total Goods		400 00
	Value Added Tax		70 00
	Total Due		470 00

TERMS
NET MONTHLY
CARRIAGE PAID
E & OE

INVOICE

Round Tubes Ltd
The Tube Works
Terry Hill Industrial Estate
BARLASTON PY3 1AJ
Tel/Fax: 0681 794238
VAT Reg No 986 3217 64

Invoice to		
TURNER & SONS LTD Unit 10 Valley Road Industrial Estate MEREFORD MR1 5PQ		

Invoice no:	109
Account:	TU 317
Date/tax point:	31 Mar 19-1
Order no:	TS 6855

Quantity	Description	Unit Price £ p	Total Amount £ p
70 lengths	Steel tube: type OP/191	2 00	140 00
	Total Goods		140 00
	Value Added Tax		24 50
	Total Due		164 50

TERMS
NET MONTHLY
CARRIAGE PAID
E & OE

STUDENT TASKS

You are to assume the role of Kevin (or Karen) Kemp and undertake the following tasks:

1. Rule up columns for Turner & Sons Ltd's sales and purchases day books. The transactions are to be recorded in the appropriate day books and, at the end of March, the books are to be totalled.

2. Rule up columns for the accounts in Turner & Sons Ltd's ledger system and open each account with the balance on 1 March 19-1. Enter the transactions, including the totals recorded in the books of prime entry, to the appropriate account in Turner & Sons Ltd's sales ledger, purchases ledger and general ledger. The accounts needed are:

    *   *Sales Ledger* – accounts for each customer
    *   *Purchases Ledger* – accounts for each supplier
    *   *General Ledger* – sales account, purchases account, VAT account

3. Balance each account at 31 March 19-1.

4. Assuming that no money settlement has been forwarded or received during March 19-1:

    *   draw up and complete statements of account for Turner & Sons Ltd's customers
    *   compile a list of the outstanding balances Turner & Sons Ltd owes its suppliers
    *   compile a list of the outstanding balances Turner & Sons Ltd is owed by its customers

    Note: a blank statement is included in Appendix 1, and may be photocopied

9 Debtors and creditors

In this chapter we shall focus on further aspects of debtors and creditors. In particular we shall look at:

- credit control
- the problem of bad debts
- recording bad debts in the accounting system
- how bad debts can be minimised
- aspects of creditors, including reconciliation of creditors' statements
- recording cash discount in debtors' and creditors' accounts

credit control

So far in this book we have taken for granted that a supplier will sell goods on credit terms (ie allow the buyer to pay later), and also that the buyer will pay up on receipt of the statement. Unfortunately these are assumptions which in reality cannot be taken for granted. When selling on credit the seller must:

- investigate a new buyer to ensure that he or she is creditworthy – ie has the financial resources to pay on the due date
- monitor existing buyers to ensure that they do pay up on time
- chase up debts which are overdue

This overall process is known as *credit control*. It is a sign of a well-run business that credit control is tight, and the debtors are chased up, and even taken to court for non-payment if the amount and the circumstances are appropriate.

We will now look at credit control through two Case Studies: the first looks at a person 'vetting' the creditworthiness of a potential buyer; the second looks at a supplier chasing up overdue debts.

Case Study 1: Selling on credit

Situation

Matthew has recently started up in business with a fruit and vegetable stall in the local market. Up until now all his sales have been paid for by his customers in cash or by cheque (collectively known as 'cash sales'). He has today been approached by Goodfood, a firm of caterers who operate a number of works canteens in the locality, to quote for all their fruit and vegetable supplies. The value of this potential contract is sales of about £300 each week; Goodfood require an invoice at the end of each week listing Matthew's sales to them for the week, and they agree to make payment not later than 30 days after the date of the invoice. What should Matthew do?

Solution

The steps that need to be taken by Matthew are:

- When approached by a previously unknown organisation wishing to buy goods on credit, the seller should ask for two references. One of these should be the buyer's bank, and the other a trader with whom the buyer has previously done business.

- The seller, Matthew, before supplying goods on credit, must take up both references and obtain satisfactory replies. (Note that it is not possible to approach a bank direct for a reference on one of their customers. It can only be done bank-to-bank, and so the seller must ask his or her own bank to approach the buyer's bank.)

- Once satisfactory replies have been received, a credit limit for the customer should be established. The actual amount of the credit limit will depend very much on the expected amount of future business – perhaps £1,000 in this example. The credit limit should not normally be exceeded.

- Matthew should ensure that invoices and monthly statements are sent out promptly.

- If a customer does not pay within a reasonable time, procedures should be followed to chase up the debt promptly; these include letters, telephone calls and even court action.

Case Study 2: Chasing debts

Situation

Matthew has found that Goodfood, despite the good references received, are not paying up, and he is owed a total of £450 which should have been paid three months ago. What should he do? He has various courses of action available to him; what he does will depend on how reluctant Goodfood are to pay.

Solution

A typical procedure used by an organisation chasing up debts, which Matthew could adopt, would be:

- Write a letter along the lines of

  "Dear Sir,

  <u>*Overdue Account*</u>
  We do not appear to have received settlement of your account with us, the balance of which is £450. We enclose an up-to-date statement and shall be grateful if you settle this overdue amount by return of post."

- If nothing is heard within seven days, then telephone and ask to speak to their Accounts Department, Purchases Ledger Section. Ask about the overdue payment. You may be told *"the cheque is in the post"* (it rarely is!) or *"can we have a copy of the last invoice –we don't seem to have received it?"* These replies can be stalling tactics to buy time; on the other hand, the telephone call may produce results and a payment in the post.

- If payment is not received as a result of the telephone call, Matthew has a number of options open to him:

  – to employ a solicitor to send Goodfood a formal demand for the money and possibly to take Goodfood to court (this is an expensive option)
  – to employ the services of a debt-collecting agency
  – to take Goodfood to the Small Claims Court (used for claims under £1,000), a time-consuming process with no guarantee of success.

Matthew should realise that taking Goodfood to court and obtaining judgement against them still does not mean he will get his money back. It is often thought that going to court will solve all problems; it often results in a large solicitor's bill and nothing from the debtor. Goodfood may not have the money, and may even be bankrupt, which means that their liabilities exceed their assets. An unsecured creditor like Matthew is unlikely to be repaid anything at all. At a time like this Matthew will probably want to cut his losses and write off the £450 as a 'bad debt', an expense to his business.

bad debts

A bad debt is a debt owing to a business or organisation which it considers will never be paid.

Let us consider a business with debtors of £10,000. This total will, most probably, be made up of a number of debtors' accounts. At any one time, a few of these accounts will be bad, and therefore the amount is uncollectable: these are *bad debts*, and they need to be written off, ie the business will give up trying to collect the debt and will accept the loss. For example, suppose that debtors' accounts with balances totalling £200 are to be written off as bad, the net debtors' figure becomes:

	£
Gross debtors	10,000
Less: bad debts written off	200
Net debtors	9,800

Bad debts are written off when they become uncollectable. This means that all reasonable efforts to recover the amount owing have been exhausted, ie statements and letters have been sent to the debtor requesting payment and legal action, where appropriate, or the threat of legal action has failed to obtain payment.

In writing off a debtor's account as bad, the business is bearing the cost of the amount due. The debtor's account is closed and the amount (or amounts, where a number of accounts are dealt with in this way) is debited to *bad debts written off account*. This account stores up the amounts of account balances written off during the year (in much the same way as an expense account).

The book-keeping transactions to write off a bad debt are:
– *debit* bad debts written off account } with amount of the bad debt
– *credit* debtor's account

For example, the following debtor's account is in the sales ledger:

Dr.		T Hughes				Cr.
19-1		£	19-1			£
5 Jan.	Sales	55	8 May	Bank		25
			6 Jul.	Cash		5

It is now 15 December 19-1 and the accounts supervisor asks you to review the debtors' accounts before the end of the financial year on 31 December. The business has sent statements and 'chaser' letters to T Hughes – the last letter was dated 30 September, and was returned marked 'gone away, not known at this address'. Nothing further has been heard from T Hughes. You take the decision to write off this account as a bad debt; the account will be closed off as follows:

Dr.		T Hughes				Cr.
19-1		£	19-1			£
5 Jan.	Sales	55	8 May	Bank		25
			6 Jul.	Cash		5
		__	15 Dec.	Bad debts written off		25
		55				55

The balance is transferred to the 'holding' account, *bad debts written off,* together with other accounts written off at the same time:

Dr.		Bad Debts Written Off Account		Cr.
19-1		£	19-1	£
15 Dec.	T Hughes	25		
15 Dec.	A Lane	85		
15 Dec.	A Harvey	90		

bad debts recovered

If, by chance, a former debtor whose account has been written off as bad, should make a payment, the book-keeping procedure is:

– *debit* cash/bank account
– *credit* either, bad debts written off account } with the amount of the payment
        or, bad debts recovered account

The latter account, *bad debts recovered*, would only be used where a business has substantial debtors and was successful in chasing its bad debts. If a recovery is a rare event – perhaps once a year – the practical accounting solution is to credit bad debts written off account. The one account you would *not* credit is the closed debtor's account – if the customer now wishes to buy goods, cash terms would be advisable for some time to come!

the book of prime entry for bad debts

We have already seen in Chapters 4 and 6 how a business uses day books (or journals) as books of prime entry for sales, purchases and returns transactions. Besides these books for routine transactions, a further book of prime entry – called the *journal* – is used as a book of prime entry for non-regular transactions, such as writing off bad debts.

The journal is a book of prime entry and is, therefore, not part of the double-entry book-keeping system. The journal is used to list the transactions that are then to be put through the accounts – we will see other uses of the journal in Chapter 11.

The journal entry to record the book-keeping transaction to write off T Hughes' account as bad (see previous page) is as follows:

Date	Details	Folio	Dr.	Cr.
19-1			£	£
15 Dec.	Bad debts written off	GL	25	
	T Hughes	SL		25
	Bad debt written off as per memo from accounts supervisor dated 10 December 19-1.			

Notes:

- The names of the accounts to be debited in the book-keeping system are written in the details column. In a journal entry, it is customary to show the debit transaction first.

- The money amounts of the debit and credit entry are stated in the columns. A journal entry always balances, ie the debit entry is equal to the credit entry.

- It is usual to include a brief narrative explaining why the transaction is being carried out.

- Each journal entry is complete in itself and is ruled off to separate it from the next entry.

minimising the risk of bad debts

Having studied the accounting for bad debts, it is appropriate to summarise the ways in which businesses selling on credit can minimise the risks. The following are some of the procedures that can be followed:

- When first approached by an unknown business or organisation wishing to buy goods on credit, the seller should ask for two references. One of these should be the buyer's bank, and the other a trader with whom the buyer has previously done business.

- The seller, before supplying goods on credit, should take up both references and obtain satisfactory replies. (Note that it is not possible to approach a bank direct for a reference on one of their customers – this can only be done bank-to-bank, and so the seller must ask his or her own bank to obtain a reference from the buyer's bank.)

- Once satisfactory replies have been received, a credit limit for the customer should be established, and an account opened in the sales ledger. The amount of the credit limit will depend very much on the expected amount of future business – for example, £1,000 might be appropriate. The credit limit should not normally be exceeded – the firm's credit controller or accountant will approve any transactions above the limit.

- Invoices and month-end statements of account should be sent out promptly; invoices should state the terms of trade (see Chapter 2), and statements should analyse the balance to show how long it has been outstanding, eg 'over 30 days, over 60 days, over 90 days' – computer-produced statements can show this automatically.

- If a customer does not pay within a reasonable time, the firm should follow established procedures in order to chase up the debt promptly. As well as telephone calls, these procedures are likely to include 'chaser' letters, the first of which points out that the account is overdue, with a later letter threatening legal action. Whether or not legal action is taken will depend on the size of the debt – for a small amount the costs and time involved in taking legal action may outweigh the benefits of recovering the money.

the use of an aged schedule of debtors

To help with credit control, many firms produce an *aged schedule of debtors* at the end of each month. This analyses individual debtor balances into the time that the amount has been owing. Thus it shows the long outstanding debts that are, potentially, bad debts, against whom early action is necessary. An aged schedule is easily produced using a computer accounting system – an example is shown in fig. 9.1

A/C	Account Name		Turnover	Credit Limit	Balance	Current	30 Days	60 Days	Older
201	Able, Baker & Clark		370.00	1000.00	164.50	164.50	0.00	0.00	0.00
202	Hitech Trading Co		320.00	750.00	376.00	376.00	0.00	0.00	0.00
204	Sixth Form College	*	1730.00	1000.00	1632.75	799.00	833.75	0.00	0.00
205	Teleservice	*	2025.00	500.00	1926.88	1880.00	46.88	0.00	0.00
208	Stone, Wall Ltd		425.00	750.00	499.38	499.38	0.00	0.00	0.00
	Totals :		4870.00	4000.00	4599.51	3718.88	880.63	0.00	0.00

COMPUTER SHOP LTD   Sales Ledger – Account Balances (Aged)   Date: 0103-2

Fig. 9.1   Aged debtors' schedule
(an asterisk indicates debtors whose balances are above the credit limit)

creditors

Creditors are people or organisations to whom the business owes money. Creditors are normally the supplier of a business.

aged creditors' schedule

An aged creditors' schedule is used by many businesses. This analyses individual creditors' balances into the time that the amount has been owing; thus the business can decide which creditors should be paid. The overall objectives of creditor management are to ensure that:

- creditors are paid within the timescales of company policy
- where cash discounts are offered, payment is made within the period covered by the cash discount *where it is financially attractive to do so*
- continuity of supplies to the business is not jeopardised by late payment to creditors

reconciliation of creditors' statements

When a statement of account (see Chapter 2) is received from a supplier, it is often necessary to reconcile, or agree, the statement balance with the creditor's account in our book-keeping records. This reconciliation can be summarised as follows:

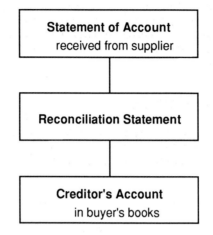

Assuming that there are no errors either on the statement of account or in the creditor's account, the discrepancies are caused by:

- *items in transit,* which have been invoiced by the supplier, but the invoice is not yet recorded by the buyer

- *payments in the post or banking system,* recorded by the buyer, but not yet received and recorded on the supplier's statement

- *purchases returns,* made by buyer but not yet recorded by the supplier

These three discrepancies are all caused by *timing differences,* ie the business document – invoice, payment, credit note – has not yet been recorded in the accounts of both buyer and seller. The reconciliation statement must take note of these.

Case Study: Reconciliation of a creditor's statement

Situation

The following creditor's account appears in the purchases ledger of A Jarvis:

Dr.			T Smith				Cr.
19-1		£		19-1			£
10 Jan.	Bank	200		1 Jan.	Balance b/d		200
30 Jan.	Bank	150		12 Jan.	Purchases		150
31 Jan.	Purchases returns	25		25 Jan.	Purchases		125
31 Jan.	Balance c/d	100					
		475					475
				1 Feb.	Balance b/d		100

Note: The credit balance of £100 on T Smith's account, in the books of A Jarvis at 1 February, indicates that Jarvis owes Smith £100.

The following statement of account is received from T Smith on 2 February:

Statement of Account: A Jarvis

		Dr.	Cr.	Balance	
19-1		£	£	£	
1 Jan.	Balance b/d	200		200	*Dr.*
9 Jan.	Invoice no. 374	150		350	*Dr.*
14 Jan.	Payment received: thank you		200	150	*Dr.*
20 Jan.	Invoice no. 382	125		275	*Dr.*
29 Jan.	Invoice no. 413	100		375	*Dr.*

Note: The debit balance of £375 on the statement from T Smith indicates that, in Smith's books, A Jarvis owes £375.

How will the creditor's account balance be reconciled with that of the statement received by A Jarvis?

Solution

Reconciliation of T Smith's statement of account
as at 31 January 19-1

	£
Balance of account at 31 January 19-1	100
Add: payment sent on 30 January, not yet appearing on statement	150
	250
Add: invoice no. 413 sent by T Smith on 29 January, not yet received	100
	350
Add: purchases returns to T Smith on 31 January, not yet appearing on statement	25
Balance of statement at 31 January 19-1	375

As each of these items are timing differences, they will correct themselves within a few days as they are entered into the accounts of buyer and seller.

recording cash discount in debtors' and creditors' accounts

We saw earlier (in Chapter 3) that *cash discount* is an allowance off the invoice amount for quick settlement, eg 2% cash discount for settlement within seven days. A business can be involved with cash discount in two ways:
- discount allowed to debtors
- discount received from creditors

(Note that, although the terms *discount allowed* and *discount received* do not use the word 'cash', they do in fact refer to cash discount.)

discount allowed

When cash discount is taken by a debtor it is entered into the accounts as shown by the following transactions:

10 Oct. 19-2   Sold goods, £100, on credit to P Henry, allowing her a cash discount of 2% for settlement within seven days
15 Oct. 19-2   P Henry pays £98 by cheque

Dr.		Sales Account		Cr.
19-2	£	19-2		£
		10 Oct. P Henry		100

Dr.		P Henry		Cr.
19-2	£	19-2		£
10 Oct. Sales	100	15 Oct. Bank		98
		15 Oct. Discount allowed		2
	100			100

Dr.		Bank Account		Cr.
19-2	£	19-2		£
15 Oct. P Henry	98			

Dr.		Discount Allowed Account		Cr.
19-2	£	19-2		£
15 Oct. P Henry	2			

Notes:
- The amount of the payment received from the debtor is entered in the bank account.
- The amount of discount allowed is entered in both the debtor's account and discount allowed account:
  – *debit* discount allowed account
  – *credit* debtor's account
- Discount allowed is an expense of the business, because it represents the cost of collecting payments more speedily from the debtors.
- The account of P Henry has been totalled to show that both the debit and credit money columns are the same – thus her account now has a nil balance.

discount received

With cash discount received, a business is offered cash discount for quick settlement by its creditors. The following transactions give an example of this:

20 Oct. 19-2   Bought goods, £200, on credit from B Lewis Ltd; 2½% cash discount is offered for settlement by the end of October
30 Oct. 19-2   Paid B Lewis Ltd £195 by cheque

Dr.		Purchases Account			Cr.
19-2		£	19-2		£
20 Oct.	B Lewis Ltd	200			

Dr.		B Lewis Ltd			Cr.
19-2		£	19-2		£
30 Oct.	Bank	195	20 Oct.	Purchases	200
30 Oct.	Discount received	5			
		200			200

Dr.	Bank Account			Cr.
19-2	£	19-2		£
		30 Oct.	B Lewis Ltd	195

Dr.	Discount Received Account			Cr.
19-2	£	19-2		£
		30 Oct.	B Lewis Ltd	5

Notes:
- The business is *receiving* cash discount from its creditor, and the amount is entered as:
  - *debit* creditor's account
  - *credit* discount received account
- Discount received account is an income account.
- The money columns of the account of B Lewis Ltd have been totalled to show that the account now has a nil balance.

summary
- Cash discount – when taken – is recorded in the debtors' and creditors' accounts.
- Discount allowed account (expenses) and discount received account (income) record the amounts of cash discount.
- The cash book (see Chapter 15) is usually used for listing the amounts of discount received and allowed – transfers are then made at the end of each month to the respective discount accounts.
- *Trade discount* is never recorded in the double-entry accounts; only the net amount of an invoice, after trade discount has been deducted, is entered in the accounts.

chapter summary

❑ A bad debt is a debt owing to a business or organisation which it considers will never be paid.

❑ Bad debts written off during the year are held in bad debts written off account.

❑ The journal book is used to list non-regular transactions, such as bad debts written off.

❑ Bad debts represent a cost which businesses that only sell goods for cash avoid. Many businesses, though, have to sell their goods on credit and they should take steps to minimise the possibility of bad debts.

❑ Information about overdue debtors is often presented in the form of an *aged debtors' schedule* which lists the acounts, amounts and the periods the debts have been outstanding.

❑ An *aged creditors' schedule* is used to ensure that payment is made to creditors within the timescales of company policy.

❑ Statements of account received from creditors may need to be reconciled with the creditor's account; discrepancies are caused by:
• items in transit
• payments in the past or banking system
• purchases returns

❑ Cash discount is an allowance off the invoice amount for quick settlement.

In the next chapter we look at how control accounts are used in business record keeping.

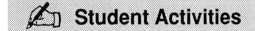 **Student Activities**

9.1 James Roberts is a debtor of your business. The balance of his account on 1 January 19-5 is £70. On 17 February he pays you £40 by cheque; on 20 March he pays you £10 in cash. All further requests for payment are ignored.

On 10 July your business is notified that he has been made a bankrupt. On 20 October a payment of 10% of the amount owing is paid to you by cheque by his trustee in bankruptcy. After receiving this amount, the accounts supervisor instructs you to write off the balance of his account as a bad debt on 21 October.

You are to show:
• the transactions on James Roberts' account in the firm's sales ledger
• the bad debts written off account in the firm's general ledger
• the journal entry made on 21 October

9.2 During November and December 19-2 the following transactions took place on Natalie Watson's account in your firm's sales ledger:

19-2

  1 Nov. Balance brought down, Natalie Watson owes your firm £320

  3 Nov. Natalie Watson pays the balance of her account by cheque, being allowed a cash discount of 2½%

10 Nov. Natalie Watson buys goods on credit from your firm for £200 (including VAT)

15 Nov. Natalie Watson returns goods £50 – a credit note is issued by your firm

20 Nov. A cheque is received from Natalie Watson for £100

  3 Dec. Cash is received from Natalie Watson for £25

22 Dec. You are told by the accounts supervisor that Natalie Watson has gone out of business and that the balance on her account is to be written off as bad

You are to show:

- the transactions on Natalie Watson's account in the firm's sales ledger
- the bad debts written off account in the firm's general ledger
- the journal entry made on 22 December

9.3 You work in the accounts department of Electralarm Ltd, a company which installs electronic alarm systems. The company address is 67 Newtown Road, West Roxton, WR6 6YP. Three months ago the company installed a domestic alarm system for Mr Tom Gunsmith, at 8 Tresham Close, West Roxton, WR3 5FG. He was sent:

- an invoice for £785.00 three months ago
- a statement of account at the end of month one
- a statement of account at the end of month two

No money has been received from Mr Gunsmith.

(a) Using today's date and assuming that the item for £785 was the only one on the statement, write an appropriate letter to Mr Gunsmith chasing up this debt.

(b) If you do not receive a reply to this letter, what courses of action are open to Electralarm Ltd? What would you chose to do?

9.4 You work as an assistant in the accounts department of JR Catering Limited, a contract caterer. Your supervisor has asked you to obtain an aged debtors' schedule from the computer. The printout shown below is the first page of the schedule. The asterisks show an account that is over its credit limit. J R Catering allows up to 30 days credit to all its customers.

Write a memorandum (using your own name and the current date) to the supervisor, Lorna Jones, setting out:

(a) the accounts that may be a source of trouble, and why

(b) corrective action that the business might take

JR CATERING LTD   SALES LEDGER - AGED DEBTORS SCHEDULE

A/C	Account Name		Turnover	Credit Limit	Balance	Current	30 Days	60 Days	Older
201	Merrion & Co		370.00	1000.00	164.50	164.50	0.00	0.00	0.00
202	KingfisherLtd		320.00	750.00	376.00	376.00	0.00	0.00	0.00
204	I Marcos	*	1730.00	1000.00	1632.75	799.00	0.00	833.75	0.00
205	Compusoft Ltd	*	2025.00	2000.00	1926.88	1880.00	46.88	0.00	0.00
208	R Weinberger		425.00	750.00	499.38	499.38	0.00	0.00	0.00
	Totals:		4870.00	5500.00	4599.51	3718.88	46.88	833.75	0.00

9.5 The following account appears in your firm's purchases ledger:

Dr.			Apple Supplies Ltd			Cr.
19-2		£	19-2			£
6 May	Bank	780	1 May	Balance b/d		800
	Discount	20	4 May	Purchases		255
10 May	Purchases returns	55	25 May	Purchases		150
30 May	Bank	195				
	Discount	5				

During the first week of June, the following statement of account was received from Apple Supplies Ltd:

19-2		£	£	£
1 May	Balance			800
2 May	Sales	255		1,055
9 May	Bank		780	
	Discount		20	255
10 May	Sales returns		55	200
23 May	Sales	150		350

You are to:

- Balance the account of Apple Supplies Ltd in your purchases ledger at 31 May 19-2
- Reconcile the balance on your purchases ledger account at 31 May 19-2 with that shown on the statement

9.6 The following account appears in your firm's purchases ledger:

Dr.			William Shaw Ltd			Cr.
19-4		£	19-4			£
10 Mar.	Purchases returns	156	1 Mar.	Balance b/d		640
12 Mar.	Bank	624	4 Mar.	Purchases		756
	Discount	16	20 Mar.	Purchases		845
25 Mar.	Purchases returns	45				
30 Mar.	Bank	780				
	Discount	20				

During the first week of April, the following statement of account was received from William Shaw Ltd:

19-4		£	£	£
1 Mar.	Balance b/d			1,080
2 Mar.	Sales	756		1,836
6 Mar.	Bank		429	
	Discount		11	1,396
10 Mar.	Sales returns		156	1,240
14 Mar.	Bank		624	
	Discount		16	600
18 Mar.	Sales	845		1,445
25 Mar.	Sales returns		45	1,400
29 Mar.	Sales	1,027		2,427

You are to:

- Reconcile the opening balance of William Shaw Ltd's account at 1 March in your purchases ledger with the statement balance at that date
- Balance the account in your purchases ledger at 31 March 19-4
- Reconcile the balance on your purchases ledger account at 31 March 19-4 with that shown on the statement

9.7   Enter the following transactions into the double-entry book-keeping accounts of Sonya Smith:

19-4

 2 Feb.   Bought goods £200, on credit from G Lewis

 4 Feb.   Sold goods £150, on credit to L Jarvis

 7 Feb.   Sold goods £240, on credit to G Patel

10 Feb.   Paid G Lewis the amount owing by cheque after deducting a cash discount of 5%

12 Feb.   L Jarvis pays the amount owing by cheque after deducting a cash discount of 2%

16 Feb.   Bought goods £160, on credit from G Lewis

20 Feb.   G Patel pays the amount owing by cheque after deducting a cash discount of 2½%

24 Feb.   Paid G Lewis the amount owing by cheque after deducting a cash discount of 5%

Notes:
- Sonya Smith is not registered for VAT
- day books are not required

10 Control accounts

Control accounts, as their name suggests, are used as 'master' accounts to control a number of subsidiary ledger accounts in the following way:

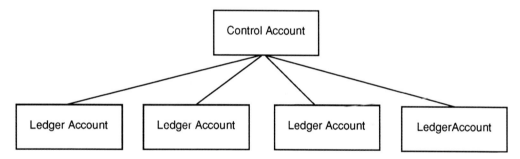

The control account (also known as a *totals account*) is used to record the totals of transactions passing through the subsidiary accounts. In this way, the balance of the control account will always be equal to the total balances of the subsidiary accounts, unless an error has occurred. Two commonly-used control accounts are:

- sales ledger control account – the total of the debtors
- purchases ledger control account – the total of the creditors

In this chapter we shall look at:

- the concept of control accounts
- the layout of sales ledger and purchases ledger control accounts
- the use of control accounts as an aid to the management of a business
- control accounts and book-keeping

the concept of control accounts

In the illustration above we have seen how a control account acts as a master account for a number of subsidiary accounts. The principle is that, if the *total* of the opening balances for subsidiary accounts is known, together with the *total* of amounts increasing these balances, and the *total* of amounts decreasing these balances, then the *total* of the closing balances for the subsidiary accounts can be calculated.

For example:

	£
Total of opening balances	50,000
Add increases	10,000
	60,000
Less decreases	12,000
Total of closing balances	48,000

The total of the closing balances can now be checked against a separate listing of the subsidiary accounts to ensure that the two figures agree. If so, it proves that the ledgers within the section are correct (subject to any errors such as misposts and compensating errors). Let us now apply this concept to one of the divisions of the ledger – sales ledger.

Fig. 10.1, on the next page, shows the personal accounts which form the entire sales ledger of a particular business (in practice there would, of course, be more than four accounts involved). The sales ledger control account acts as a totals account, which records totals of the transactions passing through the individual accounts which it controls. Notice that transactions appear in the control account *on the same side* as they appear in the individual accounts. The control account can be reconciled with the balances of the individual accounts which it controls (see below). Thus, control accounts act as an aid to locating errors: if the control account and subsidiary accounts agree, then the error is *likely* to lie elsewhere. In this way the control account acts as an intermediate checking device – proving the arithmetical accuracy of the ledger section.

Normally the whole of a ledger section is controlled by one control account, eg sales ledger control account and purchases ledger control account. However, it is also possible to have a number of separate control accounts for subdivisions of the sales ledger and purchases ledger, eg sales ledger control account A-K, purchases ledger control account S-Z, etc. It is for a business – the user of the accounting system – to decide what is most suitable, taking into account the number of accounts in the sales and purchases ledger, together with the type of book-keeping system – manual or computerised.

In the example in fig. 10.1, the control account and subsidiary accounts are agreed at the end of the month, as follows:

Reconciliation of the sales ledger control account with the closing debtor balances
as at 31 January 19-1:

	£
A Ackroyd	150
B Barnes	200
C Cox	180
D Douglas	150
Sales ledger control account	680

Note: The business will decide how often to reconcile the control account with the subsidiary accounts – weekly, monthly, quarterly or annually.

sales ledger control account

The set-out of a sales ledger control account (or debtors' control account) is shown in fig. 10.1. There are some additional items (explained below) and page 130 can be used as a 'pro-forma' layout:

Sales Ledger Control Account

Dr.		£			Cr.	£
19-1			19-1			
1 Jan.	Balances b/d	500	31 Jan.		Bank	443
31 Jan.	Sales	700	31 Jan.		Discount allowed	7
			31 Jan.		Sales returns	70
			31 Jan.		Balances c/d	680
		1,200				1,200
1 Feb.	Balances b/d	680				

A Ackroyd

Dr.		£			Cr.	£
19-1			19-1			
1 Jan.	Balance b/d	100	10 Jan.		Bank	98
5 Jan.	Sales	150	10 Jan.		Discount allowed	2
			31 Jan.		Balance c/d	150
		250				250
1 Feb.	Balance b/d	150				

B Barnes

Dr.		£			Cr.	£
19-1			19-1			
1 Jan.	Balance b/d	200	12 Jan.		Bank	195
10 Jan.	Sales	250	12 Jan.		Discount allowed	5
			25 Jan.		Sales returns	50
			31 Jan.		Balance c/d	200
		450				450
1 Feb.	Balance b/d	200				

C Cox

Dr.		£			Cr.	£
19-1			19-1			
1 Jan.	Balance b/d	50	18 Jan.		Bank	50
15 Jan.	Sales	200	29 Jan.		Sales returns	20
			31 Jan.		Balance c/d	180
		250				250
1 Feb.	Balance b/d	180				

D Douglas

Dr.		£			Cr.	£
19-1			19-1			
1 Jan.	Balance b/d	150	30 Jan.		Bank	100
20 Jan.	Sales	100	31 Jan.		Balance c/d	150
		250				250
1 Feb.	Balance b/d	150				

Fig. 10.1 An example of the use of sales ledger control account

Dr.		Sales Ledger Control Account		Cr.
	£			£
Balances b/d (large amount)		Balances b/d (small amount)		
Credit sales		Cash/cheques received from debtors		
Returned cheques		Cash discount allowed		
Interest charged to debtors		Sales returns		
Balances c/d (small amount)		Bad debts written off		
		Set-off/contra entries		
		Balances c/d (large amount)		
	——————			——————
	======			======
Balances b/d (large amount)		Balances b/d (small amount)		

Notes:

• **balances b/d**

In the layout above there is a figure for balances b/d on both the debit side *and* the credit side of the control account. The usual balance on a debtor's account is debit and so this will form the large balance on the debit side. However, from time-to-time, it is possible for some debtors to have a credit balance on their accounts. This may come about, for example, because they have paid for goods, and then returned them, or because they have overpaid in error: the business owes them the amount due, ie they have a credit balance for the time being. Such credit balances are always going to be in the minority and so they will be for the smaller amount. Clearly, if there are small credit balances at the beginning of the month, there are likely to be credit balances at the month-end, and these need to be recorded *separately* as balances carried down – do not 'net off' the two types of balances. In a balance sheet, the small credit balances should be included with creditors.

• **credit sales**

Only credit sales – and not cash sales – are entered in the control account because it is this transaction that is recorded in the debtors' accounts. The total sales of the business will comprise both credit and cash sales.

• **returned cheques**

If a debtor's cheque is returned unpaid by the bank, ie the cheque has 'bounced', then entries have to be made in the book-keeping system to record this. These entries are:

– *debit* debtor's account
– *credit* cash book (bank columns)

As a transaction has been made in a debtor's account, then the amount must also be recorded in the sales ledger control account – on the debit side.

• **interest charged to debtors**

Sometimes a business will charge a debtor for slow payment of an account. The accounting entries are:

– *debit* debtor's account
– *credit* interest received account

As a debit transaction has been made in the debtor's account, so a debit entry must be recorded in the control account.

• **bad debts written off**

The book-keeping entries for writing off a bad debt (see Chapter 9) are:

– *debit* bad debts written off account
– *credit* debtor's account

As you can see, a credit transaction is entered in a debtor's account. The control account 'masters' the sales ledger and so the transaction must also be recorded as a credit transaction in the control account.

• **set-off/contra entries**

See next page.

purchases ledger control account

The 'pro-forma' layout for the purchases ledger control account (or creditors' control account) is:

Dr.		Purchases Ledger Control Account		Cr.
	£			£
Balances b/d (small amount)		Balances b/d (large amount)		
Cash/cheques paid to creditors		Credit purchases		
Cash discount received		Interest charged by creditors		
Purchases returns		Balances c/d (small amount)		
Set-off/contra entries				
Balances c/d (large amount)	———			———
	═══			═══
Balances b/d (small amount)		Balances b/d (large amount)		

Notes:

- **balances b/d**

As with sales ledger control account, it is possible to have balances on both sides of the account. For purchases ledger, containing the accounts of creditors, the large balance b/d is always on the credit side. However, if a creditor has been overpaid, the result may be a small debit balance b/d. It may also be that there are closing balances on both sides of the account at the end of the period. In the balance sheet, any small debit balances should be included with debtors.

- **credit purchases**

Only credit purchases – and not cash purchases – are entered in the control account. However, the total purchases of the business will comprise both credit and cash purchases.

- **interest charged by creditors**

If creditors charge interest because of slow payment, this must be recorded on both the creditor's account and the control account.

- **set-off/contra entries**

See below.

set-off/contra entries

These entries occur when the same person or business has an account in both sales ledger and purchases ledger, ie they are both buying from, and selling to, the business whose accounts we are preparing. For example, M Patel Ltd has the following accounts in the sales and purchases ledgers:

SALES LEDGER

Dr.		A Smith		Cr.
	£			£
Balance b/d	200			

PURCHASES LEDGER

Dr.	A Smith		Cr.
	£	Balance b/d	£ 300

From these accounts we can see that:
- A Smith owes M Patel Ltd £200 (sales ledger)
- M Patel Ltd owes A Smith £300 (purchases ledger)

To save each having to write out a cheque to send to the other, it is possible (with A Smith's agreement) to set-off one account against the other, so that they can settle their net indebtedness with one cheque. The book-keeping entries in M Patel's books will be:

– *debit* A Smith (purchases ledger) £200

– *credit* A Smith (sales ledger) £200

The accounts will now appear as:

SALES LEDGER

Dr.		A Smith		Cr.
		£		£
Balance b/d	200	Set-off: purchases ledger	200

PURCHASES LEDGER

Dr.		A Smith		Cr.
		£		£
Set-off: sales ledger	200	Balance b/d	300

The net result is that M Patel Ltd owes A Smith £100. The important point to note is that, because transactions have been recorded in the personal accounts, an entry needs to be made in the two control accounts:

– *debit* purchases ledger control account
– *credit* sales ledger control account } with the amount set-off

sources of information for control accounts

Control accounts use totals (remember that their other name is *totals accounts*) for the week, month, quarter or year – depending on what time period is decided upon by the business. The totals come from a number of sources in the accounting system:

sales ledger control account

- total credit sales (including VAT) – from the sales day book
- total sales returns (including VAT) – from the sales returns day book
- total cash/cheques received from debtors – from the cash book (see Chapter 15)
- total discount allowed – from the discount allowed column of the cash book (see Chapter 15), or from discount allowed account
- bad debts – from the journal, or bad debts written off account

purchases ledger control account

- total credit purchases (including VAT) – from the purchases day book
- total purchases returns (including VAT) – from the purchases returns day book
- total cash/cheques paid to creditors – from the cash book (see Chapter 15)
- total discount received – from the discount received column of the cash book (see Chapter 15), or from discount received account

control accounts as an aid to management

- When the manager of a business needs to know the figure for debtors or creditors – important information for the manager – the balance of the appropriate control account will give the information immediately: there is no need to add up the balances of all the debtors' or creditors' accounts. With a computer accounting system, the control accounts can be printed at any time.

- The use of control accounts makes fraud more difficult – particularly in a manual accounting system. If a fraudulent transaction is to be recorded on a personal account, the transaction must also be entered in the control account. As the control account will be either maintained by a supervisor, and/or checked regularly by the manager, the control accounts add another level of security within the accounting system.

- We have already seen in this chapter how control accounts can help in locating errors. Remember, though, that a control account only proves the arithmetical accuracy of the accounts which it controls – there could still be errors, such as misposts and compensating errors, within the ledger section.

control accounts and book-keeping

A business must decide how to incorporate control accounts into its book-keeping system. There are two possible ways of doing this:

- *Incorporate the control accounts into double-entry book-keeping*
  This approach uses the control accounts as the double-entry system, ie the balances of the sales ledger control account and the purchases ledger control account, are recorded in the trial balance as the figures for debtors and creditors respectively. This means that the personal accounts of debtors and creditors are not part of double-entry, but are *memorandum accounts* which record how much each debtor owes, and how much is owed to each creditor. From time-to-time, the balances of the memorandum accounts will be agreed with the balance of the appropriate control account.

  The use of this approach is consistent with the way in which computerised accounts (see Chapter 19) are prepared and presented – the control account gives the total and there are separate memorandum accounts for individual debtors and creditors.

  Fig. 10.2 gives an example of sales ledger control account incorporated into the double-entry book-keeping system, while the individual debtors' accounts are kept in the form of memorandum accounts. (Fig. 10.3 shows the situation where the control account is a *memorandum* account and the debtors' accounts are part of the double-entry book-keeping system – see page 136 for further explanation.)

Control account as part of the double-entry system

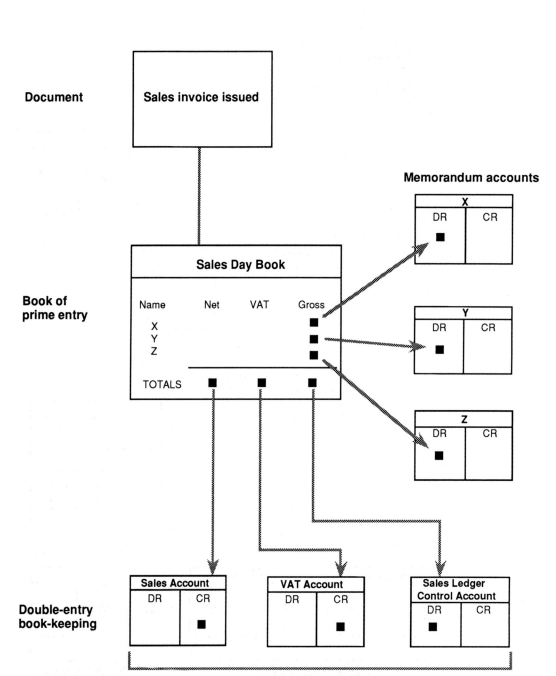

Fig. 10.2 Sales ledger control account incorporated into the double-entry book-keeping system; debtors' accounts are memorandum accounts

Control account as a memorandum account

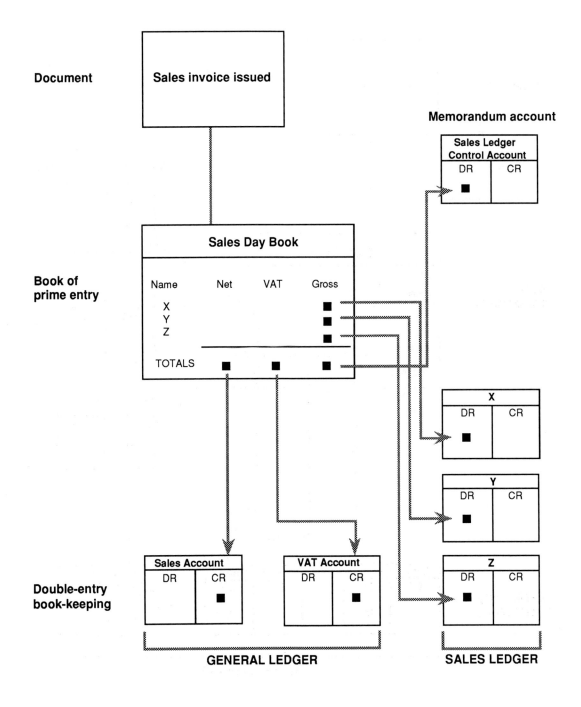

*Fig. 10.3 Sales ledger control account is a memorandum account;
debtors' accounts are part of the double-entry book-keeping system*

• *The control accounts are used as memorandum accounts*
This method uses the opposite approach: here the personal accounts of debtors and creditors are included in the double-entry book-keeping system, while the control accounts are memorandum accounts used as checking devices.

Fig. 10.3, on the previous page, gives an example of sales ledger control account being kept as a memorandum account, while the individual debtors' accounts are part of the double-entry book-keeping system.

Whichever of these two approaches is used, the principles behind the preparation of control accounts are the same.

---

chapter summary

❑   Control accounts (or *totals accounts*) are 'master' accounts, which control a number of subsidiary accounts.

❑   Two commonly used control accounts are:
   • sales ledger control account
   • purchases ledger control account

❑   Transactions are recorded on the same side of the control account as on the subsidiary accounts.

❑   Set-off/contra entries occur when one person has an account in both sales and purchases ledger, and it is agreed to set-off one balance against the other to leave a net balance. This usually results in the following control account entries:
   – *debit* purchases ledger control account
   – *credit* sales ledger control account

❑   Control accounts are an aid to management:
   • in giving immediate, up-to-date information on the total of debtors or creditors
   • by making fraud more difficult
   • in helping to locate errors

❑   Control accounts can be either:
   • incorporated into the double-entry book-keeping system
   • used as separate memorandum accounts

✍ Student Activities

10.1   Prepare a sales ledger control account for the month of June 19-1 from the following information:

19-1		£
1 Jun.	Sales ledger balances	17,491
30 Jun.	Credit sales for month	42,591
	Sales returns	1,045
	Payments received from debtors	39,024
	Cash discount allowed	593
	Bad debts written off	296

The debtors figure at 30 June should be entered as the balancing figure.

10.2   Prepare a purchases ledger control account for the month of April 19-1 from the following information:

19-1		£
1 Apr.	Purchases ledger balances	14,275
30 Apr.	Credit purchases for month	36,592
	Purchases returns	653
	Payments made to creditors	31,074
	Cash discount received	1,048
	Transfer of credit balances to sales ledger	597

The creditors figure at 30 April should be entered as the balancing figure.

10.3   The sales ledger of Rowcester Traders contains the following accounts on 1 February 19-3:

> Arrow Valley Retailers, balance £826.40 debit
> B Brick (Builders) Ltd, balance £59.28 debit
> Mereford Manufacturing Co, balance £293.49 debit
> Redgrove Restorations, balance £724.86 debit
> Wyvern Warehouse Ltd, balance £108.40 debit

The following transactions took place during February:

2 Feb.	Sold goods on credit to Arrow Valley Retailers £338.59, and to Mereford Manufacturing Co £127.48
7 Feb.	Redgrove Restorations returned goods £165.38
15 Feb.	Received a cheque from Wyvern Warehouse Ltd for the balance of the account after deduction of 2½% cash discount
17 Feb.	Sold goods on credit to Redgrove Restorations £394.78, and to Wyvern Warehouse Ltd £427.91
20 Feb.	Arrow Valley Retailers settled an invoice for £826.40 by cheque after deducting 2½% cash discount
22 Feb.	Mereford Manufacturing Co returned goods £56.29
28 Feb.	Transferred the balance of Mereford Manufacturing Co's account to the company's account in the purchases ledger
28 Feb.	Wrote off the account of B Brick (Builders) Ltd as a bad debt

You are to:

(a)   write up the personal accounts in the sales ledger of Rowcester Traders for February 19-3, balancing them at the end of the month

(b)   prepare a sales ledger control account for February 19-3, balancing it at the end of the month

(c)   reconcile the control account balance with the debtors' accounts at 28 February 19-3.

Note: VAT is to be ignored on all transactions

10.4 The purchases ledger of Rowcester Traders contains the following accounts on 1 February 19-3:

> Apple Supplies Ltd, balance £1,843.22 credit
> Beatty Brothers, £51.47 debit
> J Johnson, £675.38 credit
> Mereford Manufacturing Co, balance £478.29 credit
> Newtown Equipment Ltd, balance £684.86 credit
> W Wright, balance £987.20 credit

The following transactions took place during February:

3 Feb.	Bought goods on credit from Apple Supplies Ltd, £1,027.98, and from Beatty Brothers £150.68
6 Feb.	Paid W Wright a cheque for the balance of her account after deducting 2½% cash discount
10 Feb.	Bought goods on credit from J Johnson £328.22, and from W Wright £476.38
11 Feb.	Paid Newtown Equipment Ltd a cheque for the balance of the account
14 Feb.	Returned goods to Apple Supplies Ltd for £157.20
17 Feb.	Paid Apple Supplies a cheque for the balance of the account, after deducting 2½% cash discount
18 Feb.	Returned goods to Newtown Equipment Ltd for £105.68
24 Feb.	Paid J Johnson the amount owing by cheque, after deducting 2½% cash discount
27 Feb.	Bought goods on credit from Apple Supplies Ltd £849.36
28 Feb.	Transfer of debit balance of £364.68 in the sales ledger to Mereford Manufacturing Co's account in the purchases ledger

You are to:

(a) write up the personal accounts in the purchases ledger of Rowcester Traders for February 19-3, balancing them at the end of the month

(b) prepare a purchases ledger control account for February 19-3, balancing it at the end of the month

(c) reconcile the control account balance with the creditors' accounts at 28 February 19-3

Note: VAT is to be ignored on all transactions

10.5 Stourminster Ltd uses control accounts for its purchases ledger and sales ledger. At 1 September 19-1 the balances of the control accounts were:

	Debit £	Credit £
Purchases ledger	128	65,027
Sales ledger	106,943	558

The following transactions took place during September 19-1:

	£
Credit purchases	137,248
Credit sales	179,984
Sales returns	2,081
Purchases returns	6,349
Cash/cheques received from customers	163,481
Cash/cheques paid to suppliers	125,636
Customers' cheques dishonoured	357
Discount allowed	2,549
Discount received	1,832
Bad debts written off	528
Transfer of a credit balance from the purchases ledger to the sales ledger	2,086

At 30 September 19-1, there were debit balances in the purchases ledger of £479 and credit balances in the sales ledger of £694

You are to:

- prepare the purchases ledger control account and sales ledger control account at Stourminster Ltd for September 19-1

- balance the accounts at 30 September 19-1

11 The journal

We have already seen in Chapters 4 and 6 how a business uses day books (or journals) as books of prime entry for sales, purchases and returns transactions. Besides these books for routine transactions, a further book – called *the journal* – is used as a book of prime entry for non-regular transactions. The journal is not part of double-entry book-keeping; instead it is used to list transactions before they are entered into the accounts.

uses of the journal

The journal is used for listing transactions which are not recorded in any other book of prime entry. The categories of such transactions are:
- opening entries
- purchase and sale of fixed assets on credit
- correction of errors
- other transfers

The journal is a book of prime entry and is, therefore, not part of the double-entry book-keeping system. The journal is used to list the transactions that are then to be put through the accounts.

The reasons for using a journal are:
- to eliminate the need for remembering why non-regular transactions were put through the accounts – the journal acts as a notebook
- to reduce the risk of fraud, by making it difficult for unauthorised transactions to be entered in the accounting system
- to reduce the risk of errors, by listing the transactions that are to be put into the double-entry accounts
- to ensure that entries can be traced back to a prime document, thus providing an audit trail for non-regular transactions

opening entries

These are the transactions which open the accounts of a business. For example, a first business transaction is:

1 Jan. 19-1   Started in business with £10,000 in the bank

This non-regular transaction is entered in the journal as follows:

Date	Details	Folio	Dr	Cr
19-1			£	£
1 Jan.	Bank account	CB	10,000	
	Capital account	GL		10,000
	Opening capital introduced			

Notes:

- the names of the accounts to be debited and credited in the book-keeping system are written in the details column; it is customary to show the debit transaction first
- the money amounts of each debit and credit are stated in the appropriate columns
- a journal entry always balances
- it is usual to include a brief narrative explaining why the transaction is being carried out, and making reference to the prime document whenever possible (in assessments and examinations you should always include a narrative unless specifically told otherwise)
- each journal entry is complete in itself and is ruled off to separate it from the next entry

Here is another opening entries transaction to be recorded in the journal:

1 Feb. 19-2   Started in business with cash £100, bank £5,000, stock £1,000, machinery £2,500, creditors £850

The journal entry is:

Date	Details	Folio	Dr	Cr
19-2			£	£
1 Feb.	Cash account	CB	100	
	Bank account	CB	5,000	
	Stock account	GL	1,000	
	Machinery account '	GL	2,500	
	Creditors accounts	PL		850
	Capital account*	GL		7,750
			8,600	8,600
	Assets and liabilities at the start of business			

* Note that capital is the balancing figure, ie assets minus liabilities. The amounts will now need to be recorded in the double-entry book-keeping system.

purchase and sale of fixed assets on credit

The purchase and sale of fixed assets are non-regular business transactions which are recorded in the journal as the book of prime entry. Strictly, only *credit* transactions are entered in the journal (because cash/bank transactions are recorded in the cash book as the book of prime entry). However, a business (or an assessment/examination question) may choose to journalise cash entries: strictly, though, this is incorrect as two books of prime entry are being used.

15 Apr. 19-1   Bought a machine for £1,000 plus VAT at 17½ per cent (the buyer is registered for VAT), on credit from Machinery Supplies Ltd

Date	Details	Folio	Dr	Cr
19-1			£	£
15 Apr.	Machinery account	GL	1,000	
	VAT account	GL	175	
	Machinery Supplies Ltd*	GL		1,175
			1,175	1,175
	Purchase of machine: purchase order no. 28/19-1			

20 May 19-1   Car sold for £2,500 on credit to Wyvern Motors Ltd (no VAT chargeable).

Date	Details	Folio	Dr	Cr
19-1			£	£
20 May	Wyvern Motors Ltd*	GL	2,500	
	Car account	GL		2,500
	Sale of car, registration no X201 HAB			

* A general ledger account has been opened for the creditor (Machinery Supplies Ltd) and the debtor (Wyvern Motors Ltd). This has been done to avoid confusion with trade creditors (in the purchases ledger) and trade debtors (in the sales ledger).

correction of errors

In any book-keeping system there is always the possibility of an error. Ways to avoid errors, or ways to reveal them sooner, include:
- division of the accounting function between a number of people, so that no one person is responsible for both the debit and credit entries of a business transaction
- regular circulation of statements to debtors, who will check the transactions on their accounts and advise any discrepancies
- checking of statements received from creditors
- extraction of a trial balance at regular intervals
- the preparation of bank reconciliation statements (see Chapter 17)
- checking cash and petty cash balances (see Chapters 15 and 16) against cash held
- the use of control accounts (see Chapter 10)

Despite all of these, errors will still occur from time-to-time and, in this section, we will look at:
- correction of errors not shown by a trial balance
- correction of errors shown by a trial balance, using a suspense account

errors not shown by a trial balance

In Chapter 8 we have already seen that some types of errors in a book-keeping system are not revealed by a trial balance. These are:

- error of omission
- reversal of entries
- mispost/error of commission
- error of principle
- error of original entry (or transcription)
- compensating error

Although these errors are not shown by a trial balance, they are likely to come to light if the procedures suggested above are followed. For example, a debtor will soon let you know if her account has been debited with goods she did not buy. When an error is found, it needs to be corrected by means of a journal entry which shows the book-keeping entries that have been passed.

We will now look at an example of each of the errors not shown by a trial balance, and will see how it is corrected by means of a journal entry. (A practical hint which may help in correcting errors is to write out the 'T' accounts as they appear with the error. Then write in the correcting entries and see if the result has achieved what was intended.)

error of omission

Credit sale of goods, £100, to H Jarvis completely omitted from the accounting system; the error is corrected on 10 May 19-2

Date	Details	Folio	Dr	Cr
19-2			£	£
10 May	H Jarvis	SL	100	
	Sales account	GL		100
	Invoice no. xxx omitted from the accounts			

This type of error can happen in a very small business – often where the book-keeping is done by one person. For example, an invoice, when typed out, is 'lost' down the back of a filing cabinet. In a large business, particularly one using a computer accounting system, it *should* be impossible for this error to occur. Also, if documents are numbered serially, then none should be mislaid.

reversal of entries

A payment, on 3 May 19-2 by cheque of £50 to a creditor, S Wright, has been debited in the cash book and credited to Wright's account; the error is corrected on 12 May 19-2

Date	Details	Folio	Dr	Cr
19-2			£	£
12 May	S Wright	PL	50	
	Bank account	CB		50
	S Wright	PL	50	
	Bank account	CB		50
	Correction of £50 reversal of entries: receipt no. xxx			

To correct this type of error it is best to reverse the entries that have been made incorrectly (the first two journal entries), and then to put through the correct entries. Although it will correct the error, it is wrong to debit Wright £100 and credit bank £100. This is because there was never a transaction for this amount – the original transaction was for £50.

As noted earlier, it is often an idea to write out the 'T' accounts, complete with the error, and then to write in the correcting entries. As an example, the two accounts involved in this last error are shown with the error made on 3 May, and the corrections made on 12 May indicated by the shading (the opening credit balance of S Wright's account is shown as £50):

Dr.		S Wright			Cr.
19-2		£	19-2		£
12 May	Bank	50	1 May	Balance b/d	50
12 May	Bank	50	3 May	Bank	50
		100			100

Dr.		Bank Account			Cr.
19-2		£	19-2		£
3 May	S. Wright	50	12 May	S Wright	50
			12 May	S Wright	50

The accounts now show a net debit transaction of £50 on S Wright's account, and a net credit transaction of £50 on bank account, which is how this payment to a creditor should have been recorded in order to clear the balance on the account.

mispost/error of commission

Credit sales of £40 have been debited to the account of J Adams, instead of the account of J Adams Ltd; the error is corrected on 15 May 19-2

Date	Details	Folio	Dr	Cr
19-2			£	£
15 May	J Adams Ltd	SL	40	
	J Adams	SL		40
	Correction of mispost of invoice no. xxx			

This type of error can be avoided, to some extent, by the use of account numbers, and by persuading the customer to quote the account number or reference on each transaction. All computer accounting systems use numbers/references to identify accounts, but it is still possible to post a transaction to the wrong account.

error of principle

The cost of petrol, £15, has been debited to vehicles account; the error is corrected on 20 May 19-2

Date	Details	Folio	Dr	Cr
19-2			£	£
20 May	Vehicle running expenses account	GL	15	
	Vehicles account	GL		15
	Correction of error: voucher no. xxx			

This type of error is similar to a mispost except that, instead of the wrong *person's* account being used, it is the wrong *class* of account. In the above example, the vehicle running costs must be kept separate from the cost of the asset – vehicles.

error of original entry

Credit sale of goods, £45, to J Lamb entered in the accounts as £54; the error is corrected on 27 May 19-2

Date	Details	Folio	Dr	Cr
19-2			£	£
27 May	Sales account	GL	54	
	J Lamb	SL		54
	J Lamb	SL	45	
	Sales account	GL		45
	Correction of error: invoice no. xxx entered into the accounts wrongly			

This error could have been corrected by debiting sales, crediting J Lamb with £9, being the difference between the two amounts. However, there was no original transaction for this amount, and it is better to reverse the wrong transaction and put through the correct one.

A reversal of figures, as above, either has a difference of nine, or an amount divisible by nine. An error of original entry can also be a 'bad' figure on a cheque or an invoice, which is entered wrongly into both accounts.

compensating error

Business rates account is over-cast (over-added) by £100; sales account is also over-cast by the same amount; the error is corrected on 31 May 19-2

Date	Details	Folio	Dr	Cr
19-2			£	£
31 May	Sales account	GL	100	
	Business rates account	GL		100
	Correction of over-cast on rates account and sales account			

Here, an account with a debit balance – business rates – has been over-cast; this is compensated by an over-cast on an account with a credit balance – sales. There are several permutations on this theme, eg two debit balances, one over-cast, one under-cast; a debit balance under-cast, a credit balance under-cast.

important note
We have just looked at several journal entries in connection with the correction of errors. Remember that the journal entry lists the transactions that must then be recorded in the book-keeping system.

errors shown by a trial balance: use of suspense account

There are many types of errors revealed by a trial balance. Included amongst these are:

- omission of one part of the double-entry transaction
- recording two debits or two credits for a transaction
- recording a different amount for a transaction on the debit side from the credit side
- errors in the calculation of balances (not compensated by other errors)
- error in transferring the balance of an account to the trial balance

When errors are shown, the trial balance is 'balanced' by recording the difference in a *suspense account*. For example, on 31 December 19-1 the trial balance totals are:

	Dr	Cr
	£	£
Trial balance totals	100,000	99,850
Suspense account		150
	100,000	100,000

A suspense account is opened in the general ledger with, in this case, a credit balance of £150:

Dr.		Suspense Account		Cr.
19-1	£	19-1		£
		31 Dec. Trial balance difference		150

A detailed examination of the book-keeping system is now made in order to find the errors. As errors are found, they are corrected by means of a journal entry. The journal entries will balance, with one part of the entry being either a debit or credit to suspense account. In this way, the balance on suspense account is eliminated by book-keeping transactions. Taking the above suspense account, the following errors are found and corrected on 15 January 19-2:

- sales account is under-cast by £100
- a payment to a creditor, A Wilson, for £65, has been recorded in the bank as £56
- telephone expenses of £55 have not been entered in the expenses account
- stationery expenses £48 have been debited to both the stationery account and the bank account

These errors are corrected by journal entries:

Date	Details	Folio	Dr	Cr
19-2			£	£
15 Jan.	Suspense account	GL	100	
	Sales account	GL		100
	Under-cast on . . . . . . now corrected			
15 Jan.	Bank account	CB	56	
	Suspense account	GL		56
	Suspense account	GL	65	
	Bank account	CB		65
	Payment to A Wilson for £65 (cheque no. xxx) on . . . entered in bank as £56 in error			
15 Jan.	Telephone expenses account	GL	55	
	Suspense account	GL		55
	Omission of entry in expenses account: paid by cheque no xxx			
15 Jan.	Suspense account	GL	48	
	Bank account	CB		48
	Suspense account	GL	48	
	Bank account	CB		48
	Correction of error: payment by cheque no xxx debited in error to bank account			

After these journal entries have been recorded in the accounts, suspense account appears as:

Dr.			Suspense Account		Cr.
19-2		£	19-1		£
15 Jan.	Sales	100	31 Dec. Trial balance difference		150
15 Jan.	Bank	65	19-2		
15 Jan.	Bank	48	15 Jan. Bank		56
15 Jan.	Bank	48	15 Jan. Telephone expenses		55
		261			261

Thus all the errors have now been found, and suspense account has a nil balance.

other transfers

Any other non-regular transactions need to be recorded in the journal. Examples of such transactions in business record keeping include:
- bad debts written off
- expenses charged to owner's drawings
- goods for own use

bad debts written off

We have already seen, in Chapter 9, the double-entry book-keeping entries to write off a debtor's account as bad:

– *debit* bad debts written off account

– *credit* debtor's account

15 Dec. 19-1   Write off the account of T Hughes (see page 116), which has a balance of £25, as a bad debt

The journal entry is:

Date	Details	Folio	Dr	Cr
19-1			£	£
15 Dec.	Bad debts written off	GL	25	
	T Hughes	SL		25
	Bad debt written off as per memo from accounts supervisor dated 10 December 19-1			

expenses charged to owner's drawings

Sometimes the owner of a business uses business facilities for private use, eg telephone, or car. The owner will agree that part of the expense shall be charged to him or her as drawings, while the other part represents a business expense. The book-keeping entry to record the adjustment is:

– *debit* drawings account
– *credit* expense account, eg telephone $\Big\}$ with the amount of personal use

31 Dec. 19-3   The balance of telephone account is £600; of this, one-quarter is the estimated cost of the owner's private usage

The journal entry is:

Date	Details	Folio	Dr	Cr
19-3			£	£
31 Dec.	Drawings account	GL	150	
	Telephone account	GL		150
	Transfer of private use to drawings account			

goods for own use

When the owner of a business takes some of the goods in which the business trades for his or her own use, the double-entry book-keeping is:

– *debit* drawings account

– *credit* purchases account

15 Oct. 19-2   Owner of the business takes goods for own use, £105

The journal entry is:

Date	Details	Folio	Dr	Cr
19-2			£	£
15 Oct.	Drawings account	GL	105	
	Purchases account	GL		105
	Goods taken for own use by the owner			

chapter summary

❑   The journal is used to list non-regular transactions.

❑   The journal is a book of prime entry – it is *not* a double-entry account.

❑   The journal is used for:
  • opening entries
  • purchase and sale of fixed assets on credit
  • correction of errors
  • other transfers

❑   Correction of errors is always a difficult topic to put into practice: it tests your knowledge of book-keeping procedures and it is all too easy to make the error worse than it was in the first place! The secret of dealing with this topic well is to write down – in account format – what has gone wrong. It should then be relatively easy to see what has to be done to put the error right.

❑   Errors not shown by a trial balance: error of omission, reversal of entries, mispost/error of commission, error of principle, error of original entry (or transcription), compensating error.

❑   Errors shown by a trial balance include: omission of one part of the book-keeping transaction, recording two debits/credits for a transaction, recording different amounts in the two accounts, calculating balances, transferring balances to the trial balance.

❑   All errors are non-regular transactions and need to be corrected by means of a journal entry: the book-keeper then needs to record the correcting transactions in the accounts.

❑   When error(s) are shown by a trial balance, the amount is placed into a suspense account. As the errors are found, journal entries are made which 'clear out' the suspense account.

Student Activities

11.1   Samantha Smith owns a clothes shop. She decides to keep her accounts in the future by means of the double-entry book-keeping system. On 1 April 19-8 the financial position is as follows:

	£
Shop premises	90,000
Shop fittings	2,000
Stock	15,000
Bank overdraft	8,200
Cash	225
Debtors	565
Creditors	4,175

You are to make the opening journal entry for the above, showing clearly the capital of Samantha Smith on 1 April 19-8.

11.2 Henry Lewis is setting up the book-keeping system for his new business, which sells office stationery. He decides to use the following books of original entry:

- Journal
- Sales Day Book
- Purchases Day Book
- Sales Returns Day Book
- Purchases Returns Day Book
- Cash Book

The following business transactions take place:

(a) He receives an invoice from Temeside Traders for £956 for goods supplied on credit
(b) He issues an invoice to Malvern Models for £176 of goods
(c) He buys a computer for use in his business for £2,000 on credit from A-Z Computers Ltd
(d) He issues a credit note to Johnson Bros for £55 of goods
(c) A debtor, Melanie Fisher, settles the balance of her account, £107, by cheque
(f) He makes cash sales of £25
(g) Henry Lewis withdraws cash £100 for his own use
(h) He pays a creditor, Stationery Supplies Ltd, the balance of the account, £298, by cheque
(i) A debtor, Jim Bowen, with an account balance of £35 is to be written off as a bad debt
(j) A credit note for £80 is received from a creditor, Ian Johnson

You are to take each business transaction in turn and state:
- the name of the book of prime entry
- the name of the account to be debited
- the name of the account to be credited

Note: VAT is to be ignored.

11.3 The trial balance of Thomas Wilson balanced. However, a number of errors have been found in the book-keeping system:

(a) Credit sale of £150 to J Rigby has not been entered in the accounts
(b) A payment by cheque for £125 to H Price Ltd, a creditor, has been recorded in the account of H Prince
(c) The cost of a new delivery van, £10,000, has been entered to vehicle expenses account
(d) Purchases returns of £55 to S Mortimer, a creditor, have been entered on the wrong sides of both accounts
(e) The totals of the purchases day book and the purchases returns day book have been undercast by £100
(f) A payment for £89 from L Johnson, a debtor, has been entered in the accounts as £98

You are to take each error in turn and:
- state the type of error
- show the correcting journal entry

Note: VAT is to be ignored.

11.4 Jeremy Johnson extracts a trial balance from his book-keeping records on 30 September 19-8. Unfortunately the trial balance fails to balance and the difference, £19 debit, is placed to a suspense account pending further investigation.

The following errors are later found:

(a) A payment of £85 to Wyvern Supplies, a creditor, has been entered in the cash book but no entry has been made in the personal account.

(b) A purchases invoice for £78 has been correctly entered in the purchases day book but in the creditor's account of Henry Barton it is recorded as £87.

(c) The sales returns day book has been overcast by £100.

(d) A credit note for £25 issued to Teresa Jarvis has been entered twice in her account.

You are to:

(i) make journal entries to correct the errors

(ii) show the suspense account after the errors have been corrected

11.5 Tracey Truslove is the book-keeper for Mereford Traders Ltd. At 30 June 19-9 she is unable to balance the trial balance. The difference, £221 credit, is placed to a suspense account pending further investigation.

The following errors are later found:

(a) Purchases account is undercast by £100.

(b) A receipt from L Lewis, a debtor, for £95 has been recorded in the personal account as £59.

(c) Rent received of £205 has been debited to both the rent received account and the bank account.

(d) Motor vehicles expenses of £125 have not been entered in the expenses account.

You are to:

(i) make journal entries to correct the errors

(ii) show the suspense account after the errors have been corrected

(iii) make a further journal entry to write off as a bad debt the balance of £80 on L Branksome's account

12 Receiving payments

Organisations will normally deal with payments in three contexts:

• they will *receive payment* for goods and services they have supplied
• they will need to *bank* the payments received
• they will *make payment* for goods and services they have ordered

In this chapter we will examine the procedures for receiving payments, and the need for ensuring the *security* of the money or vouchers received. In the next two chapters we will set out the procedures for banking payments and also for making payments.

Payments can be received in a variety of ways:

• cash
• cheque
• credit card transactions
• debit card transactions

It clearly depends on the nature and the size of the organisation how the payments are made and processed. In the retail sector, for example, a newsagent will depend to a great extent on cash transactions and the cash register, a large supermarket on the other hand will use electronic tills and accept cash, cheques, and credit and debit card payments. Handling all these different forms of payment requires the same high degree of skill, and we will examine them all in turn.

cash

Cash is still used for most small transactions, and we are still nowhere near the 'cashless society' which is often talked about. For the purchaser, cash is a convenient and fast method of paying small money amounts but, for larger amounts, it is unsuitable because it is bulky to carry, liable to be lost, and a temptation to thieves. As far as the organisation accepting payments in cash is concerned, the main disadvantage of cash is the security problem, both in terms of staff theft, and also the increasing risk of armed robbery.

receiving payment in cash

For a business receiving sums of money in the form of cash it is necessary for a member of staff to count the cash received and check it against the amount due. Change will need to be given when the exact amount is not tendered (given). For example:

Sale	£3.64
Amount tendered (given) by customer	£10.00
Change to be given	£6.36

The amount of change is the difference between the amount tendered and the amount of the sale. When a cash till is in use, modern types of till will indicate the amount of change to be given after the amount tendered has been entered through the keyboard. You will know, from having bought items in shops, that many cashiers count out the change starting with the amount of the sale and working to the amount tendered. From the above example this would be done as follows:

Sale		£3.64	
Change given:	1p coin	£3.65	
	5p coin	£3.70	
	10p coin	£3.80	
	20p coin	£4.00	
	£1 coin	£5.00	
	£5 note	£10.00	Amount tendered
	£6.36		

Often when payment is made in cash, a receipt is given: this can take the form of a machine-produced receipt, such as is given in a shop, or a handwritten receipt (examples of each are shown below).

Everest Sports		retailer
15 High St Mereford		address
09 03 93 15.07		date and time of transaction
Salesperson Tina		salesperson
Tennis balls	5.99	goods purchased
Shin guards	8.99	goods purchased
TOTAL	14.98	total due
CASH	20.00	£20 (probably a £20 note) given by the customer
CHANGE	5.02	change given
Thank you for your custom		personal message to help public relations
Please retain this receipt in case of any query		advice to retain receipt in case of a problem with the goods

ENIGMA MUSIC LTD   958

13 High Street Mereford MR1 2TF
VAT reg 343 7645 23

CASH RECEIPT

Customer... *R V Williams* ....date...... *9 March 1993*

Heifitz violin and bow	*£250.00*
Music stand	*£45.00*
	£295.00
VAT (17.5%)	*£51.62*
TOTAL	*£346.62*

Fig. 12.1   Machine-produced receipt (top) and handwritten receipt (below)

Those who handle cash in a business are responsible for its safekeeping, ie it should be kept in a cash till or in a cash box. When not being used, these should be kept locked and the key retained under the control of the cashier.

At the end of the day it will be necessary to 'cash up' by balancing the amount of cash held. As most cash tills start each day with a small float of cash (to enable change to be given, if necessary, to the first customers), the amount in the till at the end of the day will be:

> cash float at start
> *plus* sales* made during the day
> *equals* amount of cash held at end of day

> * Sales for the day will be either listed on the till roll of the cash till,
>   or be found from a handwritten record of sales.

A cash float will be kept back for the next day, and the surplus will be transferred to the safe for paying into the bank next day. Alternatively, a bank paying-in slip (see Chapter 13) might be made out, and the cash, together with the paying-in slip placed in a 'wallet' to be deposited in the bank's night safe. (The night safe can be seen on the outside wall of most banks: it is opened with a special key and a wallet containing cash can be deposited by business customers outside banking hours.) The wallet will be opened by the bank next day and the contents checked and paid in to the bank account. For example:

cash float at start	£25.45
plus sales made during the day	£262.35
equals amount of cash held at end of day	£287.80**
less cash float retained for next day	£32.80
amount transferred to safe or bank's night safe	£255.00

** If the cash in the till does not agree with this figure, the discrepancy needs investigation. Regular discrepancies for significant amounts, eg £5 or £10, will lead to urgent investigations – there could be pilfering taking place if the till is often short at the end of the day, or it could be caused by poor cashiering – giving the wrong change.

cheques

Cheques are issued by banks to their personal and business *current account* customers. Building societies also issue cheques on current accounts – their customers are mainly personal. Payment by cheque is one of the most common methods of payment for all but the smallest amounts. A specimen cheque is shown in fig. 12.2 (there is more on how to write out a cheque in Chapter 14).

what is a cheque?
A cheque, as used in normal business practice, may be defined as

a written order to the bank signed by its customer (known as the 'drawer') to pay a specified amount to a specified person (known as the 'payee')

Some organisations – large retail stores, for example – have machines which print out their customers' cheques on the till. A large number of cheques, however, are still written by hand, and great care must be taken both when writing out cheques and also when receiving cheques in payment. The cheques must be examined to ensure that all the details and signatures are correct. The details that must be looked at when receiving a cheque in payment are explained on the next page.

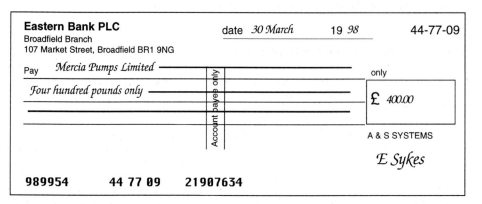

Fig. 12.2   A specimen cheque

examining the cheque

If you are receiving payment by cheque, whether it is direct from the customer over the counter or through the post on a remittance advice (see page 20), there are a number of basic checks to carry out:

- is the cheque signed? – it is invalid if it is not
- is the payee's name correct? – it should be changed and initialled by the drawer if it is not
- is the cheque in date? – a cheque becomes out of date and invalid after six months; note that if the date is missing, it may be written in
- do the words and figures agree? – the cheque may be returned by the bank if they do not

If the organisation accepting payment by cheque is inefficient and does not carry out these precautions, the cheque(s) may be returned to the organisation's bank after it has been paid in, and the amount of the cheque deducted from the organisation's bank account.   If the cheque is issued with a cheque card, different conditions apply (see page 156).

crossings

Cheques are normally crossed, as in the example shown above: they are printed with two parallel lines across the face of the cheque. If a cheque is not crossed, it is an *open* cheque. A *crossed* cheque may only be paid into a bank account; it cannot be cashed (i.e. exchanged for cash) by the payee (the person to whom the cheque is made payable). An *open* cheque, on the other hand, can be cashed by the payee at the bank branch named on the cheque. The payee in the case of an open cheque does not have to have a bank account. As you will appreciate, crossed cheques are much safer then open cheques, which if lost or stolen could be cashed by any person impersonating the payee.

endorsements

In law the payee of a cheque is entitled to sign it on the back – *endorse* it – so that it can be passed on to another person who can pay it into a bank account and receive payment. This signature on the back – the *endorsement* – should read as follows:

> *Pay Ivor Brown*
> *James Smith*

In this example James Smith, the payee, is endorsing the cheque over to Ivor Brown who will pay it into his bank account. He has actually written "Pay Ivor Brown" above his signature.

In practice nowadays this rarely happens because banks print "account payee" or "account payee only" on the front of the cheque, as is explained below.

"payee only" cheques – current banking practice

Because of the problems of fraud – people stealing cheques, forging an endorsement and paying them into their own account – banks rarely now accept endorsed cheques. A classic case was a fraudster opening a bank account in the name of "Ian Revenue" and then stealing tax cheques made payable to "I. Revenue" (the Inland Revenue) and paying them in!

As a result of this type of practice an increasing number of cheques are being printed with "only" after the space where the payee's name is written (see Fig. 12.2 on the previous page). These cheques cannot be endorsed over to another person, they can only be paid into the payee's account (if they are crossed) or cashed by the payee (if they are open). In addition most banks also print the words "account payee" or "account payee only" in the crossing of the cheque (see below). This has the same effect – these cheques can only be paid into the bank account of the payee. If you are working in an accounts department or operating a till you should *never* accept endorsed cheques when they carry these words on the front. If you do the bank will not accept them, and your business may lose the money!

crossings and endorsements

As noted above, there is often wording written or printed between the two lines of the crossing which may affect the ability of the payee to endorse the cheque and pass it on to another person. Here are some examples:

crossing	*effect*
———— *& Co.* ————	No effect at all – the cheque can be endorsed and passed on. This wording is a historical relic dating back to the nineteenth century.
———— *not negotiable* ————	The cheque can still be endorsed over, although if the cheque has been stolen and passed on, the person who pays it into their bank account may lose their money if the cheque has been 'stopped' by the person who wrote it out.
———— *account payee* ————	As we have seen above, following the passing of The Cheques Act 1992 this type of crossing effectively prevents the cheque from being endorsed, as it can only be paid into the account of the payee. You will sometimes see variations to the "account payee" wording, for example "account payee only" or "a/c payee" or "a/c payee only". These all have the same effect.
———— *Midland Bank* *Pershore* ————	This type of crossing – known a *special* crossing – means that the cheque may only be paid in at Midland Bank, Pershore. If it is paid in at another bank, payment may be refused.

You may consider that these explanations are very technical and do not relate to what you see in everyday business transactions. It is important to realise, however, that if you are in the position of receiving payment by cheque, either over a counter or through the post, these distinctions may be vital. If you spot something that is wrong – for example an "account payee" crossed cheque being handed in by someone other than the payee, you could prevent your organisation losing money from a "dud" cheque.

cheque cards

In order to encourage shops and other businesses to accept cheques more readily, banks and some building societies issue cheque cards to suitable personal and business customers (but not to limited companies). This plastic 'card' acts as a guarantee that cheques up to and including a stated limit (normally £50, sometimes £100 or £200) will be paid as long as certain conditions are fulfilled. Whereas a cheque card will only guarantee payment of cheques, many banks now issue 'payment cards' which combine the functions of

- *cheque guarantee* – guaranteeing single cheques up to a set limit
- *cash card* – enabling the holder to withdraw cash from cash machines – ATMs (automated teller machines)
- *debit card* – enabling the holder to make payment for goods and services from a bank account without writing out a cheque – examples include Switch cards and Barclay's Connect card

The rules for the use of a cheque card may be found on the reverse of the card, or they may be made available separately by the bank. The following is an example of the wording:

> XYZ Bank plc guarantees in any single transaction the payment of one cheque taken from one of its own cheque books for up to £50 provided the cheque is not drawn on the account of a Limited Company, and
>
> (1) The cheque bears the same name and code number as this card.
> (2) It is signed, before the expiry of the card, in the United Kingdom of Great Britain and Northern Ireland, the Channel Islands or the Isle of Man in the presence of the payee by the person whose signature appears on this card.
> (3) The card number is written on the back of the cheque by the payee.
> (4) The card has not been altered or defaced.

receiving payment by cheque and cheque guarantee card

If you have read the cheque card conditions set out above you will appreciate that when you accept payment by cheque and cheque guarantee card you must take great care that all the conditions are met. If you do not, the purchaser's bank may not pay the cheque, and your organisation stands to lose the money. Also, because of the large number of stolen and fraudulent cards in circulation, you must be on your guard against suspicious-looking cards and customers. The procedure is therefore as follows:

- examine the card to make sure it is not defaced – rub your finger along the signature strip, does it feel normal? – a stolen card may have been tampered with and a new signature added

- if the card is handed to you in a plastic wallet, take the card out, as it may be a forgery

- examine the card for
  - expiry date
  - amount of the guarantee
  - name agreeing with the name on the cheque
  - bank details agreeing with those on the cheque

- examine the cheque for
  - signature (this should agree with the signature on the card)
  - date
  - payee's name
  - amount in words and figures (they should agree)

- write the card number on the back of the cheque – an essential procedure, adding any other details which your organisation requires (some businesses use a rubber stamp on the back of the cheque to list the required details)

cheque card limits – a common mistake

Customers sometimes think that if the cost of the item being purchased is above the cheque guarantee limit, then a number of cheques may be issued and payment is guaranteed. *This is not correct – the cheque card guarantee covers only one cheque per transaction.* For example, if a TV costing £150 is bought with a £50 limit card, the customer may want to write out three £50 cheques. The shop should not accept these, because the cheques may be returned by the bank if the customer does not have the money. The shop should instead ask for cash or a credit or debit card. The practice of writing out separate cheques with *different dates* for one purchase is also not acceptable!

credit card

Credit cards provide a means of obtaining goods and services immediately, but paying for them later. The commonest credit cards used in the UK use the names Visa, Access, Mastercard, Eurocard. The cards are issued, upon application, to customers of banks, building societies, and retail groups. A credit limit is set on each cardholder's credit card account (which is entirely separate from his or her normal bank account). Goods and services can be obtained at shops and other outlets having computer terminals or the special machine (imprinter) for preparing sales vouchers to record the transaction. Credit cards can also be used for mail order and telephone order sales. Retailers pay to the credit card company a set percentage (up to 5%) of each transaction amount for the use of the credit card facility.

Each month a cardholder is sent a statement of the purchases made and can choose to pay off the balance of the account, or to pay part only (subject to a certain minimum amount), carrying forward the remaining balance to next month. Interest is charged on balances owing to the credit card company. An annual flat fee is normally charged to the cardholder for the use of the card.

receiving payment by credit card – 'over the counter' sales

A business will have one of two methods of receiving payment by credit card by a customer who calls in person:

- an imprinter machine, which imprints the embossed details from the credit card onto the sales voucher
- a 'swipe' machine, which is able to read the details from a credit card as it is passed through the card 'reader'

Imprinter machine
The procedure is as follows:

- check that the card has not been defaced or tampered with – check the signature strip carefully
- check that the card has not expired
- imprint the sales voucher (see Fig 12.3 on the next page)
- complete the sales voucher with date, details of goods, and total money amount
- the customer signs the imprinted sales voucher, and the signature should be compared with that on the card
- the list of stolen cards is checked
- if the payment is above a certain amount (which varies according to the type of business) it will be necessary to telephone the credit card company to obtain an authorisation code allowing the transaction to go ahead (the authorisation code is recorded on the sales voucher)
- the top copy of the sales voucher is handed to the customer, and the other three copies are retained
- of the three copies of the sales voucher which are retained, the white copy is treated in the same way as a cheque, and is kept in the till and added to the cheques and cash received to give the total sales figure; the other two copies (yellow and blue) are kept in the event of a query in the future
- the white copy of the sales voucher kept in the till is then banked along with the cash and cheques

Fig 12.3 Completed and imprinted credit card sales voucher

'Swipe' machine

The cashier or clerk should:

- 'swipe' the card through the card reader - this 'captures' the details encoded in the magnetic stripe on the reverse of the card
- having captured the data, the system checks automatically that the card number is valid
- the amount of the transaction is keyed into the electronic till, and the system (if the till is on-line) checks the cardholder's credit limit and authorises the transaction
- a telephone call to the card company may be necessary to authorise the transaction if the till is not on-line
- the till prints a two-part receipt which includes space for the cardholder's signature
- the customer signs, and the signature is compared with that on the card
- the customer is handed the top-copy of the receipt, and the other copy is kept in the event of a query in the future
- the amount of the transaction is automatically debited to the cardholder's credit card account, while the bank account of the business is credited

receiving payment by credit card – telephone and mail order sales

Buying goods and services by credit card over the telephone or by mail order is becoming increasingly common. When accepting payment by this means, the organisation must exercise the same degree of care as a shop accepting an 'over the counter' transaction. Some organisations will complete the same type of sales voucher used for an 'over the counter' transaction and send the top copy to the customer as a receipt; some organisations will use a 'swipe' machine, and send a copy of the receipt to the customer. Organisations which have a large volume of transactions will not use vouchers but instead record the details of sales on a Mail Order Schedule, a form which will provide space for recording ten transactions or more.

When accepting payment by credit card by telephone or mail order, the following details must be obtained:

- the card number
- the expiry date of the card
- the name and initials of the cardholder as shown on the card
- the cardholder's address
- the cardholder's signature (mail order only)
- authorisation of amounts over the 'floor limit' must be carried out in the normal way.

debit cards

Debit cards are issued to personal customers by banks and building societies to enable their customers to make payments from their bank accounts by Electronic Funds Transfer – see below. Examples of debit cards are Barclays' Visa 'Delta' and Midland's 'Switch' cards. Such cards are issued to selected customers of the bank; they enable a payment to be made from the person's bank account, subject to having sufficient money in the account, without the need to write a cheque.

From a seller's point of view, when a customer wishes to pay by debit card *in person*, the transaction is handled in a similar way to a credit card. As mentioned earlier, some banks have combined the functions of a debit card with that of cheque guarantee card and cash card (ATM card).

Electronic Funds Transfer

Credit cards and debit cards can be used to make electronic payments by means of a system called Electronic Funds Transfer at Point Of Sale (EFTPOS). This is a system which allows a retail outlet to debit the bank account or credit card account of the purchaser at the point of sale and, at the same time, to credit the retailer's bank account. Besides removing the need to carry a lot of cash, the system reduces the paperwork of writing out cheques or filling in credit card vouchers.

EFTPOS is operated by means of plastic cards – either *debit cards* issued by banks/building societies, or by *credit cards*. When goods are to be paid for using this method, the retailer 'swipes' the card through a card reader (as with a credit card) and the total amount is entered into an electronic checkout till. The till prints a sales slip which is signed by the customer to authenticate the transaction. The retailer checks that the signature on the sales slip is the same as that shown on the card. Details of the transaction are transmitted electronically by means of a computer link to a central computer either immediately, or later in the day. Sometimes a telephone call has to be made to authorise the transaction. The cost of the goods being purchased is checked against the amount available in the card holder's bank or building society account, or the available credit in the credit card account. If everything is in order, the customer's account is debited and the retailer's account is credited with the appropriate amount. The benefits of EFTPOS to a retail business are:
- greater efficiency, with less time taken by customers to make payment
- reduced queuing time
- less cash to handle (giving fewer security risks)
- guaranteed payment once acceptance has been made

chapter summary

❑ Common methods of payment include cash, cheque (often backed by a cheque guarantee card), credit card and debit card.

❑ Cheque payments are either received through the post or over the counter, often supported by a cheque guarantee card. Staff handling cheques must understand technical details such as crossings and endorsements, and the cheque card conditions.

❑ Credit card payments can be made in person, by post or by telephone; the procedure involves the completion of a sales voucher, schedule or the use of a 'swipe' machine.

❑ Debit card payments are becoming increasingly popular; the procedures involved are very similar to those relating to credit cards.

❑ EFTPOS (Electronic Funds Transfer at Point of Sale) enables a customer's bank or credit card account to be debited by electronic means at the point of sale, ie at the till.

✍ student activities

12.1   You operate the cash till at the firm where you work. The following are the sales for one day:

		Amount of sale £	Notes and/or coin tendered
Customer	1	8.50	£10 note
	2	3.30	£10 note
	3	2.51	£5 note
	4	1.79	£5 note
	5	0.34	£1 coin
	6	6.22	£10 note
	7	12.76	£20 note
	8	1.42	two £1 coins
	9	6.54	£10 note
	10	3.08	£5 note

You are to state:
• the amount of change to be given to each customer
• the notes and/or coin that will be given in change, *using the minimum number possible*

12.2   If the cash till in question 1 had a float of £28.71 at the start of the day, how much cash should be held in the till after the sales from question 1 had been made? Present your answer in the following form:

	£
cash float at start	28.71
plus sales made during the day	
	————
equals amount of cash held at end of day	════

12.3   You are operating a cash till at the firm where you work. Today the cash float at the start of the day is £22.30, made up as follows:

2 x £5 notes	= £10.00
6 x £1 coins	= £6.00
6 x 50p coins	= £3.00
8 x 20p coins	= £1.60
10 x 10p coins	= £1.00
8 x 5p coins	= £0.40
12 x 2p coins	= £0.24
6 x 1p coins	= £0.06
	————
	£22.30

The following are the sales which pass through the till today:

		Amount of sales £	Notes and/or coin tendered
Customer	1	7.50	£10 note
	2	3.38	£5 note
	3	2.29	two £1 coins and a 50p coin
	4	18.90	£20 note
	5	6.04	£10 note, £1 coin, two 2p coins
	6	26.36	three £10 notes
	7	4.30	four £1 coins and a 50p coin

You are to:

(a) state the amount of change to be given to each customer
(b) state the notes and/or coin that will be given in change, *using the minimum number possible*
(c) calculate the denominations of notes and coin that will remain in the till at the end of the day
(d) retain a cash float which does not exceed £30.00 (show the denominations of notes and coin); the remainder of the cash is to be banked (show denominations)
(e) prepare a summary of the day's transactions in the following form:

	£
cash float at start	22.30
plus sales made during the day	_____
equals amount of cash held at end of day	
less cash float retained for next day	
	_____
amount banked	
	======

12.4 You work as a shop counter assistant at New Era Lighting. You make a number of sales during the day (use today's date) which require the completion of a handwritten receipt. Complete the receipts set out below. Include VAT on all purchases at the current rate. All prices quoted here are catalogue prices and exclude VAT.

(a) 2 flexilamps @ £13.99, 2 60W candlelight bulbs @ 85p, to Mr George Meredith

NEW ERA LIGHTING   977
17 High Street Mereford MR1 2TF
VAT reg 141 7645 23

CASH RECEIPT

Customer...date..........................

	VAT
	TOTAL

(b) 1 standard lamp @
£149.95,
1 3 amp plug @ 99p,
to Mr Alex Bell

NEW ERA LIGHTING	978
17 High Street Mereford MR1 2TF	
VAT reg 141 7645 23	

CASH RECEIPT

Customer...date...........................

VAT	
TOTAL	

12.5 You work as an accounts clerk in the Accounts Department of Mercia Pumps Ltd., Unit 13, Severn Trading Estate, Mereford MR3 4GF.   Today is 3 April 1998.   In the morning's post are a number of cheques enclosed with remittance advices.   These cheques are illustrated below and on the next page.

Examine the cheques carefully, identify any problems and state what action (if any) you will take, and why.   Draft letters *where appropriate* for your Manager's (Mrs D Strong) signature.   You note from the remittance advices that the addresses are as follows:

(a) The Accounts Department, A & S Systems, 5 High Street, Mereford MR1 2JF

(b) Mrs P Thorne, Hillside Cottage, Mintfield, MR4 9HG

(b) The Accounts Department, C Darwin Ltd, 89 Baker Street, Mereford MR2 6RG

(c) Mr I M A King, 56 Beaconsfield Drive, Pershore MR7 5GF

(a)

Eastern Bank PLC	date *30 March* 19 *98*	44-77-09
Broadfield Branch		
107 Market Street, Broadfield BR1 9NG		

Pay   *Mercia Pumps Limited* ─────────────────────── only

Four hundred pounds only ──────────   £ *400.00*

A & S SYSTEMS

989954   44 77 09   21907634

(b)

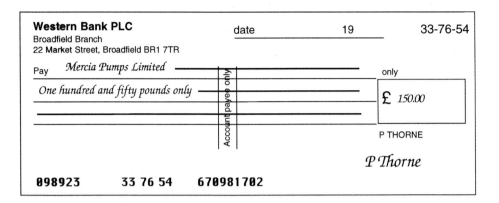

(c)

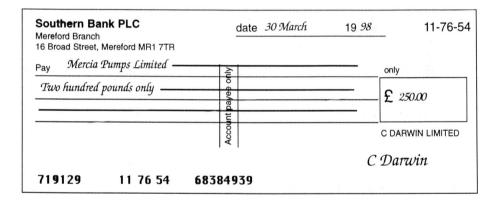

(d) Mr King has made the cheque payable to your Sales Director, John Hopkins, who says he is happy to endorse the cheque over to the company.

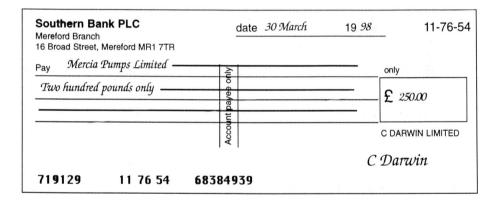

12.6 You work as a cashier at Cripplegate DIY store. The date is 20 January 1998. You deal with a number of customers who wish to make payment using cheques and a cheque card. What action would you take in the following circumstances, and why?

(a) Card limit £100, expiry May 1998, code 22-01-59. Mr King wants to buy some garden furniture costing £150.95. He has made out the following cheques in advance.

Northern Bank PLC	date *20 January* 19 *98* 22-01-59
Mereford Branch	
28 High Street, Mereford MR1 8FD	

Pay *Cripplegate DIY* — only
One hundred pounds only —
Account payee only
£ 100.00
I KING
I M King

122874   22 01 59   37537147

Northern Bank PLC	date *20 January* 19 *98* 22-01-59
Mereford Branch	
28 High Street, Mereford MR1 8FD	

Pay *Cripplegate DIY* — only
Fifty pounds 95p only —
Account payee only
£ 50.95
I KING
I M King

122875   22 01 59   37537147

(b) Card limit £200, expiry April 1998, code 33-76-54. The cheque card is handed to you in a plastic wallet and the signature on the card does not quite tally with the signature on the cheque. The customer says that he has sprained his wrist and this has affected his writing.

Western Bank PLC	date *20 January* 19 *98* 33-76-54
Broadfield Branch	
22 Market Street, Broadfield BR1 7TR	

Pay *Cripplegate DIY* — only
Two hundred pounds only —
Account payee only
£ 200.00
M ATHERSHAM
M Athersham

822321   33 76 54   61907852

12.7   Cripplegate DIY also accepts credit cards. Your floor limit is £100 and your sales number is 107 in Department 8. Complete the details on the extracts of the sales vouchers shown below, and state any further action which you might take if you think it is required. Use today's date. Note that all prices include VAT.

date		send?	take?
dept	sales no.		initials
description		£	p
TOTAL			

(a) Electrical goods at £367.60
Delivery charge £15.00

date		send?	take?
dept	sales no.		initials
description		£	p
TOTAL			

(b) Garden machinery at £125.30
Garden plants at £17.85

date		send?	take?
dept	sales no.		initials
description		£	p
TOTAL			

(c) Timber at £19.25
Paint at £29.95

date		send?	take?
dept	sales no.		initials
description		£	p
TOTAL			

(d) Garden furniture at £139.75
Building materials at £295.00
Delivery charge at £20.00

(e) As part of a training exercise your supervisor asks you to compile a checklist of the procedures to be used when accepting payment by credit card over the counter. This list should include points relating to the detection of credit card fraud, and the action to be taken when circumstances are suspicious.

The list should be set out as a memorandum to all sales staff. Use today's date.

13 Banking transactions

In this chapter we will see the way in which payments received by an organisation are prepared for paying into a bank account. We will examine:
- the preparation of cash for paying in
- the listing of cheques being paid in
- the listing and scheduling of credit card sales vouchers
- the completion of a paying-in slip

By way of introduction we will look briefly at the legal background to the bank and customer relationship, the main types of accounts offered by banks to their personal and business customers, and the bank clearing system.

bank and customer

a legal relationship

It is important to appreciate when studying and practising banking procedures that there is a distinct *legal relationship* between a bank and its customer. Normally this relationship dos not give much cause for concern; it is only when something goes wrong – for example when a bank pays a cheque which its customer has stopped – that the legal relationship becomes particularly important.

bank and customer contract

Assuming that a bank is a financial institution licensed as a bank by the Bank of England (all the well-known banks are) and a customer is a person who has an account at the bank, then in law there is said to be a *contract* between the customer and the bank. A contract may be defined as:

a legally binding agreement which is recognised in a court of law

You may wonder why a contract between a bank and a customer is important to your studies. The answer is that the bank/customer contract means that the customer has certain rights and duties to perform; including
- keeping the bank account in credit (not overdrawn, unless by arrangement)
- taking care when writing out cheques so that they cannot be altered by a fraudster
- if a payment card is issued, keeping that card safe and not leaving it where it can be stolen
- letting the bank know if anyone is forging signatures on the account

If the customer fails in any of these duties and the bank loses a substantial amount of money, *it has the right in law under the contract to take the customer to court.*

Similarly, the bank has certain rights and duties to perform under the contract, and if it fails to do so and the customer suffers sufficient loss (money or reputation), the customer can take the bank to court. Examples of the bank's duties include

- paying the customer's cheques when there is sufficient money in the account
- keeping details of the customer's account secret
- sending statements of account to the customer
- telling a customer if forgery is taking place on the account
- using care and skill when dealing with customer's accounts

Clearly a customer will not take a bank to court if a statement is not sent out! But it may do so if the bank by mistake fails to pay an business cheque issued to a supplier, and the supplier cuts off supplies to the business. This would be a breach of the *contract* between the bank and the customer. For further details of the theory of contract and the bank/customer relationship, see Chapter 24 "Business contracts".

Since March 1992, the banks have issued *Codes of Banking Practice* to their personal and business customers. A Code of Banking Practice is a document which sets out clearly the rights and duties of banks and customers. As part of your studies you should obtain a copy of a Code of Banking Practice, preferably a Code for business customers, and look carefully at what a bank expects of its customers, and what the customers should expect of the bank.

types of account

There are two main types of accounts offered by banks to personal and business customers:

- current account
- deposit (savings) account

current account

With this type of account a bank customer is issued with a cheque book and may make use of most of the services of the bank. Bank customers use a current account as a 'working account' into which receipts are paid (for example, many employees have their wages or salaries paid directly into their bank account), and out of which are paid expenses by means of cheques, standing orders, direct debits, EFT (electronic funds transfer). A business uses a current account to pay in receipts (cash, cheques and credit card vouchers), and to make payment for business expenses. Some banks are now introducing interest paying current accounts for *personal* customers.

overdraft

Banks are often prepared to grant overdraft facilities to their *current* account personal and business customers on request (deposit accounts are not allowed to go overdrawn). A business, for example, realizing that it will need overdraft facilities should contact the bank and seek agreement for an overdraft up to a certain limit for a specified time. Interest is charged on overdrawn balances.

deposit (savings) account

A deposit account is used for savings by personal customers, or excess money held by a business, and interest is paid by the bank. Current account facilities such as cheque books, standing orders, direct debits, and overdrafts are not allowed on deposit accounts for business customers. Notice of withdrawal will normally need to be given to the bank. Often, seven days' notice is required on a deposit account although, in practice, this can be overlooked, but seven days' interest will be deducted by way of penalty. Other types of account may need a longer period of notice of withdrawal, perhaps one month or three months.

Many business customers have both a current and a deposit account. A business can use a deposit account as a temporary 'home' for surplus money. When the money is needed it can be transferred easily to the firm's current account. Personal customers, as mentioned above, are increasingly using interest-paying current accounts.

cheque clearing

Every working day each bank branch receives cheques paid in by customers. These cheques take a defined time to 'clear.' The term to 'clear' means that the cheque must have passed to the bank of the issuer of the cheque for payment before the money amount of the cheque – the amount paid in – can be used by the customer. The clearance times are normally

- cheques paid in and issued by customers *of the same branch* – same day clearance
- cheques paid in by customers *of other banks and branches* – three working days' clearance

This means that if you are given a cheque by someone who has an account at your branch and you pay it in on Monday, you can draw against it, ie you can use the money on the account, on Monday, the same day. This assumes, of course, that the cheque is paid and does not 'bounce'. On the other hand, if you are given a cheque which is issued by someone who banks at another bank (or another branch of your bank), then if you pay it in on Monday, you will have to wait three working days, ie until Wednesday before the cheque is cleared, and you can use the money.

The reason for this delay is that the cheque will have to be sent to London for sorting. This long and expensive process, required by a law dating back to the last century, is illustrated below. In this case Enigma Cafe, which banks at Midland Bank in Malvern pays a cheque for £500 to their supplier, Broadheath Bakers, who then pay it into their bank, Barclays Bank in Worcester. The diagram follows the two hundred and fifty mile journey of the cheque. The two bank branches, incidentally, are seven miles apart.

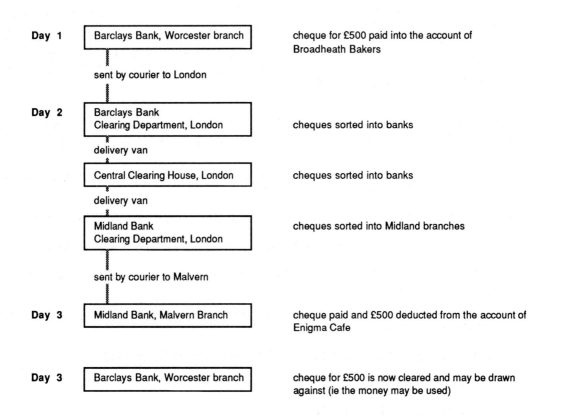

Fig. 13.1 The cheque clearing system

special clearance

Sometimes you may need to know quickly whether or not a cheque will be paid, for example, if you sell goods for £5,000 to an unknown buyer. The banks offer a special clearance service, known as a *Special Presentation*, whereby for a fee (around £10) a bank will send a cheque to the issuer's branch by *first class post*, and then telephone the following day in the morning to establish whether or not the cheque will be paid.

returned cheques

You may be in the unfortunate position of having paid in a cheque and then discovering that the cheque has been returned to your bank unpaid, and the amount of the cheque deducted from your account. Your bank will normally send it back to you by post. You will thus receive it *five* days after paying it in. It will have one of a number of answers written along the top:

* *refer to drawer* – the person who has given you the cheque (the drawer) has no money in the bank – you will have to contact him or her for an explanation! this answer is often abbreviated to "RD"
* *refer to drawer, please represent* – (abbreviated to "RDPR") – this means that there was insufficient money in the account to meet the cheque, but that the cheque has been sent through the clearing *again* (represented) in the hope that it will be paid when it reaches the issuers bank (note that in this case the cheque will *not* be sent back to the payee)
* *payment countermanded by order of drawer* – the cheque has been stopped – you should contact the drawer to find out the reason
* technical problems such *signature required*, or *words and figures differ*, or *out of date*, will mean that you will have to contact the drawer for a new cheque (if the reason is *out of date*) or a signature or an alteration (which will have to be signed by the drawer)

stopped cheques

We mentioned at the beginning of the chapter that it is the bank's duty in contract law to pay a customer's cheque as long as there is sufficient money in the account. A customer may order a bank *not* to pay a cheque; this is known as *stopping* a cheque. This often happens if a cheque is lost in the post and another cheque is issued in its place. The bank will make a charge (approximately £10) for stopping a cheque, and will return the cheque marked "payment countermanded by order of drawer" if and when it is paid in and presented for payment.

paying-in books

All business customers (and personal customers by request) are issued with a paying-in book by the bank. Details to be completed by a bank customer are:

* name of the bank and branch where the account is held (these details are normally pre-printed)

* name of the account to be credited, together with the account number (normally pre-printed)

* a summary of the different categories of notes or coins being paid in, the amount of each category being entered on the slip

* amounts and details of cheques being paid in, usually entered on the reverse of the slip, with the total entered on the front

* the cash and cheques being paid in are totalled to give the amount being paid in

* the counterfoil is completed

* the person paying-in will sign the slip

A completed paying-in slip (with counterfoil) is illustrated on the next page.

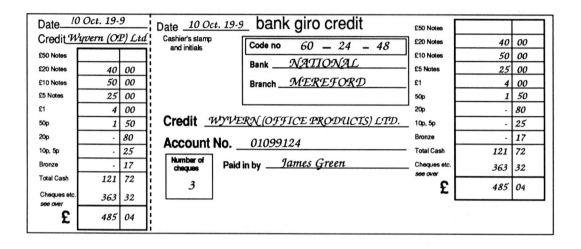

Fig. 13.2 The front of a completed paying-in slip, including counterfoil (on left)

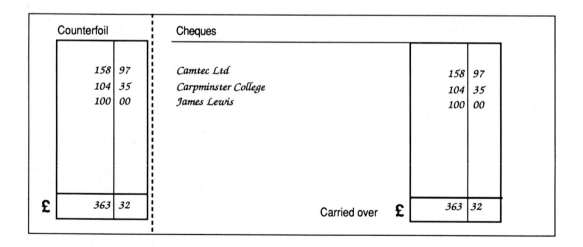

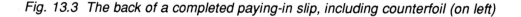

Fig. 13.3 The back of a completed paying-in slip, including counterfoil (on left)

procedures for paying in

preparing the cash

The notes should be counted, checked and sorted so that they all face the same way, usually with the Queen's head to the right of the note. Notes from Scotland and Northern Ireland are normally accepted by banks, but should be kept separate. Similarly, defaced (damaged) notes are usually accepted by the banks (it is surprising how many notes go in the washing machine).

Coins should normally be sorted and placed in separate denominations in bags as follows:

denomination	amount in bag
£1	£20
50p	£10
20p	£10
10p	£5
5p	£5
2p	£1
1p	£1

preparing the cheques

The cheques must first be examined carefully for any irregularities, such as

* *signatures* – has the drawer signed the cheque?
* *endorsements* – if the name on the payee line is not the same as the name of the account into which it is being paid, has it been suitably endorsed?
* *crossings* – if the cheque has the "account payee" wording in the crossing and your organisation is not the payee, it will not be possible to pay it in, even if it has been endorsed
* *date* – is it out of date (over six months old)? is it post-dated? – if so, it cannot be paid in
* *words and figures* – do they agree?

The details of the cheques – the amounts and the customer names – may then be listed on the back of the paying-in slip, as in the illustration on the previous page. If the volume of cheques paid in is very large, there will not be room on the paying-in slip, so the cheque details may be listed on a separate schedule. Some banks accept instead a calculator tally-roll listing the amounts, the number of cheques, and the total money amount transfered to the front of the paying-in slip. The important point is that the organisation paying in the cheques must keep a record of the cheque details in case of future queries, and in the unfortunate event of any of the cheques being returned unpaid.

paying in at the bank

At the bank the completed paying-in book is handed to the bank cashier together with the notes, coins, and cheques. The cashier counts the cash, ticks off the cheques and, if everything is correct, receipt stamps and initials the paying-in slip and counterfoil. The slip is retained by the bank for the amount to be credited to the account-holder, while the paying-in book is handed back, complete with the receipted counterfoil. A business paying-in book is sometimes larger than the paying-in slip illustrated, and sometimes there is a carbon copy behind the business paying-in slip which acts as a counterfoil.

Care must be taken when taking large amounts of cash to the bank. If possible two staff members should visit the bank. If the amount is very large, for instance the takings from a department store, a security firm may be employed to carry the cash. If the cash is received by an organisation over the weekend or, late in the day, it may be placed in a special wallet and lodged in the bank's *night safe* – a small lockable door leading to a safe in the wall of the bank.

When a business pays in money to the bank, it will record the amount in its own records, called the *cash book* (see Chapter 15).

credit card voucher clearing

As we saw in the last chapter, the sales voucher is the basic document normally produced when a credit card transaction takes place (see the illustration on page 158). The sales voucher may be produced as a result of an 'over the counter' sale or from a mail order or telephone sale. The details recorded on it will enable the credit card company to charge the amount to their customer. The voucher like a cheque, is paid in at the bank and sent to the credit card company and 'cleared'.

Although there are a number of different credit card companies – Access and Visa for example – the normal practice is for the organisation accepting payment to sign an agreement with a *separate* company which will accept *all* vouchers from cards issued by different companies. For example, a customer of The Royal Bank of Scotland may sign an agreement with a company called Roynet (owned by the Royal Bank of Scotland) and accept payment by Access and Visa and other nominated cards. The customer will pay in *all* credit card vouchers on the one paying slip and schedule (see below) at The Royal Bank of Scotland. The bank will pass them to Roynet, which will then process them by sending them to the issuing card company (Access or Visa, for example). Roynet is only one of a number of companies which will process credit card sales vouchers.

The customer paying in the vouchers is charged a set percentage fee – usually between 2% and 5% – of the total sales amount. This charge is automatically deducted from the customer's bank account by computer transfer (known as a direct debit) and a statement of charges is sent to the customer by post.

preparing credit card sales vouchers for paying-in

The vouchers are paid in after completion of a three-part *Retailer Summary*, illustrated below. In this case three sales vouchers are listed on the reverse of the summary.

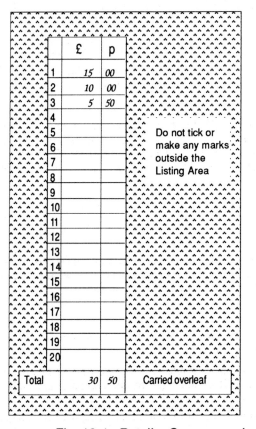

	£	p
1	15	00
2	10	00
3	5	50
4		
5		
6		
7		
8		
9		
10		
11		
12		
13		
14		
15		
16		
17		
18		
19		
20		
Total	30	50

Do not tick or make any marks outside the Listing Area

Carried overleaf

Fig. 13.4. Retailer Summary – back

Fig 13.5 Retailer Summary – front

The procedure for listing credit card sales vouchers on the retailer's summary is as follows:

- the summary is imprinted with details of the retailer using a plastic card – the Retailer's Card – supplied with the imprinter machine
- the amounts of the sales vouchers are listed on the reverse of the summary and totalled
- the total is carried forward to the front of the summary
- any refund vouchers are listed on the front of the summary
- the summary is dated, signed and totalled
- the summary is separated into its three copies – the top two are retained by the organisation and the bottom copy (the processing copy) is placed in front of the sales vouchers
- the processing copy and sales and any refund vouchers are placed in a transparent envelope and are paid into the bank on a paying-in slip, the total from the summary listed as a single item on the paying-in slip

Organisations which accept sales by mail and telephone may use *schedules* rather than sales vouchers for recording and listing the credit card transactions. The procedure for paying-in for these organisations is exactly the same, except that the *totals of the schedule(s)* are listed on the back of the Retailer Summary rather than the individual amounts of the sales vouchers as described above.

bank statements

At regular intervals the bank sends out statements of account to its customers. A business current account with many items passing through it may have weekly statements, a less active account or a deposit account may have monthly or even quarterly statements.

A bank statement is a summary showing

- the balance at the beginning of the statement – 'balance brought forward'
- amounts paid into (credited to) the account
- amounts paid out of (debited to) the account – eg cheques issued, cheques returned 'unpaid', bank charges and standing orders and direct debits (automatic computer payments – see the next chapter for an explanation of these).

The balance of the account is shown after each transaction. A specimen bank statement is shown in fig. 13.6 on the next page.

IN ACCOUNT WITH

National Bank plc

Branch..Mereford...........

TITLE OF ACCOUNT....Wyvern (Office Products) Ltd.

ACCOUNT NUMBER....01099124...................   STATEMENT NUMBER 96

DATE	PARTICULARS	PAYMENTS	RECEIPTS	BALANCE
19–9		£	£	£
1 Oct.	Balance brought forward			625.50 CR
9 Oct.	Cheque 352817	179.30		446.20 CR
10 Oct.	Credit		485.04	931.24 CR
17 Oct.	Cheque 352818	169.33		761.91 CR
23 Oct.	Credit		62.30	824.21 CR
24 Oct.	Credit		100.00	924.21 CR
26 Oct.	Cheque 352819	821.80		102.41 CR
26 Oct.	Unpaid cheque	250.00		147.59 DR
28 Oct.	Credit		108.00	39.59 DR
31 Oct.	Bank charges	25.00		64.59 DR

Fig. 13.6 A Specimen Bank Statement

You will see from the specimen bank statement that the balance of the account is indicated each time by the abbreviation 'CR' or 'DR'; the first of these means that the customer has a credit balance, ie has money in the bank, while 'DR' indicates a debit balance to show an overdraft, ie the customer has drawn more out of the bank than the available credit balance. The bank charges referred to can either be calculated on an item basis (ie the number of items passing through the account) or on a turnover basis (ie the money total of all the items paid out of the account). In addition, interest will be charged on overdrawn balances.

When a bank statement is received it should be checked and reconciled with the firm's record of bank receipts and payments – the cash book – (see Chapter 17).

chapter summary

❑ The relationship between a bank and its customer is a legal relationship of contract

❑ Banks offer two main types of account to their customers: current accounts and deposit accounts; overdrafts are available on current account

❑ The bank clearing system normally clears a cheque in three days; a special presentation of a cheque will enable the payee to find out whether the cheque is paid within twenty four hours

❑ The bank provides its business customers with paying-in books; these may be used for paying in
   • cash – which is summarised in denominations on the paying-in slip
   • cheques – which are listed on the paying-in slip, or on a schedule or tally roll listing
   • credit card vouchers – which are listed and summarised on a Retailer Summary form

✍ student activities

13.1   Make out the following paying-in slip and counterfoil for your own bank current account. (Assume that you bank at the Southern Bank, Carpminster branch, sort code no. 40-21-15; your account no. is 77078330). The items to be banked are:

Cash	two £10 notes
	two £5 notes
	five £1 coins
	six 50p coins
Cheques	£25.00
	£10.00

Note: assume the cheques have been listed and totalled on the reverse of the credit.

Date _____	Date _____	**bank giro credit**	£50 Notes		
Credit _____	Cashier's stamp and initials		£20 Notes		
£50 Notes		Code no ____ — —	£10 Notes		
£20 Notes		Bank _____	£5 Notes		
£10 Notes		Branch _____	£1		
£5 Notes			50p		
£1			20p		
50p		Credit _____	10p, 5p		
20p		Account No. _____	Bronze		
10p, 5p		Number of cheques Paid in by _____	Total Cash		
Bronze			Cheques etc. see over		
Total Cash					
Cheques etc. see over			£		
£					

13.2   The firm you work for is Eveshore Traders Ltd., which has a bank account at Barllands Bank, Eveshore (sort code no. 20-23-88). The account number is 90003174. You are required to prepare the paying-in slip and counterfoil as at today's date. The cheques are to be listed on the back of the paying-in slip. The items to be banked are:

Cash	two £20 notes	
	five £10 notes	
	eight £5 notes	
	two £1 coins	
	six 50p coins	
	four 10p coins	
	two 2p coins	
Cheques	£20.00	Maytree Enterprises
	£18.50	Bakewell Catering
	£75.25	Henderson & Co
	£68.95	Musgrave Fine Art

13.3   The firm you work for is Buxton Fine Wines, which has a bank account at Western Bank, Grantminster (sort code no. 47-21-95). The account number is 87163729. You are required to prepare the Retailers Summary and paying-in slip for ten credit card sales vouchers and a refund voucher. The documents are shown on the next page. The items to be banked are:

Sales vouchers	£45.60	£56.85
	£10.00	£56.00
	£15.50	£45.00
	£25.99	£49.50
	£67.50	£25.00
Refund voucher	£13.50	

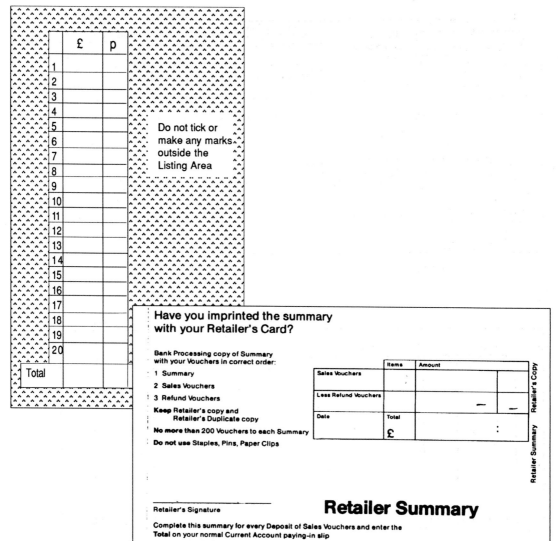

	£	p
1		
2		
3		
4		
5		
6		
7		
8		
9		
10		
11		
12		
13		
14		
15		
16		
17		
18		
19		
20		
Total		

Do not tick or make any marks outside the Listing Area

Have you imprinted the summary with your Retailer's Card?

Bank Processing copy of Summary with your Vouchers in correct order:

1 Summary

2 Sales Vouchers

3 Refund Vouchers

Keep Retailer's copy and Retailer's Duplicate copy

No more than 200 Vouchers to each Summary

Do not use Staples, Pins, Paper Clips

	Items	Amount	
Sales Vouchers			
Less Refund Vouchers			
Date	Total		
	£		

Retailer's Copy / Retailer Summary

_____
Retailer's Signature

Retailer Summary

Complete this summary for every Deposit of Sales Vouchers and enter the **Total** on your normal Current Account paying-in slip

Date_____

Credit_____

£50 Notes		
£20 Notes		
£10 Notes		
£5 Notes		
£1		
50p		
20p		
10p, 5p		
Bronze		
Total Cash		
Cheques etc. *see over*		
£		

Date _____

Cashier's stamp and initials

bank giro credit

Code no   ▬   ▬

Bank _____

Branch _____

Credit _____

Account No. _____

Number of cheques	

Paid in by _____

£50 Notes		
£20 Notes		
£10 Notes		
£5 Notes		
£1		
50p		
20p		
10p, 5p		
Bronze		
Total Cash		
Cheques etc. *see over*		
£		

13.5   Your supervisor asks you to prepare a memorandum to all Accounts staff on the subject of "Cheque Clearance". There appears to be some confusion in the office as to *when* a cheque is cleared. He asks you to make sure that you mention

(a)   the number of days it takes for a cheque to clear

(b)   whether it makes any difference if the person writing out the cheque has an account at the branch where your company banks

(c)   if there are any ways to speed up the clearance of a cheque

13.6   You are working in the Accounts Department of Martley Fruits Ltd., Maytree Farm, Martley MR7 2LX.   Part of your job is to deal with the cheques received in the post, and to prepare those cheques for banking.   During the course of a working day you deal with a number of cheques, some of which may cause problems. Your supervisor, Mark Tucker, asks you to identify the problems, and state in each case how you would deal with them.

	customer	*amount*	*comments*
(a)	Henry Young & Co	£1,245	you need to find out whether this cheque is to be paid before you can despatch the goods – rapid clearance is required
(b)	J Maxwell Ltd	£124.90	you receive this cheque from the bank; it is marked "Refer to Drawer"
(c)	James Robinson	£345.60	the cheque lacks the drawer's signature
(d)	Henry James	£450.00	the cheque lacks a date
(e)	Ivor Longway	£342.90	the date on the cheque is three months old
(f)	Ned Morgan	£837.89	the date on the cheque is ten months old
(g)	Lisa Jones	£90.00	you receive this cheque from the bank; the cheque is marked "Post dated"; on inspecting the cheque you see that the cheque is dated three months in the future
(h)	N Patel	£78.00	you receive this cheque from the bank; it is marked "Payment Countermanded by order of Drawer"
(i)	N Trebbiano	£78.98	there is no crossing on the cheque
(j)	I M A Pratt	£65.??	the words on the cheque read "sixty five pounds only", the figures "£65.65"; the amount owed is £65

When you have checked your decisions with your supervisor, he asks you to draft appropriate letters for his signature to the following customers (use today's date):

J Maxwell Ltd, 67 The Circus, Bradstreet, BD5 8GY

James Robinson, The Cedars, Parkway, PR5 3DC

Ned Morgan, 72 Malvern Crescent, Milton Park, MR6 2CS

Lisa Jones, c/o The Kings Arms, Leatherton, MR6 9SD

14 Making payments

In this chapter we will examine the different ways in which payments can be made. If you work for an organisation, you will readily appreciate that there are different types of payments involved; some will involve the issue of cheques or cash, some will involve paying money from the organisation's bank account direct to the recipient's bank account. Here are some typical examples of these different forms of payment:

issue of cheques
- paying suppliers by cheque for goods and services against invoices and statements
- paying for 'one-off' items of expenditure, for example a computer system
- paying bills (eg telephone, gas, electricity) by cheque and bank giro credit
- paying employees for expenses incurred

paying through the bank account
- paying wages
- paying *regular* suppliers for goods and services
- paying bills, for example business rates

In this chapter we will look at the practical aspects of making payments. We will also examine the systems for authorising payment and signing cheques.

paying trade suppliers by cheque

We have already seen in Chapter 3 that a supplier of goods and services is paid when the documents relating to the transaction have been checked and payment is authorised. If you are paying a supplier you should attach the cheque to a *remittance advice*. This may be a tear-off slip attached to the supplier's statement of account (see page 19), or it may be a standard form used within your organisation. An example of the latter, together with the cheque issued, is illustrated on the next page. You should note that the following details are shown:

- the date of the payment
- the amount of the cheque
- the details – ie the reference number ('your ref') and date – of the invoice(s) being paid
- the amount of any cash discount deducted for early settlement (there is none in the illustration)

In addition the remittance advice may show further details such as the cheque number, the account number of the buyer's organisation, and the buyer's order number ('our ref'). The remittance advice may also show a *deduction* made from the payment for a credit note issued by the supplier. The details will be recorded on the remittance advice in the normal way, as for an invoice.

REMITTANCE ADVICE
NIMROD DRAINAGE LIMITED
UNIT 6 Riverside Industrial Park Mereford MR4 5TF
Tel 0605 675187 Fax 0605 415181 Vat Reg 63 6252 27

Stourford Office Supplies Unit 12, Avon Industrial Estate Stourford SF5 6TD				Cheque No Date Account	000427 20 April 19-5 9873	

date	our ref.	your ref.	amount	discount	payment
18 02 -5	47621	82710	47.00	00.00	47.00
				cheque value	£ 47.00

date **20 April 19-5** **Stourford Office Supplies** **Inv 82710** £ 47.00 000427	**National Bank PLC** date **20 April** 19-5 35-09-75 Mereford Branch 10 Cathedral Street, Mereford MR1 5DE Pay **Stourford Office Supplies** ——————— only **Forty seven pounds only** ——————— **£47.00** NIMROD DRAINAGE LIMITED **E Ragle D Penny** Director Director 000427 350975 12034875

Fig 14.1 Remittance advice and cheque with counterfoil

issuing of cheques

Suppliers are normally paid monthly on the basis of the monthly statement issued rather than in response to individual invoices. A statement issued at, say, the end of March will show all the outstanding invoices; if an organisation normally pays invoices after *thirty* days, it will pay all the *February* invoices and any dated earlier than February on receipt of the statement. It will ignore any March invoices, which will be paid at the end of April. If your job is to prepare cheques and remittance advices, you will probably have a list of payments to make, with the payment amount already decided upon and authorised by a supervisor.

When writing (using ink, not pencil) or typing out the cheque you should take care to complete the
• date
• name of the payee (person receiving the money)
• amount in words
• amount in figures
• authorised signature (it may be your signature, it may be that of a more senior individual)
• counterfoil (date, amount, payee)

No room should be left for possible fraudulent additions or alterations; any blank spaces should be ruled through. If any errors are made when you are writing out the cheque, they should be corrected and an authorised signature placed close to the alteration in order to tell the bank that it is an approved correction. Large companies often, instead of writing out each cheque by hand, use cheque writing machines or computers. Clearly such a machine or computer needs to be kept under strict supervision.

paying for 'one-off' items – cheque requisition forms

So far we have looked at the payment of trade suppliers who supply on a regular basis for the normal activities of an organisation, eg merchants who supply potatoes for crisps manufacturers. The procedure for the issue of cheques in this case is reasonably straightforward. There will be times, however, when a cheque is needed for a 'one-off' purpose, for example:

* purchase of an item of equipment, authorised by the organisation
* reimbursement of 'out-of-pocket' expenses incurred by an employee
* payment of a proforma invoice (a proforma invoice is a request for payment to be made *before* the supply of the goods or services – contrast this with a normal invoice when payment *follows* supply)

The normal procedure in these cases is the completion of a cheque requisition form by the person who needs the cheque. An example is illustrated below.

Mercia Pumps Limited
CHEQUE REQUISITION FORM ─────────────────────

required by......*Tom Paget*..................Dept........*Marketing*.........

CHEQUE DETAILS ──────────────────────────────

date.....*30 March 19–5*.........................

payable to...*Media Promotions Ltd*.........................

amount £....*45.00*.........................

despatch to (if applicable)...*Media Promotions Ltd., 145 High Street,*.......
...................*Mereford, MR1 3JF*.......................

reason...*Advert in business journal*.............nominal ledger...*7556*...........

DOCUMENTATION ──────────────────────────────

invoice attached/~~to follow~~...*invoice 24516 dated 23 March 19–5*.................

receipt attached/to follow..

other...

AUTHORISATION.*Andrew Wimbush, Marketing Director*.........................

Fig. 14.2 Cheque requisition form

Note the following details:

* the cheque has been ordered by Tom Paget, but is to be sent direct to Media Promotions Ltd
* the requisition is authorised by Andrew Wimbush, the Marketing Director
* the invoice is attached
* the nominal ledger code is included – this is the category of expense for which an account is maintained in the computer accounting system of the business – 7556 is the computer account number for 'advertising account'; if the business did not have a computer accounting system the name of the nominal account – 'advertising' – would be written here

control and authorisation of payments

spending limits

In order to avoid fraud or unchecked spending within an organisation, all payments must be controlled and authorised. We have seen that incoming invoices must normally be stamped, and signed or initialled by an authorised person before being passed for payment. This is part of an overall system whereby no payment can be made without the necessary authority. The system will vary from organisation to organisation, but the following elements will be usually be found:

* the larger the payment, the more senior the person who needs to give it authority; often each level of management has a money limit imposed – for example a new vehicle costing £25,000 will be authorised at senior management level, a supplier's invoice for £250 will be paid at supervisory level

* when an item of expenditure is authorised, the person giving the authority will sign or initial and date the supporting document, eg an invoice, a cheque requisition form

cheque signatures

While an organisation will have an *internal* system of signing for and authorising expenditure, it will also have a written agreement with the bank – a *bank mandate* – which will set out who can sign cheques. A limited company or partnership may, for example, allow one director or partner to sign cheques up to £5,000, but will require two to sign cheques in excess of £5,000. It is common to have a number of different signatories to allow for partners and directors going on holiday, going sick and being otherwise unavailable for signing cheques.

cash payments

Most organisations will keep a cash float – *petty cash* – to allow for small everday items of expenditure such as taxi fares and coffee for customer reception. The operation of the petty cash system is strictly controlled and documented, and will be dealt with in Chapter 16 "Petty Cash Book". Some organisations will also use cash for the payment of wages, although this is kept to a minimum, for obvious security reasons; this will be dealt with in Chapter 22.

bank giro credits

bulk (dispersal) credits

We have already seen in Chapter 13 how money can be paid into a bank account by means of a bank paying-in slip or *bank giro credit.* So far we have looked at an organisation which pays in at its own branch, and receives the money on its own account on the same day. The banking system also allows for organisations to pay money into *other* bank accounts using a batch of *bank giro credits* which are paid in at one branch and sent through a three day clearing system (like the cheque clearing system) to another bank or branch. These giro credits are often known as *dispersal credits* and are used widely for paying wages (see Chapter 22) and settling suppliers' accounts.

single bank giro payments

There are strict regulations about sending *single* giro credits (as opposed to a batch) through the clearing. Banks will only accept *preprinted* single giro credits through the clearing system. Examples of these are fuel and credit card bills and credits from a preprinted paying-in book. You can no longer make out a *single* giro credit by hand if you want to pay money into a bank account at a bank or branch other than your own.

procedure for paying by bank giro credit

You may well be familiar as a personal bank customer with paying a bill by bank giro credit; the procedure for an organisation is exactly the same. The person or organisation making payment (or payments) prepares a cheque for the total amount to be paid (payment by cash would be very unusual for an organisation) and completes (for a single bank giro payment) the preprinted bank giro credit with a date and a signature, or a group of dispersal bank credits, if more than one bank account is to receive payment. If more than one credit is to be completed – for example if wages are being paid – it is usual to list and total the credits on a separate schedule for the benefit of the bank (see Chapter 22).

If you are using a *blank* giro credit, illustrated below, the details that need to be completed are:

- the name of the bank where the beneficiary's account is held (the beneficiary is the person receiving the money)
- the branch of bank and sort code where the beneficiary's account is held. *Note:* the sort code is a system of numbering each bank branch. (The sort code of a bank branch appears in the top right hand corner of a cheque.)
- the name and account number of the beneficiary
- the sender's name and reference
- the amount of the payment
- the date
- the counterfoil

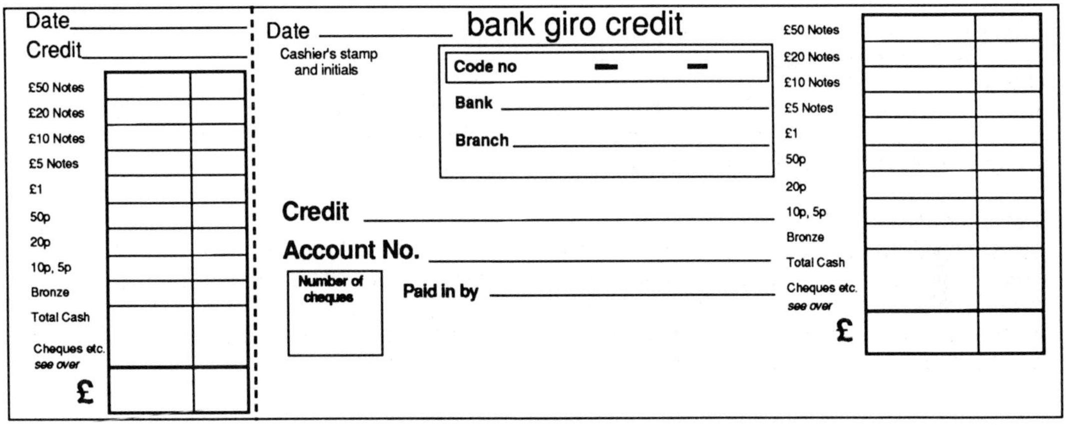

Date
Credit
£50 Notes
£20 Notes
£10 Notes
£5 Notes
£1
50p
20p
10p, 5p
Bronze
Total Cash
Cheques etc. see over
£

Date
bank giro credit
Cashier's stamp and initials
Code no
Bank
Branch
Credit
Account No.
Number of cheques
Paid in by
£50 Notes
£20 Notes
£10 Notes
£5 Notes
£1
50p
20p
10p, 5p
Bronze
Total Cash
Cheques etc. see over
£

Fig 14.3 Bank giro credit to be completed by hand

If you are using a *pre-printed* giro credit (to pay a bill, for example), all you need to do is complete the amount, date and name of person paying the bill (see fig. 9.4 below)

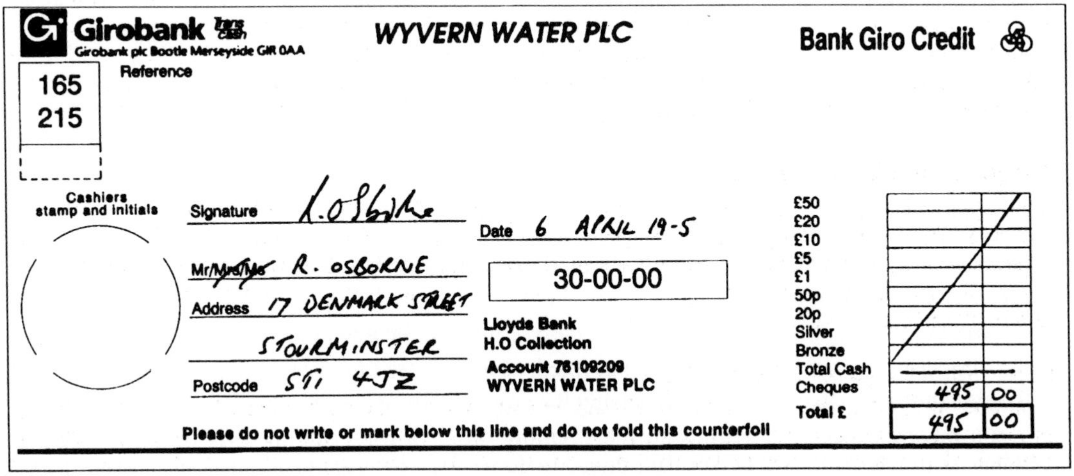

Girobank
Girobank plc Bootle Merseyside GIR 0AA
WYVERN WATER PLC
Bank Giro Credit
165
215
Reference
Cashiers stamp and initials
Signature
Date 6 APRIL 19-5
Mr/Mrs/Ms R. OSBORNE
30-00-00
Address 17 DENMARK STREET
STOURMINSTER
Lloyds Bank
H.O Collection
Account 76109209
WYVERN WATER PLC
Postcode ST1 4JZ
£50
£20
£10
£5
£1
50p
20p
Silver
Bronze
Total Cash
Cheques 495 00
Total £ 495 00
Please do not write or mark below this line and do not fold this counterfoil

Fig 14.4 Preprinted bank giro credit

BACS: standing orders and direct debits

While bank giro credits are useful for making payments through the banking system for variable amounts, for example telephone bills, the procedure is time-consuming because you need to visit the bank each time. To avoid this problem the banks have established an interbank computer transfer system (also used by building societies) called BACS (Bankers Automated Clearing Services). With this system the transfer of money is made by computer link between banks and building societies. Payment can take a number of forms:

standing order   The bank customer who needs to make regular payments completes a written authority (a mandate) instructing the bank what payments to make, to whom, and when. The bank then sets up the instructions on its computer, and the payments are made automatically by computer link on the due dates. Standing orders are useful for regular fixed payments such as loan repayments and rental payments. Personal customers use them for making mortgage repayments.

direct debit   Whilst direct debits can be used for regular payments they differ from standing orders in two ways:
- direct debits can be used for either fixed and variable amounts and/or where the time intervals between payments vary
- it is the receiver (beneficiary) of the payment who prepares the computer instructions that request the payer's bank account for payment through the banking system; a direct debit is rather like a standing order operating backwards

The direct debit system is useful for organisations such as insurance companies and credit card companies which receive a large number of variable payments. The normal procedure is for the customer making payment to complete and sign a written authority (mandate) prepared by the beneficiary (eg insurance company); this is then returned to the beneficiary, the payment details are given to the beneficiary's bank so that the computer instructions can be set up, and the original form returned to the payer's bank.

'autopay' systems   For customers who need to make regular payments of variable amounts (eg wages, payments to established suppliers) the banks have established a system whereby they set up standing orders to the regular beneficiaries. All the customer has to do each time payment is to be made is to complete and give to the bank a schedule setting out the date, beneficiaries and amounts. The bank will then input these details direct into its computer system, and payments will be made automatically via the BACS system.

For all BACS payments – standing orders, direct debits and autopay – the bank needs written instructions (a mandate) from the customer before the amounts can be deducted from the account. The details needed by the bank – some of which may be preprinted – are:
- the name of organisation or person which is to receive the money, e.g. insurance company, hire purchase company, etc.
- the details of recipient's bank, ie bank, branch, sort code number, and bank account number
- the reference number to be quoted
- the amount (unless it is not fixed, as in the case of direct debit and autopay)
- the frequency of payment (unless it is not fixed, as in the case of direct debit and autopay)
- the signature(s) of the customer authorising the amount to be debited to his/her bank account

If it is a business which is setting up the standing order or direct debit, it is important that the mandate form is signed by a person authorised to do so – it will often be the person(s) authorised to sign cheques. See the next page for examples of a standing order and a direct debit.

STANDING ORDER MANDATE _____

TO _____ BANK

ADDRESS _____

PLEASE PAY TO
BANK _____ BRANCH _____ SORT CODE ⬚⬚⬚

BENEFICIARY _____ ACCOUNT NUMBER ⬚

THE SUM OF £⬚ AMOUNTS IN WORDS _____

_____

DATE OF FIRST PAYMENT _____ FREQUENCY OF PAYMENT _____

UNTIL _____ REFERENCE _____

ACCOUNT TO BE DEBITED ⬚ NUMBER ⬚

SPECIAL INSTRUCTIONS _____

SIGNATURE(S)..**DATE**..................

....

Fig. 14.5 Bank standing order mandate

_____ **direct debit instruction** _____

Tradesure Insurance Company
PO Box 134, Helliford, HL9 6TY

Originator's Identification Number 914208

Reference (to be completed by Tradesure Insurance)..................................

Please complete the details and return this form to Tradesure Insurance

name and address of bank/building society | instructions to bank/building society

⬚

account name

⬚

- I instruct you to pay direct debits from my account at the request of Tradesure Insurance Company
- The amounts are variable and may be debited on various dates
- I understand that Tradesure Insurance Company may change the amounts and dates only after giving me prior notice
- I will inform the bank/building society if I wish to cancel this instruction
- I understand that if any direct debit is paid which breaks the terms of this instruction, the bank/building society will make a refund.

account number | sort code | signature(s) | date

⬚ | ⬚ | ⬚ | ⬚

Fig. 14.6 Direct debit mandate

company credit cards, bank drafts and CHAPS

If you work in an Accounts Office you may from time-to-time encounter other ways of making payment:

company credit cards   We have already examined the use of credit cards for making payments. Some organisations, particularly those which employ travelling representatives, may set up a company credit card scheme. This convenient and useful scheme allows nominated company representatives to have credit cards for paying for incidental expenses related to the company's business. A travelling salesperson may use one for paying for rail tickets, accommodation and food. The credit card bill is settled by the company which is then able to monitor the expenses incurred by its employees.

bank drafts   On occasions, an organisation may have to make a large purchase – for example new vehicles – and be asked to pay by bank draft. A bank draft is a bank cheque, a guaranteed means of payment which is as good as cash, but without the security risks. The draft is in effect 'purchased' from the bank by the organisation. If you need to order a bank draft, you will need to fill in a simple form provided by the bank, giving details of the amount and the payee. A fee is payable for this service.

CHAPS   A CHAPS (Clearing House Automated Payments System) payment is a high value payment system operated by the banks through their computer networks. It is used extensively by solicitors when they are arranging the purchase and sale of property for their clients. Businesses will use it for high value, same day, transfers. Once transmitted by a bank, a payment cannot be recalled. If you are asked to set up a CHAPS payment you will need to fill in a bank form giving details of the bank and account where the money is to be sent, the account from which the money is to be taken, and the amount. Remember to check the amount carefully, because if you make a mistake, the money cannot be recalled!

A similar system, known as SWIFT, exists for making payments abroad through the banks' computer network. The banks provide forms for setting up these payments which are sometimes known as IMT's (International Money Transfers). You may encounter these if your organisation is involved in paying for the import of goods from abroad.

chapter summary

❏ A business makes payment by cheque to suppliers, for 'one-off' purchases, when paying bills, and when paying employees.

❏ A business may also make payment direct to the bank account of the beneficiary by means of a bank giro credit; this method is often used for paying bills and wages.

❏ Businesses may also make use of BACS (Bankers Automated Clearing Services) to make payments through a computer system direct to the bank or building society account of the beneficiary. BACS is used for processing standing orders, direct debits, and 'autopay' payments.

❏ A business must operate a system of authorisation and control of payments.

student activities

14.1 You work in the Accounts Department of Nimrod Drainage Limited. Part of yourt day's work is the preparation of remittance advices and cheques for payments to suppliers. You are not required to sign the cheques. On 5 April 19-9 you are handed three payments to prepare:

(a) Statement from Mereford Cleaning Services, 78 Friary Park, Mereford MR4 3BJ, with a note from your Supervisor indicating the following invoices to be paid:
Invoice 1982 dated 15 February 19-9, your order number 5541, £243.50
Invoice 2019 dated 17 March 19-9, your order number 5783, £1,245.60

There is no cash discount. Complete the remittance advice and cheque set out below.

REMITTANCE ADVICE
NIMROD DRAINAGE LIMITED
UNIT 6 Riverside Industrial Park Mereford MR4 5TF
Tel 0605 675187 Fax 0605 415181 Vat Reg 63 6252 27

Cheque No
Date
Account

date	our ref.	your ref.	amount	discount	payment

cheque value £

---

date		

National Bank PLC   date   19   35-09-75
Mereford Branch
10 Cathedral Street, Mereford MR1 5DE

Pay   only

£

NIMROD DRAINAGE LIMITED

Director   Director

£

000450   000450   350975   12034875

(b) Statement from Mercia Wholesalers, Unit 12 Riverside Industrial Park, Mereford MR2 7GH, with a note from your Supervisor indicating the following invoices to be paid, and a credit note to be set off against payment:

Invoice 8765 dated 12 February 19-9, your order number 5517, £765.25
Invoice 8823 dated 19 March 19-9, your order number 5792, £3,567.80
Credit note C/N3420 dated 25 March 19-9 (your ref R/N 5168), £250.00

There is no cash discount. Complete the remittance advice and cheque set out on the next page. Note that the total of the credit note should be shown in the money column *in brackets*, indicating that it is a deduction from the payment.

REMITTANCE ADVICE
NIMROD DRAINAGE LIMITED
UNIT 6 Riverside Industrial Park Mereford MR4 5TF
Tel 0605 675187 Fax 0605 415181 Vat Reg 63 6252 27

	Cheque No
	Date
	Account

date	our ref.	your ref.	amount	discount	payment

	cheque value	£

---

date	National Bank PLC	date	19	35-09-75

Mereford Branch
10 Cathedral Street, Mereford MR1 5DE

Pay   only

£

NIMROD DRAINAGE LIMITED

Director   Director

£

000451   000451   350975   12034875

(c)   An invoice from Duplex Electronics Ltd, 78 High Street, Stourminster ST1 9WE:
Invoice 7634 dated 1 April19-9, your order number 5786, £1,250.00

On the bottom of the invoice is stamped "2.5 % cash discount for settlement within 7 days".
Your supervisor has written "PAY NOW" against these words.
Complete the remittance advice and cheque, allowing for the discount offered.

REMITTANCE ADVICE
NIMROD DRAINAGE LIMITED
UNIT 6 Riverside Industrial Park Mereford MR4 5TF
Tel 0605 675187 Fax 0605 415181 Vat Reg 63 6252 27

	Cheque No
	Date
	Account

date	our ref.	your ref.	amount	discount	payment

	cheque value	£

date		National Bank PLC	date	19	35-09-75

National Bank PLC
Mereford Branch
10 Cathedral Street, Mereford MR1 5DE

Pay _____ only

£

NIMROD DRAINAGE LIMITED

£

Director   Director

000452   000452   350975   12034875

14.2 You work in the Accounts Department of Nimrod Drainage Limited. It is 5 April 19-5. Your supervisor, Ivor Cash, hands you an invoice and asks you to prepare a cheque requisition form for the purchase of a computer, for which the company has to pay immediately. The details are :

Cheque amount £4,545.50, payee Wyvern Micros Limited on their invoice 626 dated 1 April 19-9. Reason: purchase of Intertel PC6000 workstation. Nominal account to be debited 7600.

As the amount is a large one, Ivor asks you to prepare the requisition in his name, and to send it with a covering memorandum to John Flint, Finance Director, for authorisation. The requisition should be returned to Ivor who will then process and despatch the cheque.

Nimrod Drainage Limited
CHEQUE REQUISITION FORM _____

required by..Dept..

CHEQUE DETAILS _____

date..

payable to..

amount £..

despatch to (if applicable)..

....

reason..nominal ledger..........................

DOCUMENTATION _____

invoice attached/to follow..

receipt attached/to follow..

other..

AUTHORISATION...

14.3   You work in the Accounts Department of Nimrod Drainage Limited. Your supervisor, Ivor Cash, has received a memorandum from the Personnel Department stating that a new member of staff requires an initial wages payment to be made direct to her bank account. The authorisation is in order, and the details are as follows:

Beneficiary	J Patel
Bank	Midland Bank, Stourford Branch, sort code 40 99 87, account 87875231
Payment	cheque
Amount	£78.50

You are to complete the bank giro credit shown below (which will be added to the other wages dispersal credits). Complete the bank giro credit with today's date and the company name.

14.4   You work in the Accounts Department of Nimrod Drainage Limited. You work at a clerical grade and cannot sign cheques or other payment instructions. The date is 5 April 19-5. Your supervisor, Ivor Cash, hands you two documents (shown on the next page):

- a blank standing order form provided by the bank
- a direct debit instruction received from Tradesure Insurance Company

He is in rather a rush and asks you to process the two documents, and to return them to the appropriate address with a compliments slip. He also leaves you a piece of paper with written instructions:

Hire Purchase Payments
12 monthly instalments of £350 to Broadbent Finance from 1 May 19-5, under reference BE/6637. Bank details Barclays, Eveshore, 30 98 15, Account 72627161.
Debit our Account 12034875

You are to:

(a)   complete the forms as required (look at a Nimrod Drainage cheque for your banking details)

(b)   state to which address you will send them

(c)   comment on any other procedure which you may have to carry out before sending off the forms

STANDING ORDER MANDATE

TO _____ BANK

ADDRESS _____

PLEASE PAY TO

BANK _____ BRANCH _____ SORT CODE [| |]

BENEFICIARY _____ ACCOUNT NUMBER [ ]

THE SUM OF [£ _____] AMOUNTS IN WORDS _____

_____

DATE OF FIRST PAYMENT _____ FREQUENCY OF PAYMENT _____

UNTIL _____ REFERENCE _____

ACCOUNT TO BE DEBITED [ ] NUMBER [ ]

SPECIAL INSTRUCTIONS _____

SIGNATURE(S)...**DATE**...................

....

—— direct debit instruction ——

Tradesure Insurance Company
PO Box 134, Helliford, HL9 6TY

Originator's Identification Number 914208

Reference (to be completed by Tradesure Insurance)............... PE/1982/26327 ....

Please complete the details <u>and return this form to Tradesure Insurance</u>

name and address of bank/building society

instructions to bank/building society

- I instruct you to pay direct debits from my account at the request of Tradesure Insurance Company
- The amounts are variable and may be debited on various dates
- I understand that Tradesure Insurance Company may change the amounts and dates only after giving me prior notice
- I will inform the bank/building society if I wish to cancel this instruction
- I understand that if any direct debit is paid which breaks the terms of this instruction, the bank/building society will make a refund.

account name

account number   sort code   signature(s)   date

ASSIGNMENT 4

Dealing with payments: Mereford Engineering Supplies Limited

SITUATION

You work in the office of Mereford Engineering Supplies Ltd. The company sells various types of metal products, ranging from angle iron through steel and copper rods and tubing, to sheet steel. Most of the customers are engineering companies in the area, and they have debit accounts in the sales ledger. Orders from these customers are usually made by telephone, and the goods are despatched by company lorry. In addition members of the public call in to the company to buy products, payment for which is made in cash, by cheque and by credit card. Also, some of the smaller local companies settle on cash terms as they buy goods.

One of your responsibilities is to receive payment for cash sales through a cash till, which is balanced at the end of the day, the cash sales figure for the day being advised to the company's main cashier. The cash till has a 'float' of cash in various denominations of notes and coin; this must not exceed £30, but should be greater than £25. The amount of the float is held overnight in the safe. Your tasks at the close of business each day are to:

- balance the till, ie making sure that the amount in the till agrees with the amount received during the day, plus what you started with
- advise the main cashier of the day's cash sales
- make out a bank paying-in slip for the cash and cheques to be banked (keeping back a cash float not exceeding £30, but greater than £25)
- place the paying-in slip, together with the cash and cheques in the bank night-safe wallet, which is then taken to the bank and deposited in the night safe

Today is Tuesday 6 March 19-1. You start with a cash float of £26.17 made up as follows:

£5 notes	£10.00
£1 coins	£8.00
50p coins	£3.50
20p coins	£2.60
10p coins	£1.50
5p coins	£0.30
2p coins	£0.12
1p coins	£0.15

Cash receipts for the day are:

£22.75	the customer tenders two £10 notes and a £5 note
£8.54	the customer tenders a £10 note
£11.40	the customer tenders two £5 notes, a £1 coin and a 50p coin
£27.90	the customer tenders a £20 note and a £10 note
£8.62	the customer tenders a £5 note and four £1 coins

Cheques received during the day are:

£67.50   from Mr. J. Davies
£26.82   from Miss I. Gooch
£23.85   from Mr. P. Lane
£18.22   from Mrs. S. Fields
£87.16   from Mr. A. Michaels

The first three cheques are shown below as they were originally handed to you by each customer. You noticed some errors which you asked the customer to correct before accepting them as payment. On each occasion the customer showed you his/her cheque card and, where appropriate, you wrote the cheque card number on the reverse of each cheque.

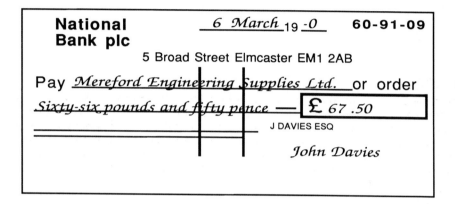

Also during the course of the day you receive payment by credit card. The sales vouchers are for the following amounts:

> £45.00
> £160.00
> £107.90
> £12.75
> £24.85

You are also involved in the making of payments to suppliers. During the day the Accounts Manager passes a statement of account to you, initialling it and saying "You can pay this one now". The statement is illustrated below. Both invoices have been checked and stamped with an authorisation stamp.

STATEMENT OF ACCOUNT ▬▬▬▬▬▬

WYVERN (OFFICE PRODUCTS) LTD
12 Lower Hyde Street
Mereford MR1 2JF
Tel: (0605) 24185 Fax: (0605) 11461
VAT Reg No 841 116011

```
Mereford Engineering Supplies
Unit 20, Riverside Estate
Mereford
MR3 5SE
```

date 28 February 19-1

Date	Reference	Debit £ p	Credit £ p	Balance £ p
19-1				
2 Jan.	Invoice no. 10381	270 10		270 10
10 Jan.	Credit note no. 11461		11 13	258 97
25 Jan.	Invoice no. 10452	388 92		647 89
	Amount now due			647 89

Registered Office: 12 Lower Hyde Street, Mereford, MR1 2JF. Registered Number: 8214612

STUDENT TASKS

1. State the change given to each cash customer, using the minimum number of notes/coins possible.

2. Indicate in red ink any changes you requested your customers to make to the cheques Which cheque(s) are not covered by the normal cheque card agreement?

3. Show the notes and coins of various denominations which are in the till at the end of the day.

4. Advise the total sales (both in cash and by cheque) for the day to the main cashier.

5. Retaining a cash float of more than £25 (but not exceeding £30), make out the bank paying-in slip and counterfoil (below) for the cash and cheques to be banked in the company's bank account (no. 01087349) with the National Bank, Mereford branch (sort code 35-09-75).

Date_____		Date _____	**bank giro credit**	£50 Notes		
Credit_____		Cashier's stamp and initials		£20 Notes		
£50 Notes			**Code no** ▬ ▬	£10 Notes		
£20 Notes			**Bank** _____	£5 Notes		
£10 Notes			**Branch** _____	£1		
£5 Notes				50p		
£1				20p		
50p		**Credit** _____		10p, 5p		
20p		**Account No.** _____		Bronze		
10p, 5p		**Number of cheques**	**Paid in by** _____	Total Cash		
Bronze				Cheques etc. *see over*		
Total Cash				**£**		
Cheques etc. *see over*						
£						

Counterfoil		Cheques		
£		Carried over **£**		

6. Balance the cash till by completing the following summary:

Tuesday 6 March 19-1

	£
Cash float at start	26.17
Add total sales (as advised to the main cashier)	_____
Less cash float retained at end of day	_____
Cash/cheques banked (total of paying-in slip)	══════

7. Complete
  • the retailer's summary (both sides – see below) for the credit card transactions
  • a paying-in slip for the summary (see the next page)

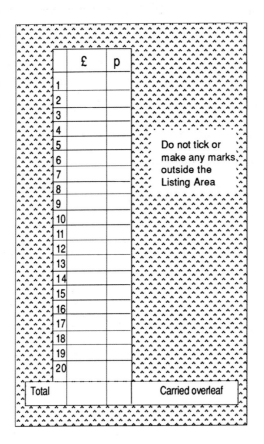

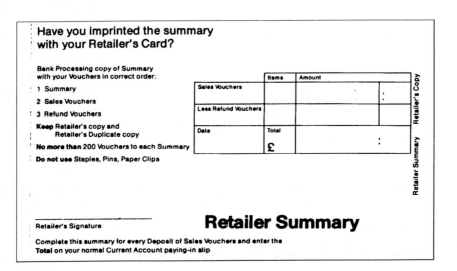

bank giro credit

Date_____		Date _____			£50 Notes	
Credit_____		Cashier's stamp and initials			£20 Notes	
					£10 Notes	

		Code no ▬ ▬	
£50 Notes		Bank _____	
£20 Notes		Branch_____	
£10 Notes			

£5 Notes

£1

50p

20p

10p, 5p

Bronze

Total Cash

Cheques etc
see over

£

Credit _____

Account No. _____

Number of cheques

Paid in by _____

£50 Notes
£20 Notes
£10 Notes
£5 Notes
£1
50p
20p
10p, 5p
Bronze
Total Cash
Cheques etc.
see over

£

---

8. Complete a remittance advice and a cheque for payment of the statement from Wyvern (Office Products) Ltd. Note that your references for the transactions are: Order no 3456 (Invoice 10381), R/N 6262 (Credit Note 11461) and Order 3783 (Invoice 10452). Your account number with Wyvern (Office Products) Limited is 4525.

REMITTANCE ADVICE
MEREFORD ENGINEERING SUPPLIES LIMITED
UNIT 20, RIVERSIDE ESTATE, MEREFORD MR3 5SE
Tel 0605 765234 Fax 0605 765233

Cheque No
Date
Account

date	our ref.	your ref.	amount	discount	payment

cheque value   £

---

date	**National Bank PLC**	date 19 35-09-75
	Mereford Branch	
	10 Cathedral Street, Mereford MR1 5DE	

Pay _____ only

_____ £

MEREFORD ENGINEERING SUPPLIES LIMITED

£

Director   Director

000750   000750   350975   01087348

15 Cash book

Cash and money in the bank is the lifeblood of any business. A firm can have an excellent product or service and be making good sales, but a shortage of cash may mean that wages and other day-to-day running expenses cannot be paid as they fall due: this could lead to the rapid failure of the business.

For most businesses, control of cash – including bank and cash transactions – takes place in the cash books, these comprise:
* cash book
* petty cash book (see next chapter)

The cash books are the books of original entry for cash and bank transactions.

Also in this chapter we look at the authorisation and payment of expenses claims – a task which is often carried out by a firm's cashier or petty cashier.

uses of the cash book

We have already used a separate cash account and bank account for double-entry book-keeping transactions. These two accounts are, in practice, brought together into one book under the title of *cash book*. This cash book is, therefore, used to record the money side of book-keeping transactions and is part of the double-entry system. The cash book is used for:

* cash transactions
    - all receipts in cash
    - most payments for cash, except for low-value expense payments (which are paid through *petty cash book:* see next chapter)

* bank transactions
    - all receipts by cheque (or payment of cash into the bank)
    - all payments by cheque (or withdrawal of cash from the bank)

The cash book is usually controlled by a cashier who:
- records receipts and payments by cheque and in cash
- makes cash payments, and prepares cheques for signature by those authorised to sign
- pays cash and cheques received into the bank
- has control over the firm's cash, either in a cash till or cash box
- issues cash to the petty cashier who operates the firm's petty cash book (see next chapter)

It is important to note that transactions passing through the cash book must be supported by documentary evidence in order to establish the audit trail (a link which can be checked and followed through the accounting system from prime document, through books of prime entry, to the double-entry accounts), and also for taxation purposes – both for Value Added Tax, and for the Inland Revenue. This applies to both receipts and payments: for example, the cashier will be responsible for issuing a formal receipt for cash (and sometimes cheques) received; payments in cash and by cheque can only be made against documents (eg an invoice received) showing the amount due – the cashier may also be required to check expenses claims before making payment. In these ways, the cash book becomes part of the audit trail, and provides evidence of receipts and payments for tax purposes.

layout of the cash book

Although a cash book can be set out in many forms to suit the requirements of a particular business, a common format is the *columnar cash book*. This is set out like other double-entry accounts, with debit and credit sides, but there may be several money columns on each side. An example of a *three column cash book* (with three money columns on each side) is shown below:

Dr.   **Cash Book**   Cr.

Date	Details	Folio	Discount allowed	Cash	Bank	Date	Details	Folio	Discount received	Cash	Bank
			£	£	£				£	£	£

The debit side is used for receipts, with one money column for cash and one for bank receipts. The credit side is used for payments with a money column for cash payments, and one for bank (cheque) payments. The third money column on each side is used to record cash *discount allowed* on the debit side, and cash *discount received* on the credit side. (To remind you, cash discount is an allowance offered for quick settlement of the amount due, eg 2% cash discount for settlement within seven days.) Note that the discount columns are *not* part of the double-entry book-keeping system – they are used in the cash book as a listing device or memorandum column and, as we will see below, are totalled at the end of the week or month, and the totals are then transferred into the double-entry system.

A *two column cash book* has money columns on each side for cash and bank only, but no other money columns.

Case Study: Cash book

Situation

The cashier at the firm for which you work, Severn Trading Co, is away on a training course this month. You are required, in her absence, to take over as the cashier. The transactions to be entered in the firm's three column cash book are:

19-1

1 Apr.	Balances at start of month: cash £300, bank £550
4 Apr.	Received a cheque from S Wright for £98 – we have allowed her £2 cash discount
7 Apr.	Paid a cheque to S Crane for £145 – he has allowed £5 cash discount
12 Apr.	Paid wages in cash £275
14 Apr.	Paid by cheque the account of T Lewis £120, deducting 2½% cash discount
17 Apr.	J Jones settles in cash her account of £80, deducting 5% cash discount
20 Apr.	Withdrew £100 in cash from the bank for use in the business
23 Apr.	Received a cheque for £45 from D Whiteman in full settlement of her account of £48
28 Apr.	Paid cash of £70 to S Ford in full settlement of our account of £75

All cheques are banked on the day of receipt.

Solution

The cash book records these transactions (as shown below) and, after they have been entered, is balanced on 30 April. (The other part of each double-entry book-keeping transaction is not shown here, but has to be carried out in order to record the transactions correctly.)

Dr.   **Cash Book**   Cr.

Date	Details	Folio	Discount allowed	Cash	Bank	Date	Details	Folio	Discount received	Cash	Bank
19-1			£	£	£	19-1			£	£	£
1 Apr.	Balances b/d			300	550	7 Apr.	J Crane		5		145
4 Apr.	S Wright		2		98	12 Apr.	Wages			275	
17 Apr.	J Jones		4	76		14 Apr.	T Lewis		3		117
20 Apr.	Bank	C		100		20 Apr.	Cash	C			100
23 Apr.	D Whiteman		3		45	28 Apr.	S Ford		5	70	
						30 Apr.	Balances c/d			131	331
			9	476	693				13	476	693
1 May	Balances b/d			131	331						

Note: The transaction on 20 April – £100 withdrawn from the bank for use in the business – involves a transfer of money between cash and bank. As each transaction is both a receipt and a payment within the cash book, it is usual to indicate both of them in the folio column with a 'C' – this stands for *contra* and shows that both parts of the transaction are in the *same* book.

balancing the cash book

We saw in Chapter 8 how accounts are balanced. The cash book is the ledger for cash account and bank account, and the procedure for balancing them is exactly the same as for other ledger accounts.

The cash book in the Case Study above is balanced in the following way:

- add the two cash columns and subtotal in pencil (ie £476 in the debit column, and £345 in the credit column); remember to erase the subtotals afterwards
- deduct the lower total from the higher (payments from receipts) to give the balance of cash remaining (£476 – £345 = £131)
- the higher total is recorded at the bottom of both cash columns in a totals 'box' (£476)
- the balance of cash remaining (£131) is entered as a balancing item above the totals box (on the credit side), and is brought down underneath the total on the debit side as the opening balance for next month (£131)
- the two bank columns are dealt with in the same way (£693 – £362 = £331)

Notice that, in the cash book shown above, the cash and bank balances have been brought down on the debit side. It may happen that the balance at bank is brought down on the credit side: this occurs when payments exceed receipts, and indicates a bank overdraft.

It is very important to appreciate that the bank columns of the cash book represent the firm's own records of bank transactions and the balance at bank – the bank statement may well show different figures (see Chapter 17).

At the end of the month each discount column is totalled separately – no attempt should be made to balance them. At this point, amounts recorded in the columns and the totals are not part of the double-entry system. However, the two totals are transferred to the double-entry system as follows:
- the total on the debit side (£9 in the example above) is debited to *discount allowed account* in the general (or nominal) ledger
- the total on the credit side (£13 in the example) is credited to *discount received account,* also in the general (or nominal) ledger

The opposite book-keeping entries will have already been entered in the debtors and creditors accounts respectively (see Chapter 9).

The accounts appear as follows:

Dr.		Discount Allowed Account			Cr.
19-1			£	19-1	£
30 Apr.	Cash Book		9		

Dr.		Discount Received Account			Cr.
19-1			£	19-1	£
				30 Apr. Cash Book	13

The two discount accounts represent an expense and an income respectively and, at the end of the firm's financial year, the totals of the two accounts will be used in the profit statement.

Where control accounts (see Chapter 10) are in use, the total of discount allowed will be credited to the sales ledger control account, while the total of discount received will be debited to the purchases ledger control account.

the cash book as a book of prime entry

The cash book performs two functions within the accounting system:
*   it is a book of prime entry for cash/bank transactions
*   it forms part of the double-entry book-keeping system

The diagram below shows the flow from:
*   prime documents
*   the cash book as a book of prime entry
*   double-entry book-keeping

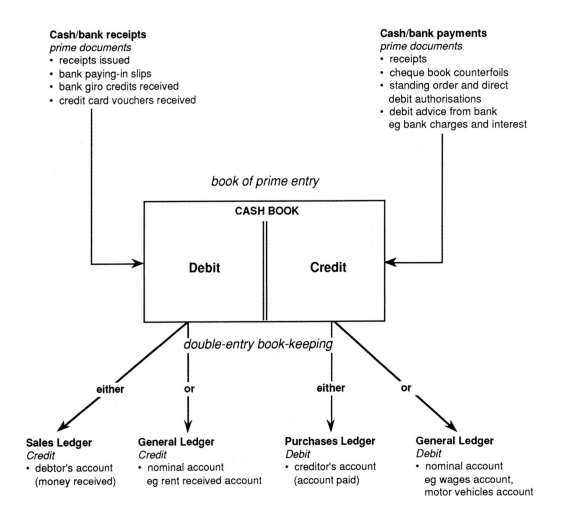

Cash/bank receipts
prime documents
*   receipts issued
*   bank paying-in slips
*   bank giro credits received
*   credit card vouchers received

Cash/bank payments
prime documents
*   receipts
*   cheque book counterfoils
*   standing order and direct debit authorisations
*   debit advice from bank eg bank charges and interest

book of prime entry

CASH BOOK

Debit   **Credit**

double-entry book-keeping

either   or   either   or

Sales Ledger
Credit
*   debtor's account (money received)

General Ledger
Credit
*   nominal account eg rent received account

Purchases Ledger
Debit
*   creditor's account (account paid)

General Ledger
Debit
*   nominal account eg wages account, motor vehicles account

checking the cash book

In business there is little point in keeping records of cash and bank transactions if we cannot, from time-to-time, prove that the records are accurate. How can we check the cash book?

cash columns

To check the cash columns is easy. It is simply a matter of counting the cash in the cash till or box, and agreeing it with the balance shown by the cash book. In the example in the Case Study on page 200, there should be £131 in the firm's cash till at 30 April 19-1. If the cash cannot be agreed in this way, the discrepancy needs to be investigated urgently.

bank columns

How are these to be checked? We could, perhaps, enquire at the bank and ask for the balance at the month-end, or we could arrange for a bank statement to be sent to us at the end of each month. However, the balance of the account at the bank may well not agree with that shown by the bank columns of the cash book. There are several reasons why there may be a difference: for example, a cheque that has been written out recently to pay a bill may not yet have been recorded on the bank statement, ie it has been entered in the cash book, but is not yet on the bank statement. To agree the bank columns of the cash book and the bank statement, it is usually necessary to prepare a *bank reconciliation statement,* and this topic is dealt with fully in Chapter 17.

cash book incorporating VAT

A cash book can be adapted to suit the needs of a business – already we have seen how a three-column cash book uses a memorandum column for discounts allowed and received. Another common layout uses a fourth money column, for VAT, as shown in the Case Study which follows. The VAT columns act as memorandum columns and, at the end of the week or month, are transferred to VAT account.

Case Study: Cash book incorporating VAT

Situation

On Monday, 2 June 19-8, the cash book of Eveshore Growers showed balances of £86 in cash and £248 in the bank. Transactions for the week were:

19-8
2 June   Paid insurance premium of £130 by cheque
3 June   Cash sales of £282, including Value Added Tax
3 June   Paid travel expenses in cash £17
3 June   Paid an invoice for £100 from A–Z Supplies by cheque after deducting £5 cash discount
4 June   Received a cheque for £117 from a debtor, P Leech, who was settling his account balance of £120 after deducting £3 cash discount
5 June   Cash sales of £423, including Value Added Tax
6 June   Cash purchase of £188, including Value Added Tax
6 June   Paid wages of £205, partly by cheque for £105 and partly in cash £100
6 June   Transferred £250 of cash into the bank

The rate of Value Added Tax is 17½%.
All cheques are banked on the day of receipt.

As cashier to Eveshore Growers, you are to:

- write up the cash book for the week commencing 2 June 19-8, using separate columns for discount, VAT, cash and bank
- balance the cash book at 6 June 19-8
- explain how the totals for the discount and VAT columns will be entered in the ledger of Eveshore Growers

Solution

Dr.　　　　　　　　　　　　　　　　　　　　**Cash Book**　　　　　　　　　　　　　　　　　　　　Cr.

Date	Details	Folio	Disc allwd	VAT	Cash	Bank	Date	Details	Folio	Disc recd	VAT	Cash	Bank
19-8			£	£	£	£	19-8			£	£	£	£
2 Jun.	Balances b/d				86	248	2 Jun.	Insurance	GL				130
3 Jun.	Sales	GL		42	282		3 Jun.	Travel exp	GL			17	
4 Jun.	P Leech	SL	3			117	3 Jun.	A–Z Supplies	PL	5			95
5 Jun.	Sales	GL		63	423		6 Jun.	Purchases	GL		28	188	
6 Jun.	Cash	C				250	6 Jun.	Wages	GL			100	105
							6 Jun.	Bank	C			250	
							7 Jun.	Balances c/d				236	285
			3	105	791	615				5	28	791	615
8 Jun.	Balances b/d				236	285							

Notes:
- The folio columns have been completed as follows:
  - GL = general ledger (or NL for nominal ledger)
  - SL = sales ledger
  - PL = purchases ledger
  - C = contra (both parts of the transaction in the same book)

- With transactions involving sales ledger (ie P Leech) and purchases ledger (ie A–Z Supplies), no amount for VAT is shown in the VAT columns. This is because VAT has been charged on invoices issued and received and was recorded in the VAT account when the sale or purchase was made.

- VAT on cash sales and purchases, and other transactions, is recorded in the two VAT analysis columns.

The discount and VAT columns:

- *discount allowed column* – the total of £3 will be debited to discount allowed account in the general (or nominal) ledger

- *discount received column* – the total of £5 will be credited to discount received account in the general (or nominal) ledger

- *VAT columns* – the total of £105 will be credited to VAT account in the general (or nominal) ledger, while the total of £28 will be debited to VAT account

analysed cash book

Many businesses use an *analysed cash book* to provide more information. An analysed cash book divides receipts and payments between a number of categories.

Receipts could be divided between:
- the main sections of a business, such as (1) furniture, and (2) carpets, for a home furnishing shop
- (1) cash sales, (2) sales ledger, ie receipts from debtors, (3) discount allowed, (4) Value Added Tax (where a business is registered for VAT)

Payments could be divided between:
- (1) cash purchases, ie immediate payment by cash or cheque, (2) purchases ledger, ie payments to creditors, (3) discount received, (4) Value Added Tax (where a business is registered for VAT)

A business will use whatever analysis columns suit it best: the cash book should be adapted to meet the needs of the business in the best possible way.

Case Study: Analysed cash book

Situation

Paul Simon runs a shop selling records, tapes, and compact discs. His business is not registered for VAT. He uses a cash book which analyses receipts between:
- records
- tapes
- compact discs

His cash book analyses payments between:
- cash purchases
- payments to creditors
- wages
- rent

The following transactions are to be entered for the first week of April 19-1:

1 Apr.	Balances from previous month: cash £55, bank £375
1 Apr.	Cash sales £150, being records £30, tapes £70, compact discs £50
2 Apr.	Paid shop rent by cheque, £85
3 Apr.	Paid wages in cash £105
3 Apr.	Cash sales £110, being records £20, tapes £40, compact discs £50
3 Apr.	Transferred £150 of cash to the bank
4 Apr.	Paid a creditor, Remus Records, £155, by cheque
4 Apr.	Cash sales £85, being tapes £45, compact discs £40
4 Apr.	Bought tapes and compact discs £120, paying by cheque
5 Apr.	Paid wages in cash, £80
5 Apr.	Cash sales £95, being tapes £45, compact discs £50
5 Apr.	Paid a creditor, Dynamic Discs Ltd, £100 by cheque
5 Apr.	Balanced the cash book at the end of the week

Solution

Dr. (Receipts)

Date	Details		Cash	Bank	Records	Tapes	CDs
19-1			£	£	£	£	£
1 Apr.	Balances b/d		55	375			
1 Apr.	Sales		150		30	70	50
3 Apr.	Sales		110		20	40	50
3 Apr.	Cash	C		150			
4 Apr.	Sales		85			45	40
5 Apr.	Sales		95			45	50
			495	525	50	200	190
6 Apr.	Balances b/d		160	65			

Cr. (Payments)

Date	Details		Cash	Bank	Cash Purchases	Creditors	Wages	Rent
19-1			£	£	£	£	£	£
2 Apr.	Rent			85				85
3 Apr.	Wages		105				105	
3 Apr.	Bank	C	150					
4 Apr.	Remus Records			155		155		
4 Apr.	Purchases			120	120			
5 Apr.	Wages		80				80	
5 Apr.	Dynamic Discs Ltd			100		100		
5 Apr.	Balances c/d		160	65				
			495	525	120	255	185	85

Notes:

• The analysed cash book analyses each receipt and payment between a number of headings. A business will adapt the cash book and use whatever analysis columns suit it best.

• The cash and bank columns are balanced in the way described on page 201; the analysis columns are totalled at the month-end. In the example above, the receipts are analysed between the three main products sold, and the monthly totals give Paul Simon useful information about the trends and progress being made by the business. The analysis columns on the payments side give the monthly totals of payments for goods bought (cash, creditors), and for the main expense items of running the business (wages, rent).

• Where a business uses control accounts (see Chapter 10) for sales ledger and purchases ledger, the weekly or monthly totals of the analysis columns for receipts from debtors (not used above) and payments to creditors can be recorded directly in the control accounts.

• For many small businesses an analysed cash book forms the main record. However, as a business grows in size it will be appropriate to develop a double-entry book-keeping system.

expenses claims

A further duty of the cashier (or the petty cashier – see Chapter 16) is the checking of *expenses claims*.

Often an employee is required to pay for expenses incurred on behalf of the business or organisation, and then to claim back the amount already paid from the business. Typically, expenses which can be reclaimed include:

• Travel, eg rail, bus, air and taxi fares, mileage allowance where a private car or motorbike has been used. (Note that the costs of travel to and from work are not paid, except under special circumstances, eg the burglar alarms go off in the middle of the night and the police request the presence of the keyholder).

• Hotel bills, including meals.

• Subsistence allowance – to cover the costs of working away from the normal place of employment, often paid at a daily rate.

• Other expenses, eg part of the employee's domestic telephone bill.

A business will establish the terms under which it will re-imburse an employee. For example, travel claims might have to be at the cheapest form of travel, such as a bus, even if the employee uses his/her private car; first-class travel is likely to be available only to senior employees. Before refunding expenses, the business will usually require proof of the expense, eg a receipt, or the travel ticket.

claims procedure

At regular intervals – perhaps monthly – an employee will be required to submit an *expenses claim* (see fig. 15.1). The procedure is likely to be:

• Employee completes and signs expenses claim form.

• Receipts for the expenses are attached to the expenses claim form.

• The form is passed to the employee's manager or section head for authorisation.

• The form is then sent to the accounts department where the amounts will be checked against the company's policies. The calculations on the form will also be checked. The various expenses will then be coded for the appropriate general ledger account, eg travel expenses, telephone expenses, etc. The book-keeping will be:
  – *debit* appropriate expense account (in the general ledger)
  – *credit* cash book (cash or bank column, as appropriate)

• The amount will either be paid direct to the employee in cash, by cheque or bank giro credit (small amounts can be paid out of petty cash – see Chapter 16), or the employee's pay will be credited and the amount paid at the next payroll run.

• The firm's general ledger expenses accounts will be debited with the cost. Where an expense includes VAT, a VAT-registered business will debit the appropriate expense account with the net amount of the expense, and debit the VAT amount to VAT account; in this way, the business claims back the VAT paid on the expense.

income tax and expenses

Most expenses are wholly incurred on behalf of the business or organisation. As such, their reimbursement does not form a part of the employee's salary, and is not subject to income tax. However, some expenses incurred are only partly used on behalf of the business, the other part is a benefit to the employee. Examples include the provision of a company car, or payment of the employee's telephone bill. The Inland Revenue lays down guidelines which, depending on the circumstances, state the employee's liability for income tax and the employee's and employer's liability for National Insurance Contributions.

WYVERN TRADERS LTD

EXPENSES CLAIM FOR THE MONTH ENDING ....

Name:

Department:

Date	Item	Travelling £	Subsistence £	Entertaining £	Miscellaneous £	Total £	OFFICE USE ONLY	
							VAT £	Net £
Total								

Signed:

Date:

Authorised by:

Date:

Fig. 15.1 Expenses claim

chapter summary

❑ The cash book records receipts (debits) and payments (credits) both in cash (except for low-value expense payments) and by cheque.

❑ A basic layout for a cash book has money columns for cash transactions and bank transactions on both the debit and credit sides, together with a further column on each side for discounts.

❑ In the discount columns are recorded cash discounts: discounts allowed (to customers) on the debit side, and discounts received (from suppliers) on the payments side.

❑ Another common cash book layout incorporates columns for VAT.

❑ The cashier may be responsible for checking expenses claims.

The bank columns of the cash book and the balance calculated are unlikely to agree exactly with the bank statement: in order to agree them it is necessary to prepare a *bank reconciliation statement* which we will look at in Chapter 17. Firstly, though, we need to look at how a business keeps records of cash payments for small items such as stationery, travel expenses, etc. This is done by means of a *petty cash book* which we shall consider in the next chapter.

Student Activities

15.1 On 1 August 19-1, the balances in the cash book of Metro Trading Co Ltd were:

Cash £276 debit
Bank £4,928 debit

Transactions for the month were:

2 Aug. Received a cheque from Wild & Sons Ltd, £398
5 Aug. Paid T Hall Ltd a cheque for £541 in full settlement of a debt of £565
8 Aug. Paid wages in cash £254
10 Aug. Withdrew £500 in cash from the bank for use in the business
12 Aug. Received a cheque for £1,755 from A Lewis Ltd in full settlement of their account of £1,775
17 Aug. Paid F Jarvis £457 by cheque
21 Aug. Received a cheque for £261 from Harvey & Sons Ltd
23 Aug. Paid wages in cash £436
24 Aug. Paid J Jones a cheque for £628 in full settlement of a debt of £661
27 Aug. Paid salaries by cheque £2,043
29 Aug. Paid telephone account by cheque £276
30 Aug. Received a cheque for £595 from Wild & Sons Ltd in full settlement of their account of £610
31 Aug. Withdrew £275 in cash from the bank for use in the business

All cheques are banked on the day of receipt.

You are to:

(a) Enter the above transactions in the three column cash book of Metro Trading Co Ltd.
(b) Balance the cash and bank columns at 31 August, and carry the balances down to 1 September.
(c) Total the two discount columns.

15.2   Walter Harrison is a sole trader who records his cash and bank transactions in a *three-column* cash book. The following are the transactions for June:

19-2

1 June   Balances: cash £280; bank overdraft £2,240

3 June   Received a cheque from G Wheaton for £195, in full settlement of a debt of £200

5 June   Received cash of £53 from T Francis, in full settlement of a debt of £55

8 June   Paid the amount owing to F Lloyd by cheque: the total amount due is £400 and you take advantage of a 2½ per cent cash discount for prompt settlement

10 June   Paid wages in cash £165

12 June   Paid A Morris in cash, £100 less 3 per cent cash discount

16 June   Withdrew £200 in cash from the bank for use in the business

18 June   Received a cheque for £640 from H Watson in full settlement of a debt of £670

20 June   Paid R Marks £78 by cheque

24 June   Paid D Farr £65 by cheque, in full settlement of a debt of £67

26 June   Paid telephone account £105 in cash

28 June   Received a cheque from M Perry in settlement of his account of £240 – he has deducted 2½ per cent cash discount

30 June   Received cash £45 from K Willis

All cheques are banked on the day of receipt.

You are to:

(a)   enter the above transactions in Harrison's three-column cash book, balance the cash and bank columns, and carry the balances down to 1 July

(b)   total the two discount columns and transfer them to the appropriate accounts

15.3   On 1 April 19-2, the balances in the cash book of Johnson Brothers were:

Cash   £85 debit

Bank   £718 credit (the business has an overdraft facility of £2,000 with Metro Bank plc)

Transactions for the month were:

3 Apr.   Paid travelling expenses of £65 in cash

5 Apr.   Paid the telephone bill of £235 (including £35 of Value Added Tax) by cheque

7 Apr.   Jim Bowen, a debtor, settles an invoice for £90, paying £85 in cash and receiving £5 discount for prompt settlement

10 Apr.   Cash sales £470 (including Value Added Tax) received by cheque and paid into the bank

14 Apr.   Paid an invoice for £190 from M Hughes by cheque for £180, £10 being received for prompt settlement

18 Apr.   Cash purchases of £94 (including Value Added Tax) paid by cheque

19 Apr.   Received a cheque for £575 from J Burrows, a debtor, in full settlement of an invoice for £600

20 Apr.   Cash sales of £188 (including Value Added Tax) received in cash

24 Apr.   Withdrew £200 in cash from the bank for use in the business

25 Apr.   Paid a cheque for £245 to Wilson Ltd, a creditor, in full settlement of an invoice for £255

27 Apr.   Paid wages in cash £350

You are to:

(a)   Enter the above transactions in the cash book of Johnson Brothers, using columns for dates, details, discount, VAT, bank and cash.

(b)   Balance the cash book at 30 April 19-2.

(c)   Show how the totals for the discount and VAT columns will be entered in the accounts in the general ledger.

15.4 John Adams is a jobbing builder and plumber; he is not registered for VAT. To help him keep his business records straight, he uses an analysed cash book. The headings used are *receipts:* building, plumbing; *payments:* cash purchases, creditors, van expenses, wages. He asks you to write up his analysed cash book for the first week of July 19-2 (all cheques are banked on the day of receipt):

1 July	Balances at start of week: cash £187.50; bank £325.10
1 July	Bought building materials £50.20, paying in cash
1 July	Paid for van repairs £78.18 by cheque
2 July	Received cash for completed building job £122.90
2 July	Received a cheque from Panton District Council £147.21 for plumbing work
3 July	Bought plumbing materials £70.80, paying in cash
3 July	Paid for petrol for van £12.50 by cheque
4 July	Received a cheque from J James for £175.20 for completed job, being building £102.10, plumbing £73.10
4 July	Paid a creditor, Builders Merchants Ltd by cheque £74.20
5 July	Received a cheque from T Lane for £33.85 for plumbing work
5 July	Withdrew cash from the bank £100.00, for use in the business
5 July	Paid wages in cash £85.22

At the end of the week, on 5 July, John Adams asks you to balance the analysed cash book, and to carry the balances down to next week

15.5 David Lewis runs a shop selling furniture, carpets and kitchen utensils. His business is registered for VAT: cash sales and purchases include VAT at 17½%. He uses a cash book which analyses receipts between:
• Value Added Tax
• furniture
• carpets
• kitchen utensils

His cash book analyses payments between:
• Value Added Tax
• cash purchases
• creditors
• expenses

The following transactions take place during the first week of May 19-1 (all cheques are banked on the day of receipt):

1 May	Balances from previous month: cash £205.75, bank £825.30
1 May	Cash sales: furniture £102.40, carpets £85.20, kitchen utensils £27.18
2 May	Paid shop rent by cheque £127.50 (no VAT)
2 May	Cash sales: furniture £125.95, carpets £104.45, kitchen utensils £83.30
2 May	Cheque received for sale of furniture £212.20
3 May	Paid in £500.00 of cash to the bank
3 May	Paid a creditor, Terry Carpets Ltd £345.80 by cheque
4 May	Cash sales: carpets £108.14, kitchen utensils £74.68
4 May	Paid wages in cash £124.29
4 May	Bought secondhand furniture £85.30, paying in cash
5 May	Cash sales: furniture £125.55, carpets £94.60
5 May	Paid a creditor, Lowland Furniture Co Ltd £195.80 by cheque
5 May	Paid shop rent in cash £127.50 (no VAT)

(a) The above transactions are to be entered in David Lewis' analysed cash book (VAT amounts should be rounded down to the nearest penny).

(b) Balance the cash book at 5 May 19-1.

(c) Show the VAT account in the general ledger.

16 Petty cash book

A petty cash book is used to record low-value cash payments for various small purchases by a business, eg small items of stationery, postages, etc. It would not be appropriate for such expenses to be entered in the main cash book, as a large number of payments would clutter it up. Instead, an amount of cash is handed by the main cashier to a member of staff, the *petty cashier,* who will be responsible for security of the money, and will make payments as appropriate.

In order to operate a petty cash system, the petty cashier needs the following:
- a *petty cash book* in which to record transactions
- a lockable *petty cash box* in which to keep the money
- a stock of blank *petty cash vouchers* (see page 215) for claims on petty cash to be made
- a *lockable desk drawer* in which to keep these items

the petty cash procedure

As an employee you are most likely to encounter the petty cash system when making claims for money for small purchases you have made. Before studying the form-filling procedures in detail, read the summary of a typical petty cash transaction set out below:

> *your supervisor asks you to go and buy a new typewriter ribbon from an office supplies shop*

> *you go to the shop and buy the typewriter ribbon; having paid for the ribbon, you retain the receipt (for £5.50) which you hand to the petty cashier on your return to the office*

> *the supervisor authorises a petty cash voucher which contains details of the purchase*

> *the petty cashier gives you £5.50 in cash*

> *the petty cashier attaches the receipt to the petty cash voucher and enters the details in the petty cash book*

what items can be passed through petty cash book?

As we have already noted, petty cash is used to make small cash payments for expenses incurred by the business. Examples of the type of payments made from petty cash include:

- stationery items
- small items of office supplies
- casual wages
- window cleaning
- bus, rail and taxi fares (incurred on behalf of the business)
- meals and drinks (incurred on behalf of the business)
- postages
- tips and donations

Note that petty cash should not be used to pay for private expenses of employees, eg tea, coffee, and milk, unless the business has agreed these in advance. Usually the petty cashier will have a list of approved expenses which can be reimbursed.

A business will also decide on the maximum value of each transaction that can be paid out of petty cash; for example, £20 is a common maximum.

Case Study: Petty cash expenses

Situation

You are working as a clerk for Wyvern Engineering Co. Ltd. One of your duties is that of petty cashier. Which of the following expenses would you allow to be paid out of petty cash?

- envelopes for use in the office, £2.50
- postage on an urgent parcel of engineering parts, £3.75
- bus fare to work claimed by typist, £1.20
- car mileage to work of office manager called in late at night when the burglar alarm went off (false alarm!), £5.50
- tea and coffee for use in the office, £3.70
- office window cleaning, £2.80
- pot plant bought for reception area, £5.50
- floppy disks for computer, £35.00
- donation to local charity by the business, £5.00
- meal allowance paid to a member of staff required to work during the lunch hour, £3.50

Solution

For most expenses it is clear whether or not they can be drawn from petty cash. However, there are points to consider for some of the expenses.

Envelopes:	pay from petty cash
Postage:	pay from petty cash
Bus fare to work:	this is a personal expense and cannot be drawn from petty cash

Car mileage:	travel to work is a personal expense, as seen with the previous item; however, as this expense was a special journey in the middle of the night in order to resolve a business problem, it can be paid from petty cash
Tea and coffee:	this is a personal expense of employees and cannot normally be paid out of petty cash; however, if the ingredients were used to make drinks for official visitors and customers, it can be paid from petty cash
Office window cleaning:	pay from petty cash
Pot plant:	pay from petty cash (but plants for the general office cannot be bought with the company's money)
Floppy disks:	this is a business expense but, in view of the amount (too large for petty cash), it should be paid by cheque from the cash book
Donation:	pay from petty cash
Meal allowance:	pay from petty cash, provided that it is company policy to make an allowance in these circumstances

Note: before payment can be made in each case, it must be authorised by an official of the company – see petty cash voucher (on next page).

the imprest system

Most petty cash books operate on the *imprest system*. With this method the petty cashier starts each week (or month) with a certain amount of money – the imprest amount. As payments are made during the week (or month) the amount of money will reduce and, at the end of the period, the cash will be made up by the main cashier to the imprest amount. For example:

Started week with imprest amount	£100.00
Total of petty cash amounts paid out during week	£80.50
Cash held at end of week	£19.50
Amount drawn from cashier to restore imprest amount	£80.50
Cash at start of next week, ie imprest amount	£100.00

If, at any time, the imprest amount proves to be insufficient, further amounts of cash can be drawn from the cashier. Also, from time-to-time, it may be necessary to increase the imprest amount so that regular shortfalls are avoided.

petty cash voucher

The petty cashier, who is likely also to have other tasks within the firm, is responsible for control of the petty cash, making cash payments when appropriate, keeping records of payments made, and balancing the petty cash book at regular intervals.

Payments out of petty cash are made only against correct documentation – usually a petty cash voucher (see fig. 16.1). Petty cash vouchers are completed as follows:

* details and amount of expenditure
* signature of the person making the claim and receiving the money
* signature of the person authorising the payment to be made

- additionally, most petty cash vouchers are numbered, so that they can be controlled, the number being entered in the petty cash book
- any relevant documentation, eg receipt, should be attached to the petty cash voucher

<table>
<tr><td colspan="3"></td><td>No <u>807</u></td></tr>
</table>

Petty Cash Voucher   No <u>807</u>

Date <u>*11 May 19-1*</u>

For what required	AMOUNT £	p
Envelopes	1	55
10 Floppy disks	6	10
	7	65

Signature _____ *T. Harris* _____

Passed by _____ *D. Adams* _____

Fig. 16.1   An example of a petty cash voucher

layout of a petty cash book

Receipts	Date	Details	Voucher No.	Total Payment	Analysis columns				
					VAT	Postages	Stationery	Travel	Ledger
£				£	£	£	£	£	£

The layout shows that:

- receipts from the main cashier are entered in the column on the extreme left
- there are columns for the date and details of all receipts and payments
- there is a column for the petty cash voucher number
- the total payment (ie the amount paid out on each petty cash voucher) is in the next column
- then follow the analysis columns which analyse each transaction entered in the 'total payment' column (note that VAT may need to be calculated – see below)

A business or organisation will use whatever analysis columns are most suitable for it and, indeed, there may be more columns than shown in the example.

petty cash and VAT

Value Added Tax is charged by VAT-registered businesses on their taxable supplies. Therefore, there will often be VAT included as part of the expense paid out of petty cash. However, not all expenses will have been subject to VAT. There are four possible circumstances:

- VAT has been charged at the standard rate
- VAT has not been charged because the supplier is not VAT-registered
- the zero rate of VAT applies, eg food and drink (but not meals which are standard-rated), books, newspapers, transport (but not taxis and hire cars)
- the supplies are exempt (eg financial services, postal services)

Often the indication of the supplier's VAT registration number on a receipt or invoice will tell you that VAT has been charged at the standard rate.

Where VAT has been charged, the amount of tax might be indicated separately on the receipt or invoice. However, for small money amounts it is quite usual for a total to be shown without indicating the amount of VAT. An example of a receipt which does not show the VAT content is illustrated below. The receipt is for a box of envelopes purchased from Wyvern Stationers Ltd. It shows:

- the name of the retailer
- the VAT registration number of the retailer
- the price of the item – £4.70
- the amount of money given – a £10 note
- the amount of change given – £5.30
- the date and time of the transaction

a till receipt

```
Wyvern Stationers Ltd
VAT No 454 7106 52

Qty 1            4.70
Total            4.70

Cash            10.00
Change           5.30

11/03/93        09:30
```

What it does not show, however, is the VAT content of the purchase price – it only shows the price after the VAT has been added on.

How do you calculate purchase price before the VAT is added on? The formula, with VAT at 17½%, is:

price including VAT ÷ 1.175 = price before VAT is added on

in this case: £4.70 ÷ 1.175 = £4.00 = price before VAT is added on

The VAT content is therefore £4.70 less £4.00 = 70p

Here £0.70 will be entered in the VAT column in the petty cash book, £4.00 in the appropriate expense column, and the full £4.70 in the total payment column.

Remember that, when calculating VAT amounts, fractions of a penny are ignored, ie the tax is rounded down to a whole penny.

Case Study: Petty cash book

Situation

You work in the accounts office of Wyvern Traders. One of your tasks is to keep the petty cash book, which is operated on the imprest system. There are a number of transactions (all of which, unless otherwise indicated, include VAT at 17½%) to be entered for the week in the petty cash book:

19-1
10 Apr. Started the week with an imprest amount of £50.00
10 Apr. Paid stationery £3.76 on voucher no. 47
10 Apr. Paid taxi fare £2.82 on voucher no. 48
11 Apr. Paid postages £0.75 (no VAT) on voucher no. 49
12 Apr. Paid taxi fare £4.70 on voucher no. 50
12 Apr. Paid J Jones, a creditor, £6.00 (no VAT shown in petty cash book – amount will be on VAT account already) on voucher no. 51
13 Apr. Paid stationery £3.76 on voucher no. 52
13 Apr. Paid postages £2.85 (no VAT) on voucher no. 53
14 Apr. Paid taxi fare £6.11 on voucher no. 54
14 Apr. Cash received to restore imprest amount, and petty cash book balanced at the end of the week

Solution

The petty cash book is written up as follows:

| Receipts | Date | Details | Voucher No. | Total Payment | Analysis columns | | | | |
					VAT	Postages	Stationery	Travel	Ledger
£ 50.00	19-1 10 Apr.	Balance b/d		£	£	£	£	£	£
	10 Apr.	Stationery	47	3.76	0.56		3.20		
	10 Apr.	Taxi fare	48	2.82	0.42			2.40	
	11 Apr.	Postages	49	0.75		0.75			
	12 Apr.	Taxi fare	50	4.70	0.70			4.00	
	12 Apr.	J Jones	51	6.00					6.00
	13 Apr.	Stationery	52	3.76	0.56		3.20		
	13 Apr.	Postages	53	2.85		2.85			
	14 Apr.	Taxi fare	54	6.11	0.91			5.20	
				30.75	3.15	3.60	6.40	11.60	6.00
30.75	14 Apr. 14 Apr.	Cash received Balance c/d		50.00					
80.75				80.75					
50.00	14 Apr.	Balance b/d							

Notes:

- The totals of the analysis columns add up to the total payment
- the amount of cash received from the main cashier to restore the imprest amount is the same as the total paid out during the week
- The petty cashier will give the firm's book-keeper details of the total of each analysis column – see below – so that the amounts can be recorded in the double-entry book-keeping system

petty cash and double-entry book-keeping

In the petty cash book looked at in the Case Study above, each analysis column has been totalled. In order to record the amounts in the double-entry system, the total of each column is debited to the relevant account in the general ledger. For example:

Dr.		Postages Account		Cr.
19-1	£	19-1		£
14 Apr. Petty cash book	3.60			

Thus, from the petty cash book, debits are passed to the general ledger accounts as follows:
- VAT account, £3.15
- postages account, £3.60
- stationery account, £6.40
- travel expenses account, £11.60

The amount in the ledger analysis column is debited to the appropriate creditor's account – in this case, the account of J Jones in the purchases ledger must be debited with £6.00

Total debits in the example are £30.75 and this is the amount that needs to be drawn from the main cashier on 14 April. The petty cashier will need to complete a requisition form either for the cash itself, or for a cheque made payable to cash. If the latter, the petty cashier will have to take the cheque to the bank and obtain the cash. An example of a cheque requisition is shown below:

Wyvern Traders
Request for cheque

Amount:	*£30.75*
Payee:	*Cash*
Date:	*14 April 19-1*
Details:	*Reimbursement of petty cash*
Signature:	*Jane Watkins, petty cashier*
Authorised by:	*Natalie Wilson, supervisor*
Cheque no:	*017234*

The cheque is credited in the firm's cash book, so completing double-entry book-keeping. If a trial balance is extracted on 14 April (after the analysis columns have been debited to the respective accounts, and a credit entered in the cash book to restore the imprest amount) the balance of petty cash, £50.00, must be included as a debit balance in the trial balance.

Case Study: Control of petty cash

Situation

You are a junior clerk in the office of Osborne Engineering Ltd. As part of your duties you are required to be the petty cashier.

The office manager is reviewing the way in which work is carried out in the office. She asks you to set out the procedures for the operation and control of petty cash. She explains that this will be of help to the person who takes over from you when you go on holiday. She also says that she doesn't require details of how to balance the petty cash book.

Solution

The main procedures for the operation and control of petty cash are:

- Ensure that you start each week with the imprest amount of cash which has been agreed with the office manager.
- Keep the petty cash in a locked cash box, and keep control of the keys.
- Provide petty cash vouchers (in number order) on request.
- Pay out of petty cash against correctly completed petty cash vouchers ensuring that:
    - the voucher is signed by the person authorising payment
    - the voucher is signed by the person receiving the money
    - a receipt (if possible) is attached to the petty cash voucher, and that receipt and petty cash voucher are for the same amount
- Write up the petty cash book (to include calculation of VAT amounts when appropriate).
- Store the petty cash vouchers safely – file them in numerical order. The vouchers will need to be kept for at least seven years in the company's archives. They may be needed by the firm's auditors or in the event of other queries. Completed petty cash books will also need to be retained.
- Expect a surprise check of petty cash from the office manager – at any one time the cash held plus amounts of petty cash vouchers should equal the imprest amount.
- At the end of each week (or month) balance the petty cash book and draw an amount of cash from the cashier equal to the amount of payments made, in order to restore the imprest amount.
- Present the petty cash book and cash in hand for checking by the office manager.
- Advise the accounts clerk of the totals of each analysis column, so that he/she can enter the amount of each expense in the book-keeping system.
- Deal with any discrepancies promptly; these can include:
    - a receipt and petty cash voucher total differing – raise the matter with the person who made the purchase and adjust the cash accordingly
    - a difference between the totals of the analysis columns and the total payments column in the petty cash book – check the addition of the columns, check the figures against the vouchers, check your VAT calculations (does the VAT plus the analysis column amount equal the total payment amount?)
    - a difference between the cash in the petty cash box and the balance shown in the petty cash book – if this is not an arithmetic difference it may be a case of theft, and should be reported promptly to the office manager.

chapter summary

❏   The petty cash book records payments for a variety of low-value business expenses.

❏   The person responsible for maintaining the petty cash book is the petty cashier.

❏   Most petty cash books operate on the imprest system.

❏   Payment can only be made from the petty cash book against correct documentation – usually a petty cash voucher, which must be signed by the person authorising payment.

❏   Where a business is registered for Value Added Tax, it must record VAT amounts paid on petty cash purchases in a separate column in the petty cash book.

❏   At regular intervals – weekly or monthly – the petty cash book will be balanced; the main cashier will restore the imprest amount of cash and the total of each analysis column will be debited to the relevant account.

The next chapter looks at how a *bank reconciliation statement* is prepared in order to agree the bank columns of the cash book with the balance shown on the bank statement.

Student Activities

16.1   You work as a clerk in the office of Temeside Printers Ltd. One of your duties is that of petty cashier. Which of the following expenses will you allow to be paid out of petty cash?

(a)   postage on a parcel of printing sent to a customer, £3.85
(b)   a rubber date stamp bought for use in the office, £4.60
(c)   rail fare to work claimed by the office manager's secretary, £2.50
(d)   donation to charity, £5.00
(e)   tea and coffee for use by office staff, £5.50
(f)   mileage allowance claimed by works foreman who had to visit a customer, £4.80
(g)   meal allowance paid to typist who had to work her lunch hour, £4.00
(h)   window cleaning, £3.50
(i)   purchase of shelving for the office, £35.00
(j)   taxi fare claimed for delivering an urgent parcel of printing to a customer, £6.25

16.2   You are going on holiday and handing your job as petty cashier to a colleague who is not familiar with the security and safety aspects of the job, although she can manage the paperwork. Prepare a checklist of the security and safety aspects of the job so that she can learn them more easily. Write them out as numbered points rather than as solid text – they will be more easily remembered in this format.

16.3   As petty cashier, prepare the following petty cash vouchers under today's date for signature by the person making the claim. You are authorised to approve payments up to £10.00.

Voucher no. 851: £4.45 claimed by Jayne Smith for postage (no VAT) on an urgent parcel of spare parts sent to a customer, Evelode Supplies Ltd.

Voucher no. 852: £2.35 (including VAT) claimed by Tanya Howard for air-mail envelopes bought for use in the office. Show on the petty cash voucher the amount of VAT.

No ___851_____

Petty Cash Voucher

Date _____

For what required	AMOUNT £	

Signature _____
Passed by _____

No ___852_____

Petty Cash Voucher

Date _____

For what required	AMOUNT £	

Signature _____
Passed by _____

16.4   The business for which you work is registered for VAT. The following petty cash amounts include VAT at 17½% and you are required to calculate the amount that will be shown in the VAT column and the appropriate expense column (remember that VAT amounts should be rounded down to the nearest penny):

(a)   £9.40
(b)   £4.70
(c)   £2.35
(d)   £2.45
(e)   £5.60
(f)   £3.47
(g)   £8.75
(h)   94p
(i)   99p
(j)   £9.41

16.5   On returning from holiday, you are told to take over the petty cash book. This is kept on the imprest system, the float being £75.00 at the beginning of each month. Analysis columns are used for VAT, travelling expenses, postages, stationery, meals, and miscellaneous.

Enter the following transactions for the month. The voucher amounts include VAT at 17½% unless indicated. You can assume that all payments have been authorised by the office manager:

19-1
1 Aug.   Balance of cash £75.00
2 Aug.   Voucher no. 39: taxi fare £3.80
4 Aug.   Voucher no. 40: parcel postage £2.35 (no VAT)
7 Aug.   Voucher no. 41: pencils £1.26
10 Aug.   Voucher no. 42: travel expenses £5.46 (no VAT)
12 Aug.   Voucher no. 43: window cleaner £8.50 (no VAT)
14 Aug.   Voucher no. 44: large envelopes £2.45
17 Aug.   Voucher no. 45: donation to charity £5 (no VAT)
18 Aug.   Voucher no. 46: rail fare £5.60 (no VAT); meal allowance £5.00 (no VAT)
20 Aug.   Voucher no. 47: recorded delivery postage £0.75 (no VAT)
23 Aug.   Voucher no. 48: roll of packing tape £1.50
25 Aug.   Voucher no. 49: excess postage paid £0.55 (no VAT)
27 Aug.   Voucher no. 50: taxi fare £5.40
31 Aug.   Cash received from cashier to restore imprest amount to £75.00

16.6   Prepare a petty cash book with analysis columns for VAT, postages, travelling expenses, meals, and sundry office expenses. Enter the following transactions for the week. The voucher amounts include VAT at 17½% unless indicated.

19-1
1 June   Balance of cash £100.00
1 June   Postages £6.35 (no VAT), voucher no. 123
2 June   Travelling expenses £3.25 (no VAT), voucher no. 124
2 June   Postages £1.28 (no VAT), voucher no. 125
3 June   Envelopes £4.54, voucher no. 126
3 June   Window cleaning £5.50, voucher no. 127
4 June   Taxi fare £4.56, meals £10.85, voucher no. 128
4 June   Postages £8.56 (no VAT), packing materials £3.25, voucher no. 129
4 June   Taxi fare £4.50, meals £7.45, voucher no. 130
5 June   Marker pens £2.55, envelopes £3.80, voucher no. 131
5 June   Cash received from cashier to restore imprest amount to £100.00

ASSIGNMENT 5

Petty cash book, using spreadsheets

SITUATION

You are working in the accounts department of Deansway Trading Co, a VAT-registered company. One of your responsibilities is to maintain the petty cash records under the supervision of the office manager.

At present the petty cash book is kept on a handwritten system, with an imprest amount of £100. The petty cash book is balanced at the end of each week, and the imprest amount is restored to £100.

You have been asked by the office manager to set up and run a computerised system using a spreadsheet.

STUDENT TASKS

1. Using a spreadsheet package, design a suitable layout for recording petty cash transactions. The following example can be used as a guide:

Receipts	Date	Details	Voucher No	Total Payment	Analysis columns				
					VAT	Postages	Travel	Meals	Stationery
£				£	£	£	£	£	£

   Note: spreadsheet formulas must be used in the calculation of totals and balances

2. Print out the following:
   • the blank spreadsheet mask
   • the spreadsheet contents, showing formulas

3. Using the information on the attached petty cash vouchers, which have been authorised by the office manager, you are to enter the relevant details for the:
   • week commencing 1 May 19-1 (vouchers on page 224)
   • week commencing 8 May 19-1 (vouchers on pages 225 and 226)

   Notes:
   (a) The imprest amount at the beginning of each week is £100.
   (b) Some payments are not subject to VAT and the office manager has marked these; all other payments *include* VAT.
   (c) Print out the completed spreadsheet *at the end of the first week* and submit it to the office manager (your tutor) for checking.

4. Print out the completed spreadsheet (showing both weeks) at the end of the exercise and submit all your material to the office manager (your tutor).

Vouchers for the week commencing 1 May 19-1

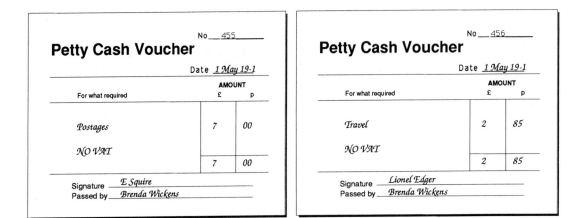

Petty Cash Voucher	No 455		
	Date *1 May 19-1*		
		AMOUNT	
For what required		£	p
Postages		7	00
NO VAT			
		7	00
Signature *E Squire*			
Passed by *Brenda Wickens*			

Petty Cash Voucher	No 456		
	Date *1 May 19-1*		
		AMOUNT	
For what required		£	p
Travel		2	85
NO VAT			
		2	85
Signature *Lionel Edger*			
Passed by *Brenda Wickens*			

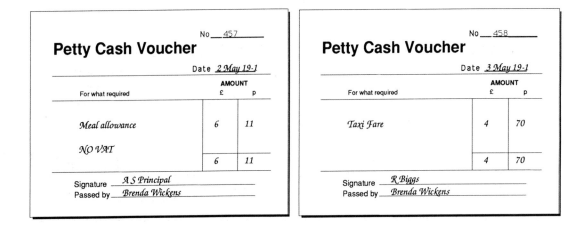

Petty Cash Voucher	No 457		
	Date *2 May 19-1*		
		AMOUNT	
For what required		£	p
Meal allowance		6	11
NO VAT			
		6	11
Signature *A S Principal*			
Passed by *Brenda Wickens*			

Petty Cash Voucher	No 458		
	Date *3 May 19-1*		
		AMOUNT	
For what required		£	p
Taxi Fare		4	70
		4	70
Signature *R Biggs*			
Passed by *Brenda Wickens*			

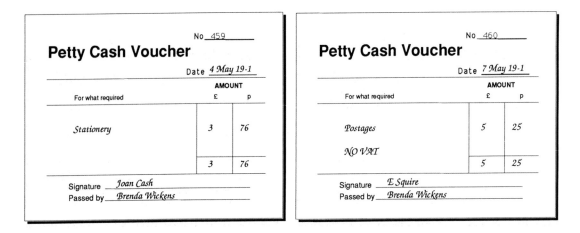

Petty Cash Voucher	No 459		
	Date *4 May 19-1*		
		AMOUNT	
For what required		£	p
Stationery		3	76
		3	76
Signature *Joan Cash*			
Passed by *Brenda Wickens*			

Petty Cash Voucher	No 460		
	Date *7 May 19-1*		
		AMOUNT	
For what required		£	p
Postages		5	25
NO VAT			
		5	25
Signature *E Squire*			
Passed by *Brenda Wickens*			

**Vouchers for the week commencing 8 May 19-1
(continued on next page)**

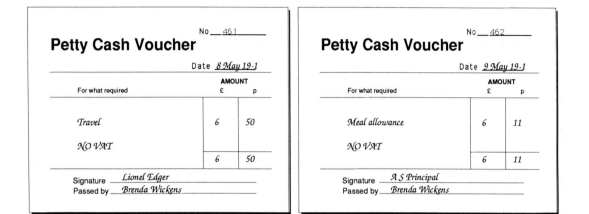

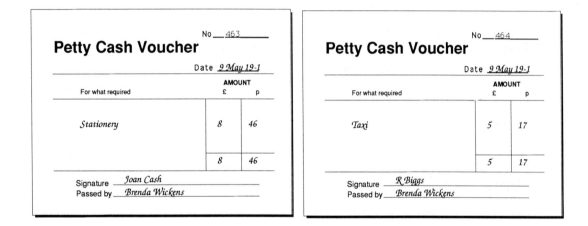

Petty Cash Voucher

No. 465

Date 10 May 19-1

For what required	AMOUNT £	p
Stationery	4	70
	4	70

Signature _Joan Cash_
Passed by _Brenda Wickens_

Petty Cash Voucher

No. 466

Date 10 May 19-1

For what required	AMOUNT £	p
Travel	3	50
NO VAT		
	3	50

Signature _Lionel Edger_
Passed by _Brenda Wickens_

Vouchers for the week commencing 8 May 19-1 (continued)

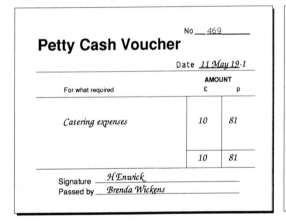

Petty Cash Voucher   No. 467

Date *10 May 19-1*

For what required	AMOUNT £	p
Postages	4	50
NO VAT		
	4	50

Signature *E Squire*
Passed by *Brenda Wickens*

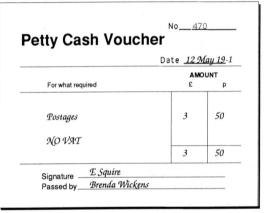

Petty Cash Voucher   No. 468

Date *11 May 19-1*

For what required	AMOUNT £	p
Bus fares	3	80
NO VAT		
	3	80

Signature *T Sawyer*
Passed by *Brenda Wickens*

Petty Cash Voucher   No. 469

Date *11 May 19-1*

For what required	AMOUNT £	p
Catering expenses	10	81
	10	81

Signature *H Enwick*
Passed by *Brenda Wickens*

Petty Cash Voucher   No. 470

Date *12 May 19-1*

For what required	AMOUNT £	p
Postages	3	50
NO VAT		
	3	50

Signature *E Squire*
Passed by *Brenda Wickens*

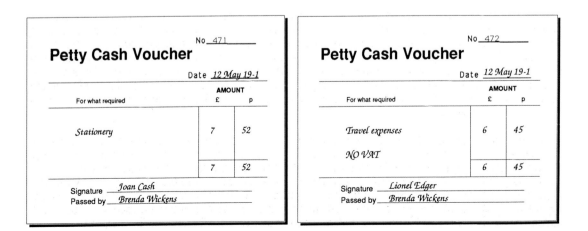

Petty Cash Voucher   No. 471

Date *12 May 19-1*

For what required	AMOUNT £	p
Stationery	7	52
	7	52

Signature *Joan Cash*
Passed by *Brenda Wickens*

Petty Cash Voucher   No. 472

Date *12 May 19-1*

For what required	AMOUNT £	p
Travel expenses	6	45
NO VAT		
	6	45

Signature *Lionel Edger*
Passed by *Brenda Wickens*

17 Bank reconciliation statements

In Chapter 15 we saw that the bank columns of the cash book record the business' own internal record of the bank transactions, and the balance at the end of the week or month. However, the bank statement received from the bank may show a rather different balance. There are two main reasons for this:

- *timing differences* caused by unpresented cheques, ie the time delay between, for example, writing out (drawing) a cheque and recording it in the cash book, and the cheque being entered on the bank statement
- *the cash book has not been updated* with items which appear on the bank statement and should also appear in the cash book, eg bank charges

Assuming that there are no errors, both cash book and bank statement are correct, but need to be reconciled with each other, ie the closing balances need to be agreed.

timing differences

The two main timing differences between the bank columns of the cash book and the bank statement are:
- cheques drawn, not yet recorded on the bank statement
- amounts paid into the bank, not yet recorded on the bank statement

The first of these – unpresented cheques – is caused because, when a cheque is written out, it is immediately entered on the payments side of the cash book, even though it may be some days before the cheque passes through the bank clearing system and is recorded on the bank statement. Therefore, for a few days at least, the cash book shows a lower balance than the bank statement in respect of this cheque. When the cheque is recorded on the bank statement, the difference will disappear. We have looked at only one cheque here, but a business will often be issuing many cheques each day, and the difference between the cash book balance and the bank statement balance may be considerable.

With the second timing difference – amounts paid in, not yet recorded on the bank statement – the firm's cashier will record a receipt in the cash book as he or she prepares the bank paying-in slip. However, the receipt may not be recorded by the bank on the bank statement for a day or so, particularly if it is paid in late in the day (when the bank will put it into the next day's work), or if it is paid in at a bank branch other than the one at which the account is maintained. Until the receipt is recorded by the bank the cash book will show a higher bank account balance than the bank statement. Once the receipt is entered on the bank statement, the difference will disappear.

These two timing differences are involved in the calculation known as the *bank reconciliation statement*. The business cash book *must not be altered* for these because, as we have seen, they will correct themselves on the bank statement as time goes by.

updating the cash book

Besides the timing differences described above, there may be other differences between the bank columns of the cash book and the bank statement, and these *do* need to be entered in the cash book to bring it up-to-date. For example, the bank might make an automatic standing order payment on behalf of a business – such an item is correctly debited by the bank, and it might be that the bank statement acts as a reminder to the business cashier of the payment: it should then be entered in the cash book.

Examples of items that show in the bank statement and need to be entered in the cash book include:

receipts
- standing order and BACS (Bankers' Automated Clearing Services) receipts credited by the bank, eg payments from debtors (customers)
- bank giro credit (credit transfer) amounts received by the bank, eg payments from debtors (customers)
- dividend amounts received by the bank
- interest credited by the bank

payments
- standing order and direct debit payments
- bank charges and interest
- unpaid cheques debited by the bank (ie cheques from creditors paid in by the business which have 'bounced' and are returned by the bank marked 'refer to drawer')

For each of these items, the cashier needs to check to see if they have been entered in the cash book; if not, they need to be recorded (provided that the bank has not made an error). If the bank has made an error, it must be notified as soon as possible and the incorrect transactions reversed by the bank in its own accounting records.

the bank reconciliation statement

This forms the link between the balances shown in the cash book and the bank statement:

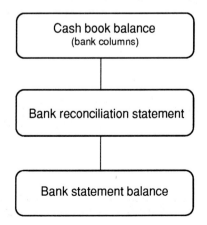

Upon receipt of a bank statement, reconciliation of the two balances is carried out in the following way:

- tick off the items that appear in *both* cash book and bank statement
- the unticked items on the bank statement are entered into the bank columns of the cash book to bring it up-to-date (provided none are errors made by the bank)
- the bank columns of the cash book are now balanced to find the revised figure
- the remaining unticked items from the cash book will be the timing differences
- the timing differences are used to prepare the bank reconciliation statement, which takes the following format (with example figures):

XYZ TRADING LTD
Bank Reconciliation Statement as at 31 October 19-1

		£	£
Balance at bank as per cash book			525
Add: cheques drawn, not yet recorded on the bank statement			
J Lewis	cheque no. 0012378	60	
ABC Ltd	cheque no. 0012392	100	
Eastern Oil Co	cheque no. 0012407	80	
			240
			765
Less: amounts paid in, not yet recorded on the bank statement		220	
		300	
			520
Balance at bank as per bank statement			245

Notes:

- The layout shown above starts from the cash book balance, and works towards the bank statement balance. A common variation of this layout is to start with the bank statement balance and to work towards the cash book balance (see page 232).

- If a bank overdraft is involved, brackets should be used around the numbers to indicate this for the cash book or bank statement balance. The timing differences are still added or deducted, as appropriate.

- Once the bank reconciliation statement agrees, it should be filed because it proves that the cash book (bank columns) and bank statement were reconciled at a particular date. If, next time it is prepared, it fails to agree, the previous statement is proof that reconciliation was reached at that time.

Case Study: Bank reconciliation statement

Situation

The cashier of Severn Trading Co has written up the firm's cash book for the month of February 19-2, as follows (the cheque number is shown against payments):

Cash Book

Dr.   Cr.

Date	Details	Cash	Bank	Date	Details	Cash	Bank
19-2		£	£	19-2		£	£
1 Feb.	Balances b/d	250.75	1,340.50	3 Feb.	Appleton Ltd 123456		675.25
7 Feb.	A Abbott		208.50	5 Feb.	Wages	58.60	
9 Feb.	Sales	145.25		12 Feb.	Rent 123457		125.00
13 Feb.	Sales	278.30		14 Feb.	Transfer to bank C	500.00	
14 Feb.	Transfer from cash C		500.00	17 Feb.	D Smith & Co 123458		421.80
20 Feb.	Sales	204.35		23 Feb.	Stationery	75.50	
21 Feb.	D Richards Ltd		162.30	24 Feb.	G Christie 123459		797.55
26 Feb.	Sales	353.95		27 Feb.	Transfer to bank C	500.00	
27 Feb.	Transfer from cash C		500.00	28 Feb.	Balances c/d	98.50	954.00
28 Feb.	P Paul Ltd		262.30				
		1,232.60	2,973.60			1,232.60	2,973.60
1 Mar.	Balances b/d	98.50	954.00				

The cash balance of £98.50 shown by the cash columns on 1 March has been agreed with the cash held in the firm's cash box. The bank statement for February 19-2 has just been received:

National Bank plc

Branch ..... Bartown ....

TITLE OF ACCOUNT .... Severn Trading Co ....

ACCOUNT NUMBER .... 67812318 ....

STATEMENT NUMBER 45

DATE	PARTICULARS	PAYMENTS	RECEIPTS	BALANCE
19-2		£	£	£
1 Feb.	Balance brought forward			1,340.50 CR
9 Feb.	Credit		208.50	1,549.00 CR
10 Feb.	Cheque no. 123456	675.25		873.75 CR
16 Feb.	Credit		500.00	1,373.75 CR
17 Feb.	Cheque no. 123457	125.00		1,248.75 CR
23 Reb.	Credit		162.30	1,411.05 CR
24 Feb.	Bank Giro Credit: J Jarvis Ltd		100.00	1,511.05 CR
26 Feb.	Cheque no. 123458	421.80		1,089.25 CR
26 Feb.	Direct Debit: A-Z Finance Co	150.00		939.25 CR
28 Feb.	Credit		500.00	1,439.25 CR
28 Feb.	Bank Charges	10.00		1,429.25 CR

Note that the bank statement is prepared from the bank's viewpoint: thus a credit balance shows that the customer is a creditor of the bank, ie the bank owes the balance to the customer. In the customer's own cash book, the bank is shown as a debit balance, ie an asset.

Solution

As the month-end balance at bank shown by the cash book, £954.00, is not the same as that shown by the bank statement, £1,429.25, it is necessary to prepare a bank reconciliation statement. The steps are:

1. Tick off the items that appear in *both* cash book and bank statement.

2. The unticked items on the bank statement are entered into the bank columns of the cash book to bring it up-to-date. These are:
   - *receipt*   24 Feb. Bank Giro Credit, J Jarvis Ltd £100.00
   - *payments* 26 Feb. Direct Debit, A-Z Finance Co £150.00
              28 Feb. Bank Charges, £10.00

   In double-entry book-keeping, the other part of the transaction will need to be recorded in the accounts, eg in J Jarvis Ltd's account in the sales ledger, etc.

3. The cash book is now balanced to find the revised balance:

Dr.		£		Cash Book (bank columns)		Cr. £
19-2			19-2			
	Balance b/d	954.00	26 Feb.	A-Z Finance Co		150.00
24 Feb.	J Jarvis Ltd	100.00	28 Feb.	Bank Charges		10.00
			28 Feb.	Balance c/d		894.00
		1,054.00				1,054.00
1 Mar.	Balance b/d	894.00				

4. The remaining unticked items from the cash book are used in the bank reconciliation statement:
   - *receipt*   28 Feb. P Paul Ltd £262.30
   - *payment* 24 Feb. G Christie (cheque no 123459) £797.55

   These items are timing differences, which should appear on next month's bank statement.

5. The bank reconciliation statement is now prepared, starting with the re-calculated balance of £894.00.

SEVERN TRADING CO
Bank Reconciliation Statement as at 28 February 19-2

	£
Balance at bank as per cash book	894.00
Add: cheque drawn, not yet recorded on the bank statement	797.55
	1,691.55
Less: amount paid in, not yet recorded on the bank statement	262.30
Balance at bank as per bank statement	1,429.25

With the above, a statement has been produced which starts with the amended balance from the cash book, and finishes with the bank statement balance, ie the two figures are reconciled.

Notes:
- *Cheque drawn, not yet recorded on the bank statement* is added back to the cash book balance because, until it is recorded by the bank, the cash book shows a lower balance than the bank statement.
- *Amounts paid in, not yet recorded on the bank statement* are deducted from the cash book balance because, until they are recorded by the bank, the cash book shows a higher balance than the bank statement.

preparing a bank reconciliation statement: a summary

In order to help you with the Student Activities at the end of the chapter, here is a step-by-step summary of the procedure. Reconciliation of the cash book balance with that shown on the bank statement should be carried out in the following way:

1.   From the bank columns of the cash book tick off, in both cash book and bank statement, the *receipts* that appear in both.

2.   From the bank columns of the cash book tick off, in both cash book and bank statement, the *payments* that appear in both.

3.   Identify the items that are unticked on the bank statement and enter them in the cash book on the debit or credit side, as appropriate. (If, however, the bank has made a mistake and debited or credited an amount in error, this should not be entered in the cash book, but should be notified to the bank for them to make the correction. The amount will need to be entered on the bank reconciliation statement: see section below, *dealing with unusual items on bank statements:* bank errors.)

4.   The bank columns of the cash book are now balanced to find the up-to-date balance. This new balance from the cash book forms the starting figure for the bank reconciliation statement.

5.   In the bank reconciliation statement *add* the unticked *payments* shown in the cash book – these will be cheques drawn, not yet recorded on the bank statement.

6.   In the bank reconciliation statement, *deduct* the unticked *receipts* shown in the cash book – these are amounts paid in, not yet recorded on the bank statement.

7.   The resultant money amount on the bank reconciliation statement is the balance at bank as per bank statement.

The layout which is often used for the bank reconciliation statement is that shown on the previous page. The layout starts with the cash book balance and finishes with the bank statement balance. However, there is no reason why it should not commence with the bank statement balance and finish with the cash book balance: with this layout it is necessary to *deduct* cheques drawn, not yet recorded on the bank statement, and to *add* amounts paid in, not yet recorded. The bank reconciliation statement of Severn Trading Co (see previous page) would then appear as:

	£
Balance at bank as per bank statement	1,429.25
Less: cheque drawn, not yet recorded on the bank statement	797.55
	631.70
Add: amount paid in, not yet recorded on the bank statement	262.30
Balance at bank as per cash book	894.00

dealing with unusual items on bank statements

out-of-date cheques
As noted above, these are cheques that are more than six months' old. Where a business has a number of out-of-date – or 'stale' – cheques which have not been debited on the bank statement, they will continue to appear on the bank reconciliation statement. As the bank will not pay these cheques, they can be written back in the cash book, ie debit cash book (and credit the other double-entry account involved).

stopped or cancelled cheques

* *Cheques received* will have been entered as a receipt in the cash book, paid into the bank and returned by the bank because the drawers have stopped them. They should be entered as payments in the cash book on the credit side (and debit the account of the drawer of each cheque, most probably in the sales ledger).

* *Cheques drawn by the business* will have been entered as payments in the cash book, and later stopped. They should be entered as receipts on the debit side (and credit the account of the payee of each cheque, most probably in the purchases ledger).

bank errors

Errors made by the bank can include:

* A cheque debited to the bank account which has not been drawn by the business – look for a cheque number on the bank statement that is different from the current cheque series: care, though, as it could be a cheque from an old cheque book.

* A bank giro credit (or other credit) shown on the bank statement for which the business is not the correct recipient. If in doubt, the bank will be able to give further details of the sender of the credit.

* Standing orders and direct debits paid at the wrong time or for the wrong amount. A copy of all standing order and direct debit mandates sent to the bank should be kept by the business in case reference needs to be made to them.

When an error is found, it should be queried immediately with the bank. The item and amount should not be entered in the firm's cash book until the issue has been resolved. If, in the meantime, a bank reconciliation statement is to be prepared, the bank error should be shown separately:

* if working from the cash book balance to the bank statement balance, deduct payments and add receipts that the bank has applied to the account incorrectly

* if working from the bank statement balance to the cash book balance, add payments and deduct receipts that the bank has applied to the account incorrectly

bank charges and interest

From time-to-time the bank will debit business customers' accounts with an amount for:

– service charges, ie the cost of operating the bank account
– interest, ie the borrowing cost when the business is overdrawn.

Often these charges and interest are debited either monthly or quarterly; some banks notify customers before debiting the customer's account. All banks publish details of their service charges: these usually comprise a set fee, eg £10 per month, plus a charge for each transaction passed through the account during the period, eg 60p per item.

Interest is usually calculated at a set number of percentage points above the bank's base rate, eg a business customer might borrow at '4 over base': with base rate at 10%, this means that overdraft interest is charged at 4 + 10 = 14%. Overdraft interest is calculated on a daily basis and is debited to the account along with the charges. Base rate varies from time-to-time: the current rate can be found in the financial pages of newspapers.

While bank charges and interest need to be recorded as payments in a firm's cash book, it makes sense to carry out a rough check to ensure that the correct amount has been debited to the bank statement.

reconciliation of opening cash book and bank statement balances

If you look back to the Case Study on page 230, you will see that both the cash book (bank columns) and the bank statement balance both *started* the month with the same balance: 1 February 19-2 £1,340.50. In reality, it is unlikely that the opening cash book and bank statement balances will be the same. It will be necessary, in these circumstances, to prepare an *opening* bank reconciliation statement in order to prove that there are no errors between cash book and bank statement at the start of the month. This is set out in the same format as the end-of-month bank reconciliation statement, and is best prepared immediately after ticking off the items that appear in both cash book and bank statement. The earliest cheques drawn and amounts paid in, but not yet recorded on the bank statement will comprise the opening bank reconciliation statement. Of course, where last month's bank reconciliation statement is available, such as in a business situation, there is no need to prepare an opening reconciliation.

importance of bank reconciliation statements

1. A bank reconciliation statement is important because, in its preparation, the transactions in the bank columns of the cash book are compared with those recorded on the bank statement. In this way, any errors in the cash book or bank statement will be found and can be corrected (or advised to the bank, if the bank statement is wrong).

2. The bank statement is an independent accounting record, therefore it will assist in deterring fraud by providing a means of verifying the cash book balance.

3. By writing the cash book up-to-date, the organisation has an amended figure for the bank balance to be shown in the trial balance.

4. Unpresented cheques over six months old – out-of-date cheques – can be identified and written back in the cash book (any cheque dated more than six months' ago will not be paid by the bank).

chapter summary

❏   A bank reconciliation statement is used to agree the balance shown by the bank columns of the cash book with that shown by the bank statement.

❏   Certain differences between the two are timing differences. The two main timing differences are:
   • cheques drawn, not yet recorded on the bank statement
   • amounts paid into the bank, not yet recorded on the bank statement
   These differences will be corrected by time and, most probably, will be recorded on the next bank statement.

❏   Certain differences appearing on the bank statement need to be entered in the cash book to bring it up-to-date. These include:

Receipts	• standing order and BACS receipts credited by the bank
	• bank giro credit amounts received by the bank
	• dividend amounts received by the bank
	• interest credited by the bank
Payments	• standing order and direct debit payments
	• bank charges and interest
	• unpaid cheques debited by the bank

❏   The bank reconciliation statement makes use of the timing differences.

❏   Once prepared, a bank reconciliation statement is proof that the cash book (bank columns) and the bank statement were agreed at a particular date.

Student Activities

17.1   The bank columns of Tom Reid's cash book for December 19-5 are as follows:

19-5	Receipts	£	19-5	Payments		£
1 Dec.	Balance b/d	280	9 Dec.	W Smith	345123	40
12 Dec.	P Jones	30	13 Dec.	Rent	345124	50
18 Dec.	H Homer	72	18 Dec.	Wages	345125	85
27 Dec.	J Hill	13	20 Dec.	B Kay	345126	20
			31 Dec.	Balance c/d		200
		395				395

He received his bank statement which showed the following transactions for December 19-5:

BANK STATEMENT

		Payments	Receipts	Balance
19-5		£	£	£
1 Dec.	Balance brought forward			280 CR
12 Dec.	Credit		30	310 CR
15 Dec.	Cheque no. 345123	40		270 CR
17 Dec.	Cheque no. 345124	50		220 CR
20 Dec.	Credit		72	292 CR
23 Dec.	Cheque no. 345125	85		207 CR

You are required to prepare a bank reconciliation statement to agree the cash book figure with the bank statement.

17.2   The bank columns of P Gerrard's cash book for January 19-1 are as follows:

19-1	Receipts	£	19-1	Payments		£
1 Jan.	Balance b/d	800.50	2 Jan.	A Arthur Ltd	001351	100.00
6 Jan.	J Baker	495.60	10 Jan.	C Curtis	001352	398.50
31 Jan.	G Shotton Ltd	335.75	12 Jan.	Donaldson & Co	001353	229.70
			13 Jan.	Bryant & Sons	001354	312.00
			23 Jan.	P Reid	001355	176.50
			31 Jan.	Balance c/d		415.15
		1,631.85				1,631.85

He received his bank statement which showed the following transactions for January 19-1:

BANK STATEMENT

		Payments	Receipts	Balance
19-1		£	£	£
1 Jan.	Balance brought forward			800.50 CR
5 Jan.	Cheque no. 001351	100.00		700.50 CR
6 Jan.	Credit		495.60	1,196.10 CR
13 Jan.	Bank Giro Credit: T K Supplies		716.50	1,912.60 CR
18 Jan.	Cheque no. 001352	398.50		1,514.10 CR
23 Jan.	Direct Debit: Omni Finance Co Ltd	207.95		1,306.15 CR
24 Jan.	Cheque no. 001353	229.70		1,076.45 CR

You are required to:
(a)   write the cash book up-to-date at 31 January 19-1
(b)   prepare a bank reconciliation statement at 31 January 19-1

17.3 The bank columns of Jane Doyle's cash book for May 19-6 are as follows:

19-6	Receipts	£	19-6	Payments		£
1 May	Balance b/d	300	2 May	P Stone	867714	28
7 May	Cash	162	14 May	Alpha Ltd	867715	50
16 May	C Brewster	89	29 May	E Deakin	867716	110
24 May	Cash	60				
31 May	Cash	40				

She received her bank statement which showed the following transactions for May 19-6:

BANK STATEMENT

		Payments	Receipts	Balance
19-6		£	£	£
1 May	Balance brought forward			326 CR
1 May	Credit		54	380 CR
4 May	Cheque no. 867714	28		352 CR
5 May	Cheque no. 867713	80		272 CR
7 May	Credit		162	434 CR
17 May	Standing order: A-Z Insurance Co	25		409 CR
17 May	Credit		89	498 CR
18 May	Cheque no. 867715	50		448 CR
25 May	Credit		60	508 CR
31 May	Bank Charges	10		498 CR

You are required to:

(a) write the cash book up-to-date at 31 May 19-6

(b) prepare an opening bank reconciliation statement at 1 May 19-6

(c) prepare a bank reconciliation statement at 31 May 19-6

17.4 On 28 February 19-1 the bank column of A Wilson's cash book showed that there was £600 in the bank.

A bank statement for February 19-1 showed that the following items had not been entered in the cash book:

- the sum of £1,500 received from P Jones by bank giro credit
- the transfer of £1,000 from Wilson's private bank deposit account into his business bank account
- bank charges £25

When the bank statement was further checked against the cash book the following items were discovered:

- cheques issued in favour of creditors totalling £5,300 had not yet gone through the bank account
- cash and cheques £4,100 had been entered in the cash book but not yet credited by the bank

You are required to:

(a) write the cash book up-to-date at 28 February 19-1

(b) prepare a bank reconciliation statement at 28 February 19-1 which shows the balance appearing on the bank statement

17.5 Wyvern Wholesalers requires the bank statement and cash book balances (bank columns) to be reconciled. You are given the following information as at 30 April 19-3:

- the bank columns of the cash book show a balance of £900 in the bank
- cheques for £120, £150 and £40 have been sent out in payment to various suppliers but have not yet been paid into the bank by those suppliers; they are recorded in the cash book
- a direct debit payment of £45 has been recorded by the bank, but has not yet been entered in the cash book
- a cheque for £500 has been recorded as a receipt in the cash book, but has not yet been paid into the bank account
- bank charges amounting to £20 appear on the bank statement, but have not yet been entered in the cash book
- a bank giro credit from a customer for £150 appears on the bank statement, but has not yet been entered in the cash book
- the bank statement shows a closing bank balance of £795 CR.

You are required to:
(a)   write the cash book up-to-date at 30 April 19-3
(b)   prepare a bank reconciliation statement at 30 April 19-3

17.6 You work in the office of H James (Precision Engineering) Ltd. One of your tasks at the end of each month is to reconcile the bank columns of the company's cash book with the bank statement. As you will be away on holiday over the next month-end, the office manager has asked you to write clear instructions in the form of a memo for the person who is to undertake this task in your absence.

ASSIGNMENT 6

Cash book and bank reconciliation: Speciality Paints Ltd

SITUATION

You work as a trainee in the office of Speciality Paints Ltd, a company which buys special types of paints and other finishes from the manufacturers and sells them in your area to local businesses. This week the cashier, who is responsible for keeping the company's cash book is away on holiday. You have been asked to carry out her work for the week commencing 8 March 19-2.

At the start of the week the cash book has a balance at bank of £802.50, and cash in hand of £120.68. The following are the transactions to be entered in the cash book for the week:

Cheques received from debtors
8 Mar.   £178.55 from Wyvern County Council, after deducting £2.85 cash discount to which the debtor is entitled
10 Mar.   £451.20 from J Jones & Co
12 Mar.   £321.15 from Building Supplies Ltd, after deducting £5.25 cash discount to which the debtor is entitled

Note: all cheques received are banked on the day of receipt.

Cheques drawn
8 Mar.   Cheque no. 123451 for £210.50, payee ITI Paint Division Ltd, a creditor, after deducting £4.95 cash discount
9 Mar.   Cheque no. 123452 for £100.00, payee Cash (the cash was drawn for use in the business)
9 Mar.   Cheque no. 123453 for £169.75, payee BT (payment of the telephone bill*)
10 Mar.   Cheque no. 123454 for £394.20, payee Wages
11 Mar.   Cheque no. 123455 for £129.45, payee Paint Manufacturing Co Ltd, a creditor, after deducting £3.30 cash discount

* Assume that BT is a creditor of Speciality Paints Ltd and, therefore, that VAT on the telephone bill has already been recorded in the accounts.

Cash received from debtors
9 Mar.   £27.50 from T Lewis
12 Mar.   £28.25 from H Simms, after deducting £0.28 cash discount to which he is entitled

Cash paid
11 Mar.   £88.50 for casual labour

At the end of the week, the following bank statement is received:

National Bank plc

Branch Mereford

TITLE OF ACCOUNT Speciality Paints Ltd

ACCOUNT NUMBER 12345678

STATEMENT NUMBER 45

DATE	PARTICULARS	PAYMENTS	RECEIPTS	BALANCE
19-2		£	£	£
8 Mar.	Balance brought forward			967.00 CR
8 Mar.	Cheque		178.55	1,145.55 CR
9 Mar.	123450	164.50		981.05 CR
9 Mar.	123452	100.00		881.05 CR
9 Mar.	Standing order: Wyvern Hire Purchase Co Ltd	85.50		795.55 CR
10 Mar.	123454	394.20		401.35 CR
10 Mar.	Cheque		451.20	852.55 CR
10 Mar.	Bank giro credit:Johnson Bros		125.50	978.05 CR
11 Mar.	123451	210.50		767.55 CR
11 Mar.	874111	25.00		742.55 CR
12 Mar.	Bank charges	12.50		730.05 CR
12 Mar.	Balance carried forward			730.05 CR

STUDENT TASKS

1. Rule up a cash book with columns for discount, cash and bank.

2. Enter the transactions for the week (listed on the previous page).

3. Using the bank statement, write the cash book (bank columns) up-to-date with any items appearing on the bank statement that need to be recorded in the cash book.

4. Balance the cash book at 12 March 19-2, and show the discount accounts as they will appear in the firm's general ledger.

5. Prepare bank reconciliation statements at:
   - 8 March 19-2 (in order to agree the opening cash book and bank statement balances)
   - 12 March 19-2

6. Write
   - an explanation of how you would check that the bank charges are correctly calculated.
   - a memorandum to the office manager regarding any matter that you consider should be queried with the bank.

18 Stock control

Stock is a valuable asset held by a business. Businesses purchase *stock* for two purposes:

- to buy in raw materials or goods *for resale* – items which are processed or used to provide income and profit for the business, eg goods on a shop's shelves, components on the factory production line, sheep in a farmer's field

- to provide items of stationery and equipment which are *consumed within the business,* eg paper, biros, paperclips, staplers, computer disks

Both types of stock have to be purchased. Larger businesses will operate a Purchasing Department with buyers who negotiate the best possible deals, while in smaller businesses the responsibility usually falls on an individual.

Stock also has to be stored and controlled. A business needs to know *how much* stock it has at any one time, and it needs to ensure that the stock is stored securely so that it is not pilfered. A business also needs to know *when* stock needs to be re-ordered, and *how much* needs to be ordered. You will know how frustrating it is when a shop runs out of an item that you want.

In this chapter we will concentrate on stock that is *consumed* within a business, eg stationery. It should be noted that the principles we will outline apply equally to stock held for resale. Items used up within a business are usually controlled by a member of staff and kept under lock and key in a cupboard or a stockroom. A term you will come across when dealing with stock is 'inventory.' An inventory is a detailed list of the stock items held by an organisation.

We will look in detail at:

- ordering stock from the storeroom by means of a requisition form

- the recording of the receipt and issue of items of stock from the stockroom on stock record cards

- the maintenance of suitable levels of stock

- accepting incoming deliveries of stock and dealing with the paperwork involved

- counting the stock by means of a stock check (also known as a stock take)

- agreeing (reconciling) your stock check with the stock records

- ensuring the security of stock

- keeping stock records on a computer

requisition form - ordering stock for office use

If you work in an office, your first encounter with office stock will probably be the need to order an item - such as copying paper – which has either run out, or has nearly run out. The normal office procedure is for the person requiring the stock to complete a *requisition form*, an example of which is illustrated below. The person ordering the paper is Lou Jones and the organisation is Wyvern (Office Products) Ltd.

REQUISITION FORM

From ...*Lou Jones*...........................   No. ...*007*.........

Dept ...*Administration*...................

Quantity	Description	Ref. No.
10	reams photocopying paper	P1026

Signed .....*L. Jones*............... Authorised ....Date.........................

The form is completed with the following details
- the name of the person ordering the stock
- the name of the department or section in which that person works
- a reference number for the order
- the quantity of the stock required
- the stock item and reference number (the number shown in the catalogue – see Appendix 3)
- the signature of the person ordering the stock

The person requiring the stock will obtain the supervisor's authorisation (signature) and the form will then be dated and forwarded to the person handling stock issue – possibly a full time storekeeper. The stock will then be sent to the person who requested it.

The storekeeper will need to record the transaction, *either*
- by entering the details on a stock record card (if a manual recording system is used), *or*
- by entering the details onto a computer terminal (if the stock records are computerised)

We will now examine in detail the records used to record items of stock held. We will concentrate on the manual method - based on the *stock record card*. Computerised stock control works on the same principles as the manual system.

stock records

A well organised business will have a stock control section where staff keep records of all stock held on individual *stock record cards*. The stock held may either be for resale by the business, or may be for internal issue (as discussed in this Chapter). A separate card is made out for each stock item. When articles are issued (or sold), the number of items taken out of stock is deducted from the total on the stock card, and when new supplies are received, these are added to the total. A typical stock record card is shown below. The stock item is A4 photocopying paper which is used within the business, Wyvern (Office Products) Ltd., and also sold to its customers. As yet there is no stock entered on the card.

STOCK RECORD CARD

Stock Description A4 white photocopying paper

Stock units ..... reams

Stock Ref. No. P1026

Location row A, bin 6

Minimum 1,500 reams

Maximum 10,000 reams

Re-order level 4,500 reams

Re-order quantity 5,000 reams

DATE	GOODS RECEIVED		GOODS ISSUED		BALANCE
	Reference	Quantity	Reference	Quantity	

• **stock description**   refers to the description of the stock, eg photocopying paper

• **stock units**   refers to how the stock is stored or packed, eg photocopying paper would be packed in reams (packets of 500 sheets);

• **stock reference no.**   refers to the identification number allocated to the stock by the business - it will be found on the stock inventory and on the catalogue and price list

• **location**   refers to where the stock can be found in the stores, eg row A, bin 6 refers to the location in the storeroom or warehouse

• **minimum**   is the minimum level of the number of items to be kept in stock

• **maximum**   is the maximum level of the number of items to be kept in stock

• **re-order level**   is the level to which the stock falls before the business reorders more items

- **re-order quantity**   is the amount which is normally re-ordered

- **goods received**   the two columns record the purchase order reference and the quantity of items received

- **goods issued**   the two columns record the requisition reference (see section below) and the number of items issued

- **balance**   is the number of items which remain in stock

stock levels

Businesses normally set the following stock levels, which are indicated on the stock record cards:
- minimum stock level
- maximum stock level
- re-order level

The person responsible for setting stock levels must therefore ensure that:
- the minimum level is not so low that the business runs out of that item of stock
- the maximum level is not so high that too much money is tied up in stock

minimum stock level
Stock should not be allowed to fall below this level. The setting of this level acts as a safeguard against stock falling to a dangerously low level following delays or disruptions of deliveries from suppliers.

maximum stock level
This is a 'ceiling' stock level to prevent overstocking. It will be fixed bearing in mind the cost to the company of acquiring the stock, the space available for storage, and the expected demand.

re-order level
Re-order level is the level to which stock falls before an order for further stock is placed. This level is normally higher than the minimum level and is calculated so that the replacement order will be delivered before the stock balance has reached the minimum level. This level is normally calculated as follows:

*average daily issue of stock x number of days for delivery from supplier **plus** the minimum stock level*

for example,

        A4, white photocopying paper
        average daily issue   300 reams
        normal delivery   10 days
        minimum stock   1,500 reams
        maximum stock   10,000 reams

        Re-order level = 300 (daily issue) x 10 (number of days delivery) + 1,500 (minimum stock)
        = 300 x 10 + 1,500
        = 3,000 + 1,500
        = 4,500 reams

When the balance of stock reduces to 4,500 reams, a purchase order is forwarded to the suppliers of the paper. When the paper arrives (10 days later) the number of reams and the Purchase Order no. are entered on the Stock Record Card.

checking incoming deliveries of stock

Suppose that the storekeeper needs to order some stock; the photocopying paper may, for instance, have reached the reorder level of 4,500 reams.   An order will have to be placed with the organisation's supplier for the normal reorder quantity – in this case 5,000 reams.   The procedure for this will vary from organisation to organisation; it will often be the responsibility of a Purchasing Department or section.   When the items – eg reams of paper – are eventually delivered, they will be accompanied by a delivery note.   The example illustrated below will accompany the delivery of photocopying paper ordered by Wyvern (Office Products) Ltd.

━━━━━━ DELIVERY NOTE ━━━━━━

Stourford Office Supplies
Unit 12, Avon Industrial Estate, Stourford SF5 6TD
Tel 0807 765434 Fax 0807 765123

Wyvern (Office Products) Ltd 12, Lower Hyde Street Mereford MR1 2JF	Delivery Note No 27648 Date 9 April 19-9 Your Order No 17901 Delivery Van Delivery

product code	quantity	description
3564749	5,000 reams	white photocopying paper

received
signature... name (capitals)...

date...

---

delivery note
The details on the delivery note, which the van driver will normally give to you, will include
• the *supplier's* reference number for the delivery note
• the date of issue
• *your* order number
• the method of delivery
• the description and quantity of the goods together with the *supplier's* product code
• a section for you to sign when you have checked the consignment

checking the consignment against the delivery note
You will need to check the incoming goods carefully:
• check the condition of the goods
• check that the right goods have been delivered
• check that the right quantity of goods have been delivered

Only when you are satisfied on all these points should you sign and write your name in capital leters on the delivery note.   The driver will normally hand you one copy and keep one copy.   If there are any discrepancies (short delivery, wrong goods) they should be noted on the delivery note *before you sign it* so that both the supplier and your organisation will know that there is a problem.   Lastly - *ensure that the delivery note is passed to the person responsible for ordering the goods* - it will need to be checked against the original order and the invoice (demand for payment) when it is received.

worked example: Wyvern (Office Products) Ltd.

In this case study we look at the stock records relating to reams of A4 white phoptocopying paper in the warehouse of Wyvern (Office Products) Ltd. This organisation, as we saw earlier, sells stationery to its customers and also issues it internally when requisition forms are issued within the organisation. The object of the Case Study is to show you how the stock cards are updated for

- requisitions
- receipt of orders

On 1 April 19-9, Wyvern's stock records indicate that the company has a stock balance of 3,000 reams of A4 photocopying paper. Assuming that Wyvern has just started a new stock record card for this paper, the stock record card would appear as follows:

STOCK RECORD CARD

Stock Description A4 white photocopying paper

Stock units reams

Stock Ref. No. P1026

Location row A, bin 6

Minimum 1,500 reams

Maximum 10,000 reams

Re-order level 4,500 reams

Re-order quantity 5,000 reams

DATE	GOODS RECEIVED		GOODS ISSUED		BALANCE
	Reference	Quantity	Reference	Quantity	
19-9 1 Apr.					3,000

requisitions

During the first week of April the stores have received the following requisitions for this paper

2 April	Requisition no. 101	200 reams
4 April	Requisition no. 104	300 reams
5 April	Requisition no. 116	400 reams
6 April	Requisition no. 121	250 reams

How will these requisitions be recorded on the stock record card? The stock record card is illustrated on the next page. Note that

- the Balance column on the right is the running total of the number of reams held by the business
- the Reference under 'Goods Issued' is the requisition number in each case

STOCK RECORD CARD

Stock Description ..A4 white photocopying paper...

Stock units ....reams..........................

Stock Ref. No. ......P1026.........................

Location ....row A, bin 6.......................

Minimum ....1,500 reams.............

Maximum ....10,000 reams..............

Re-order level ....4,500 reams.............

Re-order quantity ..5,000 reams..........

DATE	GOODS RECEIVED		GOODS ISSUED		BALANCE
	Reference	Quantity	Reference	Quantity	
19-9					
1 Apr.					3,000
2 Apr.			REQ 101	200	2,800
4 Apr.			REQ 104	300	2,500
5 Apr.			REQ 116	400	2,100
6 Apr.			REQ 121	250	1,850

receipt of the stock order

Wyvern (Office Products) Ltd. have previously placed an order with their supplier, Stourford Office Supplies Ltd., for 5,000 reams of this paper (the standard re-order quantity). This order is delivered to the warehouse on 9 April. The Purchase Order Number is 17901.

The stock record card will be amended as follows:

STOCK RECORD CARD

Stock Description ..A4 white photocopying paper...

Stock units ....reams..........................

Stock Ref. No. ......P1026.........................

Location ....row A, bin 6.......................

Minimum ....1 500 reams.............

Maximum ....10 000 reams..............

Re-order level ....4 500 reams.............

Re-order quantity ...5 000 reams..........

DATE	GOODS RECEIVED		GOODS ISSUED		BALANCE
	Reference	Quantity	Reference	Quantity	
19-9					
1 Apr.					3,000
2 Apr.			REQ 101	200	2,800
4 Apr.			REQ 104	300	2,500
5 Apr.			REQ 116	400	2,100
6 Apr.			REQ 121	250	1,850
9 Apr.	Purchase Order 17901	5,000			6,850

stock checks and inventory reconciliation

the stock inventory

A business will regularly (often twice yearly) check that the numbers of items of stock held in the storeroom or warehouse is the same as the numbers recorded on the stock record cards. The way to check the stock is to count it - this is known as a *stock check* or *stock take*. If you have worked in a shop you may well be familiar with the periodic counting of the items on the shelves. The numbers of items actually held is recorded on a *stock list* by the person doing the stock check. The stock list is also known as a *stock inventory*. An extract from a stock inventory is illustrated below; it shows the A4 paper referred to in the case study. The list will, of course, contain many items when the stock take has been completed.

stock inventory as at 31 December 19-9 checker H Ramsay						
product code	item description	location	unit size	units counted	stock card balance	discrepancy
P1026	A4 white photocopying paper	A6	ream	6,850	6,850	

the inventory reconciliation

The object of the stock check is to see if the stock record cards accurately represent the level of stock held. The two columns on the stock inventory – 'units counted' and 'stock card balance' enable this comparison to be carried out; the process is known as an *inventory reconciliation*. It is an important process because

- an accurate stock figure can then be given to the accountants so that they can value the stock
- it will highlight any discrepancies which can then be investigated

Discrepancies should be noted in the far right hand column of the stock inventory.

dealing with discrepancies

Why should there be discrepancies, and what action should you take? Differences can occur for a number of reasons:

- someone has made a mistake on the stock record card - failed to record a stock movement or failed to calculate the balance correctly
- someone has been helping themselves to the stock without authorisation
- damaged stock has been disposed of without any record having been made
- stock has been stolen

If you find a discrepancy you should

- correct the error on the stock record card – e. g. write on the next available line '31 December Stock take - amended balance 6,800 ' if, for instance, you find that there are 6,800 reams of copy paper rather than the 6,850 shown in the balance column of the stock record card
- notify your supervisor and any other people who may need to know, eg your storekeeper and your auditors (the accountants who will check your stock taking method and figures)

dealing with damaged and obsolete stock

When you check the stock you may find damaged stock and obsolete stock:

- *damaged stock* can include broken items (eg torn paper) or soiled items (eg stained paper)
- *obsolete stock* can include computer ribbons or disks which are unusable because you may have new machines, or headed notepaper which is printed with a telephone number which has changed

Whatever the circumstances, the stock no longer has any use and will have to be thrown away or used for some other purpose (e.g. scrap paper). The important point is that you will have to amend your stock records for the damaged or obsolete stock. This will involve:

- deducting the stock items from the stock inventory and making a suitable comment in the right-hand comments column (see illustration below)
- amending the stock record card to show a reduced balance; the entry might read as follows: '31 December Stock Take - 50 reams damaged - amended balance 6,800'

stock inventory as at 31 December 199−		checker *H Ramsay*				
product code	item description	location	unit size	units counted	stock card balance	discrepancy
P1026	A4 white photocopying paper	A6	ream	6,800	6,850	50 reams damaged

safety and security of stock

It is important to ensure that stock is stored safely and securely.

safety

Safety in the workplace is one of the employer's duties, and maintenance of safety instructions is the responsibility of the employee. You should observe the following precautions:

- no smoking!
- inflammable materials such as thinners should be stored in sealed containers and away from heat
- heavy items should be stored on the lower shelves
- use a safe stepladder or stool when taking down items from high shelves
- store the stock neatly and do not leave packing materials lying around
- issue the old stock before the new stock to avoid wear and tear - place new stock at the *back* of the shelf on receipt from the suppliers - this process is known as FIFO (first in, first out)

security

Stock may be pilfered if left unattended, and therefore security in the storeroom is essential:

- the storeroom should be kept locked and access to the keys restricted
- issue of stock should be controlled by nominated staff
- stock should only be issued on receipt of a properly authorised requisition form
- the stock record cards should be updated on each issue or receipt of stock

stock records on the computer

advantages of computer records

We have described the maintenance of stock records in terms of *manual* records - stock record cards and stock inventories. Many organisations use computers to maintain stock records. The advantages of using a computer are well known: they are accurate, they will store large amounts of information and can provide the management of an organisation with information and reports in a short space of time. Here are some of the advantages of computerised stock control:

- automatic updating of stock balance levels
- printouts and display of the current stock levels
- indication of when minimum, maximum or re-order levels are reached
- automatic production, in some cases, of a Purchase Order for re-order of stock
- valuation of stock held
- printouts of suppliers' names and addresses

how the system works

The person dealing with the receipt and issue of stock will have access to a computer terminal. All the details that would normally be written on a stock record card by hand are input into the computer. When the time comes for a stock check, the computer will print out an inventory list with the balances of all the stock items; the person counting the stock will then have to reconcile the actual quantity with the computer total. If there is a discrepancy it will have to be reported in the normal way, and the computer records adjusted, just as the stock record cards would be amended in a manual system.

bar codes

Some larger organisations operate their stock control system by means of bar codes which identify individual stock items. You will no doubt be familiar with the bar code system operated by supermarkets and other retailers: each item is 'read' with a special pen at the cash till. The pen identifies the stock item by its bar code and relays the information through the cash till to the computer which indicates what the correct selling price is. There is a bar code on the back of this book. If you bought the book at a larger bookshop you may have seen them read the code with a special pen at the checkout. If enough copies of the book are sold by the bookseller, and the re-order level is reached, the bookshop's computerised stock control system will automatically send out an order to Osborne Books (the publisher) for a fresh supply of books.

chapter summary

❑ Businesses order stock for resale and also for consumption within the business.

❑ Stock is ordered by means of a stock requisition form.

❑ The level of stock is recorded on a stock record card which also indicates
- the level to which stock should fall at which fresh stock should be ordered
- the amount of stock that should be re-ordered

❑ Incoming deliveries of stock should be checked carefully against the delivery note.

❑ The stock levels are monitored regularly by means of a stock check, and any discrepancies are noted and reported.

❑ Stock must be kept safely and securely.

❑ Stock records are increasingly being maintained on computer, a process aided by the bar-coding of stock items.

✍ Student Activities

18.1 (a) A form used for ordering stock for use in an office is a   ....

(b) Stock levels and movements are recorded on a   ....

(c) Goods arriving at the organisation will be accompanied by a ....

(d) A person carrying out a stock check will record the stock on an ....

(e) The process of comparing stock on the shelves with stock in the records is known as   ....

Choose from: • delivery note • requisition form • stock record card • inventory list
• inventory reconciliation

18.2 Design a notice to be displayed in your stock storage area setting out the safety precautions to be observed when storing and handling stock.

18.3 Calculate the maximum and minimum stock levels from the following information:
- total stock should never exceed 40 days' usage
- daily usage 4 units
- 12 days' stock should always be held

18.4 Calculate, for stock items D and E, the re-order stock level and the re-order quantity to replenish stock levels to the maximum level, from the following information:
- daily usage of D = 3 units, of E = 4 units
- total stock should never exceed 95 days' usage
- 10 days' stock should always be held
- there is space available in the store for 350 units of each item of stock
- normal delivery time is 7 days

18.5
(a)   Prepare a stock record card from the following information:
- *product:* A4 Yellow Card, code A4/Y3, location row 7, bin 5
- *units:* reams
- *maximum stock:* 35 days' usage
- *daily usage:* 3 units
- *normal delivery time:* 10 days
- *minimum stock:* 12 days' stock
- *opening balance on 1 May 19-2:* 84 reams

(b)   Calculate maximum, minimum and re-order levels of stock, together with re-order quantity (to replenish stock to the maximum level)

(c)   Bearing these figures in mind, enter the following requisitions on the stock record card, remembering to re-order when necessary and to show the order on the card arriving ten days later (Purchase order 126):

2 May	Requisition 184	18 reams
3 May	Requisition 187	20 reams
10 May	Requisition 188	10 reams
16 May	Requisition 394	20 reams
20 May	Requisition 401	11 reams
22 May	Requisition 422	6 reams

18.6 You work for Martley Machine Rental Ltd.; you receive a delivery of stock to the storeroom. It is accompanied by a delivery note which was signed by the person receiving the goods from the van driver. You now check the delivery note (illustrated below) against the original purchase order (also illustrated below) and notice some discrepancies. You are to

(a) make a list of the discrepancies

(b) write a letter to the supplier pointing out the problems and asking for the correct stock

Note: it would be normal for faulty or incorrect goods to be returned to the supplier.

PURCHASE ORDER
MARTLEY MACHINE RENTAL LTD
67 Broadgreen Road
Martley MR6 7TR
Tel 090655 6576 Fax 090655 6342

Stourford Office Supplies Unit 12 Avon Industrial Estate Stourford SF5 6TD	No Date Delivery	47700 13 March 19-9 to above address

catalogue	quantity	description
3564749	15 reams	100gsm white Supalaser paper
5366788	150	Fax roll FR1-396
5526754	100 boxes	Banmate 2000 fine point ball point pens
5423786	15	Mercury staplers, colour black

authorised signature......*C J Farmer*....................................... date......*13 March 19-9*...............

━━ DELIVERY NOTE ━━
Stourford Office Supplies
Unit 12, Avon Industrial Estate, Stourford SF5 6TD
Tel 0807 765434 Fax 0807 765123

Martley Machine Rental Ltd 67 Broadgreen Road Martley MR6 7TR	Delivery Note No Date Your Order No Delivery	26754 26 March 19-9 47700 Van Delivery

product code	quantity	description
3564749	50 reams	100 gsm white Supalaser paper
5366789	150	Fax roll FR1-399
5526754	100	Banmate 2000 fine point ball point pens
5423788	15	Mercury staplers, colour red

received
signature...name (capitals)...

date...

18.7   You are doing a stock check of items in the office stationery store. Your stock record cards show the following balances:

item	units	location	product code
white copy paper	65 reams	A6	P4252
headed notepaper	10 reams	A7	E6272
plain DL envelopes	10 boxes of 1000	A8	E7262
window DL envelopes	7 boxes of 1000	A9	E9161
ball point pens - black	20 boxes of 50	B1	P9712
ball point pens - red	5 boxes of 50	B2	P8161
pencils HB	10 boxes of 50	B3	P6173
correction fluid	76 bottles	C1	T6694
thinner	25 bottles	C2	T6695
notepads	125	C3	P4256

You note the following on your stock count:

white copy paper	63 reams OK, 2 reams damp and wrinkled
headed notepaper	10 reams,
	but 2 reams out of date - with old company name
plain DL envelopes	8 boxes of 1000, 2 boxes of 800
window DL envelopes	7 boxes of 1000
ball point pens - black	18 boxes of 50 - 2 boxes missing
ball point pens - red	5 boxes of 50
pencils HB	10 boxes of 50
correction fluid	75 bottles
thinner	25 bottles
notepads	127

(a)   You are to prepare an inventory list, showing any discrepancies, using the following format (use your own name as checker and today's date).

stock inventory as at .... **checker** ....

product code	item description	location	unit size	units counted	stock card balance	discrepancy

(b)   State what action you would take when you have noted any discrepancies on the stock inventory.

19 Computer accounting

Many small businesses and almost all large businesses use computers to handle their accounting records.

Computers are ideal where there are large quantities of routine data; common uses in accounting are:
- preparing invoices to be sent out to customers
- keeping the sales ledger (debtors' accounts) up-to-date
- keeping the purchases ledger (creditors' accounts) up-to-date
- stock control
- recording receipts and payments
- payroll, ie handling the information on wages and salaries of employees

In addition to handling routine data, computers are able to print out management reports, including the production of a trial balance and financial statements. These give information on various aspects of the business, and should enable the business to be run more efficiently.

computer accounting programs

For accounting purposes there are basically two types of accounting programs: the simple *cash trader* program, and the *complete ledger* system.

cash trader programs
These simple systems assume that the business keeps only a cash book, and needs to keep track of money received and money spent, and to analyse the expenditure. Such programs are inexpensive and are suitable for small businesses which deal on a cash-only basis.

complete ledger systems
These are more suitable for the larger business, and common applications include:
- invoicing
- sales ledger (ie the debtors' accounts)
- purchases ledger (ie the creditors' accounts)
- nominal ledger
- stock control
- payroll

Often, such programs for business record keeping are fully integrated so that a business transaction can be recorded in a number of different records at the same time. For example, when an invoice is prepared for the sale of goods, an integrated program will reduce the stock of goods held and will record, in the sales ledger, that an increased amount is now owed by the debtor concerned.

Integrated programs include a *nominal ledger* (also known as general ledger) which brings together the totals from the other records, and can also be used to record fixed assets and expenses, and produce a trial balance and other financial statements. The nominal ledger also usually includes the cash book. Fig. 19.1 shows the various programs that can be brought together in an integrated system.

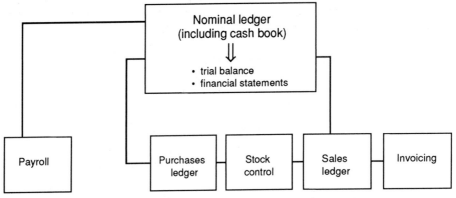

Fig. 19.1 An integrated computer accounting system

computer accounting in practice

The rest of this chapter looks at the practical application of computers to:

- sales ledger
- purchases ledger
- nominal (general) ledger

While the chapter follows the use of Sage™ Book-keeping and Accounting programs, most other accounting programs designed for use with personal computers operate in a similar way.

To work through this chapter you will need:

- a personal computer with either twin floppy disk drives, or a hard disk drive
- a printer
- a computer accounting program, such as Sage 'Book-keeper', 'Accountant', 'Accountant Plus', or 'Financial Controller'

In order to demonstrate the use of computer accounting, we will use the book-keeping transactions of a new business called Computer Shop Ltd.

After each set of transactions, the trial balance is given so that you can check the accuracy of your work as you make progress.

getting started

Firstly you will need to have configured the accounting program to suit the type of computer being used, following the instructions in the manual. When this has been done, the procedures are as follows:

Twin floppy disk drive
- switch on the computer and printer
- insert the operating system disk in the 'A' drive (usually on the left-hand side); press any key
- if necessary, key in the date and time
- the A prompt (A>) will now be showing
- remove the operating system disk and insert the program disk in the 'A' drive, and your own data disk (configured to suit your computer) in the 'B' drive
- key in SAGE (in upper or lower case) and press return

Hard disk drive
- switch on the computer and printer
- at the C prompt (C >) key in SAGE (in upper or lower case) and press return

The business name and address (or College name and address) will appear on the screen. Press return. The date will now appear and can be altered now if you wish. Press return and key in the password: this is set initially as LETMEIN. Press return to take you to the main menu, (other choices may appear, depending on the program you are running.

```
SALES LEDGER
PURCHASE LEDGER
NOMINAL LEDGER
UTILITIES
QUIT
```

Important note: To quit the program, always return to this menu and select [Quit]: by doing this the data files will be correctly updated. Never quit by just switching off or resetting the computer.

situation

Computer Shop Ltd is a new business which has just been set up by its owner, Richard Brown. The business operates from premises in St Nicholas Street, Mereford, where Richard sells computer hardware and software. He buys his stocks of hardware and software on credit terms from a number of suppliers. The business is registered for Value Added Tax.

Richard Brown intends that his main customers are to be the business community in Mereford. To these he must offer credit terms. In order to seek business, he has recently visited a number of firms and schools in the area offering the services of his company on credit terms of a 30 day payment period. A number of these have asked him to open an account for them.

You have just been appointed as an assistant in the shop and Richard Brown has asked you to set up an accounting system using the computer hardware and accounting software available to you.

purchases ledger

Details of suppliers
Richard Brown has arranged to purchase hardware and software on credit from the following:

Supplier's name and address	For your use – account number or short name*
Axis Supplies Ltd Unit 21 Ringway Trading Estate Barchester BR2 9JT	101 or AXIS
Bell Computers Ltd The Old Foundry Clapton-on-Sea CL9 8AJ	102 or BELL

* Note: With the Sage programs, any combination of up to six numbers and/or letters – selected by the user – identify each purchases ledger (and sales ledger) account.

Computer Supplies Ltd 35-40 Granbury Road Leeton LT1 8RZ	103 or COMP
Granta Trading Co Ltd Unit 6 Camside Industrial Estate Cambury CB5 2AQ	104 or GRANTA
Kingsway Technical Ltd 126 The Parade Kingsway Denham DM3 9PQ	105 or KINGS
Pratt and Co Ltd 28 Avon Lane Eveshore MR10 9HP	106 or PRATT

opening accounts in the purchases ledger

- From the main menu, select [Purchase Ledger]; press return.

- From the purchase ledger menu, select [Supplier Details], press return.

- The program will ask you for an account reference – for the first account, key in either the account number, 101, or the short name, AXIS, and press return. (If the account reference has already been used, details of the account will show on the screen.) Press return.

- The program will ask "Is this a new account: No Yes". The cursor will be positioned over the word No; move the cursor to the word Yes by pressing the [→] key, and then press return.

- Now enter the name and address of the supplier. If you make any errors use the arrow keys to move up or down the screen, and make the corrections.

- Ignore other details that could be completed.

- When all the details of the first account have been entered on screen, press [ESC]. The program now asks "Do you want to: Post Edit Abandon" – notice that the cursor is already positioned over Post, which is the default, ie the answer the computer expects. If the details are correct, simply press return and the data files will be updated.

- Repeat the process for the other supplier accounts.

- Return to the main menu by pressing [ESC] twice.

purchases account in the nominal ledger

As Richard Brown's business buys computer hardware and software, it is appropriate to open separate purchases accounts in the nominal ledger for each of these aspects of his business.

Your data disk will already include a standard layout for nominal ledger, with accounts already numbered. The purchases accounts are 5000, 5001, 5002, 5003: we will use the first two numbers for hardware purchases and software purchases respectively. However, we need to name them as such.

- From the main menu, select [Nominal Ledger].

- From the nominal ledger menu, select [Nominal Account Structure], press return; then, select [Account Names] from the sub-menu.

- You are now asked for an account reference: key in 5000.

- Change the account name by keying in Hardware Purchases and press return.

- Press [ESC] and, at the prompt, select Post and press return.
- Repeat the process for account reference 5001, which is to be called Software Purchases.
- To return to the main menu, press [ESC] three times.

using the purchases ledger
Richard Brown's business, Computer Shop Ltd, has the following credit purchases transactions for his first month in business:

Note: All purchases are subject to Value Added Tax. The amounts shown below need the addition of VAT: the program will calculate the amounts and will post them to the VAT account. (This chapter has been worked using a VAT rate of 17½ per cent.)

January
2	Bought software £500 from Axis Supplies Ltd, their invoice no 1341
3	Bought hardware £600 from Bell Computers Ltd, invoice no 1005
5	Bought software £350 from Granta Trading Co Ltd, invoice no T7648
7	Bought software £200 from Pratt and Co Ltd, invoice no A81721
8	Bought hardware £425 from Kingsway Technical Ltd, invoice no 900817
12	Bought software £200 from Axis Supplies Ltd, invoice no 1397
18	Bought hardware £365 from Granta Trading Co Ltd, invoice no T7721
22	Bought software £85 from Computer Supplies Ltd, invoice no 9987
27	Bought software £125 from Pratt & Co Ltd, invoice no A81795

Starting from the main menu, the purchases ledger transactions are entered as follows:
- Select [Purchase Ledger]; press return.
- Select [Batched Data Entry]; press return.
- Select [Purchase Invoices]; press return, and the data entry screen now appears.

data entry screen
- The cursor is in the 'A/C' column; enter the account number or short name of the first account you need. As this is Axis Supplies Ltd, key in 101 or AXIS (depending on how you opened the accounts earlier); press return. Note that the supplier's account name appears at the top of the screen. (Pressing function key F4 – the Search Key – will show on screen a list of the suppliers' accounts.)
- The cursor will have moved automatically to the 'Date' column. Key in the required date, eg 020192 (2 January 1992), or press function key F5 to display the system date.
- The cursor will have moved to the 'Inv' column; key in the supplier's invoice number 1341 (up to six numbers/letters can be entered); press return.
- The cursor will now be under the column 'N/C' – this stands for nominal code and here we must enter the nominal account number involved in the other half of the book-keeping transaction. As it is software that has been bought from Axis Supplies Ltd, the nominal code is 5001; enter this and press return. (Pressing function key F4 will show on screen a list of nominal account codes. The up and down arrow keys – or 'Pg Up' and 'Pg Dn' keys – can be used to move the highlight to the correct account. Return is pressed to accept the selected account.) Note that the name of the nominal account used shows at the top of the screen below the name of the supplier.
- The next column is 'Dep' (department); press return to miss this out.
- In the 'Details' column can be entered Software (in this first transaction), or Hardware. Alternatively, the items on the invoice can be described (in up to 19 characters). Press return.
- In the 'Nett Amt' column enter the amount before VAT: for this first transaction it is £500. Press return.

- In the 'Tc' (tax code) column, key in T1 and press return. VAT will be calculated and displayed at the standard rate – currently 17½ per cent. (Other tax codes available are T0 for zero-rated and T2 for exempt goods.) Function key F9 can also be used to input the T1 tax code. Press return.

- Note that the batch total (top right-hand side of the screen) shows the total (value of goods, plus VAT) of the screen transactions.

- The cursor will now be at the start of the next line and you should enter the other credit purchases of Richard Brown's business.

- When all the other transactions have been entered, ensure that the cursor is on a blank line, and press [ESC]. The prompt "Do you want to: Post Edit Abandon" appears. If all the details are correct, select Post and press return. The data files will now be updated. (If any items need to be edited, move the cursor by using the arrow keys, amend the details, press return, and then move the cursor back to a clear line before pressing [ESC].)

- Press [ESC] to return to the purchase ledger sub-menu

reports

The following reports can be displayed on screen, printed or filed on disk:

- Day book, showing purchases invoices
- Transaction history (for each account) – an asterisk against a money amount indicates that it has not yet been paid
- Account balances (aged) – after the first screen use the [→] key to display the aged balances

Select each in turn and follow the screen prompts. Where the prompt asks for account references or dates, press return. (If the data files were larger than those created so far, we would need to be more selective to avoid being inundated with information.) At the prompt "Display, Print or File" press return for the information to be shown on screen, or enter P for the information to be printed, and press return. (The computer will remind you to switch on the printer).

Do ensure that you print out the day book. When you have finished with reports, press [ESC] twice to return to the main menu.

trial balance

Choose [Nominal Ledger] from the main menu, and then [Trial Balance] which can be displayed on screen, or printed (key in 'P') as follows:

Ref	Account Name	Debit	Credit
2100	CREDITORS CONTROL ACCOUNT		3348.77
2200	TAX CONTROL ACCOUNT	498.77	
5000	HARDWARE PURCHASES	1390.00	
5001	SOFTWARE PURCHASES	1460.00	
		3348.77	3348.77

Note that, instead of showing the balance of the account of each creditor, a total of all suppliers' accounts is shown under the heading *Creditors Control Account*. Control accounts are used where there is a need to show a total for a ledger section. *Tax Control Account* shows the balance of Value Added Tax – the amount of VAT is recorded automatically as each transaction is entered. In the trial balance above, the tax authorities currently owe £498.77 to Richard Brown's company.

sales ledger

details of credit customers

The following customers have asked Richard Brown, the owner of Computer Shop Ltd, to open credit accounts for them:

Customer's name and address and credit limit (decided by Richard Brown)	*For your use – account number or short name**
Able, Baker & Clark Orchard House The Green St Peters Mereford MR3 8AK Credit limit £1000	201 or ABLE
Hitech Trading Co Unit 16 Factory Estate Eveshore MR10 8PW Credit limit £750	202 or HITECH
Jones & Co Ltd 123 High Street Mereford MR1 2DB Credit limit £500	203 or JONES
Sixth Form College Whittington Avenue Mereford MR2 7QH Credit limit £1000	204 or SIXTH
Teleservice 78 Bruton Road Mereford MR2 4PT Credit limit £500	205 or TELE
Wyvern County Council County Hall Eveshore Road Mereford MR4 8AP Credit limit £2500	206 or WCC

* Note: With the Sage programs, any combination of up to six numbers and/or letters – selected by the user – identify each sales ledger (and purchases ledger) account.

opening accounts in the sales ledger

- From the main menu, select [Sales Ledger]; press return.
- From the sales ledger menu, select [Customer Details]; press return.
- Key in the first account number, 201, or the short name, ABLE. Follow the same procedure as with purchase ledger. Remember to key in the credit limit for each customer.
- After the customer details have been entered, return to the main menu by pressing [ESC] twice.

sales account in the nominal ledger

Two separate sales accounts are to be opened in the nominal ledger, one for hardware sales, the other for software sales. Follow the same procedure as for opening purchases accounts. The sales accounts to be opened are numbered:

    4000   Hardware sales

    4001   Software sales

Return to the main menu by pressing [ESC] three times.

using the sales ledger

Richard Brown's business, Computer Shop Ltd, has the following credit sales transactions for his first month in business (all sales are subject to VAT):

January
6	Sold software £100 to Able, Baker & Clark, invoice no 1001
10	Sold software £300 to Teleservice, invoice no 1002
13	Sold hardware £600 to Sixth Form College, invoice no 1003
15	Sold software £125 to Jones & Co Ltd, invoice no 1004
17	Sold hardware £700 to Wyvern County Council, invoice no 1005
20	Sold software £50 to Hitech Trading Co, invoice no 1006
23	Sold software £125 to Teleservice, invoice no 1007
24	Sold hardware £450 to Sixth Form College, invoice no 1008
27	Sold software £130 to Able, Baker & Clark, invoice no 1009

These transactions are entered to the sales ledger in a similar way as purchases are entered in the purchases ledger:

• Select [Sales Ledger] from the main menu; press return.

• Select [Batched Data Entry]; press return.

• Select [Sales Invoices]; press return, and the data entry screen now appears.

• Enter the transactions in a similar way as purchases are entered in the purchases ledger.

• When all transactions have been entered, press [ESC] and, at the prompt, select Post and press return: the data files will now be updated.

• Press [ESC] to return to the sales ledger sub-menu.

reports

The following reports can be displayed on screen, printed or filed on disk:

• Day book, showing sales invoices

• Transaction history (for each account) – an asterisk indicates items that have not yet been paid

• Account balances (aged) – after the first screen use the [→] key to display the aged balances

• Statements

Ensure that you print out the day book.

For sales ledger, an aged analysis of debtor balances is particularly useful as a management report in order to see the amounts owing analysed in terms of 'current, 30 days, 60 days, 90 days, older'. Overdue debts can be identified and action taken to chase for payment.

Statements can be printed on commercially available forms: they can then be dispatched to the customers.

Press [ESC] twice to return to the main menu.

trial balance

Choose [Nominal Ledger] from the main menu, and display or print the trial balance which now appears as:

Ref	Account Name	Debit	Credit
1100	DEBTORS CONTROL ACCOUNT	3031.51	
2100	CREDITORS CONTROL ACCOUNT		3348.77
2200	TAX CONTROL ACCOUNT	47.26	
4000	HARDWARE SALES		1750.00
4001	SOFTWARE SALES		830.00
5000	HARDWARE PURCHASES	1390.00	
5001	SOFTWARE PURCHASES	1460.00	
		5928.77	5928.77

Note that the *Debtors Control Account* totals the individual debtor balances; *Tax Control Account* shows the net balance of Value Added Tax – in the trial balance above, the tax authorities currently owe £47.26 to Richard Brown's company.

recording receipts and payments

All receipts and payments pass through nominal account no 1200 'Bank Account': this is already open in the nominal ledger.

receipts

Richard Brown's business has the following receipts from customers in the first month:

January
15	Received a cheque for £117.50 from Able, Baker & Clark
20	Received a cheque for £352.50 from Teleservice
24	Received a cheque for £400.00 from Sixth Form College
30	Received a cheque for £146.88 from Jones & Co Ltd

These receipts are entered as follows:

- Choose [Sales Ledger] from the main menu, and then [Receipts].

- Press return to accept the nominal code of Bank (account no 1200).

- The data entry screen requires the account reference of the debtor, date of payment, cheque number (press return if not giving a number), and the amount of the cheque.

- The screen now displays the outstanding transactions on the debtors account (or the first ten transactions, if there are more). At the bottom of the screen is asked "Method of Payment: Automatic Manual" with the cursor positioned over the default of Automatic.

automatic allocation

This goes through the transactions in numerical order and pays off outstanding invoices until either the amount of the receipt reaches zero or there are no more invoices to pay off. If there is insufficient money to pay off an invoice in full, the remaining money will be used to partially pay the invoice. Press [ESC] if you are satisfied with the allocations made, and then press return at the prompt "Do you want to: Post Edit Abandon" to post the receipts.

manual allocation

This is selected in order to allocate payment to a particular invoice, either in full or partially. Simply move the cursor up or down by using the arrow keys. Now select one of the four payment options: 'Full, Part, Discount, or Cancel'. If part payment is selected, the amount needs to be keyed in. Once the allocations have been made, press [ESC], and then press return at the prompt "Do you want to: Post Edit Abandon" to post the receipts.

- After posting receipts, return to the main menu by pressing [ESC] twice.

payments

Richard Brown makes the following payments to suppliers in the first month:

January
22	Paid Pratt & Co Ltd a cheque for £235.00, cheque no 860005
27	Paid Axis Supplies Ltd a cheque for £587.50, cheque no 860006
31	Paid Bell Computers Ltd a cheque for £705.00, cheque no 860009

These payments are entered as follows:

- Select [Purchase Ledger] from the main menu, and then [Payments].

- Press return to accept the nominal code of 'Bank'.

- At the data entry screen, follow the same procedure as for receipts (enter the cheque number).

- Choose between either automatic or manual allocation, and post the payments.

- Return to the main menu by pressing [ESC] twice.

trial balance

Choose [Nominal Ledger] from the main menu, and display or print the trial balance which now appears as:

Ref	Account Name	Debit	Credit
1100	DEBTORS CONTROL ACCOUNT	2014.63	
1200	BANK CURRENT ACCOUNT		510.62
2100	CREDITORS CONTROL ACCOUNT		1821.27
2200	TAX CONTROL ACCOUNT	47.26	
4000	HARDWARE SALES		1750.00
4001	SOFTWARE SALES		830.00
5000	HARDWARE PURCHASES	1390.00	
5001	SOFTWARE PURCHASES	1460.00	
		4911.89	4911.89

Note that the bank is overdrawn.

recording returned goods

Most computer accounting systems do not use separate purchases returns and sales returns accounts to record returned goods. Instead, they credit purchases account with purchases returns, and debit sales with sales returns.

purchases returns
Richard Brown's business has the following purchases returns in the first month:

January
20   Returned software to Axis Supplies Ltd for £50, plus VAT, and received a credit note reference CN251
31   Returned hardware to Granta Trading Co Ltd for £120, plus VAT, and received a credit note reference 8524

These are entered as follows:
* Choose [Purchases Ledger] from the main menu, then [Batched Data Entry].
* From the sub-menu, select [Purchase Credit Notes].
* The data entry screen is the same as for purchases invoices.
* When the entries have been recorded, press [ESC] and post the transactions.
* Press [ESC] three times to return to the main menu.

sales returns
Richard Brown's business has the following sales returns in the first month:

January
24   Wyvern County Council returns hardware £300, plus VAT; credit note no. CN101
27   Hitech Trading Co returns software £50, plus VAT; credit note no. CN102

These are entered as follows:
* Choose [Sales Ledger] from the main menu, then [Batched Data Entry].
* From the sub-menu, select [Sales Credit Notes].
* The data entry screen is the same as for sales invoices.
* When the entries have been recorded, press [ESC] and post the transactions.
* Press [ESC] twice to return to the main menu.

trial balance
Choose [Nominal Ledger] from the main menu, and display or print the trial balance which now appears as:

Ref	Account Name	Debit	Credit
1100	DEBTORS CONTROL ACCOUNT	1603.38	
1200	BANK CURRENT ACCOUNT		510.62
2100	CREDITORS CONTROL ACCOUNT		1621.52
2200	TAX CONTROL ACCOUNT	78.76	
4000	HARDWARE SALES		1450.00
4001	SOFTWARE SALES		780.00
5000	HARDWARE PURCHASES	1270.00	
5001	SOFTWARE PURCHASES	1410.00	
		4362.14	4362.14

other nominal account transactions

The standard default layout for nominal ledger comprises many accounts which are already numbered. In this section we will enter transactions to expenses accounts, capital and loans, and fixed assets.

expenses

Richard Brown pays the following business expenses by cheque in his first month:

January
10   Paid travelling expenses (nominal account no 7400) £25.00, cheque no 860003
19   Paid staff salaries (account no 7003) £645.00, cheque no 860004
20   Paid stationery (account no 7504) £70.50 *including* VAT (see below), cheque no 860007
31   Paid shop rent (account no 7100) £176.25 *including* VAT (see below), cheque no 860008

The various expenses of the business, eg salaries, rent, electricity, etc do not usually pass through the purchase ledger. They are paid direct by cheque, and so the double-entry book-keeping is:
– *debit* appropriate expense account (with amount excluding VAT, if any)
– *debit* VAT account (with amount of VAT, if any)
– *credit* bank account

To see the nominal ledger accounts which are already open on your data disk:
• From the main menu select [Nominal Ledger], then [Nominal Account Structure], then [Account Names].
• Press function key F4 to see the existing accounts: use the arrow keys – or 'Pg Up' and 'Pg Dn' keys – to move up or down the list.
• Press [ESC] to remove the display.
• Press [ESC] twice to return to the main menu.

Where expenses are paid by cheque, transactions are entered by using the bank payments routine, as follows:
• From the main menu choose [Nominal Ledger], then [Bank Transactions], then [Bank Payments].
• At the data entry screen, press return to accept the nominal account no 1200 for Bank. Enter the nominal account number for the expense and check that the correct account name shows towards the top of the screen.
• Enter the other details: note that the VAT tax code for travelling expenses will be T0 (zero-rated), while that for salaries will be T9 (outside the scope of VAT). With stationery and rent, which are subject to VAT at 17½ per cent, the amount paid *includes* VAT. The program can calculate the VAT amount:
   – enter the amount of the cheque (eg £70.50 for stationery) in the 'Nett Amnt' column
   – enter the tax code in the 'Tc' column, as T1 (or use function key F9)
   – in the 'Tax Amnt' column, press the shift *and* [<] keys (later versions of the programs use function key F10 to deduct VAT at the standard rate)
   – the program will deduct tax from the figure in the net column and show the changed net value and amount of VAT
• When the entries have been recorded, press [ESC] and post the transactions.
• Press [ESC] three times to return to the main menu.

Note: Some business expenses may be made through purchase ledger if a creditor's account is opened. For example, a business may have an account open in the name of the local garage to which petrol, servicing and repair costs are credited, with settlement being made at the end of each month.

capital and loans

Richard Brown's business, Computer Shop Ltd, has the following capital and loans transactions:

January

1	Started in business with ordinary share capital (nominal account no 3000) of £10,000, received by cheque
10	Received a loan (account no 2300) of £5,000, by cheque

These are entered through the bank receipts routine, as follows:

- From the main menu choose [Nominal Ledger], then [Bank Transactions], then [Bank Receipts]; press return.
- At the data entry screen, enter the transactions: use the tax code T9 for both ordinary share capital and the loan (both transactions are outside the scope of VAT).
- When the entries have been recorded, press [ESC] and post the transactions.
- Press [ESC] three times to return to the main menu.

fixed assets

Richard Brown's business buys the following fixed assets:

January

4	Bought office equipment (nominal account no 0030) for £2,350 *including* VAT, paying by cheque no 860001
8	Bought a delivery van (nominal account no 0050) for £9,400 *including* VAT, paying by cheque no 860002

These are entered in a similar way to expenses (see previous page) using the bank payments routine. Note that both of these purchases *include* VAT at the standard rate (tax code T1), so use the automatic tax calculation method described in the expenses section above.

trial balance

Choose [Nominal Ledger] from the main menu, and display or print the trial balance which now appears as:

Ref	Account Name	Debit	Credit
0030	OFFICE EQUIPMENT	2000.00	
0050	MOTOR VEHICLES	8000.00	
1100	DEBTORS CONTROL ACCOUNT	1603.38	
1200	BANK CURRENT ACCOUNT	1822.63	
2100	CREDITORS CONTROL ACCOUNT		1621.52
2200	TAX CONTROL ACCOUNT	1865.51	
2300	LOANS		5000.00
3000	ORDINARY SHARES		10000.00
4000	HARDWARE SALES		1450.00
4001	SOFTWARE SALES		780.00
5000	HARDWARE PURCHASES	1270.00	
5001	SOFTWARE PURCHASES	1410.00	
7003	STAFF SALARIES	645.00	
7100	RENT	150.00	
7400	TRAVELLING	25.00	
7504	OFFICE STATIONERY	60.00	
		18851.52	18851.52

If your trial balance fails to agree with that shown on the previous page, choose [Utilities] from the main menu, and then [Audit Trail]. Print out all the transactions for January and 'tick' them off against the transactions in this chapter. Errors can be corrected, as described below.

saving data files to disk

As you worked through the chapter, each time you posted transactions the data files were updated, either on the floppy disk in drive 'B' or on the hard disk. There is no requirement to save data at regular intervals during the processing. However, in a business, it makes good sense to save data at regular intervals throughout the day to a back-up disk. With accounting data, we cannot consider to be correctly posted until it is backed-up on a separate disk.

correction of errors

The audit trail (from the Utilities sub-menu) lists all of the transactions and gives each a reference number. When an error is located from the audit trail, the Utilities sub-menu Data File Utilities provides a Posting Error Corrections routine. Selecting this offers two choices:

- Reverse Posting
- Correct Posting

Reverse posting cancels out an incorrect posting, ie it deletes the effect of the transaction from the book-keeping records. The number of the wrong transaction from the audit trail is entered; the program will then indicate the accounts affected and will ask "Proceed with Correction?: No Yes". If the error correction is proceeded with, a transaction will be recorded on the audit trail. As reverse posting only cancels an incorrect transaction; it will then be necessary to post the correct transaction (which adds another transaction to the audit trail).

Correct posting allows certain details of a previously-posted transaction to be altered, eg account code, date, reference, tax code. The audit trail number of the transaction is entered and, if the transaction exists, the details are displayed on screen. The arrow keys are used to move the cursor to the information that is to be changed. The cursor can only be placed on information which may be changed. Press return. After details have been changed, press [ESC] and return. The program will state the corrective posting to be made and will then ask "Proceed with Correction?: No Yes". This error correction routine will usually add two transactions to the audit trail, depending on the correction carried out. Press [ESC] to return to the main menu.

allocation of credit notes

Credit notes posted to accounts need to be allocated against invoices – at present outstanding invoices and credit notes on debtors' and creditors' accounts are indicated with an asterisk.

allocating sales credit notes
- From Sales ledger, choose [Receipts]. Accept the nominal code for Bank by pressing return.
- Enter the debtor's account reference and the date.
- Press return to enter the cheque amount as zero. Transactions on the debtor's account will now be showing on the screen.
- Select Manual allocation of receipts, and press return.
- Select the credit note first and pay it off in full by pressing return; this will cause the cheque balance to increase by the amount of the credit note.

- Now pay off the invoice – either in full or in part – by moving the cursor to it, and pressing return.
- Press [ESC], and then press return at the prompt "Do you want to: Post Edit Abandon" to allocate the credit note.
- Return to the main menu by pressing [ESC] twice.

allocating purchases credit notes
- From Purchases ledger choose [Payments]. Accept the nominal code for Bank by pressing return.
- Enter the creditor's account reference and the date.
- Press return to enter the cheque amount as zero. Transactions on the creditor's account will now be showing on the screen.
- Select Manual allocation of payments and press return.
- Select the credit note first and pay it off in full by pressing return; this will cause the cheque balance to increase by the amount of the credit note.
- Now pay off the invoice – either in full or in part – by moving the cursor to it, and pressing return.
- Press [ESC], and then press return at the prompt "Do you want to: Post Edit Abandon" to allocate the credit note.
- Return to the main menu by pressing [ESC] twice.

chapter summary

❏   We have used a computer accounting program to:
  • open debtors' accounts in the sales ledger
  • open creditors' accounts in the purchases ledger
  • enter business transactions in the sales ledger, purchases ledger and nominal ledger

❏   We have seen some of the reports that can be produced:
  • day books
  • transaction history for each account
  • statements of account for debtors
  • aged account balances
  • trial balance
  • audit trail

❏   It has only been possible to look at the main features of computer accounting. It may be that you will wish to investigate other aspects of the program. In addition you may have the opportunity to use other computer accounting programs, eg
  • invoicing
  • stock control

Later in the book (Chapter 23) we shall use a computer accounting program for the payment of wages and salaries – the payroll of a business.

ASSIGNMENT

7

Computer accounting: Computer Shop Limited

SITUATION

You are the assistant to Richard Brown, the owner of Computer Shop Ltd. You are required to enter the transactions for February into a computer accounting system. Before commencing you must ensure that you have worked through Chapter 19, recording the transactions for January, and ensure that your trial balance agrees with that shown on page 265.

STUDENT TASKS

Starting with your data disk with January's transactions, you are to enter the following transactions of Richard Brown's business for the month of February:

1. Open new accounts in the purchases ledger for:

    • Software Supplies, Unit 10, Newtown Trading Estate, Newtown NT1 7AJ
      Account no 107 or SOFT

    • Trade Tech Ltd, 45-50 The High Road, Dunton DT4 7AL
      Account no 108 or TRADE

2. Enter the following credit purchases transactions for the month (all subject to VAT at 17½ per cent):
    February
4	Bought software £150 from Software Supplies, invoice no. AB452
5	Bought hardware £220 from Trade Tech Ltd, invoice no. H3974
7	Bought hardware £550 from Granta Trading Co Ltd, invoice no. T7849
10	Bought software £200 from Axis Supplies Ltd, invoice no. 1529
15	Bought hardware £320 from Kingsway Technical Ltd, invoice no. 901072
18	Bought hardware £525 from Bell Computers Ltd, invoice no. 1149
20	Bought software £110 from Computer Supplies Ltd, invoice no. 10105
23	Bought hardware £610 from Granta Trading Co Ltd, invoice no. T7927
25	Bought software £500 from Software Supplies, invoice no. AB641

    • Print the day book for February, showing purchases invoices (transaction numbers† 38 to 46)
    • Print the trial balance
    † *Note:* transaction numbers referred to assume that no errors/corrections have occurred.

3. Open new accounts in the sales ledger for:

    • Adams & Co, The Old Rectory, Church Street, Eveshore MR8 7PP
      Account no 207 or ADAMS; credit limit £500

    • Stone, Wall Ltd, Builders Merchants, Station Yard, Mereford MR2 1BT
      Account no 208 or STONE; credit limit £750

4. Enter the following credit sales transactions for the month (all subject to VAT at 17½ per cent):

   February
2	Sold software £350 to Adams & Co, invoice no. 1010
4	Sold hardware £1,100 to Wyvern County Council, invoice no. 1011
5	Sold software £425 to Stone, Wall Ltd, invoice no. 1012
8	Sold hardware £750 to Teleservice, invoice no. 1013
10	Sold hardware £630 to Sixth Form College, invoice no. 1014
12	Sold software £320 to Hitech Trading Co, invoice no. 1015
16	Sold hardware £450 to Sixth Form College, invoice no. 1016
20	Sold software £250 to Able, Baker & Clark, invoice no. 1017
24	Sold hardware £850 to Teleservice, invoice no. 1018

   - Print the day book for February, showing sales invoices (transaction numbers† 47 to 55)
   - Print the trial balance

   † *Note*: transaction numbers referred to assume that no errors have occurred and been corrected.

5. Enter the following returns for the month (all subject to VAT at 17½ per cent):

   February
   Purchases returns
18	Returned software to Software Supplies for £50, and received a credit note reference 3219
27	Returned hardware to Kingsway Technical Ltd for £220, and received a credit note reference CN681

   Sales returns
20	Sixth Form College returns hardware £400; credit note no. CN103 issued
26	Able, Baker & Clark return software £110; credit note no. CN104 issued

   - Print the trial balance

6. Enter the following receipts and payments for the month of February

   Receipts
4	Received a cheque for £152.75 from Able, Baker & Clark
19	Received a cheque for £411.25 from Adams & Co
20	Received a cheque for £100.00 from Teleservice
28	Received a cheque for £1,762.50 from Wyvern County Council

   Payments
5	Paid Axis Supplies Ltd a cheque for £176.25, cheque no 860010
10	Paid Kingsway Technical Ltd a cheque for £499.38, cheque no 860013
18	Paid Pratt & Co Ltd a cheque for £146.88, cheque no 860015
28	Paid Computer Supplies Ltd a cheque for £229.13, cheque no 860016

   - Print the trial balance

7. Enter the following nominal account transactions for the month of February

   Payments
6	Paid stationery £152.75 *including* VAT, cheque no 860011
10	Paid advertising £293.75 *including* VAT, cheque no 860012
15	Paid travelling expenses £30.00 (zero-rated – use tax code T0), cheque no 860014
28	Paid staff salaries £650.00 (outside the scope of VAT – use tax code T9), cheque no 860017
28	Bought office equipment £587.50 *including* VAT, cheque no 860018

   Receipts
15	Received a loan £1,500 (outside the scope of VAT – use tax code T9)

   - Print the trial balance. What is the significance of the balance of VAT account?

8. Print out the aged account balances from the sales ledger at 1 March. Which account should be brought to the attention of Richard Brown, the owner of Computer Shop Ltd? What action would you advise him to take?

20 Calculation of wages

In this chapter we will look at the different methods of calculating pay, the employer's records of employees' attendance and the voluntary deductions made from pay. To illustrate these procedures we will show in a Case Study how an employer works out how much to pay a new employee for the first two weeks at work.

The income a person receives from being employed is often referred to in terms of 'wages' or 'salary'. Over the years a tradition has been established of describing them as follows:

wages   payment made to manual employees normally working in the areas of production or service; payment is made weekly and is paid in cash or by transfer to a bank or building society account

salary   payment made to non-manual employees normally working in the areas of administration and management; payment is usually made monthly and paid directly into the employees' bank or building society accounts.

A further distinction is drawn between 'gross pay' and 'net pay'.

gross pay   wages or salary paid by the employer *before* deductions are made

net pay   the wages or salary actually received by the employee *after* compulsory and voluntary deductions

Note that employees normally speak about earning '£10,000 a year' (gross pay) but actually receiving '£700 a month' (net pay).

different methods of calculating pay

The methods of calculating wages and salaries can vary between different employers and different employees within the same company. The following methods are commonly used for calculating wages and salaries:
- *salary payment* – an agreed annual amount
- *time rate payment* – an hourly rate
- *basic rate plus bonus* – an incentive scheme based on productivity
- *piece rate payment* – based on the number of items produced
- *commission* – payment related to the sales achieved

salary payment

An annual salary is agreed between employer and employee and an equivalent amount is either paid in weekly or monthly amounts.

example: Mr Harris and Miss White
Mr Harris, Production Manager, and Miss White, Receptionist, have just agreed new rates of pay with their employer. Mr Harris is to receive £24,000 per year, Miss White is to receive £7,800. Their gross (before deductions) income is as follows:

Mr Harris, monthly paid, will earn £24,000 ÷ 12, ie £2,000 per month gross

Miss White, weekly paid, will earn £7,800 ÷ 52, ie £150 per week gross

time rate payment

A payment rate for each hour worked is agreed and the employee will be paid according to the number of hours worked. It is common with this system to pay a higher rate of pay when an employee works overtime. Overtime is any time worked beyond what is normal for the working day, or time worked on a day not normally worked. A normal working week usually consists of five days, each of seven or eight working hours.

example: Ron Bourne
Ron Bourne, a storekeeper, is paid at the rate of £5.00 per hour for an eight hour day, five days a week. Overtime is paid at the rate of time and a quarter (ie 1¼ x £5.00) for weekday work and time and a half (ie 1½ x £5.00) for weekend work. During one week Ron Bourne worked the following hours:

Monday	8 hours
Tuesday	9 hours
Wednesday	8 hours
Thursday	9 hours
Friday	8 hours
Saturday	4 hours

Ron's working hours for the week are therefore as follows:

Basic hourly rate 5 days x 8 hours	=	40 hours
Weekday overtime (Tuesday and Thursday)	=	2 hours
Weekend overtime (Saturday)	=	4 hours

Ron's gross pay for the week is worked out as follows:

Basic hourly rate (40 hours x £5.00)	=	£200.00
Weekday overtime (2 hours x £5.00 x 1¼)	=	£12.50
Weekend overtime (4 hours x £5.00 x 1½)	=	£30.00
Gross pay for the week		£242.50

basic rate bonus payment

Many businesses operate bonus schemes as an incentive to workers to reach and exceed set targets. An employer will fix the amount of work to be completed in a certain time; if the work target is exceeded, bonus payments will be paid. The bonus payment will be paid either individually to each worker based on his or her performance, or paid as an average bonus to every worker based on the amount by which the target has been exceeded. The bonus, often referred to as a 'productivity bonus', can be paid either as a specific amount of money or as a percentage of the basic pay.

Example: Ron Bourne

If we suppose that Ron Bourne, in addition to receiving the gross pay of £242.50 calculated in the previous example, was awarded in that week a productivity bonus of 5% on basic pay. His gross pay will be increased by that bonus.

The bonus is calculated (on basic pay) as follows:

Basic weekly pay (£200) x 5% ($5/_{100}$)   =   £10.00

His gross pay will therefore be:

Basic pay	£200.00
Weekly overtime	£12.50
Weekend overtime	£30.00
Bonus	£10.00
	£252.50

piece rate payments

Piece rate payment is another form of incentive to employees to work more quickly. The employer will agree a rate of pay for each article produced or operation completed and the employees will be paid only for the work that they have completed. Normally, however, there is an agreement between employer and employees that a minimum wage will be paid regardless of the work completed. An agreement of this nature is to provide the employee with a wage when the employer cannot provide work.

example: Fred Parry and Helen Morse on piece rate

Fred Parry and Helen Morse work at Lowe Electronics which produces electronic alarms. The employer and employees have come to an agreement that piecework rates will be paid as follows:

- 'Red alert' alarm   =   £2.00 per unit
- 'Klaxon' alarm   =   £1.50 per unit

The company has also agreed a minimum of £80 per week.

During one week Fred worked hard and produced 80 'Red alert' alarms whereas Helen Morse had a machine breakdown and only managed 40 'Klaxon' alarms. What are they paid?

Fred Parry: 80 x £2.00   =   £160

Helen Morse: 40 x £1.50 = £60, *but* because
of £80 agreed minimum wage   =   £80

commission

Commission payment is normally made to employees engaged in selling goods. A sales person receives commission on the sales that are made during a specific period. The commission is usually paid as a percentage of the total sales made. Commission could be paid in addition to a basic salary, or instead of a salary.

example: Jane Summers and Joan Dudley on commission

Jane Summers, Area Sales Manager of a mail order company, receives a basic £750 per month salary plus commission at the rate of 5% on all the sales in her area. Joan Dudley, working for the same organization, sells direct to the customer and earns commission at the rate of 20% of her total sales.

During the past month:

- Jane Summers' area sales were £20,000
- Joan Dudley's direct sales were £2,500

Their monthly pay is calculated as follows:

Jane Summers' pay = basic + commission
= basic + (total sales x commission rate)
= £750 + (£20,000 x 5%)
= £750 + £1,000
= £1,750 per month

Joan Dudley's pay = commission only
= sales x commission rate
= £2,500 x 20%
= £500 per month

records of attendance

In order that an employer can calculate wages, particularly where hourly paid workers are employed, a record of attendance must be kept. Employees' attendance records take a number of different forms which include the following:

- *time book* – a simple 'signing in' book
- *clock cards* – a card used in conjunction with a time 'clock'
- *time sheets* – records used by employees who work away from the premises
- *computerised 'clock cards'* – a card which records the hours on a computer

time book

A 'time book' is often used in offices and is a simple ruled book in which staff enter against an allocated number:

- their time of arrival
- their signature
- their time of departure

clock cards

With this method, each employee who works regularly on the business premises has a *clock card* which is kept in a rack next to a time recorder clock. On arrival at work, the employee removes the card from the 'out section' of the rack and inserts the card into the time recorder clock, which stamps the arrival time on the card in the appropriate place. The card is then removed from the time recorder clock and placed in the 'in section' of the rack indicating that the employee is at work. When the employee leaves work, the card is stamped in the recorder clock and then placed in the 'out section' rack ready for when she or he works the next shift.

The clock cards are used to calculate weekly wages by the wages department of the business which will be able to see the actual hours worked by each employee.

example: J Hicks' clock card
J Hicks works for Mereford Metal Castings Ltd. as a lathe operator. He works a standard 40 hour week and is paid £5.50 per hour. He is paid time-and-a-half for overtime. His clock card for a typical working week appears below. Note that he has worked two hours overtime (on Tuesday and Thursday) and takes an hour for lunch each day when he 'clocks off' to go to the works canteen.

No.	701				
Name	J Hicks				
Week ending: 20 January 19–9					

Day	In	Out	In	Out	TOTAL HOURS
M	0800	1230	1330	1700	8.00
Tu	0800	1230	1330	1800	9.00
W	0800	1230	1330	1700	8.00
Th	0800	1230	1330	1800	9.00
F	0800	1230	1330	1700	8.00
Total					42.00

	£
Ordinary time: ..40... hrs @ £.5..50	220.00
Overtime: ..2....... hrs @ £.8.25.	16.50
TOTAL GROSS WAGES	236.50

Note how the wages department has used the bottom of the clock card to calculate his gross wages of £236.50 by adding his basic pay of £220.00 and 2 hours' overtime of £16.50.

time sheets

This method is normally associated with employees who work away from the business premises on contract work, or for hourly paid staff who do not 'clock in' with clock cards. The employee completes his or her record of attendance on a specially prepared time sheet, indicating the hour of attendance each day. The foreman or supervisor in charge will normally check and sign the time sheet before it is passed to the wages department. Illustrated below is a typical time sheet. Note that time is split into three categories:

- time spent working
- time spent travelling
- time spent 'waiting' to do the job in hand, eg if a machine to be serviced is not immediately accessible to the travelling maintenance engineer

TIME SHEET (in hours)							
Name .... Works No: .... Week ending							
Job No.	Mon	Tues	Wed	Thu	Fri	Sat	Sun
Sub-total							
Travel							
Waiting							
Total							
Supervisor .... **Date**							

computer cards

Employers using this method require staff to carry computer cards to and from their place of work and to insert the card in a computersied time clock on arrival or departure. This computerised system automatically records their hours of work.

This method of recording attendance is normally used by businesses which operate a flexitime system. Flexitime is a method that allows staff to arrive at work when they like and leave when they like, provided they are present during a prescribed 'core' time (say, between 10 am and 4 pm). Staff will still need to complete the normal number of hours per week but can arrange their own hours of attendance. With this system, it is also possible to carry forward time worked in excess of the normal time or time owed to the company provided the amount does not exceed a set figure.

Using the computer card system, the daily attendance hours are automatically calculated, totalled for the week and compared with the normal weekly figure. Wages for the week are worked out on the basis of the normal weekly figure.

deductions from gross pay

As we saw earlier in the chapter, *gross pay* is the total wage earned by an employee. It is the basic wage plus any additional payments such as overtime and bonuses. The *net pay* is the amount the employee receives after the employer has made certain deductions. There are a number of deductions an employer can make from gross pay. Some are compulsory and some are voluntary.

compulsory deductions

An employer will deduct the following government taxes:

• Income Tax

• National Insurance Contributions

Income tax is collected by a government department known as the *Inland Revenue*. National Insurance Contributions are collected by the Inland Revenue on behalf of the Department of Social Security. These tax deductions are explained in the next section.

voluntary deductions

An employer may deduct the following at the request of the employee:

• payments to charity by means of GAYE (Give As You Earn) – deducted *before* the tax calculations are made

• pensions/superannuation scheme payments, deducted *after* the tax calculations have been made

• SAYE (Save as You Earn) savings schemes, deducted *after* the tax calculations have been made

income tax

Income tax is a tax on the income received by an individual. 'Income' for tax purposes includes pay, tips, bonuses, and benefits in kind (eg company car, cheap loans), pensions, most State Benefits, and interest and dividends from investments.

If you are in employment the Income tax on your pay is deducted by the employer from your gross pay by means of a scheme known as PAYE (Pay As You Earn). This scheme, as its title suggests, enables you to spread out your taxation evenly over the year instead of having to pay it in one amount. If you are *self-employed*, you estimate your own income tax liability by means of the self-assessment scheme – this will involve you in making lump sum payments to the Inland Revenue.

taxable income: the personal allowance

Income which is liable to tax is known as *taxable income*. Taxable income is calculated by deducting the *personal allowance* from gross income.

Employees do not, fortunately, have to pay tax on all their income. In order to help the lower paid, the Government gives a *personal allowance*, an amount which can be earned during the tax year (6 April – 5 April), on which no tax is paid at all.

The personal allowance, which is set in the Chancellor's annual budget, is normally increased in line with inflation each year, and is fixed for each tax year. The amount of the personal allowance varies, depending on factors such as whether you are single or married, or over a certain age. The two basic personal allowances, fixed for the tax year from 6 April 1998 to 5 April 1999 are:

• personal allowance   £4,195

• married couple's allowance   £1,900

A single male or female may therefore earn up to £4,195 without deduction of tax. Married couples are taxed separately as individuals and each will receive a personal allowance of £4,195. Additionally a married couple's allowance may be given to the husband, *or* to the wife, *or* split between the two.

income tax calculations

It is the responsibility of the employer to see that the employee pays the right amount of tax through the PAYE system.

There are three rates of income tax applicable to taxable income (for the tax year 1998/1999)
- Lower Rate Tax: 20%, charged on the first £4,300 of taxable income
- Basic Rate Tax: 23%, charged on the remaining taxable income up to £27,100
- Higher Rate Tax: 40%, charged on taxable income *above* £27,100

If, therefore, you are fortunate to receive taxable income that exceeds £27,100, you have to pay income tax at 40% *on the excess* and income tax at 20% on the first £4,300 and 23% on £22,800.

If we take two employees of the same business, an unmarried accounts clerk earning £15,000 gross per year and an unmarried financial director earning £40,000 per year, it is straightforward to work out how much income tax they pay. Remember that taxable income in each case is gross income less the personal allowance of £4,195. The figures are quoted to the whole £ (pence are ignored).

	accounts assistant		**finance director**	
		nearest £		*nearest £*
Gross pay		15,000		40,000
Less personal allowance		4,195		4,195
Taxable pay		10,805		35,805
Income tax @ 20%	4,300 @ 20% =	860	4,300 @ 20% =	860
Income tax @ 23%	6,505 @ 23% =	1,496	22,800 @ 23% =	5,244
Income tax @ 40%		nil	8,705 @ 40% =	3,482
TOTAL INCOME TAX		2,356		9,586

These tax calculations cannot, however, be taken in isolation, as the employer will also, as we will see, deduct National Insurance Contributions, and the Inland Revenue may make further adjustments by means of a *tax code*.

tax codes and allowances

adjusting allowances

The Inland Revenue in certain circumstances will adjust the tax allowance given. It may be *increased* if expenses are incurred by the employee in the course of employment. It may be *decreased* (more commonly) to take account of perks such as company cars and mobile phones. The effect of decreasing the allowance is that the employee pays *more* tax as there is *less* tax free allowance. If the employee has a substantial 'value' of taxable perks – eg a £50,000 Mercedes provided by the employer – the allowance may be decreased so much that it becomes negative.

calculation of the tax code

How does the employer know what allowances have been given to the employee and how much tax to deduct? The Inland Revenue gives each employee a *tax code*, a number which is used by the employer to calculate the taxable pay. The tax code incorporates *all* the tax allowances, including the personal allowance, *and is quoted less the final digit*. The tax code for the accounts clerk mentioned above would be the total of the allowances (£4,195) less the final digit, ie 419. It will also be followed by the letter 'L' which indicates that it includes the personal allowance.

The range of letters which can follow the number in the tax code is as follows:

    L   = a code incorporating a single person's allowance
    H   = a code incorporating a married couple's allowance
    P   = a code where a person aged between 65 and 74 receives the single person's allowance
    V   = a code where a person aged between 65 and 74 receives the married couple's allowance
    T   = a code used generally

Other letters used include:

    BR = a code where a person has *no* allowance and is taxed at <u>B</u>asic <u>R</u>ate
    D   = all income is taxed at the higher rate of tax
    NT = no tax at all is deducted
    K   = a letter which comes before the code number indicating that a person's taxable benefits (eg a company car) exceed their allowances!

Occasionally, if an employee starts work and has no tax code, the employer will use the 'emergency code', the personal allowance. The tax code will be notified separately to the employer and the employee by the Inland Revenue on Form P6.

PAYE (Pay As You Earn)

When the Inland Revenue has allocated the tax code to the employee, the tax is, in principle, easy to calculate. The employer's task of collecting the tax on a weekly or a monthly basis is less simple. What happens for instance if an unmarried employee starts work, for the first time, halfway through the tax year? No tax will be payable, unless the employee earns over the basic personal allowance, in that year. How is the employer to know how much to deduct, and when? The Inland Revenue makes the calculation of tax and the collection of National Insurance Contributions on a *weekly or monthly* basis possible for the employer through the PAYE (Pay As You Earn) system.

Calculation of tax through the PAYE system is normally carried out in what is known as a *cumulative* way, ie an employer works out how much tax an employee has to pay using figures for pay and tax deducted since the start of the tax year (April 6). Occasionally the Inland Revenue will require an employer to use a *non-cumulative* method, ie to ignore previous pay and tax. This is also called the Week 1 or Month 1 basis.

The workings of the PAYE system using the Tax Tables provided by the Inland Revenue are illustrated in full in the Case Study on page 280, but first it is necessary to look at National Insurance Contributions, the other compulsory deduction made by the employer from gross pay.

National Insurance Contributions (NIC)

Both the employer and the employee have to pay Class 1 National Insurance Contributions (NIC) when an employee earns over a certain amount (the 'lower earnings limit'). The employer will have to pay to the Inland Revenue the employee's National Insurance Contributions by deduction from gross pay through the PAYE system. If the employee has a company car, the employer also has to pay yearly (in June) a Class 1A contribution on the taxable benefit, but the employee makes no contribution.

Payment of National Insurance enables the employee in time of need to claim benefits from the State such as retirement pension and sickness benefits. The amount contributed depends on earnings. As mentioned above, there is a 'lower earnings limit' (£64 per week in 1998/1999): once an employee earns over this amount, NICs are payable on total pay (not just the amount over £64). Also, if an employee earns over £485 a week (1998/1999) no NICs are payable by the employee on the excess, although they *are* payable by the employer. It should also be noted that employees under 16, women over 60 and men over 65 do not have to pay NICs.

The complete range of 'non-contracted out' National Insurance rates (which are commonly used) is set out on the next page. The rates are for the 1998/1999 tax year.

National Insurance Contributions (1998/1999)

Total weekly earnings	Employee	Employer
Under £64	Nil	Nil
£64 to £109.99	2% on earnings up to £64, plus 10% on earnings between £64 and £485	3%
£110 to £154.99		5%
£155 to £209.99		7%
£210 to £485		10%
Over £485	2% on £64, 10% on £421	10%

NIC may be worked out by the employer either by using the percentages set out above and a calculator, or by using up-to-date tables issued by the Department of Social Security.

operating the PAYE system

On the next five pages we set out a Case Study of an employer, Mays Mail Order, calculating the wages of an employee for the first two weeks of the tax year, using the PAYE system. Before starting the calculations, however, it is important to examine the records and documents that will be needed by the employer. Any employer that operates PAYE must

- calculate the correct amount of gross pay for each employee – a clear record of hours worked and rates of pay to be applied must be maintained
- calculate the correct amount of income tax to be deducted from the employee's gross pay
- calculate the correct amount of National Insurance Contributions to be paid by the employee *and* the employer
- keep records of the pay and deductions
- pay the Inland Revenue the amounts of income tax and National Insurance Contributions collected each month (normally any month's deductions are payable by the 19th of the following month)
- send a summary (Form P35) to the Inland Revenue at the end of each tax year, showing all payments and deductions (see Chapter 21 for details)

documention of PAYE

An employer operating PAYE will need the following:

gross pay figures	the employer will need a written record of the gross pay due
P11	a standard deduction sheet for working out the net pay, issued by the Inland Revenue
NIC tables	tables issued by the Department of Social Security showing the National Insurance Contributions for both employer and employee on a weekly or monthly basis; Table A is the standard rate table
Pay Adustment Tables	tables 'A' issued by the Inland Revenue showing the amount of 'free pay' that is available on a weekly or monthly basis, ie pay on which no tax is payable (see Fig 20.2 on page 281 for an example)
Taxable Pay Tables	tables issued by the Inland Revenue showing the amount of tax that is due on taxable pay each week or month; there are three tables:

- Table B: tax at basic rate, plus a subtraction table for the lower rate band (see Fig 20.1 on the next page for an example)
- Table LR : when tax is only due at the lower rate
- Table D: when tax is also due at the higher rate of 40% (used in conjunction with Table C)

Table B

Tax Due on Taxable Pay from £1 to £99

Total TAXABLE PAY to date £	Total TAX DUE to date £	Total TAXABLE PAY to date £	Total TAX DUE to date £
1	0.23	56	12.88
2	0.46	57	13.11
3	0.69	58	13.34
4	0.92	59	13.57
5	1.15	60	13.80
6	1.38	61	14.03
7	1.61	62	14.26
8	1.84	63	14.49
9	2.07	64	14.72
10	2.30	65	14.95
11	2.53	66	15.18
12	2.76	67	15.41
13	2.99	68	15.64
14	3.22	69	15.87
15	3.45	70	16.10
16	3.68	71	16.33
17	3.91	72	16.56
18	4.14	73	16.79
19	4.37	74	17.02
20	4.60	75	17.25
21	4.83	76	17.48
22	5.06	77	17.71
23	5.29	78	17.94
24	5.52	79	18.17
25	5.75	80	18.40
26	5.98	81	18.63
27	6.21	82	18.86
28	6.44	83	19.09
29	6.67	84	19.32
30	6.90	85	19.55
31	7.13	86	19.78
32	7.36	87	20.01
33	7.59	88	20.24
34	7.82	89	20.47
35	8.05	90	20.70
36	8.28	91	20.93
37	8.51	92	21.16
38	8.74	93	21.39
39	8.97	94	21.62
40	9.20	95	21.85
41	9.43	96	22.08
42	9.66	97	22.31
43	9.89	98	22.54
44	10.12	99	22.77
45	10.35		
46	10.58		
47	10.81		
48	11.04		
49	11.27		
50	11.50		
51	11.73		
52	11.96		
53	12.19		
54	12.42		
55	12.65		

Where the exact amount of taxable pay is not shown, add together the figures for two (or more) entries to make up the amount of taxable pay to the nearest £1 below

Tax Due on Taxable Pay from £100 to £26,100

Total TAXABLE PAY to date £	Total TAX DUE to date £	Total TAXABLE PAY to date £	Total TAX DUE to date £	Total TAXABLE PAY to date £	Total TAX DUE to date £	Total TAXABLE PAY to date £	Total TAX DUE to date £
100	23.00	6600	1518.00	13100	3013.00	19600	4508.00
200	46.00	6700	1541.00	13200	3036.00	19700	4531.00
300	69.00	6800	1564.00	13300	3059.00	19800	4554.00
400	92.00	6900	1587.00	13400	3082.00	19900	4577.00
500	115.00	7000	1610.00	13500	3105.00	20000	4600.00
600	138.00	7100	1633.00	13600	3128.00	20100	4623.00
700	161.00	7200	1656.00	13700	3151.00	20200	4646.00
800	184.00	7300	1679.00	13800	3174.00	20300	4669.00
900	207.00	7400	1702.00	13900	3197.00	20400	4692.00
1000	230.00	7500	1725.00	14000	3220.00	20500	4715.00
1100	253.00	7600	1748.00	14100	3243.00	20600	4738.00
1200	276.00	7700	1771.00	14200	3266.00	20700	4761.00
1300	299.00	7800	1794.00	14300	3289.00	20800	4784.00
1400	322.00	7900	1817.00	14400	3312.00	20900	4807.00
1500	345.00	8000	1840.00	14500	3335.00	21000	4830.00
1600	368.00	8100	1863.00	14600	3358.00	21100	4853.00
1700	391.00	8200	1886.00	14700	3381.00	21200	4876.00
1800	414.00	8300	1909.00	14800	3404.00	21300	4899.00
1900	437.00	8400	1932.00	14900	3427.00	21400	4922.00
2000	460.00	8500	1955.00	15000	3450.00	21500	4945.00
2100	483.00	8600	1978.00	15100	3473.00	21600	4968.00
2200	506.00	8700	2001.00	15200	3496.00	21700	4991.00
2300	529.00	8800	2024.00	15300	3519.00	21800	5014.00
2400	552.00	8900	2047.00	15400	3542.00	21900	5037.00
2500	575.00	9000	2070.00	15500	3565.00	22000	5060.00
2600	598.00	9100	2093.00	15600	3588.00	22100	5083.00
2700	621.00	9200	2116.00	15700	3611.00	22200	5106.00
2800	644.00	9300	2139.00	15800	3634.00	22300	5129.00
2900	667.00	9400	2162.00	15900	3657.00	22400	5152.00
3000	690.00	9500	2185.00	16000	3680.00	22500	5175.00
3100	713.00	9600	2208.00	16100	3703.00	22600	5198.00
3200	736.00	9700	2231.00	16200	3726.00	22700	5221.00
3300	759.00	9800	2254.00	16300	3749.00	22800	5244.00
3400	782.00	9900	2277.00	16400	3772.00	22900	5267.00
3500	805.00	10000	2300.00	16500	3795.00	23000	5290.00
3600	828.00	10100	2323.00	16600	3818.00	23100	5313.00
3700	851.00	10200	2346.00	16700	3841.00	23200	5336.00
3800	874.00	10300	2369.00	16800	3864.00	23300	5359.00
3900	897.00	10400	2392.00	16900	3887.00	23400	5382.00
4000	920.00	10500	2415.00	17000	3910.00	23500	5405.00
4100	943.00	10600	2438.00	17100	3933.00	23600	5428.00
4200	966.00	10700	2461.00	17200	3956.00	23700	5451.00
4300	989.00	10800	2484.00	17300	3979.00	23800	5474.00
4400	1012.00	10900	2507.00	17400	4002.00	23900	5497.00
4500	1035.00	11000	2530.00	17500	4025.00	24000	5520.00
4600	1058.00	11100	2553.00	17600	4048.00	24100	5543.00
4700	1081.00	11200	2576.00	17700	4071.00	24200	5566.00
4800	1104.00	11300	2599.00	17800	4094.00	24300	5589.00
4900	1127.00	11400	2622.00	17900	4117.00	24400	5612.00
5000	1150.00	11500	2645.00	18000	4140.00	24500	5635.00
5100	1173.00	11600	2668.00	18100	4163.00	24600	5658.00
5200	1196.00	11700	2691.00	18200	4186.00	24700	5681.00
5300	1219.00	11800	2714.00	18300	4209.00	24800	5704.00
5400	1242.00	11900	2737.00	18400	4232.00	24900	5727.00
5500	1265.00	12000	2760.00	18500	4255.00	25000	5750.00
5600	1288.00	12100	2783.00	18600	4278.00	25100	5773.00
5700	1311.00	12200	2806.00	18700	4301.00	25200	5796.00
5800	1334.00	12300	2829.00	18800	4324.00	25300	5819.00
5900	1357.00	12400	2852.00	18900	4347.00	25400	5842.00
6000	1380.00	12500	2875.00	19000	4370.00	25500	5865.00
6100	1403.00	12600	2898.00	19100	4393.00	25600	5888.00
6200	1426.00	12700	2921.00	19200	4416.00	25700	5911.00
6300	1449.00	12800	2944.00	19300	4439.00	25800	5934.00
6400	1472.00	12900	2967.00	19400	4462.00	25900	5957.00
6500	1495.00	13000	2990.00	19500	4485.00	26000	5980.00
						26100	6003.00

Fig. 20.1 Example of a Taxable Pay Table

TABLE A - PAY ADJUSTMENT

WEEK 1
Apr 6 to Apr 12

Code	Total pay adjustment to date £	Code	Total pay adjustment to date £	Code	Total pay adjustment to date £	Code	Total pay adjustment to date £	Code	Total pay adjustment to date £	Code	Total pay adjustment to date £	Code	Total pay adjustment to date £	Code	Total pay adjustment to date £	Code	Total pay adjustment to date £
0	NIL																
1	0.37	61	11.91	121	23.45	181	34.99	241	46.52	301	58.06	351	67.68	401	77.29	451	86.91
2	0.56	62	12.10	122	23.64	182	35.18	242	46.72	302	58.25	352	67.87	402	77.49	452	87.10
3	0.75	63	12.29	123	23.83	183	35.37	243	46.91	303	58.45	353	68.06	403	77.68	453	87.29
4	0.95	64	12.49	124	24.02	184	35.56	244	47.10	304	58.64	354	68.25	404	77.87	454	87.49
5	1.14	65	12.68	125	24.22	185	35.75	245	47.29	305	58.83	355	68.45	405	78.06	455	87.68
6	1.33	66	12.87	126	24.41	186	35.95	246	47.49	306	59.02	356	68.64	406	78.25	456	87.87
7	1.52	67	13.06	127	24.60	187	36.14	247	47.68	307	59.22	357	68.83	407	78.45	457	88.06
8	1.72	68	13.25	128	24.79	188	36.33	248	47.87	308	59.41	358	69.02	408	78.64	458	88.25
9	1.91	69	13.45	129	24.99	189	36.52	249	48.06	309	59.60	359	69.22	409	78.83	459	88.45
10	2.10	70	13.64	130	25.18	190	36.72	250	48.25	310	59.79	360	69.41	410	79.02	460	88.64
11	2.29	71	13.83	131	25.37	191	36.91	251	48.45	311	59.99	361	69.60	411	79.22	461	88.83
12	2.49	72	14.02	132	25.56	192	37.10	252	48.64	312	60.18	362	69.79	412	79.41	462	89.02
13	2.68	73	14.22	133	25.75	193	37.29	253	48.83	313	60.37	363	69.99	413	79.60	463	89.22
14	2.87	74	14.41	134	25.95	194	37.49	254	49.02	314	60.56	364	70.18	414	79.79	464	89.41
15	3.06	75	14.60	135	26.14	195	37.68	255	49.22	315	60.75	365	70.37	415	79.99	465	89.60
16	3.25	76	14.79	136	26.33	196	37.87	256	49.41	316	60.95	366	70.56	416	80.18	466	89.79
17	3.45	77	14.99	137	26.52	197	38.06	257	49.60	317	61.14	367	70.75	417	80.37	467	89.99
18	3.64	78	15.18	138	26.72	198	38.25	258	49.79	318	61.33	368	70.95	418	80.56	468	90.18
19	3.83	79	15.37	139	26.91	199	38.45	259	49.99	319	61.52	369	71.14	419	80.75	469	90.37
20	4.02	80	15.56	140	27.10	200	38.64	260	50.18	320	61.72	370	71.33	420	80.95	470	90.56
21	4.22	81	15.75	141	27.29	201	38.83	261	50.37	321	61.91	371	71.52	421	81.14	471	90.75
22	4.41	82	15.95	142	27.49	202	39.02	262	50.56	322	62.10	372	71.72	422	81.33	472	90.95
23	4.60	83	16.14	143	27.68	203	39.22	263	50.75	323	62.29	373	71.91	423	81.52	473	91.14
24	4.79	84	16.33	144	27.87	204	39.41	264	50.95	324	62.49	374	72.10	424	81.72	474	91.33
25	4.99	85	16.52	145	28.06	205	39.60	265	51.14	325	62.68	375	72.29	425	81.91	475	91.52
26	5.18	86	16.72	146	28.25	206	39.79	266	51.33	326	62.87	376	72.49	426	82.10	476	91.72
27	5.37	87	16.91	147	28.45	207	39.99	267	51.52	327	63.06	377	72.68	427	82.29	477	91.91
28	5.56	88	17.10	148	28.64	208	40.18	268	51.72	328	63.25	378	72.87	428	82.49	478	92.10
29	5.75	89	17.29	149	28.83	209	40.37	269	51.91	329	63.45	379	73.06	429	82.68	479	92.29
30	5.95	90	17.49	150	29.02	210	40.56	270	52.10	330	63.64	380	73.25	430	82.87	480	92.49
31	6.14	91	17.68	151	29.22	211	40.75	271	52.29	331	63.83	381	73.45	431	83.06	481	92.68
32	6.33	92	17.87	152	29.41	212	40.95	272	52.49	332	64.02	382	73.64	432	83.25	482	92.87
33	6.52	93	18.06	153	29.60	213	41.14	273	52.68	333	64.22	383	73.83	433	83.45	483	93.06
34	6.72	94	18.25	154	29.79	214	41.33	274	52.87	334	64.41	384	74.02	434	83.64	484	93.25
35	6.91	95	18.45	155	29.99	215	41.52	275	53.06	335	64.60	385	74.22	435	83.83	485	93.45
36	7.10	96	18.64	156	30.18	216	41.72	276	53.25	336	64.79	386	74.41	436	84.02	486	93.64
37	7.29	97	18.83	157	30.37	217	41.91	277	53.45	337	64.99	387	74.60	437	84.22	487	93.83
38	7.49	98	19.02	158	30.56	218	42.10	278	53.64	338	65.18	388	74.79	438	84.41	488	94.02
39	7.68	99	19.22	159	30.75	219	42.29	279	53.83	339	65.37	389	74.99	439	84.60	489	94.22
40	7.87	100	19.41	160	30.95	220	42.49	280	54.02	340	65.56	390	75.18	440	84.79	490	94.41
41	8.06	101	19.60	161	31.14	221	42.68	281	54.22	341	65.75	391	75.37	441	84.99	491	94.60
42	8.25	102	19.79	162	31.33	222	42.87	282	54.41	342	65.95	392	75.56	442	85.18	492	94.79
43	8.45	103	19.99	163	31.52	223	43.06	283	54.60	343	66.14	393	75.75	443	85.37	493	94.99
44	8.64	104	20.18	164	31.72	224	43.25	284	54.79	344	66.33	394	75.95	444	85.56	494	95.18
45	8.83	105	20.37	165	31.91	225	43.45	285	54.99	345	66.52	395	76.14	445	85.75	495	95.37
46	9.02	106	20.56	166	32.10	226	43.64	286	55.18	346	66.72	396	76.33	446	85.95	496	95.56
47	9.22	107	20.75	167	32.29	227	43.83	287	55.37	347	66.91	397	76.52	447	86.14	497	95.75
48	9.41	108	20.95	168	32.49	228	44.02	288	55.56	348	67.10	398	76.72	448	86.33	498	95.95
49	9.60	109	21.14	169	32.68	229	44.22	289	55.75	349	67.29	399	76.91	449	86.52	499	96.14
50	9.79	110	21.33	170	32.87	230	44.41	290	55.95	350	67.49	400	77.10	450	86.72	500	96.33
51	9.99	111	21.52	171	33.06	231	44.60	291	56.14								
52	10.18	112	21.72	172	33.25	232	44.79	292	56.33								
53	10.37	113	21.91	173	33.45	233	44.99	293	56.52								
54	10.56	114	22.10	174	33.64	234	45.18	294	56.72								
55	10.75	115	22.29	175	33.83	235	45.37	295	56.91								
56	10.95	116	22.49	176	34.02	236	45.56	296	57.10								
57	11.14	117	22.68	177	34.22	237	45.75	297	57.29								
58	11.33	118	22.87	178	34.41	238	45.95	298	57.49								
59	11.52	119	23.06	179	34.60	239	46.14	299	57.68								
60	11.72	120	23.25	180	34.79	240	46.33	300	57.87								

Pay adjustment where code exceeds 500

1. Where the code is in the range 501 to 1000 inclusive proceed as follows:

   a. Subtract **500** from the code and use the balance of the code to obtain a pay adjustment figure from the table above.

   b. Add this pay adjustment figure to the figure given in the box alongside to obtain the figure of total pay adjustment to date * **£ 96.16**

2. Where the code **exceeds 1000** follow the instructions on **page 2**.

Fig. 20.2 Example of a Pay Adjustment Table (Week 1 of the tax year)

CROWN COPYRIGHT

Case Study: Bill Baker's first wages

Bill Baker, aged 18, works as a telesales operator at May's, a mail order company based in Mereford. His terms of employment are a 40 hour week at £6.00 per hour and a rate of time-and-a-half for overtime. His employer uses a swipe card system for recording time worked. He is paid on a weekly basis. The Inland Revenue have sent May's a Form P9 (T) stating that Bill's tax code for the current tax year is 419L.

In the first two weeks of the tax year Bill worked the following hours:

| week 1 | 40 hours normal rate |
| week 2 | 40 hours normal rate plus 8 hours at overtime rate |

How does Bill's employer, May's, work out his take-home ('net') pay for these two weeks? His employer has a number of basic documents to work from:

- Bill's *computer printout* showing the hours worked (recorded by the swipe card)
- *P11 deduction sheet* on which to work out all the calculations for tax deductions from gross pay (see fig. 20.3 on page 285)
- *National Insurance Contributions 'Table A'*
- *Pay Adjustment Tables* showing the employer how much pay, depending on Bill's tax code, is not subject to Income Tax - this is the Free Pay (see the previous page)
- *Taxable Pay Tables* showing the employer how much tax is payable on Bill's taxable income (see page 280)

The basis of the calculation is the P11 deduction sheet and we will show how, step-by-step, this will be completed, first with the Income Tax calculations and secondly with the National Insurance calculations.

Income Tax Calculations

Step one: calculate gross pay for week one

Establish how much gross pay Bill has earned:
Hours worked x rate per hour = gross pay
    40 x £6 = £240

Enter £240 in column 2 (pay for the week) of the deduction sheet
Enter £240 also in column 3 (total pay to date, ie £240)

Step two: calculate free pay to date

Calculate the free pay, ie untaxed pay, from the Pay Adjustment Tables on the page for week 1
Locate Bill's tax code of 419 and read off total free pay of £80.75

Enter £80.75 in column 4a of the deduction sheet

Step three: calculate taxable pay to date

Deduct total free pay from the gross pay to date (column 3 minus column 4a)
In this case £240 less £80.75 = £159.25

Enter £159.25, the taxable pay, in column 5 of the deduction sheet

Step four: calculate tax due to date

Select Table B of the Taxable Pay Tables, and find the tax due on £159 (pence are ignored). As there is not a figure for taxable pay of £159 this will be done by splitting £159 into £100 and £59, and adding up the tax due on these two amounts, ie £23.00 plus £13.57 = £36.57.

This figure, which shows tax at basic rate, now has to be adjusted for the amount of lower rate tax. This is done by deducting from it the figure shown in Table B (Lower Rate Relief) on the right-hand page of the tax table under 'Weekly Pay' for week no. 1, ie £2.48 the calculation is £36.57 – £2.48 = £34.09.

Enter £34.09 in column 6 ('tax due to date') of the deduction sheet

As this is the first week at work for Bill, this 'tax due to date' is also the tax for week one.

Enter £34.09 in column 7

Normally at this stage Bill's employer will work out his National Insurance Contribution. We will explain this shortly, but first we will see how the Income Tax is worked out for week two, because the employer will need to base his calculations on the figures for week one. The procedure is as follows:

Step five: calculate gross pay for week two

As Bill worked eight hours overtime in the second week his gross pay will be as follows:

Normal rate:	40 hours x £6	=	£240
Overtime rate:	8 hours x £9	=	£72
Total gross pay		=	£312

Enter £312 in column 2 of the deduction sheet in the line for Week 2

Enter £312 + £240 (last week's pay) = £552, in column 3 ('Total pay to date')

Step six: calculate free pay to date (week 2)

The figure will be obtained from the Pay Adjustment Table for Week 2. In this case, free pay to date against Bill's code of 419 is £161.50. 'Free pay to date' means the amount of money Bill has earned since he started on which he does not have to pay tax.

Enter £161.50 in column 4a of the deduction sheet

Step seven: calculate taxable pay to date (week 2)

As in week one, deduct free pay to date from total pay to date (column 3 minus column 4a), i.e. £552 – £161.50 = £390.50

Enter £390.50 in column 5 of the deduction sheet

Step eight: calculate tax due to date (week 2)

Select Table B of the Taxable Pay Tables, and find the tax due on £300 and £90 (pence are ignored): the tax amount is £69 plus £20.70 = £89.70.

This figure of £89.70, which shows tax at basic rate, now has to be adjusted for the amount of taxable pay taxed at lower rate. This is done by deducting from it the figure shown in Table B (Lower Rate Relief) on the right-hand page of the tax table under 'Weekly Pay' for week no. 2, ie £4.96: the calculation is £89.70 minus £4.96 = £84.74.

Enter £84.74 in column 6 ('tax due to date') of the deduction sheet

Note that this tax figure is not the tax that has to be paid in Week 2; it is the 'total due to date'; some of it will have been paid in Week 1.

Step nine: calculate the tax due for week two

As £34.09 of the tax 'due to date' was paid in week one, tax for week two is calculated as follows:
Total tax due to date minus tax paid to date, ie £84.74 minus £34.09 = £50.65

Enter £50.65 in column 7 of the deduction sheet

As mentioned earlier, Bill's employer will also work out on the same deduction sheet his National Insurance Contributions on a weekly basis. It must be stressed that this calculation, explained below, is a completely separate process and is an additional deduction from Bill's gross earnings.

National Insurance Contributions

Both Bill Baker and his employer, May's Mail Order will pay National Insurance Contributions. In their case, the contributions are 'not contracted-out'. As you will see from the illustration of the P11 deduction sheet on the next page there are columns for:
- earnings on which contributions are calculated – column 1a
- total of employer's and employee contributions – column 1b
- employee's contribution – column 1c

The figures for these columns should be copied from columns 1a, 1b, and 1c of the 'Table A' National Insurance Contributions tables which are available from the Department of Social Security.

Alternatively the figures could be calculated (using a calculator) by referring to the percentages shown in the National Insurance Tables. In this case the figures are as follows:

	column 1a (earnings)	column 1b (total contributions)	column 1c (employee's contribution)
	£	£	£
week one	240.00	42.98	18.93
week two	312.00	57.38	26.13

P11	Name: *William Baker*					Tax Code: *419L*		
Month no	**Week no**	Pay in the week or month 2	Total pay to date 3	Total Free Pay to date 4a	Total taxable pay to date (Column 3 minus 4a) 5	Total tax due to date 6	Tax deducted or refunded in the week or month 7
	1	240.00	240.00	80.75	159.25	34.09	34.09
	2	312.00	552.00	161.50	390.50	84.74	50.65
	3						
1	4						
	5						
	6						
	7						
2	8						

P11(extract)

For employer's use	Earnings on which employee's contributions are payable 1a	Total of employee's and employer's contributions payable 1b	Employee's contributions payable 1c	**Month no**	**Week no**
	240.00	42.98	18.93		1
	312.00	57.38	26.13		2
					3
				1	4
					5
					6
					7
				2	8

Fig 20.3 P11 Deduction Sheet for Bill Baker (extracts)

Note: for ease of illustration this form has been divided in half; in reality the sheet is horizontal in format. Income Tax and National Insurance Contributions would appear on one line for each week (or each month, if the employee was paid monthly).
The form shown here is a representation only – it has been simplified to make it clearer.

Bill's Net Pay Calculation

	Week One		Week Two	
	£	£	£	£
Gross Pay		240.00		312.00
Deductions				
Income Tax	34.09		50.65	
National Insurance	18.93		26.13	
Total Deductions		53.02		76.78
Net Pay		186.98		235.22

The table set out above summarises the deductions made from Bill's gross pay and shows that his net pay (what he actually received) was £186.98 in week one and £235.22 in week two. Bill's employer would set out this information in full each week on a *payslip*. In the next chapter we will examine payslips and the way in which wages are paid to employees.

The tax and National Insurance Contributions collected by May's through the PAYE system will be paid to the Inland Revenue on a payslip, together with the employer's National Insurance Contributions by the 19th of the *next* month.

chapter summary

❏ The basis of wage and salary calculations can vary between employees within the same organisation. An employee can be paid a basic wage only or can receive additional income in the form of overtime or a bonus.

❏ An employer, in order to be able to calculate wages, must keep records of attendance for all employees. Different organisations have different methods to suit their own requirements. These include:
- time books
- clock cards
- time sheets
- computer cards

❏ Income Tax and National Insurance Contributions are compulsory deductions from an employee's gross pay.

❏ An employee can also make voluntary deductions such as pension payments, savings scheme (SAYE) contributions, or voluntary givings (GAYE) payments.

❏ The amount of Income Tax which an employed person will pay will depend on the personal allowance, tax coding and total earnings.

❏ The PAYE system operated by employers calculates these deductions on a weekly or a monthly basis.

✍ student activities

Note: a modified blank P11 deductions sheet (which may be photocopied) is included in Appendix 1

20.1   Using the following words, complete the sentences listed below.

List of words to be used to complete the sentences:

net pay	gross pay
income tax	pension schemes
commission	overtime
piece rate	tax code
taxable pay	National Insurance Contributions
savings	

(a) .... is based on the principle of the more items the operators produce the greater the pay received.

(b) Compulsory deductions from an employee's gross pay include .... and ....

(c) National Insurance Contributions are calculated on an employee's ....

(d) Income tax is payable on an employee's ....

(e) A salesman will normally receive a .... payment on sales.

(f) Voluntary deductions from an employee's pay include ...., and ....

(g) The amount of income tax deducted from a wage depends upon the employee's ....

(h) .... rates are paid to workers who work beyond the normal number of hours for the working week.

(i) .... is the amount of pay employees take home in their pay packets.

20.2   Calculate the following employees' gross wage for the week, assuming that they are paid at an hourly rate of £6 for the first 40 hours and time-and-a-quarter for hours in excess of 40.

Employee	Hours worked during week
H. Marsh	35
D. Hall	42
E. Bristow	48
P. Patel	50

20.3 Joe Johnson works for a company which pays its employees working in the production area a bonus based on piece work rate. Joe receives a flat rate of £5.00 per hour and a weekly bonus of 50p for every article produced in excess of 100. Calculate Joe's gross wages for each of the following weeks:

	hours worked	items produced
Week 1	30	90
Week 2	40	100
Week 3	40	120
Week 4	45	160

> NOTE: FOR THE NEXT TWO ACTIVITIES YOU WILL NEED TO OBTAIN COPIES
> OF TAX AND NATIONAL INSURANCE TABLES.

20.4 You have just been appointed wages clerk at Bright's Breweries. Although most of the wages have been calculated by your predecessor, you have been left to calculate the wages of six new employees for the week beginning 6 April. The details are:

Employee	Gross Pay
J. Whitbread	£195.00
R. Banks	£210.50
L. Foster	£201.50
S. Watney	£200.50
F. Loveday	£250.75
R. Sisson	£275.50

You are to draw up deduction sheets (P11's) for each employee (or photocopy the example in Appendix 1), and

(a) calculate their income tax using Pay Adjustment Tables and Taxable Pay Tables (the employees all have the basic personal allowance)

(b) calculate National Insurance Contributions (not Contracted out) from National Insurance Table 'A' tables, or by using the percentage method

(c) calculate their net pay for the week

20.5 During the following week in the business referred to in question 4, the gross wages earned by the six employees are:

J. Whitbread	£215.00
R. Banks	£198.50
L. Foster	£198.45
S. Watney	£214.90
F. Loveday	£202.85
R. Sisson	£212.75

You are to use the deduction sheets drawn up in question 4, and calculate for each employee for week two:

(a) income tax

(b) National Insurance Contributions

(c) net weekly pay

21 Wages – statutory benefits and returns

In this chapter we turn to the duty in law (statutory duty) of employers to pay certain benefits to employees:

- *Statutory Sick Pay (SSP)* to most employees over the age of 16 who are away sick from work for four or more days in a row
- *Statutory Maternity Pay (SMP)* to female employees who are away from work to have a baby

Some of this money paid out by the employer can be reclaimed by deducting it from the National Insurance Contributions (NICS) due each month:

- *SSP* – a certain amount is recoverable if SSP paid out exceeds a certain percentage of total NICS paid for the month
- *SMP* – between 92% and 100%, depending on the size of the business

In this chapter we also look at the forms that have to be returned by an employer to the Inland Revenue, both *monthly* and *annually*.

We conclude by looking at some of the other Inland Revenue forms that an employer will encounter when staff join the business, and also leave the business.

Statutory Sick Pay (SSP)

Statutory Sick Pay (SSP) must by law be paid to most employees who are away sick from work for four or more days in a row. It is paid for *qualifying* days (days that 'qualify' for SSP) after the employee has been ill for three *waiting* days. In order to qualify for SSP the employee has to earn at least the amount at which National Insurance Contributions become payable. Some employers may 'top up' or replace this payment to provide the employee with full pay for the period of sickness, but here the employer stands the cost of the 'top up' or replacement pay. The object of the scheme is for the State to ensure that sick employees receive an income while they are incapacitated, whether it be because of serious illness or a bad curry.

The Department of Social Security issues tables setting out the rate of SSP and SMP. For example, in the tax year 1998/1999 the weekly rate of SSP was £57.70. If the employee worked a five day week (5 qualifying days) he or she would receive a daily rate of £57.70 divided by 5, ie £11.54.

Employees who are *not* entitled to SSP include:

- people who earn less than the NIC Lower Earnings Limit (ie they do not pay National Insurance)
- women over 60, men over 65
- employees contracted to work for less than three months
- people receiving Statutory Maternity Pay (SMP)
- people outside the European Community

procedure when an employee reports sick

If, for example, an employee called Bob is off sick, he will normally notify the employer if he cannot get to work, then:

- if he is off for less than seven days he will on return to work fill in an Employee's Statement of Sickness (Form SC2), or the employer's internal form saying what was wrong with him
- if he is off work for more than seven days he will need a doctor's note

questions for the employer to ask to determine level of SSP

How many days has the employee been off sick?

- 1 to 3 days – no SSP is payable – the employer is responsible for any sick pay
- 4 days or more – this is a Period of Incapacity for Work (PIW), and SSP is probably payable

Has the employee had another Period of Incapacity for Work (PIW) within the last eight weeks?

If this is the case (the SSP Tables issued by the Department of Social Security will help here), then this will affect the number of days for which SSP is payable. In effect one PIW will *link* with an earlier one, and SSP will be payable for the *whole* of the later PIW, including the first three days (see below).

For how many days is SSP payable?

SSP is payable for *qualifying* days. A *qualifying* day is a day on which an employee normally works, ie usually Monday to Friday. SSP is never payable for the first three days of a Period of Incapacity for Work (PIW), unless the PIW links with an earlier PIW (ie if the employee has received SSP within the previous eight weeks). In simple terms, normally if an employee is off sick, he is paid SSP from the fourth working day.

What is the daily rate of SSP?

The daily rate of SSP is the weekly rate divided by the number of qualifying days in that week.

Now look at the following examples:

example one

Bob falls ill with the 'flu' on Monday morning and keeps to his bed until the next Sunday afternoon. He normally works Monday to Friday, ie the qualifying days are Monday to Friday. He has not been off sick in the previous six months. When will he receive SSP? After the three waiting days.

PIW						
MONDAY	TUESDAY	WEDNESDAY	THURSDAY	FRIDAY	SATURDAY	SUNDAY
waiting day	waiting day	waiting day	qualifying day	qualifying day	non-qualifying day	non-qualifying day
NO SSP	NO SSP	NO SSP	SSP PAID	SSP PAID	NO SSP	NO SSP

example two

Two weeks later Bob has a relapse, and is off sick for a further Monday to Friday. He now has two linking Periods of Incapacity for Work (PIWs), and so there are no waiting days in the second PIW.

PIW						
MONDAY	TUESDAY	WEDNESDAY	THURSDAY	FRIDAY	SATURDAY	SUNDAY
qualifying day	qualifying day	qualifying day	qualifying day	qualifying day	non-qualifying day	non-qualifying day
SSP PAID	SSP PAID	SSP PAID	SSP PAID	SSP PAID	NO SSP	NO SSP

problems with weekends and SSP

Confusion is sometimes caused by weekends (or non-working days) when calculating eligibility for SSP. Remember the following:

- a Period of Incapacity for Work (PIW) can include non-working days, eg the weekend
- but . . . calculations for SSP are based on *qualifying* days, ie working days
- and . . . the first three qualifying days (ie not normally Saturday or Sunday) are *waiting* days for which SSP is *not* payable

For example, if Bob falls ill on a Sunday, and there is no previous linking PIW, the PIW begins on Sunday, but the first of the three qualifying days is Monday, and he will receive SSP from Thursday, the first qualifying day, as in example one on the previous page.

recovery of SSP by the employer – Percentage Threshold Scheme (PTS)

If the employer qualifies under the Percentage Threshold Scheme (PTS), the employer can reclaim a certain amount of SSP. How does the employer qualify? If the employer in any one month pays out in SSP more than 13% of gross Class 1 National Insurance contributions then the employer can recover the excess. For example, suppose total gross monthly National Insurance contributions are £1,000 and the employer pays out £200 in SSP, an excess of £70 has been paid. (13% of £1,000 is £130, and £200 minus £130 is £70). This £70 can be reclaimed by deducting it from the monthly payment of NICS to the Inland Revenue.

Statutory Maternity Pay (SMP)

Statutory Maternity Pay (SMP) is paid to an employee who is away from work to have and look after a baby, even if she does not intend to return to work. It is payable for a period of up to 18 weeks. Like SSP it is payable by the employer and recoverable by deduction from National Insurance contributions paid by the employer to the Inland Revenue. Unlike most SSP, most or all of SMP is recoverable, plus an allowance for NIC *paid on the SMP.*

procedure when an employee becomes pregnant

If an employee reports that she is pregnant, an employer should

- ask for medical evidence of the due date of the baby (normally on Form MATB1 from the doctor)
- look at the SMP Tables issued by the Department of Social Security and find the expected week of confinement (when the baby is due) in Column 1, then read off in Column 2 the *qualifying week* (15 weeks before the confinement week); this qualifying week is critical for the payment of SMP (see below)

does the employee qualify for SMP?

In order to qualify for SMP, a woman must

- be continuously employed for at least 26 weeks into the qualifying week (see above)
- be paid at least the lower earnings limit for NIC (ie she must be paying NICs)
- still be pregnant in the 11th week before the due date, or have had the baby by then
- stop working for the employer when payment is to be made
- remain within the EC, and not be taken into legal custody!
- give 21 days' notice of the start of the Maternity Pay Period

how much SMP?

- *higher rate* – for the first six weeks of payment: 90% of the employee's average weekly earnings

- *lower rate* – payable for the rest of the Maternity Pay Period, at rates set out in the DSS Statutory Maternity Pay Tables (£57.70 per week for the 1998/1999 tax year)

what is the time schedule for payment of SMP?

The choice of the timing of the Maternity Pay Period (MPP), ie when SMP is paid, lies with the pregnant woman. She may, for instance want to carry on working as long as possible, and use the time off work and MPP for the period of sleepless nights *after* the birth. There are, however, certain constraints:

- the MPP cannot start *before* the eleventh week before the Expected Week of Confinement
- the latest MPP can start is the Sunday after the birth of the child

Look at the diagram in fig. 21.1 set out below – time runs horizontally:

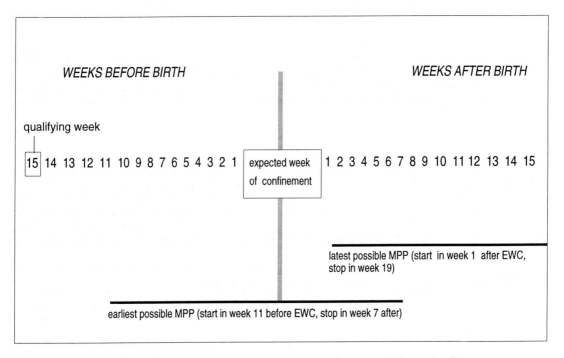

Fig. 21.1 Time schedule for payment of Statutory Maternity Pay

recovery of SMP by the employer

SMP is recorded on the employee's P11 deductions sheet, together with SMP recovered; NIC and income tax are deducted where appropriate. SMP is recovered when the monthly return of NIC and income tax is made to the Inland Revenue (see page 293). An additional percentage of gross SMP is also recoverable at the same time to compensate for NIC contributions made.

employer's maternity pay schemes

It must be stressed that SMP is a state benefit and may be 'topped up' by an employer's maternity payment scheme which may be offered as part of the pay package offered with a job. SMP represents the minimum benefit payable, and must be paid where the woman qualifies for it.

month-end returns

So far in this chapter we have looked at Statutory Sick Pay and Statutory Maternity Pay – additional items which will be included on the P11 deduction sheet explained in the last chapter. We now turn to examine how the income tax and National Insurance Contributions collected through the PAYE system and recorded on the P11 deduction sheet are sent to the Inland Revenue each month.   The payments will normally comprise:

tax deducted from employees in the month

plus	National Insurance Contributions deducted from employees in the month
plus	employer's National Insurance Contributions for the month
less	any tax refunded to employees in the month
less	any SSP or SMP recoverable
less	any compensation for NIC paid on SMP

The Inland Revenue supplies the employer with all the necessary paperwork:

Form P32

The Inland Revenue provide the employer with a large yellow sheet known as Form P32. This records week-by-week or month-by-month all the items listed in the above formula, and calculates the total that has to be sent the Inland Revenue each month. The employer does not *have* to use this form, but it is a very useful aid, and can also be used when calculating the figures for the annual return on Form P35 (see the next section).

P30B Payslip

The Inland Revenue provides the employer with a book of payslips, one payslip for each month (see fig 21.2 below). The employer completes the payslip with the amount of income tax and net National Insurance, figures already calculated on Form P32. The payslip is then sent with a payment – a cheque normally – to reach the Inland Revenue by the 19th of the following month. The payslip can be sent by post, through the bank credit clearing, or through the Post Office using Girobank or cash settlement. Businesses which make small PAYE payments can make settlement quarterly rather than monthly.

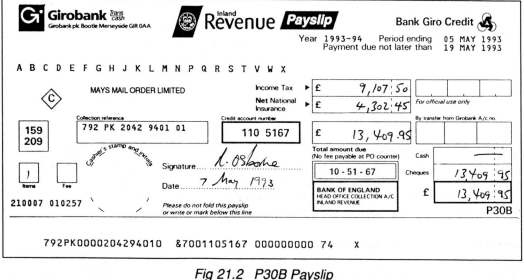

Fig 21.2   P30B Payslip
CROWN COPYRIGHT

year-end returns

At the end of each tax year, and by 19 May, an employer must send to the Inland Revenue:
- Form P14 for each employee
- Form P35 'Employer's Annual Return'

Form P14

This form, illustrated in fig. 21.3 below, summarises the pay and deductions for each employee for the tax year ending 5 April. It includes details of
- the employee and the National Insurance Number
- National Insurance Contributions (both employee's and employee's plus employer's)
- any SSP and SMP paid
- total pay for the year
- income tax deducted in the year
- pay and tax in any previous employment in the tax year

The form comes in three parts, the top two copies are sent to the Inland Revenue with Form P35 (see below), and the bottom copy is given to the employee as a P60. The information on Form P14 is taken from the totals of the employee's P11 deduction sheet and from the personnel records.

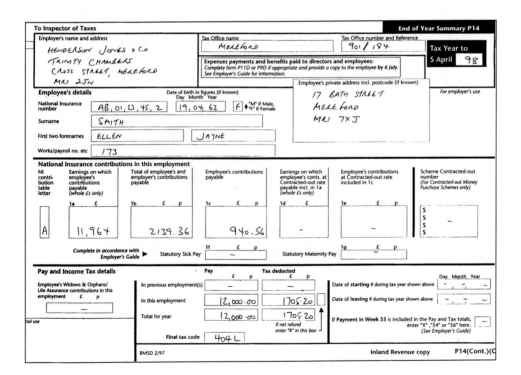

Fig. 21.3 Form P14 (P60)
CROWN COPYRIGHT

Form P35

The principal annual return of an employer is Form P35, the 'Employer's Annual Return', which has to be sent to the Inland Revenue by 19 May, together with Forms P14 and any other supplementary forms, eg information about casual employees (P38A) and directors' and employees' benefits (P11D). Look at the illustration on the next two pages, and then read the notes that follow.

Inland Revenue

Tax district reference   084

Employer's Annual Return
6 APR 1992 – 5 APR 1993

Collection reference
792 PK 2042 9301

Return to
220004 008008 AA 008008

HM Inspector of Taxes
WORCESTER
BLOCK A GOVERNMENT BUILDINGS
WHITTINGTON ROAD
WORCESTER   WR5 2LE

ENIGMA MUSIC PUBLICATIONS LIMITED

JAEGER HOUSE
BROADHEATH ROAD
WORCESTER WR7 OTE

Telephone
number   0905 357575

Your reference

PAYE, National Insurance Contributions, Statutory Sick Pay and Statutory Maternity Pay

This statement, declaration and certificate will help check that you made the right PAYE payments during the year. See your *Employer's Basic Guide to PAYE* (P8 cards) for guidance. Contact your Tax Office if you need further help.

You are required by law to:

• complete and sign this form
• send it to your Tax Office with the DSS and Inland Revenue copies of the *End of Year Summary* (form P14) for each employee you were required to complete a *Deductions*

Working Sheet (form P11) for during the year. You should do this by: 19 MAY 93

You may be charged penalties if you miss the deadline and penalised or prosecuted if you make false statements.

You should send any payment due to the Inland Revenue Accounts Office immediately. Interest is chargeable on amounts not paid by 19 April. Do not send payment with this form - see your payslip booklet for instructions.

Checklist

Tick the boxes. You must answer each question.

1 Have you enclosed an *End of Year Summary* (form P14) for every person in your paid employment, either on a casual basis or otherwise, during the above tax year?

No _____   Yes ✓

If no, please make a declaration on an *Employer's Supplementary Return* (form P38A).

2 Did you agree to bear any tax for any employee?

No ✓   Yes _____

3 So far as you know, did anyone else pay expenses or provide benefits or vouchers exchangeable for money, goods or services to any of your employees because they were employed by you during the year?

No ✓   Yes _____

4 Did anyone employed by a person or company outside the UK work for you in the UK for 30 or more days in a row?

No ✓   Yes _____

If yes, have you included them in the list on the back of this form or on any continuation sheets?

No _____   Yes _____

5 Have you paid any of an employee's pay to someone other than that employee (for example, to a school)?

No ✓   Yes _____

If yes, have you included it in the payments shown on that employee's *End of Year Summary* (form P14)?

No _____   Yes _____

Declaration and Certificate

This declaration and certificate covers any documents authorised by the Inland Revenue as substitutes for the forms mentioned below.

I declare and certify that for the above tax year:
(tick one box for each section)

• I enclose an *End of Year Summary* (form P14) for each employee for whom I was required to complete a *Deductions Working Sheet* (form P11) during the year ✓

• completed *Employer's Supplementary Returns* (form P38A)

are enclosed ✓   are not due _____

• completed *Expenses and Benefits Statements* (forms P11D and/or form P11D(b))

are enclosed ✓   will be sent later _____   are not due _____

• completed *Returns of Expenses Payments and Income from which Tax Cannot be Deducted* (form P9D) for employees earning at a rate of less than £8,500 per annum

are enclosed _____   will be sent later _____   are not due ✓

(If you are a new employer we may not have sent you any forms P11D or P9D. If you are paying expenses or providing benefits refer to the *Employer's Further Guide to PAYE* (booklet P7). Ask your Tax Office for these forms if you need them.)

All the details on this form and any forms enclosed are fully and truly stated to the best of my knowledge and belief.
Signature of employer

E. Agle   E. RAGLE

Capacity in which signed
COMPANY SECRETARY

Date
(day/month/year)
01.05.93

Fig. 21.4 Employer's Annual Return (P35) – front
CROWN COPYRIGHT

Deductions Working Sheets

You should list below the individual *Deductions Working Sheets* (forms P11) which you have filled in during the year and which contain a figure under any of the headings.

You should prepare continuation sheets if there is not enough space to list all your employees. Enter only the figures for ' this employment '.

Employee's name Put an asterisk (*) beside the name if the person is a director	National Insurance contributions (NIC). Enter the total of employee's and employer's NIC	Statutory Sick Pay (SSP) paid	Statutory Maternity Pay (SMP)	Income tax deducted or refunded. Write 'R' beside amount to show a net refund
* ALICE RASLE	£ 762.45	£ .	£ .	£ 500.—
* GOWARD RASLE	£ 4085.08	£ .	£ .	£ 4975.00
DORA PENNY	£ 367.68	£ .	£ .	£ 201.14
	£ .	£ .	£ .	£ .
	£ .	£ .	£ .	£ .
	£ .	£ .	£ .	£ .
	£ .	£ .	£ .	£ .
	£ .	£ .	£ .	£ .
	£ .	£ .	£ .	£ .
	£ .	£ .	£ .	£ .

Calculation of National Insurance contributions and income tax now due

	National Insurance contributions (NIC)	Statutory Sick Pay (SSP) paid	Statutory Maternity Pay (SMP)	Income tax
Totals from this page (remember to deduct any amounts marked 'R')	A £ 5215.21	£ .	£ .	£ 5676.14
Totals from continuation sheets	B £ —.—	£ .	£ .	£ .
Totals paid (A+B)	C £ 5215.21	£ .	£ .	£ 5676.14
Received from the Inland Revenue to pay SSP or SMP	D £ —.—			
Total SSP recovered (1991-92 onwards) - see your *Employer's Payment Record* (form P32)*		E £ —.—		
NIC compensation on SSP (only complete if form is used for 1990-91 or earlier)**		F £ —.—		
NIC compensation on SMP - see your *Employer's Payment Record* (form P32)			G £ —.—	
Received from the Inland Revenue to refund tax				H £ —.—
Tax deducted from subcontractors - see your *Contractor's Statement* (form SC35)				I £ —.—
	C+D	E(1991-92 onwards) C+F (1990-91 or earlier)	C+G	C+H+I
Totals	J £ 5215.21	£ —.—	£ —.—	£ 5676.14
Total SSP recovered/compensation	K £ —.—			
Total SMP recovered/compensation	L £ —.—			
NIC payable to Accounts Office (J minus K minus L)	M £ 5215.21			
NIC already paid	N £ 5215.21			
NIC now due (M minus N)	O £ NIL.			
Tax already paid				P £ 5676.14
Tax now due (J minus P)				Q £ NIL.

*The current rules for Statutory Sick Pay recovery are in booklet NI268.

**NIC compensation on Statutory Sick Pay due and paid after 5 April 1991 is abolished.

Claim for payments for contracted-out pensions

I claim payment under Section 7 of the Social Security Act 1986 for each employee on whose *End of Year Summary* (form P14) I have entered a scheme contracting-out number. So far as I know, none of these employees is in an employment which has been contracted-out by reference

to any other scheme since 1 January 1986. My employer's contracting-out number, where applicable, is:

£ —

(You will find the number on the Occupational Pensions Board's Certificate)

Fig. 21.5 Employer's Annual Return (P35) – back
CROWN COPYRIGHT

Form P35 – explanatory notes

The P35 summarises all the P14s that you are sending to the Inland Revenue. It contains:

- a declaration by the employer that all the figures are accurate and complete
- a list of all the P11 deduction sheets completed completed during the year
- a calculation of National Insurance Contributions and income tax due for the year (figures which can be taken from the P32 yellow summary sheet) and any amount outstanding at the year-end

The P35 also refers to supplementary forms which may also have to be sent. These include:

P38A   A return of any casual employment taken on by the employer during the tax year

P11D   A return of expenses and benefits in kind (eg company cars, holidays) provided to employees who earn over £8,500 per year or who are company directors (or both)

P9D   A return of expenses and benefits in kind (eg company cars, holidays) provided to employees earning under £8,500 per year and who are not company directors

other pay and tax records: P45 and P46

Form P45

When an employee leaves a business, the employer is required to complete form P45. This form gives the following information about the employee:

- tax (PAYE) reference of employee
- National Insurance number of employee
- name and address of employee
- date of leaving
- tax code at date of leaving
- total pay to date during the tax year
- total tax to date during the tax year

Form P45 is in three parts, with parts 2 and 3 being carbon copies of part 1. The employer sends part 1 to the local tax office and parts 2 and 3 are given to the departing employee. When starting a new job, the employee hands these two parts to the new employer, who keeps part 2, completes further information on part 3 and sends it to the local tax office.

Form P46

A Form P46 is used when a new employee has no P45 (eg a school or college leaver) and is starting a job which will last for more than one week. The employee will normally have to sign one of two declarations:

- *Declaration A* states that this is the first job of the employee since leaving full-time education
- *Declaration B* states that the job is the only or main job of the employee

Form P46 should then be sent to the Inland Revenue, and if the employee is earning more than the PAYE threshold a Form P15 (Coding Claim Form) should be given to the employee to complete and send to the Inland Revenue so that a tax code can be issued. Until the tax code has been issued the employee should be given what is known as an Emergency Tax Code – 344L (1993/1994 tax year).

If the employee is unable to sign P46 (if for example he has another job), it should be returned to the tax office unsigned, and the employee should be taxed on code BR (ie basic rate).

chapter summary

❏ Statutory Sick Pay (SSP) is paid by employers to most employees who are away sick from work for four or more days in a row.

❏ SSP is payable only for qualifying days in a Period of Incapacity for Work (PIW). The first three days of an unlinked PIW are waiting days for which SSP is not payable.

❏ Statutory Maternity Pay is paid by employers to women who are away from work to have a baby; it is normally payable for 18 weeks to eligible employees.

❏ Some SSP and most SMP is normally recoverable from the Inland Revenue; the claims are set against National Insurance Contributions and tax due under the PAYE system.

❏ Monthly income tax and NIC due to the Inland Revenue are listed on Form P32, and the money due is sent off on a payslip P30B.

❏ A yearly return of pay and deductions for each employee is sent by the employer to the Inland Revenue on Form P14. A copy (P60) is given to the employee.

❏ A Form P35, a summary of all the P14s is also sent annually to the Inland Revenue. It also refers to any other payments made or benefits given to employees by the employer.

❏ Form P45 is given to an employee who leaves an employer; it is retained and given to the new employer in due course.

❏ Form P46 is completed by a new employee who has no P45.

✍ Student Activities

You work as payroll clerk at Osborne Biscuits, a food company which employs 350 people on weekly payroll, including production line workers, packers and other clerical staff. Your particular area of work is dealing with payment of SSP and SMP. Set out below are some of the transactions with which you will have to deal.

Note: the company works a Monday to Friday working week; Saturday and Sunday are *not* qualifying days for SSP; the daily SSP rate is therefore the weekly rate divided by *five*. The company does *not* operate its own sickness pay scheme nor a maternity pay scheme.

21.1 It is a Friday pay day in the current month. Calculate the Statutory Sick Pay due, where appropriate, for the employees listed below for the period Monday to Friday. Use current rates. State in each case:
- the waiting days, where applicable
- the qualifying days, where applicable, for which SSP is payable

(a) Bill Taylor, reported sick on Monday, still off sick on Friday; not off sick for the last six months; weekly pay £150.

(b) James Mason, reported sick on Monday, still off sick on Friday; not off sick for the last three months; weekly pay £250.

(c) Christine Thompson, reported sick on Monday still off sick on Friday; off sick for ten days (SSP paid) a month ago; weekly pay £150.

(d) Caroline Morgan, reported sick on Monday still off sick on Friday; off sick for ten days (SSP paid) a month ago; weekly pay £250.

(e) Bruno Hicks, reported sick on Wednesday, still off sick on Friday; never reported sick before; weekly pay £150.

(f) Luigi Brunello, reported sick on Tuesday, still off sick on Friday; not off sick for four months; weekly pay £150.

(g) Tom Talbot, reported sick on Tuesday, still off sick on Friday; off sick for ten days (SSP paid) a month ago; weekly pay £250.

(h) Trevor Davies, reported sick on Monday still off sick on Friday; off sick for ten days (SSP paid) a month ago; weekly pay £250. He claims that he started his illness last Saturday, and wants this to be taken into consideration.

(i) Vicky Mostyn, who is on maternity leave on SMP and two weeks away from the expected week of confinement, is rushed into hospital on Monday with high blood pressure; her husband Martin phones in to ask for sick pay.

(j) Andrea O'Shea, a student on a temporary one month contract, earning £50 a week, reported sick on Monday, still off sick on Friday. She has not been off sick before.

21.2 It is the third week of April. You receive the following enquiries about Statutory Maternity Pay. State how you would deal with them. Where appropriate calculate the rate of SMP that will be received. Use the SMP Tables produced by the Department of Social Security.

(a) Denise Jones is expecting a baby; her form MATB1 states that it is due in the third week in November. She has been working for Osborne Biscuits for 10 years, and her current average weekly pay is £200. She wants to know if she is eligible for SMP, when she can give up work, the period of time for which she will receive SMP, and how much she will receive.

(b) Angelica Rice is also expecting a baby; her form MATB1 states that it is due in the second week in December. She has been working for Osborne Biscuits for 12 months, and her current average weekly pay is £150. She wants to know if she is eligible for SMP, when she can give up work, the period of time for which she will receive SMP, and how much she will receive.

(c) Emma Stephenson is expecting a baby; her form MATB1 states that it is due in the last week in November. She has been working for Osborne Biscuits since March of the same year, and her current average weekly pay is £200. She wants to know if she is eligible for SMP, when she can give up work, the period of time for which she will receive SMP, and how much she will receive.

21.3 A new colleague joins the payroll team of Osborne Biscuits and asks:

(a) on what Inland Revenue forms will SSP and SMP will be recorded?

(b) how much (if any) will the employer will get back from the Inland Revenue?

(c) how is it reclaimed?

(d) how is it paid?

What would your answers be?

21.4 Set out in the form of a memorandum to payroll staff a list of the Inland Revenue forms that will be needed for the annual return. Include with the list a brief description of the purpose of each of the forms and the main details that will be included on it. Use your own name and today's date.

21.5 As payroll clerk at Osborne Biscuits you occasionally deal with personnel leaving and joining the firm. What documentation and details would you need for:

(a) Sean O'Mallory who is leaving Osborne Biscuits to join Pitman Pasta Products.

(b) Heather Farmer who has just joined you as Marketing Assistant, having just completed a full-time course at Mereford University. She has not worked or claimed benefit since finishing her studies.

In you answer state what will happen to the documentation used.

22 Payment of wages

In the previous two chapters we looked at the way in which an employer calculates gross pay, deductions and net pay. We also looked at the forms and returns an employer will encounter when dealing with the payroll. In this chapter we will examine payroll as it affects the employee. We will explain:

- the payslip
- the methods used to pay wages

We will also look at the internal records an employer maintains to record wages and deductions, and the entries relating to payroll that need to be made in the accounting system of a business.

pay slip

An employer normally gives to each employee written details of earnings and deductions. This is set out in the form of a payslip which shows:

- the name of the employee

- the current tax code for the employee

- the period for which the pay is calculated

- the basic pay

- any overtime and/or bonus payments

- total gross pay (ie basic pay, plus overtime/bonus)

- details of compulsory deductions, ie income tax, National Insurance Contributions

- details of voluntary deductions, ie savings schemes, donations to charity, pensions

- cumulative totals (since the beginning of the tax year on 6 April) of gross pay, income tax and National Insurance Contributions

A specimen pay slip for the second week in the tax year is illustrated on the next page in fig. 22.1.

OSBORNE ELECTRONICS LTD			Pay Advice	Week 2
payments			**deductions**	
		£		£
Basic pay		180.00	Income tax	51.22
Overtime		80.00	National Insurance	27.09
Bonus		60.00	Superannuation	9.00
TOTAL GROSS PAY		320.00	SAYE	00.00
			TOTAL DEDUCTIONS	87.31
Gross pay to date		620.00		
Taxable pay to date		446.26	TOTAL NET PAY	232.69
Date	**Employee**	**Code**	Income tax to date	97.84
18.04.97	J Smithers	404L	National insurance to date	52.18

Fig. 22.1 Specimen payslip for the second week in the tax year

payroll

At the end of each week or month, an employer prepares a list of the earnings, deductions and net pay of each employee. This list is known as the *payroll,* and is the master internal record for these items. A typical payroll is illustrated on page 304.

Payroll details can be either recorded manually on specially ruled payroll sheets, or can be entered and stored on computer disc.

A ready-to-use payroll exercise on a computer system is set out in Chapter 23 of this book .

The payroll, as well as acting as a permanent record, can be used to give:

- total amounts the employer has to pay out in wages and salaries (used in the accounting records of the business – see pages 310 to 311)
- totals for employees' income tax and National Insurance Contributions which the employer has to forward to the Inland Revenue each month and at the end of the tax year on Form 35.
- a breakdown of the overtime and bonus payments

When employees are paid in cash, a separate sheet is needed for *cash analysis.* A cash analysis is required so that an employer can withdraw from the bank the exact quantities of bank notes and coin required to pay wages due to employees. A cash analysis is illustrated on page 305.

In the Case Study which follows, the payroll is for a business which pays wages in cash only.

Case Study: Payroll paid in cash

Situation

Caroline Hughes is employed by Bright Kitchens Ltd, a retail outlet which supplies and fits kitchen units in customers' homes. Part of Caroline's job is to complete the payroll for the hourly paid fitters who install the units. Bright Kitchens Ltd. have six fitters who are all paid a basic gross wage of £105.00 per week, plus overtime at a rate of time-and-a-half, and a weekly bonus based on company sales. All the fitters are paid in cash. The six fitters are:

Works Number	Name
111	P. Waite
112	D. Land
113	A. Brooks
114	G. Johnson
115	S. Barber
116	T. Lord

How does Caroline prepare the payroll for the week ending 21 July 19-1?

Solution

Caroline collects from the company's manager details of hours worked and the bonus to be paid to each fitter. In addition to the basic gross wage of £105.00 for the week, a bonus of £15.00 is to be paid, and overtime payments are:

- £15.57 for P. Waite, A. Brooks and G. Johnson
- £11.81 for S. Barber and T. Lord

These earnings are entered onto the weekly payroll sheet shown in fig. 22.2 on page 304.

Next Caroline calculates the compulsory deductions (income tax, National Insurance Contributions) and voluntary deductions (savings scheme) for each fitter. The amounts are:

	Income tax £	National Insurance £	Savings Scheme £
P. Waite	14.25	9.19	5.00
D. Land	17.25	7.79	5.00
A. Brooks	18.50	9.19	-
G. Johnson	14.50	9.19	-
S. Barber	13.50	8.85	5.00
T. Lord	12.25	8.85	5.00

These deductions are entered onto the payroll sheet (fig. 22.2) on page 304.

Caroline totals each earnings and deductions column and completes the following cross-checking of totals to ensure she has not made any calculation errors:

- add the basic earnings, plus overtime and bonus totals and compare with total gross pay:
  £630 + £70.33 + £90 = £790.33 (total gross pay)

- add the individual deduction column totals and compare with total deduction column:
  £90.25 + £53.06 + £20.00 = £163.31 (total deductions)

- subtract total deductions from total gross pay and compare with total net pay:
  £790.33 - £163.31 = £627.02 (total net pay)

In addition to the payroll calculations, Caroline is required to complete a cash analysis. This is prepared so that the exact amount of notes and coin can be ordered from the bank to be able to pay each employee the net pay amount. As employees do not like high value bank notes (it is difficult to pay for the bus fare home on pay day with a £50 note!), Caroline is instructed to use bank notes up to and including £20 in value.

Caroline uses a cash analysis sheet (see fig. 22.3) and enters the net earnings for each employee in the column on the right-hand side. The analysis of notes and coin is then made, entering the *number* of notes and coin required on the sheet. The *money amount* for each note and coin is entered as the total.

Caroline lists each column total and compares the total with the net pay amount.

29 x £20 notes	=	£580.00
1 x £10 notes	=	£10.00
4 x £5 notes	=	£20.00
13 x £1 coins	=	£13.00
4 x 50p coins	=	£2.00
7 x 20p coins	=	£1.40
3 x 10p coins	=	£0.30
4 x 5p coins	=	£0.20
3 x 2p coins	=	£0.06
6 x 1p coins	=	£0.06
Total net pay	=	<u>£627.02</u> agrees with payroll

A cheque is written out for this amount, and the appropriate amounts of notes and coin are requested from the bank to enable the pay packets to be made up.

Bright Kitchens Ltd.   Week ending: 21 July 19-1   Week Number: 16

| Work Number | Name | Earnings | | | | | Deductions | | | Employer's National Insurance Contributions | Net Pay |
		Basic £	Overtime £	Bonus £	Total Gross Pay £	PAYE (Income Tax) £	National Insurance £	Savings Scheme £	Total Deductions £	£	£
111	P. Waite	105.00	15.57	15.00	135.57	14.25	9.19	5.00	28.44	12.19	107.13
112	D. Land	105.00	-	15.00	120.00	17.25	7.79	5.00	30.04	10.84	89.96
113	A. Brooks	105.00	15.57	15.00	135.57	18.50	9.19	-	27.69	12.19	107.88
114	G. Johnson	105.00	15.57	15.00	135.57	14.50	9.19	-	23.69	12.19	111.88
115	S. Barber	105.00	11.81	15.00	131.81	13.50	8.85	5.00	27.35	11.83	104.46
116	T. Lord	105.00	11.81	15.00	131.81	12.25	8.85	5.00	26.10	11.83	105.71
	TOTALS	630.00	70.33	90.00	790.33	90.25	53.06	20.00	163.31	71.07	627.02

Fig. 22.2 Payroll: Employees paid weekly in cash

NAME	£20	£10	£5	£1	50p	20p	10p	5p	2p	1p	TOTAL (£ p)
P. Waite	5		1	2			1		1	1	107.13
D. Land	4		1	4	1	2		1		1	89.96
A. Brooks	5		1	2	1	1	1	1	1	1	107.88
G. Johnson	5	1		1	1	1	1	1	1	1	111.88
S. Barber	5			4		2		1		1	104.46
T. Lord	5		1		1	1				1	105.71
TOTAL (£ p)	580.00	10.00	20.00	13.00	2.00	1.40	0.30	0.20	0.06	0.06	627.02

Fig. 22.3   Cash Analysis Sheet

methods of payment of wages and salaries

cash payment

Many manual workers still have their wages paid in bank notes and coin. The cash is placed inside a wage packet marked with the name and pay reference or clock number of the employee. Details showing how the payment is made up and the deductions that have been made are provided to each employee. These details can be shown on a separate pay slip (see page 301) or written on the wage packet itself. Most wage packets are designed so that the employee can check the contents of the packet before it is opened.

An employer paying wages in cash can either sub-contract the work to a security firm which will make up the wage packets, or it can be completed by the company's own staff. Preparing wage packets involves collecting sufficient notes and coin from the bank to make up the exact amount for each pay packet. It is normal practice to telephone the bank in advance to tell them the exact denominations of notes and coin needed; these details are taken from a cash analysis (see previous Case Study).

cheque payment

This method requires the employer to write out individual cheques made payable to each employee for the net pay earned. Larger employers may well use a computerised wages (or payroll) system which can print out the payment cheques for each employee. The employer encloses the cheque in each pay packet with the pay advice slip and distributes them to employees who can then either cash them at the employer's bank or pay them into a bank or building society account.

bank giro credits

Almost all salaried staff, and quite a number of manual employees, have their wages and salaries paid directly into their bank or building society account. This reduces the security problem of cash handling by the employer, and the fear of loss or theft of the wage packet by the employee. Employers can make direct payments by means of bank giro credits (see Chapter 14). The employer gives each employee a pay slip, stating earnings and deductions, the net pay figure on the pay slip being the amount credited to the employee's bank or building society account.

The procedure for the payment of the giro credits through the banking system is for the employer to list the giro credits on a separate schedule and to take the credits, schedule and a cheque for the total of all the credits to the bank. These are then processed through the banking system. It is quite common for the employer's computer to work out the net pay, and print out the credits and payslips for the employees. The Case Study on the next page shows the bank giro system working on a small scale (three employees); it is quite possible that a large business would process literally hundreds of credits in this manner.

BACS payment of wages

As an alternative to using the bank giro credit system, an employer can make use of BACS (Bankers Automated Clearing Services), which is the banks' computerised payment transfer system (see Chapter 14). With this system an employer, using his own computer will prepare a magnetic tape or disc containing the banking and money amount details relating to each wage payment. This data is then sent, by courier or by telephone link, to BACS in London, who run it through their computer, crediting the employees' and debiting the employer's bank account on the same day.

If an employer does not have a suitable computer to prepare the tape or disc for BACS, a computer bureau or a bank may be used to send the payments through the banking system via BACS. All the employer has to do is to provide the bureau or bank with a schedule listing the employees' pay and the date of payment. The bureau or bank will already have been given the employees' banking details which will be held permanently on computer file. An example of a bank BACS payment system is National Westminster Bank's 'Autopay' system.

Case Study: bank giro credits for payment of wages

Electra Engineering Co Ltd has a bank account at the Southern Bank, Mereford branch(sort code no. 40-21-14); the number of the account is 11772375. The company has only three weekly-paid employees who have asked for their wages to be paid direct to their bank accounts. Their net pay this week has been calculated by the wages clerk as follows:

F Fleming	£212.76
G Green	£194.21
H Harman	£178.45

The details of their bank accounts are:

F Fleming   National Bank
         Mereford branch
         Sort code 60-24-48
         Account no. 01087138

G Green   Barllands Bank
         Eveshore branch
         Sort code 20-23-88
         Account no. 31286328

H Harman   Northern Bank
         Redgrove branch
         Sort code 30-18-34
         Account no. 23156382

The wages clerk asks you, as her assistant, to prepare the bank giro credit slips for these payments, together with a summary sheet, as at today's date, 27 March 19-1.

These documents are set out below.

FROM ___ Southern ___ **Bank plc**
___ Mereford ___ BRANCH

bank giro credit

Date ___ 27 March 19-1 ___

CODE NO	BANK AND BRANCH TITLE	ACCOUNT	AMOUNT
60-24-48	NATIONAL MEREFORD	F. FLEMING A/C No.01087138	£212.76

By order of ___ Electra Engineering Co. Ltd. ___

FROM ___ Southern ___ **Bank plc**
___ Mereford ___ BRANCH

bank giro credit

Date ___ 27 March 19-1 ___

CODE NO	BANK AND BRANCH TITLE	ACCOUNT	AMOUNT
20-23-88	BARLLANDS EVESHORE	G. GREEN A/C No.31286328	£194.21

By order of ___ Electra Engineering Co. Ltd. ___

FROM	Southern	**Bank plc**	**bank giro credit**

Mereford _____ BRANCH

Date __ 27 March 19-1 __

CODE NO	BANK AND BRANCH TITLE	ACCOUNT	AMOUNT
30-18-34	NORTHERN REDGROVE	H. HARMAN A/C No.23156382	£178.45

By order of _Electra Engineering Co. Ltd._

BANK GIRO CREDITS   Date __ 27 March 19-1 __

To SOUTHERN BANK plc
__MEREFORD__ BRANCH

Please distribute the credit slips attached
Our cheque for £585.42 is enclosed

for and on behalf of
Electra Engineering Co. Ltd.
_____*Jane Lewis*_____ signed
Director

CODE NO	BANK AND BRANCH TITLE	ACCOUNT	AMOUNT
60-24-48	NATIONAL MEREFORD	F. FLEMING A/C No. 01087138	£212.76
20-23-88	BARLLANDS EVESHORE	G. GREEN A/C No. 31286328	£194.21
30-18-34	NORTHERN REDGROVE	H. HARMAN A/C No. 23156382	£178.45
		TOTAL £	585.42

To enable these payments to be made, Electra Engineering Co Ltd must write out a cheque for £585.42, which is the *total* of the three payments. All these documents will be handed to Electra Engineering Co Ltd's bank for processing.

payroll and the accounting system

We have seen how a business calculates and pays the wages of its employees. We also need to appreciate how the paying of wages, pensions, tax and National Insurance Contributions by a business is recorded in the double-entry book-keeping system.

Clearly 'wages' or the cost of employing staff is an expense to the business and will appear in the profit statement among other expenses such as advertising, insurance and so on. The final cost to a business of employing staff is not, however, just the wages paid; adjustments have to be made for:

* income tax collected by the employer under PAYE and paid monthly to the Inland Revenue
* employees' National Insurance Contributions (NIC) collected by the employer under PAYE and paid monthly to the Inland Revenue
* employer's NIC paid monthly to the Inland Revenue
* employer's National Insurance Class 1A payments due each June to the Inland Revenue in respect of company cars and petrol benefits provided to company employees (note that the employee does not have to pay any NIC for these benefits)
* Statutory Sick Pay and Statutory Maternity Pay payments made by the employer and set off against (deducted from) NIC payments
* pension contributions deducted from *employees'* pay and paid to pension funds when a pension is contributory, ie the employee pays a set percentage of gross income
* pension contributions provided by the *employer* and paid to pension funds, ie where a pension is not contributory (the employee pays nothing) or where both employer *and* employee contribute

This list may seem long and complex, but in essence the book-keeping entries are straightforward. A common practice is to put all the entries through a 'wages and salaries control' account, as in the Case Study below. It must be stressed, however, that there is no 'set' method, and the system used will depend on the size and sophistication of the business.

In the Case Study below we look at an employer who employs ten staff on monthly payroll, and examine the likely book-keeping entries that will be made. We stress that these entries are 'likely' – different businesses may well set up different accounts, as mentioned above.

Case Study: Broadwater Designs Limited

Situation

Broadwater Designs Limited is a small business employing ten staff on a monthly payroll. The usual pay day is the 21st of the month. Payroll figures for July 19-1 are:

* gross wages	£10,000
* net wages paid to employees	£7,270
* income tax collected by PAYE	£1,500
* NIC (employees' contribution) collected by PAYE	£730
* NIC (employer's contribution)	£1,041
* pension: paid by the employees by deduction from pay	£500

The questions that can be asked are:
What payments are due to whom?
What entries will be made in the double-entry book-keeping system?

solution

payments due

employees will receive net wages of £7,270; this is calculated by deducting income tax, NIC and the employees' pension contributions from gross pay, ie
£10,000 – £1,500 – £730 – £500 = £7,270.

Inland Revenue will receive income tax and NIC collected from employees, plus the employer's NIC, ie £1,500 + £730 + £1,041 = £3,271, paid by the 19th of the next month.

Pension Fund (an independent investment company) will receive the employees' contributions of £500 in the month following the payment of wages.

book-keeping entries

It is from the payroll record that the double-entry book-keeping transactions for wages and salaries are made. A *salaries and wages control account,* which is a double-entry book-keeping account, is credited with the total of *all* the payments due as listed above: net pay, the amount due to the Inland Revenue, and the pension payment. The double-entry transactions are as follows:

- Transfer of totals to the control account:
  £7,270 (net pay) + £3,271 (Inland Revenue) + £500 (pensions) = £11,041
  — debit wages and salaries account £11,041 (the expense to the business)
  — credit wages and salaries control account £11,041

- Payment of wages and salaries, ie net pay:
  — debit wages and salaries control account £7,270
  — credit bank account £7,270

- Transfer to the Inland Revenue account of income tax (£1,500) and NIC (£730 + £1,041) = £3,271. This represents money that is *due to* the Inland Revenue, and will be paid by the 19th of the following month – it is a *creditor* account.
  — debit wages and salaries control account £3,271
  — credit Inland Revenue account £3,271

- Transfer of pension contributions of £500 deducted from gross pay. This represents money that is *due to* the Pension fund, and will be paid in the following month – it is a *creditor* account. Note that the Pension fund may either be operated by the employer or as here by a separate specialist investment company.
  — debit wages and salaries control account £500
  — credit pension contributions account £500

The double-entry accounts appear as follows:

Dr.			Wages and Salaries Control Account		Cr.
19-1		£	19-1		£
21 Jul.	Bank	7,270	21 Jul.	Wages and salaries	
21 Jul.	Inland Revenue account	3,271		(payroll for the month)	11,041
21 Jul.	Pension contributions	500			
		11,041			11,041

Dr.	**Wages and Salaries Account**		Cr.

19-1		£	19-1		£
21 Jul.	Wages and salaries control account	11,041			

Note: This figure is the sum of the gross pay of £10,000 plus the employer's National Insurance Contribution of £1,041. It is an expense of the business.

Dr.	**Inland Revenue Account**		Cr.

19-1		£	19-1		£
			21 Jul.	Wages and salaries control account	3,271

Note: This account shows the amount *due* to the Inland Revenue for income tax and National Insurance Contributions. Payment is made on a monthly basis, in the month after the wages payment. After payment has been made (debit Inland Revenue account, credit bank account), the account will have a nil balance.

Dr.	**Pension Contributions Account**		Cr.

19-1		£	19-1		£
			21 Jul.	Wages and salaries control account	500

Note: This account shows the amount due to the pension fund. Payment is normally made on a monthly basis, in the month after the wages payment. After payment has been made (debit pension contributions account, credit bank account), the account will have a nil balance.

chapter summary

- ❏ When payment is made an employer gives each employee a payslip which gives details of earnings and all deductions.
- ❏ An employer will keep payroll records of all its employees.
- ❏ An employer making payment of wages in cash will need to prepare a cash analysis sheet to ensure that sufficient notes and coin are available to make up each wage packet.
- ❏ An employer can pay wages and salaries by the following methods:
  - cash payment
  - cheques
  - bank giro credit
  - BACS payment
- ❏ An employer will transfer the payroll figures into the accounting system of the business so that the expense of employing staff can be quantified for the profit statement.

✎ student activities

22.1   Using the following words and form numbers, complete the sentences listed below:

List of words and form numbers to complete the sentences:
cash	P45
bank giro credit	P60
payslip	BACS
payroll	

(a)   An employer can pay employees' wages directly into their bank accounts by means of a
....

(b)   The form which is given annually to each employee showing the total amount of tax deducted during the previous twelve months is form ....

(c)   A .... gives details of an employee's gross earnings, deductions, and net pay.

(d)   When leaving an employer, the employee is handed form ....

(e)   A cash analysis sheet is used by employers who pay their employees in ....

(f)   A .... details and totals the gross earnings, deductions and net pay of all employees.

(g)   Wages can be processed through the banks' computer network by means of ....

22.2   A friend of yours has just started her first job. Her employer has asked how she would like her wages paid. The employer has offered her the following methods of payment:

• payment in cash
• payment by cheque
• payment directly into her bank or building society account

Advise your friend on the advantages and disadvantages of each method of payment.

22.3   Rule up and complete a payroll sheet from the following details of weekly pay:

	A Adams £ p	B Barnes £ p	C Cutts £ p	D Dodds £ p
Basic pay	110.00	110.00	110.00	110.00
Overtime	13.75	-	13.75	6.88
Bonus	10.00	10.00	10.00	10.00
PAYE (Income Tax)	13.75	15.00	13.50	10.25
National Insurance (Employees' contribution)	9.02	7.79	9.02	8.40
National Insurance (Employer's contribution)	12.01	10.84	12.01	11.38
Union fees	1.20	1.20	1.20	1.20

22.4   From the information contained in question 22.3, prepare a cash analysis on the basis of the following instruction:

Each employee's pay packet to be made up in the highest value bank notes and coin available, but no bank notes in excess of £20 are to be used.

22.5   Repeat question 22.4 using the following instruction:

Each employee's pay packet to be made up in the highest value bank notes and coin available with the following exceptions:

• no bank notes in excess of £20 to be paid
• no more than three £20 notes to be paid
• at least four £5 notes to be paid
• at least five £1 coins to be paid

22.6   Rule up and compile a payroll sheet from the following details of weekly pay:

Name	F Fleming	G Singh	H Hock	L Mehta	M Mann	P Potts
	£ p	£ p	£ p	£ p	£ p	£ p
Basic pay	96.00	104.00	110.50	110.50	110.50	126.00
Overtime	-	24.00	20.00	20.00	15.00	10.00
PAYE (Income Tax)	8.50	13.50	10.75	10.25	16.75	18.50
National Insurance (Employee's contribution)	5.63	8.51	8.73	8.73	8.28	9.23
National Insurance (Employer's contribution)	6.75	11.56	11.74	11.74	11.29	12.28
Savings scheme	10.00	10.00	5.00	5.00	5.00	10.00

22.7   From the information contained in question 22.6, prepare a cash analysis sheet using the following instruction:
Each employee's pay packet to be made up in the highest value bank notes and coin available, with the following exceptions:
• no bank notes in excess of £20 to be paid
• no more than three £20 notes to be paid
• at least four £5 notes to be paid
• at least five £1 coins to be paid

22.8   Wichenford Fine Foods employs five staff. The monthly figures for the PAYE payroll are as follows:
• gross wages	£5,000
• income tax	£750
• NIC (employees)	£350
• NIC (employer)	£500
• pension (deducted from pay)	£300

You are to advise the owner, Samuel Palmer, on the following points:

(a)   At present the employees are paid by cheque. Mr Palmer wants to know if there are any other suitable methods – how would they work? (Note: all the employees have bank accounts)

(b)   What accounts would you advise Mr Palmer to open up in his book-keeping system for payroll, and how would the month's figures set out above be posted to these accounts?

ASSIGNMENT

8

Payroll:
Super Blinds Limited

SITUATION

Sue Walker works in the general office of Super Blinds Ltd., a company which assembles and fits all types of blinds – vertical, horizontal, venetian, etc – mainly for business customers, but also for domestic customers. Part of Sue's job is to keep payroll records and to prepare wage slips for the three hourly-paid assembly employees and the two installation fitters. These employees are all paid weekly in cash.

The assembly workers are employed at the company's factory unit in Mereford. They use a clock recording machine to record hours worked and are paid at the rate of £4.00 per hour. The installation fitters travel around the country and use time sheets to record their hours worked. They are paid at the rate of £5.00 per hour.

The company's normal working hours for Monday to Friday are: 8.00 am to 12.30 pm, and 1.30 pm to 5.00 pm. Overtime is paid at the rate of time-and-a-quarter for weekday working, time-and-a-half for weekend working. The company operates a bonus scheme based on overall sales of the company. Each week a percentage bonus figure is calculated and all weekly paid employees are paid the percentage of their gross pay as a bonus. Sue has just received the time sheets and clock cards for the week 6 April to 12 April 19-1. The sales bonus for this week has been calculated at 10% of gross pay.

TIME SHEET (in hours)

Name A. Good   Works No: 215.   Week ending 12 April 19-1

Job No.	Mon	Tues	Wed	Thu	Fri	Sat	Sun
S 621	5	8	8				
S 622				6	8	4	
Sub-total	5	8	8	6	8	4	
Travel	3	1	1	3		3	
Waiting	–	–	–	–	–	–	
Total	8	9	9	9	8	7	

Supervisor ....P. Collins.......   Date .13 April 19-1...

TIME SHEET (in hours)

Name N. Hall   Works No: 216.   Week ending 12 April 19-1

Job No.	Mon	Tues	Wed	Thu	Fri	Sat	Sun
S 621	5	8	8				
S 622				4	8	4	
Sub-total	5	8	8	4	8	4	
Travel	3	1	1	4	1	2	
Waiting	–	–	–	–	–	–	
Total	8	9	9	8	9	6	

Supervisor ....P. Collins........   Date .13 April 19-1...

No.	111				
Name	H Ford				
Week ending:	12 April 19-1				

Day	In	Out	In	Out	TOTAL HOURS
M	0800	1230	1330	1700	
Tu	0800	1230	1330	1700	
W	0800	1230	1330	1700	
Th	0800	1230	1330	1700	
F	0800	1230	1330	1700	
Sa	0800	1300			
Su					
Total					

Ordinary time: .... hrs @ £.........

Weekday overtime: .... hrs @ £...........

Weekend overtime: .... hrs @ £...........

TOTAL GROSS WAGES

£

No.	112				
Name	J White				
Week ending:	12 April 19-1				

Day	In	Out	In	Out	TOTAL HOURS
M	0800	1230	1330	1700	
Tu	0800	1230	1330	1900	
W	0800	1230	1330	1800	
Th	0800	1230	1330	1700	
F	0800	1230	1330	1700	
Sa	0900	1300			
Su					
Total					

Ordinary time: .... hrs @ £.........

Weekday overtime: .... hrs @ £...........

Weekend overtime: .... hrs @ £...........

TOTAL GROSS WAGES

£

No.	113				

Name   J Thorne

Week ending: 12 April 19-1

Day	In	Out	In	Out	TOTAL HOURS
M	0800	1230	1330	1700	
Tu	0800	1230	1330	1900	
W	0800	1230	1330	1700	
Th	0800	1230	1330	1700	
F	0800	1230	1330	1700	
Sa					
Su					
Total					

Ordinary time: .... hrs @ £.........

Weekday overtime: .... hrs @ £..........

Weekend overtime: .... hrs @ £..........

TOTAL GROSS WAGES

£

STUDENT TASKS

You are to assume the role of Sue Walker (or Steve Walker if you prefer) and complete the following tasks:

1. Photocopy from Appendix 1 (or draw up) blank P11 deduction sheets for each employee and, having calculated the hours worked by each employee, calculate their gross pay, compulsory deductions, and net pay. Obtain the appropriate Tax Tables and National Insurance Tables from your local tax office. Assume that each employee has the personal allowance, and the appropriate tax code.

2. Complete pay slips for each employee. The specimen pay slip shown below can be used as a guide.

Super Blinds Limited		Pay Advice	
Payments		**Deductions**	
	£		£
Basic Pay		Income Tax	
Overtime		National Insurance	
Bonus		TOTAL DEDUCTIONS	
TOTAL GROSS		NET PAY	
Gross pay to date		Income Tax to date	
Taxable Pay to date		National Insurance to date	

Date	**Employee's name**	**Tax Code**	**Tax Period**

3. Draw up and complete a payroll sheet (see Appendix 1) for the five weekly-paid employees.

4. Draw up and complete a cash analysis (see Appendix 1) assuming the following:

    • no bank notes in excess of £20 to be paid
    • no more than seven £20 notes to be paid
    • at least two £5 notes to be paid
    • at least two £1 coins to be paid

5. During the week 13 April –19 April, assembly employees H Ford and J White and the two fitters record a normal 40 hour week with no overtime, and receive an 8% bonus. Complete their P11 deduction sheets for this second week.

6. On the Tuesday of the week 13 April – 19 April, J Thorne reports sick, and stays off for the rest of the week. The company's qualifying days are Monday to Friday, and J Thorne has no linked PIW. what Statutory Sick Pay would he receive?

7. Post the payroll transactions for the week 6 April – 12 April into the double-entry book-keeping system of the business on 13 April.   You should rule up the following accounts, and record the transactions on the appropriate day:

    • wages and salaries control account

    • wages account

    • inland revenue account

    • bank account

    Note: do *not* post entries for the payment to the Inland Revenue in respect of National Insurance Contributions and income tax, as this will not be paid until the beginning o f May.

23 Computer payroll

This chapter looks at the application of computers to payroll, ie the calculation of wages and salaries.

While the chapter follows the use of the Sage™ Payroll program, most other payroll programs designed for use with personal computers operate in a similar way.

To work through this chapter you will need:
- a personal computer with, preferably, a hard disk drive or, alternatively, twin floppy disk drives
- a printer
- a computer payroll program, such as Sage 'Sterling Payroll'

In order to demonstrate the use of computer payroll, we will follow the calculation of wages and salaries of Wyvern Mail Order Ltd for one tax year (from 6 April 1993 to the following 5 April). The chapter uses the tax year 1993-94, but you can easily use the current year – just key in the year date you are using whenever it is needed by the program.

An example printout is given at intervals for you to monitor your progress. However, it is unlikely that you will have exactly the same figures on your printout: this is because payroll programs are revised each year to take note of changes in tax rates, National Insurance Contributions and personal allowances. Your tutor or trainer will be able to check your printout for accuracy, based on the particular version and date of the software you are using.

getting started

Technical note
For the purposes of this chapter, the following information should be specified during installation and initialisation of the program (with SAGE Payroll, during the SAGELOAD program):

- The company name and address is:
  WYVERN MAIL ORDER LTD
  UNIT 42
  NEWTOWN INDUSTRIAL ESTATE
  MEREFORD MR4 8TH

- Records are needed for ten employees

- The chapter uses data for the tax year 1993-94; for simplicity, it has been assumed that changes in income tax bandwidths which took place from 18 May 1993 were in force from 6 April 1993.

Firstly you will need to have configured the payroll program to suit the type of computer being used, following the instructions in the manual. If you are at a college or training establishment, this will have been done for you already.

Once the program has been configured, the procedures are as follows:

Hard disk drive
• switch on the computer and printer
• at the C prompt (C>) key in SAGE or PAY (in upper or lower case) and press return; if this doesn't work, try keying in CD SAGE, press return, then key in SAGE or PAY and press return.

Twin floppy disk drives
• switch on the computer and printer
• insert the operating system disk in the 'A' drive (usually on the left-hand side); press any key
• if requested to do so, key in the date and time
• the A prompt (A>) will now be showing
• remove the operating system disk and insert the program disk in the 'A' drive, and your own payroll data disk (configured to suit your computer) in the 'B' drive
• key in SAGE (in upper or lower case) and press return

The date will appear on the screen and should be altered to 6 April 1993 (or the current year): this is done by keying in 060493 (or the current year). Remember that 6 April is the first day of the tax year. Press return.

Now key in the password: this is set initially as LETMEIN. Press return.

The main menu now appears as:

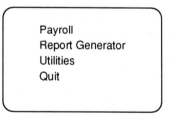

Payroll
Report Generator
Utilities
Quit

Important note: To quit the program, always return to this main menu (keep pressing escape [ESC] until you get to it) and select [Quit]. By doing this the data files will be correctly updated. Never quit by just switching off, or resetting the computer.

On the main menu, [Payroll] will already be highlighted; press return to take you to the payroll menu. This appears as:

Employee Details
Processing Payroll
Statutory Sick Pay
Statutory Maternity Pay
Government Parameters
Company Details

It is from this payroll menu that much of the program operates, and you will need to start from it, or return to it after entering data, on a number of occasions.

situation

Wyvern Mail Order Ltd is a recently-established supplier of kitchenware and utensils. It operates from a modern warehouse: Unit 42, Newtown Industrial Estate, Mereford MR4 8TH. The company publishes a mail order catalogue which is advertised in quality weekend newspapers. Orders are received from the public and despatched from the warehouse by carrier.

At 6 April 1993 (or the current year) there are six employees on the company's payroll. All employees are paid monthly.

You are the office clerk – your name is John (or Jane) Smith. You have been asked by the manager, Tina Mason, to set up a payroll system using the computer hardware and payroll software available to you. The computer payroll is to be used from 6 April 1993 (or the current year).

company details

Before starting payroll activities we must key in to the program details about the company. This is done as follows:

- From the main menu, select [Company Details]; press return.

Department names
- From the company details menu, select [Department Names]; press return.
- Enter the details of the following departments of Wyvern Mail Order Ltd:
    1. DIRECTORS
    2. SALES
    3. WAREHOUSE
    4. OFFICE
- Return to the company details menu by pressing [ESC] once.

By setting up the different departments of the company, we can analyse staff costs for each department.

Payment types
- From the company details menu, select [Payment Types]; press return.
- We now need to list the various types of payment made by the company – eg basic pay, overtime, bonus – and tell the computer whether each is subject to income tax, National Insurance Contributions, and pension contributions.

For Wyvern Mail Order Ltd the screen should be completed as follows:

Description	Tax	Nat. Ins.	Pension
1: BASIC	Y	Y	Y
2: OVERTIME	Y	Y	N
3: BONUS	Y	Y	N
4: COMMISSION	Y	Y	N

Note: In some pension schemes contributions will be based on the amount of basic pay plus overtime/bonus/commission.

- Press [ESC] once to return to the company details menu.

Adjustment types

- From the company details menu, select [Adjustment Types]; press return.

- Any adjustments made to a person's pay can now be listed. Such adjustments might include allowances for clothing, lunch, travel and subsistence (meals, and other expenses whilst working away), or deductions such as union subscriptions, social club subscriptions. We must tell the computer whether each adjustment is a plus or a minus to a person's pay, and whether the adjustment affects calculations for income tax, National Insurance Contributions and pension contributions.

For Wyvern Mail Order Ltd the screen should be completed as follows:

Description	+/–	Tax	N. I.	Pen
1: CLOTHING ALLOW	+	Y	Y	N
2: LUNCH ALLOWANCE	+	Y	Y	N
3: TRAVEL EXPS	+	N	N	N
4: UNION SUBSCRIPT	–	N	N	N
5: SOCIAL CLUB SUB	–	N	N	N

- Return to the payroll menu by pressing [ESC] twice.

Note that other company information can be entered from the company details menu:
- Company information: the bank account details of the company.
- Pension schemes: the rates applicable to the pension scheme (if any) operated by the company.
- Cash analysis limits: minimum quantities for cash analysis. This is used when paying wages in cash – it ensures, for example, that a person with net pay of £200 doesn't receive four £50 notes, but a spread of more useful denominations of notes and coins.

employee details

The details of employees of Wyvern Mail Order Ltd can now be entered.
- From the payroll menu, select [Employee Details]; press return.
- From the employee details menu, select [Add a New Employee]; press return.
  Note that:
  - [Add a New Employee] is used when setting up the information for a new employee
  - [Amend Employee Details] is used to change information about an existing employee
- Press return to accept the lower employee number of 1, and again to accept the upper employee number of 10. (The program should have already been set up during the installation process with ten employees.)
- The first employee record appears on the screen.
- The employee records are held by the program on <u>four</u> separate screens:

  screen 1: personal details of employee, eg name, address, date started in employment, current tax code, National Insurance number

  screen 2: department in which employed, Statutory Sick Pay qualifying days, rates of pay and overtime, adjustments screen 3: employee's bank account details, and pay from previous employment (if any)

screen 4: cumulative figures of pay and adjustments for the tax year to date

By using the [Pg Dn] or [Pg Up] keys each of these screens can be viewed.

- The first employee record is for Tina Mason, who is the manager of the company. Complete screen 1 as follows:

Employee No.	:	1 On HOLD: NO		Start Date	:	010890
				Leave Date	:	
Forenames	:	TINA		Holiday Return	:	
Surname	:	MASON				
				Tax Code	:	370L
Address	:	THE FIRS		Effective from	:	060493
"	:	WELSH ROAD		N.I. Number	:	AL459231B
"	:	MEREFORD WELLS		N.I. Category	:	A
"	:	MR8 4BT		Contracted-Out	:	N
				SCON Ref.	:	0
Works Number	:	1		Effective from	:	060493
Payment Type	:	GM				
Pension Ref.	:	0		Marital Status	:	M
Auto SSP/SMP	:	Y		Male/Female	:	F
Date of Birth	:	150446		Director	:	N

Notes:

– After keying in the employee's surname, use the space bar to delete any letters remaining of 'UNUSED EMPLOYEE'.

– After keying in the works number, use the space bar to delete any other numbers.

– When keying in the tax code you will be asked to 'Confirm Amendment' – use the right arrow key to move the cursor to 'Yes', and press return.

– The payment type is made up of two letters. The first is the way in which payment is made: C = cash; G = giro (ie bank giro credit); Q = cheque. The record letter indicates the frequency of payment: W = weekly; 2 = 2 weekly; 4 = 4weekly; M = monthly.

– The date 060493 can be entered, or the current year if you are using a different tax year from 1993-94.

- Press [Pg Dn] to go to the next screen.
- Complete screen 2 as follows:

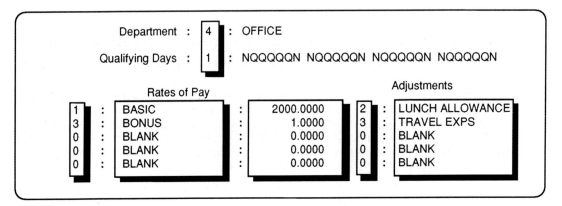

Department	:	4	:	OFFICE
Qualifying Days	:	1	:	NQQQQQN NQQQQQN NQQQQQN NQQQQQN

		Rates of Pay					Adjustments
1	:	BASIC	:	2000.0000	2	:	LUNCH ALLOWANCE
3	:	BONUS	:	1.0000	3	:	TRAVEL EXPS
0	:	BLANK	:	0.0000	0	:	BLANK
0	:	BLANK	:	0.0000	0	:	BLANK
0	:	BLANK	:	0.0000	0	:	BLANK

Notes:

– Qualifying days are used in the calculation of Statutory Sick Pay: N = a non-qualifying day; Q = a qualifying day.

– The basic rate of pay of '2000.0000' means that this employee earns gross pay of £2,000.

• Press [Pg Dn] to go to the next screen.

• Complete screen 3 as follows:

```
         Bank name  :  │  WESTERN BANK
  Branch Address 1  :  │  HIGH STREET
      "       "  2  :  │  MEREFORD

  Branch Sort Code  :  │  60–20–44

      Account Name  :  │  J & MRS T MASON
    Account Number  :  │  63482145
```

Note that this screen needs to be completed only when payment is to be made by bank giro credit. Ignore the details of previous and current employment.

• Press [Pg Dn] to go to the next screen.

• There is no information to be entered on this screen, as we are starting the payroll at the beginning of the tax year.

• Press [F10] twice. The program now asks "Post Edit Abandon" – notice that the cursor is already positioned over 'Post', which is the default, ie the answer the computer expects. If you are sure that you have entered the details correctly, press return and the employee record for Tina Mason will be completed.

• The second employee record now appears on screen.

• From the details given in fig. 23.1 (on the next two pages), complete the employee records for employees 2–6. Where information is not given, do not make an entry on the computer. When you have keyed in the information for each employee, press [F10] twice in order to show the "Post/Edit/Abandon" options – if the details are correct, press return to complete the employee record.

• Press [Esc] twice to return to payroll menu when all records have been entered.

Note that:

– Employee number 5 is 'yourself', ie John (or Jane Smith); complete the details as appropriate.

– The date 060493 can be entered, or the current year if you are using a different tax year from 1993-94.

– The words "On HOLD: NO" indicate that the employee will be included in the payroll run. "On HOLD: YES" would be used, for example, for a student who had previously worked for the firm and was now back at college, but expected to return at the next college holiday period – when he or she returns, the 'On HOLD' can be altered to 'NO' and he or she will be included in the next payroll run.

Employee No.	2 On HOLD: NO	3 On HOLD: NO
Forenames	PHILIP JOHN	LINDA
Surname	FLEMING	MEHTA
Address	24 VINCENT STREET	165 VICTORIA AVENUE
"	MEREFORD	MEREFORD
"	MR2 8AB	MR5 2AJ
"		
Works Number	2	3
Payment Type	QM	QM
Pension Ref.	0	0
Auto SSP/SMP	Y	Y
Date of Birth	110849	081069
Start Date	010890	011092
Tax Code	525H	360L
Effective from	060493	060493
N.I. Number	AB452124C	YL639427D
N.I. Category	A	A
Contracted-Out	N	N
SCON Ref	0	0
Effective from	060493	060493
Marital Status	M	M
Male/Female	M	F
Director	N	N
Department	3: WAREHOUSE	3: WAREHOUSE
Qualifying Days	1: NQQQQQN NQQQQQN	1: NQQQQQN NQQQQQN
	NQQQQQN NQQQQQN	NQQQQQN NQQQQQN
Rates of Pay	1: BASIC : 1000.0000	1: BASIC : 800.0000
" " "	2: OVERTIME : 12.0000	2: OVERTIME : 8.0000
" " "	3: BONUS : 1.0000	3: BONUS : 1.0000
Adjustments	1: CLOTHING ALLOW	1: CLOTHING ALLOW
"	4: UNION SUBSCRIPT	5: SOCIAL CLUB SUB
Bank Name		
Branch Address		
" "		
Branch Sort Code		
Account Name		
Account Number		

Fig. 23.1 Details for employee records

4 On HOLD NO	5 On HOLD NO	6 On HOLD NO
MICHAEL	JOHN (or JANE)	DAVID BRYAN
MANN	SMITH	BARNES
THE OLD RECTORY	217 LONDON ROAD	94 STATION ROAD
ELMLEY HACKETT	MEREFORD WELLS	MEREFORD
EVESHORE	WYVERN	MR2 7HT
EV8 9AP	MR8 3AK	
4	5	6
GM	GM	QM
0	0	0
Y	Y	Y
070265	311274	230575
010191	010992	010293
550H	350L	344L
060493	060493	060493
JZ459238A	PA623391B	JN668834C
A	A	A
N	N	N
0	0	0
060493	060493	060493
M	S	S
M	M (or F)	M
N	N	N

2: SALES	4: OFFICE	3: WAREHOUSE
1: NQQQQQN NQQQQQN	1: NQQQQQN NQQQQQN	1: NQQQQQN NQQQQQN
NQQQQQN NQQQQQN	NQQQQQN NQQQQQN	NQQQQQN NQQQQQN
1: BASIC :1800.0000	1: BASIC : 800.0000	1: BASIC : 600.0000
4: COMMISSION: 1.0000	2: OVERTIME : 8.0000	2: OVERTIME : 6.0000
	3: BONUS : 1.0000	3: BONUS : 1.0000
3: TRAVEL EXPS	2: LUNCH ALLOW	1: CLOTHING ALLOW
5: SOCIAL CLUB SUB	5: SOCIAL CLUB SUB	4: UNION SUBSCRIPT
NATIONAL BANK	EASTERN BANK	
CORN EXCHANGE	ORIENT WAY	
EVESHORE	MEREFORD WELLS	
30–81–34	40–46–90	
M MANN	J SMITH	
08749615	76349517	

Fig. 23.1 Details for employee records (continued)

processing the payroll

There are three stages to be followed for routine computer processing of payroll:

- *entering payments*, recording the amount earned by each employee during the week or month
- *running the payroll*, printing out a summary of payments to be made, followed by printing of payslips and, where appropriate, printing of bank giro credits and cheques
- *backing up the date*, copying the data to a back up disk

month 1 – April

Entering payments

- From the main menu select [Processing Payroll]; press return.
- Enter the date at which the payroll is to be run – for April 1993 key in 300493; press return.
- Confirm that the tax year is "93 to 94" (or the current year) by highlighting 'Yes'; press return.
- Highlight [Monthly]; the program will respond with "OK to process"; press return.
- At the new screen, press return for both lower employee number and upper employee number, ie we are going to process the payroll for all employees of Wyvern Office Supplies Ltd. Respond to the prompt "Clear payments file" with 'Yes'; press return.
- The processing payroll menu will now be on screen; select [Enter Payments] and press return.
- The payments record for the first employee, Tina Mason, will appear.
- Enter '1' in the BASIC box and press return. Notice how the program immediately enters the basic pay of the employee and makes the deductions to show the net pay in the bottom right-hand corner of the screen.
- Press [F10] to bring up the payments record for the second employee – Philip Fleming.
- Enter '1' in the BASIC box and press return. The program calculates the deductions and shows Philip's net pay.
- Repeat the process of pressing [F10] to take you to the next employee and entering '1' in the BASIC box for the other employees of Wyvern Office Supplies Ltd.
- When you have completed entering the payments for all the employees, press [F10] or [ESC] to return to the processing payroll menu.

Running the payroll

- From the processing payroll menu, select [Payment Summary]; press return.
- At the prompt "Printer File or View", press return; switch on the printer; press return. The program will print out a three-part report showing:
  - gross pay, deductions, etc, and net pay for each employee
  - National Insurance Contributions: employee's and employer's contributions
  - a summary of the year-to-date figures
- From the processing payroll menu, select [Payslips].
- Press return at the various prompts and print out the payslips (there is no need to print a test pattern, unless you are printing on pre-printed payslips and wish to ensure that the printer is aligned correctly).
- Check from the reports you have printed that everything has been entered correctly – any amendments can be made through the 'Enter Payments' routine (see above). This is a last opportunity to correct any errors before the payroll records are permanently updated.

- From the processing payroll menu, select [Update Records]. Respond to the prompts as follows:
  - Print check report   No
  - Backup Data Files   No*
  - Update Records   Yes

  * for a business it is *essential* to back up data files (see below) before updating, and your tutor or trainer may require you to take back ups in order to demonstrate your computer 'housekeeping' skills.

  After updating, press any key to continue.
- At the processing payroll menu, select [Collector of Taxes].
- At the various prompts, enter tax month 1, and the report can be printed. The report shows the amount due to the Collector of Taxes in respect of income tax and National Insurance Contributions. Note that this report is printed after the payroll records for the month have been updated permanently.
- Press [ESC] to return to the payroll menu and, if you are stopping at this point, press [ESC] again and select [Quit].

Having completed the basics of the first month's payroll – we will look at producing bank giro credits and cheques in a later month. Fig. 23.2 (on page 328) gives an example of the payments summary print out; fig. 23.3 (page 329) shows the payslip for Tina Mason; fig. 23.4 (page 329) gives the report showing the amount due to the Collector of Taxes for month 1.

Backing up the data
It is a standard computer procedure to take back up copies of files that have been worked on, ie files on the working disk – hard disk or floppy disk – saved from time-to-time to another disk. With computer payroll it is essential to take back up copies of the data files at the end of each month. With SAGE Payroll, this is done before the records are updated (on the Update Records screen – see above). The back up is best taken on a separate floppy disk which must then be labelled clearly, eg

Program	*SAGE Payroll*
Date of back up	*30 April 1993*
Pre- or post update	*Pre-update*
Tax week/month	*Month 1*
Payment frequency	*Monthly*

If mistakes are discovered after updating, it will be necessary to restore the data from the back up copy (which deletes later data) and process the payroll again. For example, if an error was discovered in processing May's payroll which relates to April's payroll, the data from the above back up would have to be used; the error would need to be corrected (using the 'Enter Payments' routine), and May's payroll will need to be processed again. The effect of updating the records is to update them *permanently*; as you can appreciate, there would be a lot of extra work to do if an error was not discovered for, say, three months. To restore a back up, it is necessary to go to the main menu (if you are at the payroll menu, press [ESC]), and select [Utilities], then [Backup Utilities], then [Restore Data Files]. You will be prompted to insert the disk containing the data files at the date of the back up that you wish to restore.

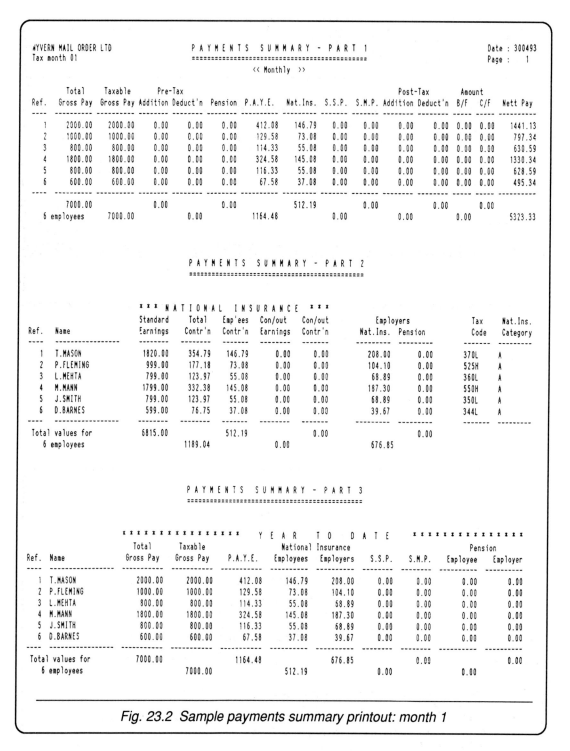

Fig. 23.2 Sample payments summary printout: month 1

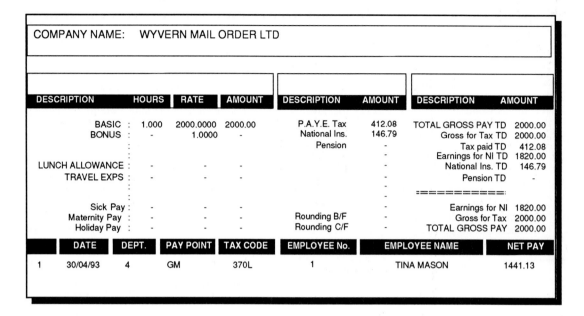

COMPANY NAME: WYVERN MAIL ORDER LTD

DESCRIPTION	HOURS	RATE	AMOUNT	DESCRIPTION	AMOUNT	DESCRIPTION	AMOUNT
BASIC :	1.000	2000.0000	2000.00	P.A.Y.E. Tax	412.08	TOTAL GROSS PAY TD	2000.00
BONUS :	-	1.0000	-	National Ins.	146.79	Gross for Tax TD	2000.00
:				Pension	-	Tax paid TD	412.08
					-	Earnings for NI TD	1820.00
LUNCH ALLOWANCE :	-	-	-		-	National Ins. TD	146.79
TRAVEL EXPS :	-	-	-		-	Pension TD	-
:					-	============	
Sick Pay :	-	-	-		-	Earnings for NI	1820.00
Maternity Pay :	-	-	-	Rounding B/F	-	Gross for Tax	2000.00
Holiday Pay :	-	-	-	Rounding C/F	-	TOTAL GROSS PAY	2000.00

	DATE	DEPT.	PAY POINT	TAX CODE	EMPLOYEE No.	EMPLOYEE NAME	NET PAY
1	30/04/93	4	GM	370L	1	TINA MASON	1441.13

Fig. 23.3 Sample payslip: month 1

WYVERN MAIL ORDER LTD   Date : 300493
Collector of Taxes (Monthly Payslip Returns)

Record of deductions from gross National Insurance   Record of Payments

	(1) S.S.P.	(2) NIC comp'n	(3) S.M.P.	(4) NIC comp'n	(5) Total Ded.	(1) Income Tax	(2) Gross N.I.	(3) Total Ded.	(4) Net N.I.	(5) Total Due
Weekly	0.00	0.00	0.00	0.00	0.00	0.00	0.00	0.00	0.00	0.00
2 Weekly	0.00	0.00	0.00	0.00	0.00	0.00	0.00	0.00	0.00	0.00
4 Weekly	0.00	0.00	0.00	0.00	0.00	0.00	0.00	0.00	0.00	0.00
Monthly	0.00	0.00	0.00	0.00	0.00	1164.48	1189.04	0.00	1189.04	2353.52
Totals	0.00	0.00	0.00	0.00	0.00	1164.48	1189.04	0.00	1189.04	2353.52

NIC compensation percentage   Employee range   Date range

S.S.P. : 0.00   S.M.P. : 4.50   0001 - 0010   Week : 060493 - 050593   Month : 060493 - 050593

Fig. 23.4 Sample Collector of Taxes' report: month 1

It is good practice to keep back up copies of the last four months' payroll transactions *as a minimum*. Some businesses may well keep back up copies for the whole of the tax year. Clearly the back up disks should be kept in a safe place away from the computer area – the best place is in a fireproof safe designed especially for the storage of computer data.

exercise: processing the payroll for May

In this exercise, you are to process the payroll at the end of month 2, ie 31 May 1993 (or the current year). As there are no changes to the gross monthly pay for each employee of Wyvern Mail Order Ltd you can follow the procedures we have used for entering payments and running the payroll. (At the 'Processing Payroll' menu, where the program asks "Clear Payments File?", select 'No' – the default; this will retain the gross monthly pay figures that we entered in April, and you can go straight to the payment summary screen.)

After running the payroll and checking that everything is correct, you can update the records (taking a back up copy before update if your tutor or trainer asks you to do so). Finally, the Collector of Taxes' report can be printed out for month 2 (at prompt 'Enter Tax Month from', key in '2', and at prompt 'Enter Tax month to', key in '2').

Having set up payroll records and processed two straightforward months, we can pause and look at some of the data held by the program:

- From the payroll menu, select [Employee Details].
- From the employee details menu, select [Amend Employee Details].
- From amend employee details menu, select [Cumulative Values] – this will take us to the fourth screen of the employee records.
- Respond to the screen prompts by pressing return twice.
- On screen will be the cumulative values for employee number 1, Tina Mason, for the two months' payroll that has been processed, for example:

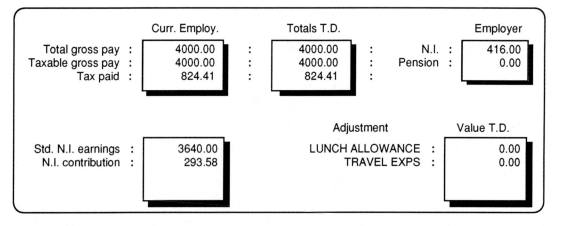

	Curr. Employ.		Totals T.D.			Employer
Total gross pay :	4000.00	:	4000.00	:	N.I. :	416.00
Taxable gross pay :	4000.00	:	4000.00	:	Pension :	0.00
Tax paid :	824.41	:	824.41	:		

			Adjustment		Value T.D.
Std. N.I. earnings :	3640.00		LUNCH ALLOWANCE :		0.00
N.I. contribution :	293.58		TRAVEL EXPS :		0.00

- The cumulative values for other employees can be inspected by using the F10 key to move forward, and the F9 key to move backwards.
- Press [ESC] three times to return to the payroll menu.

month 3 – June

For this month we will add a few extra details when processing the payroll. Firstly, though, we will carry out a check to see if the program can spot an operator error.

- From the payroll menu, select [Processing Payroll]
- Enter the payroll run date as 310593 (or the current year) – even though we have already processed May's payroll; press return.
- Confirm the tax year.
- Choose [Monthly] and note that the program tells us that May's payroll has been run already.
- Press [ESC] to return to the payroll menu: we will now process the payroll for the month of June.
- From the payroll menu, select [Processing Payroll]; press return.
- Enter the payroll run date as 300693 (or the current year); press return.
- Confirm the tax year; press return.
- Choose [Monthly] and, when the program responds with "OK to process", press return.
- Press return at the prompts for the lower and upper employee numbers; at the prompt "Clear payments file", respond with 'No'; press return.
- The processing payroll menu will now be on screen; select [Enter Payments] and press return. We will now enter some overtime, bonus, and commission payments for the employees of Wyvern Mail Order Ltd.
- On screen will be the payments record for the first employee, Tina Mason. Basic pay will already show; use the arrow key to move to the bonus line. Enter a bonus of £100 (no £ sign needed) in the bonus section; notice how the deductions are immediately re-calculated to give a new net pay figure.
- Press [F10] to move to the payments record for the next employee, Philip Fleming. Enter 5 in the overtime section (ie this employee has worked 5 hours of overtime), and £25 (no £ sign) in the bonus section. Press [F10] to go to the next employee (or [F9] if you want to go back to an earlier employee).
- Now enter the following:

  Linda Mehta – 5 hours' overtime; £20 bonus

  Michael Mann – commission £135

  John (or *Jane*) *Smith* – 3 hours' overtime; £25 bonus

  David Barnes – 4 hours' overtime; £10 bonus

- Press [F10] or [ESC] to return to the processing payroll menu.
- From the processing payroll menu, follow the routine we have used earlier and print
  - the payments summary
  - payslips
- From the processing payroll menu, select [Cheque Analysis] and print a list of cheques to be written out for those employees who wish to be paid by cheque. You can then select [Print Cheques], respond to the prompts, and print out the cheques. A large company would have cheques pre-printed on continuous stationery and the details would be printed at this stage; a smaller company can take a plain paper printout, and then transfer the details manually to cheques, which are then ready for signature.
- For those employees of Wyvern Mail Order Ltd who prefer to be paid by bank giro credit direct into their bank accounts, the [Giro Analysis] and [Print Giros] options from the processing payroll menu can be followed in a similar way to the cheques routine.

- If any employees are paid in cash, a cash analysis can be printed from the processing payroll menu to show how much cash and which denominations of notes and coin need to be drawn from the bank to make up the pay packets.

- From the processing payroll menu, update the records as we have done previously, and then print out the Collector of Taxes report for month 3.

- Press [ESC] to return to the payroll menu, having completed the payroll for month 3.

exercise: processing the payroll for July

In this exercise, you are to process the payroll at the end of month 4, ie 31 July 1993 (or the current year). As well as the standard gross monthly pay for each employee of Wyvern Mail Order Ltd, there are the following overtime, bonus, and commission payments to enter:

Tina Mason – bonus £80
Philip Fleming – 4 hours' overtime; £20 bonus
Linda Mehta – 3 hours' overtime; £15 bonus
Michael Mann – commission £95
John (or *Jane*) *Smith* – 2 hours' overtime; £20 bonus
David Barnes – 3 hours' overtime; £15 bonus

Print out the payments summary, payslips, giros and cheques; update the records; print the Collector of Taxes' report for month 4.

month 5 – August

For this month, as well as the material already covered, we will record additions and deductions to pay such as clothing, lunch, and travel allowances, union and social club subscriptions.

- From the payroll menu, select [Processing Payroll].

- Enter the payroll run date as 310893 (or the current year); press return.

- Confirm the tax year; press return.

- Choose [Monthly] and, when the program responds with "OK to process", press return.

- Press return at the prompts for the lower and upper employee numbers; at the prompt "Clear payments file", respond with 'No'; press return.

- The processing payroll menu will now be on screen; select [Enter Payments] and press return.

- On screen will be the payments record for the first employee, Tina Mason. Enter a bonus of £90 and press return; then press [Pg Dn] to take you to the second screen. Enter a lunch allowance of £10 and travel expenses of £15.

- Press [F10] twice to go to the next employee, Philip Fleming. Enter 7 hours' overtime and a bonus of £27.50. Press [Pg Dn] and enter a clothing allowance of £8.50 and a union subscription of £5. Press [F10] twice to go to the next employee.

- Now enter the following:

    Linda Mehta – 6 hours' overtime; £20 bonus; clothing allowance £8.50; social club subscription £4.50.

    Michael Mann – commission £110; travel expenses £63.50; social club subscription £4.50.

    John (or *Jane*) *Smith* – 4 hours' overtime; £25 bonus; lunch allowance £12.50; social club subscription £4.50.

    David Barnes – 5 hours' overtime; £20 bonus; clothing allowance £8.50; union subscription £5.

- Press [F10] or [ESC] twice to return to the processing payroll menu.
- From the processing payroll menu, follow the routine we have used earlier and print
    - the payments summary
    - payslips
    - cheque analysis and cheques
    - giro analysis and giros
- Update the records
- Print the Collector of Taxes report for month 5.

exercise: processing the payroll for September

In this exercise, you are to process the payroll at the end of month 6, ie 30 September 1993 (or the current year). As well as the gross monthly pay for each employee of Wyvern Mail Order Ltd, there are the following items to enter:

Tina Mason – bonus £75; lunch allowance £15; travel expenses £25
Philip Fleming – 4 hours' overtime; bonus £30; clothing allowance £9; union subscription £5.50
Linda Mehta – 3 hours' overtime; bonus £25; clothing allowance £9; social club subscription £5
Michael Mann – commission £85; travel expenses £70; social club subscription £5
John (or *Jane*) *Smith* – 5 hours' overtime; bonus £30; lunch allowance £10; social club subscription £5
David Barnes – 4 hours' overtime; bonus £25; clothing allowance £9; union subscription £5.50

Print out the payments summary, payslips, cheques and giros; update the records; print the Collector of Taxes' report for month 6.

changes in employees

This section shows how to record
- changes in details of employees
- new employees
- employees leaving

We shall then process the payroll for October.

changes in details of employees

- From the payroll menu, select [Employee Details]; press return.
- From the employee details menu, select [Amend Employee Details]; press return, and select [Full Details]; press return.

- Press return at the prompts for the lower and upper employee numbers.

- Now make the following alterations and, at the "Post Edit Abandon" menu, select 'Post':

Tina Mason
- The Inland Revenue has advised that her tax code is to be 380L, as from 1 October (you will be asked by the program to confirm the amendment).

Philip Fleming
- He has moved house: his new address is The Old Barn, Teme Lane, Little Mereford MR8 4AD.
- His overtime rate is now £13 per hour.

Linda Mehta
- She now wishes to be paid by bank giro credit (payment type GM); her bank account details are:

Bank name:	Midtown Bank
Branch address:	Broad Street
	Mereford
Branch sort code:	56–21–35
Account name:	L Mehta
Account number:	63214982

- Her basic pay is now £850 per month.

Michael Mann
- Add a bonus (code 3) to his rates of pay (remember to key in the amount as '1').

- After posting the above alterations, press [ESC] three times to return to the payroll menu.

new employees

On 1 October two new employees, Rebecca Adams and Peter Singh, join the staff of Wyvern Mail Order Ltd. Their details are entered onto the computer payroll program as follows:

- From the payroll menu, select [Employee Details]; press return.

- From the employee details menu, select [Add a New Employee]; press return.

- Press return at the prompts for the lower and upper employee numbers.

- The next available blank employee record (for employee no 7) appears on screen.

- Enter the details of Rebecca Adams, as detailed in fig. 23.5 (on the next page). Rebecca has brought a P45 from her previous employer, and the following details should be completed at screen 3:

Taxable Gross Pay:	3750.00
Tax paid:	455.33

- Press [F10] twice; the "Post Edit Abandon" menu will now be on screen – select 'Post' and press return.

- Now enter the details of Peter Singh in the same way. Enter the following details from his P45 at screen 3:

Taxable Gross Pay:	6595.50
Tax paid:	936.25

- After posting the details, press [ESC] twice to return to the payroll menu.

Employee No.	7 On HOLD NO	8 On HOLD NO
Forenames	REBECCA JEAN	PETER JOHN
Surname	ADAMS	SINGH
Address	8 NELSON STREET	FARM COTTAGE
"	MEREFORD	LOWER HANBURY
"	MR3 4TK	REDGROVE
"		RD10 0AB
Works Number	7	8
Payment Type	QM	GM
Pension Ref.	0	0
Auto SSP/SMP	Y	Y
Date of Birth	140875	050367
Start Date	011093	011093
Tax Code	350L	540H
Effective from	011093	011093
N.I. Number	JV147293D	BJ321749C
N.I. Category	A	A
Contracted-Out	N	N
SCON Ref	0	0
Effective from	011093	011093
Marital Status	S	M
Male/Female	F	M
Director	N	N
Department	4: OFFICE	3: WAREHOUSE
Qualifying Days	1: NQQQQQN NQQQQQN	1: NQQQQQN NQQQQQN
	NQQQQQN NQQQQQN	NQQQQQN NQQQQQN
Rates of Pay	1: BASIC : 550.0000	1: BASIC : 900.0000
" " "	2: OVERTIME : 5.0000	2: OVERTIME : 10.0000
" " "	3: BONUS : 1.0000	3: BONUS : 1.0000
Adjustments	2: LUNCH ALLOWANCE	1: CLOTHING ALLOW
"		4: UNION SUBSCRIPT
Bank Name		SOUTHERN BANK
Branch Address		MARKET STREET
" "		REDGROVE
Branch Sort Code		20–33–44
Account Name		P J & MRS R SINGH
Account Number		49561284

Fig. 23.5 Details of new employees joining on 1 October

employees leaving

David Barnes (employee no 6) has handed in his notice – he will leave on 31 October. We will see how to deal with this situation after we have processed the payroll for October.

processing the payroll: month 7 – October

Having already recorded a number of changes in details of employees, and set up employee records for the two staff who joined Wyvern Mail Order Ltd this month, we will now process the payroll on 31 October.

- Go through the routines we have followed previously and, at the processing payroll menu; select [Enter Payments]. Now record the following:

  Tina Mason – bonus £60; lunch allowance £12; travel expenses £30.

  Philip Fleming – 3 hours' overtime; bonus £15; clothing allowance £9; union subscription £5.50.

  Linda Mehta – 3 hours' overtime; bonus £15; clothing allowance £9; social club subscription £5.

  Michael Mann – commission £70; bonus £15; travel expenses £60; social club subscription £5.

  John (or *Jane*) *Smith* – 4 hours' overtime; bonus £20; lunch allowance £15; social club subscription £5.

  David Barnes – 5 hours' overtime; bonus £20; clothing allowance £9; union subscription £5.50.

  Rebecca Adams – 2 hours' overtime; bonus £5; lunch allowance £7.50 (remember to enter '1' in her basic pay box).

  Peter Singh – 2 hours' overtime; bonus £5; clothing allowance £9; union subscription £5.50 (remember to enter '1' in his basic pay box).

- Press [ESC] twice to return to the processing payroll menu.
- From the processing payroll menu, follow the routines we have used earlier and print
  - the payments summary
  - payslips
  - cheque analysis and cheques
  - giro analysis and giros
- Update the records.
- Print the Collector of Taxes report for month 7.
- Press [ESC] to return to the payroll menu: we will now record the fact that David Barnes is leaving on 31 October.
- From the payroll menu select [Employee Details].
- From the employee details menu, select [Remove an Employee].
- David Barnes is employee no 6, so respond to the prompts with his number, and date of leaving. Print the details – the printout will give us the information to complete his form P45.
- Press [ESC] and return to the payroll menu.

Notes:

- Having removed an employee, do not re-use the employee number – 6 in this case – again for the remainder of the current tax year.
- Fig. 23.6 (on the next page) shows the printout of information in order to complete David Barnes' P45.

```
WYVERN MAIL ORDER LTD          P45 Details              Date : 311093
                              =============


                          PAYE reference : BLANK

                 National Insurance Number : JN 66 88 34 C

                            Surname : BARNES
                          Forenames : DAVID BRYAN

                    Date of Leaving : 31/10/1993

                          Tax Code : 344L

   ----------------------------------------------------------------

             Last entries on Deductions Working Sheet

                    Tax Month : 07

             Total Pay to Date :    4442.50
             Total Tax to Date :     534.58

   ----------------------------------------------------------------


                       Current Employment

                    Total Pay :    4442.50
                    Total Tax :     534.58

   ----------------------------------------------------------------


                    Works Number : 6

                 Department :  3 - WAREHOUSE

   ----------------------------------------------------------------


          Employee's Address : 94 STATION ROAD
                             : MEREFORD
                             : MR2 7HT
                             :

   ----------------------------------------------------------------
```

Fig. 23.6 Printout of P45 information for employee leaving

exercises

The payroll for the next three months, ie November, December and January is in the form of exercises which consolidate the material that we have worked through earlier.

processing the payroll for November (month 8)

As well as the gross monthly pay for each employee of Wyvern Mail Order Ltd, there are the following items to enter at 30 November 1993 (or the current year):

Philip Fleming
– His basic pay is now £1050 per month

Linda Mehta
– The Inland Revenue has advised that her tax code is to be 355L, as from 1 November

John (or *Jane*) *Smith*
– You have changed your bank account to:

Bank name:	National Bank
Branch address:	High Street
	Mereford
Branch sort code:	30–17–54
Account name:	J Smith
Account number:	08493216

Tina Mason – bonus £75; lunch allowance £15; travel expenses £40.

Philip Fleming – 5 hours' overtime; bonus £20; clothing allowance £9; union subscription £5.50.

Linda Mehta – 2 hours' overtime; bonus £15; clothing allowance £9; social club subscription £5.

Michael Mann – commission £80; bonus £20; travel expenses £70; social club subscription £5.

John (or *Jane*) *Smith* – 1 hour's overtime; bonus £15; lunch allowance £15; social club subscription £5.

Rebecca Adams – 3 hours' overtime; bonus £10; lunch allowance £8.

Peter Singh – 3 hours' overtime; bonus £10; clothing allowance £9; union subscription £5.50.

Print out the payments summary, payslips, cheques and giros; update the records; print out the Collector of Taxes report for month 8.

processing the payroll for December (month 9)

On 1 December two new employees, John Howard and Tracey Simmonds, join the staff of Wyvern Mail Order Ltd. Their details are given in Fig. 23.7 (on the next page). Their P45s from their former employers show:

John Howard

Taxable gross pay	£6105.27
Tax paid	£592.25

Employee No.	9 On HOLD NO		10 On HOLD NO
Forenames	JOHN		TRACEY
Surname	HOWARD		SIMMONDS
Address	68 ACACIA AVENUE		MILL COTTAGE
"	MEREFORD		MILL LANE
"	MR3 6BJ		MEREFORD
"			MR6 5DH
Works Number	9		10
Payment Type	GM		QM
Pension Ref.	0		0
Auto SSP/SMP	Y		Y
Date of Birth	151072		110673
Start Date	011293		011293
Tax Code	540H		350L
Effective from	011293		011293
N.I. Number	TD369142B		AK247913C
N.I. Category	A		A
Contracted-Out	N		N
SCON Ref	0		0
Effective from	011293		011293
Marital Status	M		S
Male/Female	M		F
Director	N		N
Department	3: WAREHOUSE		3: WAREHOUSE
Qualifying Days	1: NQQQQQN NQQQQQN		1: NQQQQQN NQQQQQN
	NQQQQQN NQQQQQN		NQQQQQN NQQQQQN
Rates of Pay	1: BASIC : 825.0000		1: BASIC : 825.0000
" " "	2: OVERTIME : 8.5000		2: OVERTIME : 8.5000
" " "	3: BONUS : 1.0000		3: BONUS : 1.0000
Adjustments	1: CLOTHING ALLOW		1: CLOTHING ALLOW
"	4: UNION SUBSCRIPT		4: UNION SUBSCRIPT
Bank Name	EASTERN BANK		
Branch Address	HIGH STREET		
" "	MEREFORD		
Branch Sort Code	40–42–64		
Account Name	J & MRS T HOWARD		
Account Number	34728917		

Fig. 23.7 Details of new employees joining on 1 December

Tracey Simmonds
Taxable gross pay   £4829.36
Tax paid   £602.98

As well as the gross monthly pay for each employee, there are the following items to enter at 31 December 1993 (or the current year):

Rebecca Adams
– The Inland Revenue has advised that her tax code is to be 375L, as from 1 December.

Peter Singh
– His basic pay is now £925 per month
– His overtime rate is now £10.25 per hour

Tina Mason – bonus £65; lunch allowance £20; travel expenses £20.

Philip Fleming – no overtime; bonus £15; clothing allowance £10; union subscription £6.

Linda Mehta – 3 hours' overtime; bonus £12.50; clothing allowance £10; social club subscription £5.

Michael Mann – commission £70; bonus £25; travel expenses £80; social club subscription £5.

John (or *Jane*) *Smith* – 2 hours' overtime; bonus £17.50; lunch allowance £10; social club subscription £5.

Rebecca Adams – 2 hours' overtime; bonus £12.50; lunch allowance £7.

Peter Singh – 2 hours' overtime; bonus £12.50; clothing allowance £10; union subscription £6.

John Howard – (enter '1' in the basic box) 2 hours' overtime; bonus £10; clothing allowance £10; union subscription £6.

Tracey Simmonds – (enter '1' in the basic box) 2 hours' overtime; bonus £10; clothing allowance £10; union subscription £4.

Print out the payments summary, payslips, cheques and giros; update the records; print the Collector of Taxes' report for month 9.

processing the payroll for January (month 10)

Peter Singh (employee no 8) has handed in his notice and will leave the company on 31 January.

The Inland Revenue has advised that, in order to implement tax changes announced by the Chancellor of the Exchequer, all 'H' and 'L' tax codes are to be increased by 15 – eg 350L becomes 365L – from 1 January. This can be effected in one of two ways:

• Select [Employee Details] and go to each employee's record to make the alteration. The program will prompt you to key in the 'effective from' date – for this change it is 010194 (or the current year).

• Alternatively, the change can be effected globally. To do this, the computer date on entering the payroll program *must be set at the date of the change*, ie, for this change 010194 (or the current year). Switch to the *main menu*, select [Utilities], [Global Changes], and then [Tax Codes] – use 'Manual', then 'Suffix' (eg 'H' and 'L' tax codes), then 'Increase'.

As well as the gross monthly pay for each employee, there are the following items to enter at 31 January 1994 (or the current year):

John (or *Jane*) *Smith* – you are now allowed to claim travel expenses.

Tina Mason – bonus £60; lunch allowance £15; travel expenses £15

Philip Fleming – 3 hours' overtime; bonus £25; clothing allowance £10; union subscription £6.

Linda Mehta – 2 hours' overtime, bonus £15; clothing allowance £10; social club subscription £5.50.

Michael Mann – commission £60; bonus £20; travel expenses £65; social club subscription £5.50.

John (or *Jane*) *Smith* – 3 hours' overtime; bonus £20; lunch allowance £8; social club subscription £5.50; travel expenses £12.50.

Rebecca Adams – no overtime; bonus £10; lunch allowance £6.

Peter Singh – 4 hours' overtime; bonus £15; clothing allowance £10; union subscription £6.

John Howard – 3 hours' overtime; bonus £15; clothing allowance £10; union subscription £6.

Tracey Simmonds – 3 hours' overtime; bonus £12.50; clothing allowance £10; union subscription £4.

Print out the payments summary, payslips, cheques and giros; update the records; print the Collector of Taxes' report for month 10. Record the employee leaving, and print out the details for his P45.

Statutory Sick Pay and Statutory Maternity Pay

Statutory Sick Pay (SSP)
Under the SSP scheme, employees who are off work due to illness for four days or more at a time are paid a minimum level of sick pay by the employer. Some employers may 'top up' this payment, but at least employees know that they will receive pay when they are off sick. With a computer program, such as SAGE Payroll, it is only necessary to record the dates of sickness of employees: the program will make all the calculations, and work out the pay that is due. We will see the entries necessary for SSP when we process the payroll for February (see below).

Statutory Maternity Pay (SMP)
SMP is paid by an employer to an employee who is away from work to have a baby – certain rules apply about eligibility for payments. The employer is able to claim most of the SMP payments plus an additional percentage of the total gross SMP as compensation for National Insurance Contributions paid by the employer on SMP. The employer reduces the total amount from monthly National Insurance Contributions and tax payments. We will see how to record SMP on the computer when we process the payroll for February (see below).

processing the payroll: month 11 – February

For this month there are SSP and SMP details to record for the employees of Wyvern Mail Order Ltd:

- Go through the routines we have followed previously – the payroll will be processed on 28 February 1994 (or the current year) – and, at the processing payroll menu, select [Enter Payments].

- Press [F10] to get to the payments screen for Philip Fleming.

- Using the arrow keys, move the cursor to the statutory sick pay line; press [F3].

- The Statutory Sick Pay diary will now be on screen. Philip was off sick between 7 February and 14 February: enter these two dates (remember to include the year, eg 070294) as the start and finish dates, pressing return after each. Enter 'A' as the type; press return. The prompt on the screen asks "Block fill", answer 'Yes' and press return. His absences are now recorded on the SSP diary.

- Press [ESC] to return to the payments screen for the employee. Note that SSP has been calculated.

- Move the cursor to the basic pay line, and press [F3].

- The program prompts "Adjust for SSP/SMP"; respond with 'Yes' (this means that the employee's basic pay will be reduced by the amount of SSP paid); press return.

- Now press [F10] four times to move to the payments screen for Rebecca Adams.

- Follow the procedures listed above to record that Rebecca was off sick between 18 and 20 February. Note however that, as Rebecca was ill for three days, no SSP shows on her payment record (there is no need, therefore, to adjust her basic pay for SSP).

- Now press [F9] three times to move back to the payments screen for Linda Mehta. Linda has given you the appropriate notice that she wishes to commence a period of maternity leave from 1 February.

- Using the arrow keys, move the cursor to the statutory maternity pay line; press [F3]. Complete the maternity details screen as follows:

Date baby due:	080494 (or current year)
Medical evidence:	Y
Average Pay:	Press [F3], and respond 'Yes'
Employment ended:	010294 (or current year)
Min. hours per week:	34
Fair dismissal:	N

The program will automatically calculate the SMP due to Linda.

- Press [ESC] to return to her payments screen; enter '0' in the basic pay, overtime and bonus boxes; also, enter '0' on the next screen against her clothing allowance and social club subscription.

- Press [ESC] and allow a tax refund, if prompted.

- Move on to the payments screen for Michael Mann and try to enter SMP for this employee (with the same details above) ...

- Now enter the following items for the other employees of Wyvern Mail Order Ltd:

Tina Mason – bonus £50; lunch allowance £10; travel expenses £20.

Philip Fleming – 2 hours' overtime; bonus £20; clothing allowance £10; union subscription £6.

Michael Mann – commission £65; bonus £15; travel expenses £70; social club subscription £5.50.

John (or *Jane*) *Smith* – 2 hours' overtime; bonus £15; lunch allowance £10; social club subscription £5.50; travel expenses £10.

Rebecca Adams – 2 hours' overtime; bonus £12.50; lunch allowance £11.

John Howard – 4 hours' overtime; bonus £12.50; clothing allowance £10; union subscription £6.

Tracey Simmonds – 4 hours' overtime; bonus £15; clothing allowance £10; union subscription £4.

Print out the payments summary, payslips, cheques and giros; update the records; print the Collector of Taxes' report for month 11.

exercise

This final exercise – processing the payroll for March – consolidates the material that we have covered so far.

processing the payroll for March (month 12)

You are to process the payroll at the end of month 12, ie 31 March 1994 (or the current year).

Record the following changes:

Philip Fleming
– The Inland Revenue has advised that his tax code is to be 560H, as from 1 March.

Rebecca Adams
– She now wishes to be paid by bank giro credit; her bank account details are:

Bank name:	Midshires Savings Bank
Branch address:	Market Place
	Mereford
Branch sort code:	70–24–96
Account name:	R J Adams
Account number:	47358921

John Howard
– His basic pay is now £875 per month.
– His overtime rate is now £9 per hour.

Tracey Simmonds
– Her basic pay is now £875 per month.
– Her overtime rate is now £9 per hour.

Linda Mehta – look at her payments record and check that Statutory Maternity Pay has been calculated by the program for the month; allow a tax refund, if prompted.

The following absences need to be recorded:

Michael Mann – from 14 March to 20 March

John Howard – from 11 March to 13 March

Tracey Simmonds – from 2 March to 5 March, and 18 March to 21 March

As well as the gross monthly pay for each employee, there are the following items to enter:

Tina Mason – bonus £75; lunch allowance £15; travel expenses £25

Philip Fleming – 5 hours' overtime; bonus £30; clothing allowance £11; union subscription £6.50 (remember to put his basic pay back to '1', after being off sick last month).

Michael Mann – commission £80; bonus £40; travel expenses £65; social club subscription £5.50.

John (or *Jane*) *Smith* – 4 hours' overtime; bonus £25; lunch allowance £14; social club subscription £5.50; travel expenses £12.50.

Rebecca Adams – no overtime; bonus £15; lunch allowance £8.

John Howard – 4 hours' overtime; bonus £15; clothing allowance £11; union subscription £6.50.

Tracey Simmonds – 3 hours' overtime; bonus £18; clothing allowance £11; union subscription £4.

Print out the payments summary, payslips, cheques and giros; update the records; print the Collector of Taxes' report for month 12.

This now completes the payroll transactions for Wyvern Mail Order Ltd for the whole of the tax year (which ends on 5 April).

year-end procedures

At the end of each tax year, the employer is required to produce information for both the employee and the Inland Revenue.

With SAGE Payroll, the year-end procedures are:

- From the *main menu*, select [Utilities], then [Year End].

- From the year end routines menu, print the following (the end of the tax year is 5 April 1994 – or current year):

  - *P11 Deduction Form*
    This provides a printout of the entries for the year that would be written on the deductions Working Sheet when the payroll is calculated manually. Fig. 23.8 (below) shows a sample printout of the P11 Deduction Form.

```
Employer Name : WYVERN MAIL ORDER LTD        P 1 1   D E D U C T I O N   C A R D              Reference :   1
Tax Ref/Dist. : BLANK                        ====================================           Surname : MASON
Payment Type  : Giro                                   << Monthly >>                         Forenames : TINA


               Current     Prev's-1   Prev's-2   Prev's-3                  Current    Prev's-1   Prev's-2   Prev's-3
               ---------   ---------  ---------  ---------                 ---------  ---------  ---------  ---------
   Tax Code :  395L        380L       370L         xxx     N.I. Letter :  A            xxx        xxx        xxx
Date Applied : 010194-09   011093-06  060493-01    xxx     Date Applied : 060493-01    xxx        xxx        xxx

N.I. No. : AL459231B   D.O.B. : 150446   Works No. : 1     SCON : S4xxxxxxx   Leaving Date :   xxx   Year to 5th April 1994


xxxxxxxxxx National Insurance xxxxxxxxxx
Standard  Total    Emp'ees  Con/out  Con/out                Wk/Mth Pay-For    Total-Pay Free-Pay Taxable-Pay Total-Tax  Tax-Ded'd
Earnings  Contr'n  Contr'n  Earnings Contr'n  S.S.P.  S.M.P. No  Week/Month   To-Date   To-Date  To-Date     Due-To-Date or-Ref'd
--------  -------  -------  -------  -------  -------  ------- -- ---------    --------- -------- ----------- ----------- ---------
1820.00   354.79   146.79   0.00     0.00     0.00    0.00   01  2000.00      2000.00   309.09   1690.91     412.08      412.08
1820.00   354.79   146.79   0.00     0.00     0.00    0.00   02  2000.00      4000.00   618.18   3381.82     824.41      412.33
1820.00   365.19   146.79   0.00     0.00     0.00    0.00   03  2100.00      6100.00   927.27   5172.73     1261.75     437.34
1820.00   363.11   146.79   0.00     0.00     0.00    0.00   04  2080.00      8180.00   1236.36  6943.64     1694.08     432.33
1820.00   365.19   146.79   0.00     0.00     0.00    0.00   05  2100.00      10280.00  1545.45  8734.55     2131.41     437.33
1820.00   364.15   146.79   0.00     0.00     0.00    0.00   06  2090.00      12370.00  1854.54  10515.46    2566.25     434.84
1820.00   362.28   146.79   0.00     0.00     0.00    0.00   07  2072.00      14442.00  2221.94  12220.06    2982.08     415.83
1820.00   364.15   146.79   0.00     0.00     0.00    0.00   08  2090.00      16532.00  2539.10  13992.64    3414.66     432.58
1820.00   363.63   146.79   0.00     0.00     0.00    0.00   09  2085.00      18617.00  2856.78  15760.22    3846.25     431.59
1820.00   362.59   146.79   0.00     0.00     0.00    0.00   10  2075.00      20692.00  3299.20  17392.80    4243.83     397.58
1820.00   361.03   146.79   0.00     0.00     0.00    0.00   11  2060.00      22752.00  3629.12  19122.88    4665.91     422.08
1820.00   364.15   146.79   0.00     0.00     0.00    0.00   12  2090.00      24842.00  3959.04  20882.96    5095.50     429.59
--------  -------  -------  -------  -------  -------  ------- --             ---------- -------- ----------- ----------- ---------
21840.00           1761.48           0.00             0.00                   0.00      <-Prev employment->  0.00
          4345.05           0.00              0.00                           24842.00  <-This employment->  5095.50
========  ======== ======= ======== ======= ======= =======                 ==========               ==========
                                                                            24842.00  <--Total To Date-->  5095.50


                   -------------------------------------------------------------
                   | Nat.Ins.  Standard    Total     Emp'ees   Con/out   Con/out   |
                   | Category  Earnings    Contr'n   Contr'n   Earnings  Contr'n   |
                   | --------  --------    -------   -------   --------  -------   |
                   |    A      21840.00    4345.05   1761.48   0.00      0.00      |
                   | ========  ========== ========= ========= ========= ========= |
                   | Totals    21840.00    4345.05   1761.48   0.00      0.00      |
                   -------------------------------------------------------------
```

Fig. 23.8 Sample printout of the P11 Deduction Form

- *P14/P60 Certificate*

  This form (illustrated on page 294) gives totals of gross pay, income tax and National Insurance Contributions for employees who have worked for the company during the tax year, and for whom a P11 has been completed. The P14 (top copies of the form) is sent to the Inland Revenue, while the P60 (the bottom copy) is handed to the employee.

  A large organisation would use pre-printed P14/P60 forms on continuous stationery and print them out direct from the computer; a smaller company will print out the details on plain paper, and then transfer the details manually to the Certificates.

- *P35 Year End Summary*

  The P35 form (illustrated on pages 295 and 296) summarises the P14s, giving the cumulative totals for each employee of income tax, National Insurance Contributions, Statutory Sick Pay, and Statutory Maternity Pay. The P35 has to be sent to the Inland Revenue after the end of each tax year, together with the P14s.

- A back up copy of the data files should now be taken – if your trainer or teacher requires you to do so.

- From the year-end routines menu, select [Clear Year–TD Totals]; press return; accept April 1994 (or the current year) by pressing return. A warning comes on the screen stating that cumulative values will be set to zero, and that employees who have left will be deleted. Press return to clear the current year data, and again to accept the lower and upper employee numbers. The program then works through each employee in turn and, upon completion, returns you to the year-end routines menu.

- Press [ESC] twice to return to the main menu – we have now completed one year's computer payroll and the program is ready for processing the first payroll of the next tax year!

---

chapter summary

❑ We have used a computer payroll program to:
  - set up company details
  - set up employee details
  - process the payroll
  - calculate Statutory Sick Pay and Statutory Maternity Pay

❑ We have seen some of the reports that can be produced:
  - monthly payments summary
  - payslips
  - cheques and giros
  - monthly Collector of Taxes report
  - information for P45
  - year-end reports

❑ It has only been possible to look at the main features of computer payroll. It may be that you will wish to investigate other aspects of the program, eg
  - weekly paid employees
  - changes in rates of income tax and National Insurance Contributions
  - pension contributions
  - National Insurance Contributions for directors

The use of a computer payroll accounting program relieves office staff of a large number of repetitive and time-consuming calculations. Nevertheless, computer payroll needs to be used carefully to avoid operator errors, and the importance of regular backing up of data cannot be stressed too strongly.

24 Business contracts

In this book we have dealt with:

- the procedures involved in the buying and selling of goods and services
- dealings by businesses with the banks
- the paying of wages to employees

It is likely that part of your course involves the understanding of the background to these three areas. This will essentially be an appreciation of the *legal framework* which enables these activities to take place and which states what can happen if there is a dispute, for example, between a buyer and a seller or an employer and an employee. The agreement between the parties in these cases is known as a *contract*. In this chapter we will look at

- the elements of a contract
- contracts of sale
- contracts between a business and its bank
- contracts of employment

a contract defined

what is a contract?

a contract is a legally binding agreement enforceable in a court of law

Contracts, which may be in writing, or by word of mouth (oral), are agreements between two parties. Examples include:

- a written contract which you sign if you buy a house
- a written contract for a loan agreement if you borrow money
- a written contract of employment which you may have to sign if you get a job
- an oral contract if you buy goods in a shop
- an oral contract if you order goods over the telephone
- an oral contract if you hire a decorator to paint your house

In each case somebody does something for which some kind of payment is made. A contract is a agreement with legal consequences because if the work done is not satisfactory, or if the payment is not made, the wronged party can take the other person to court for *breach of contract*.

You may rightly wonder how all this affects you in the workplace. The answer is that the principles of contract affect any person carrying out normal business activities. For example if you quote an incorrect price to a customer, they may be able to hold your business to that price, under the terms of the contract of sale. If you fail to finish a job for a customer, they may be able to go to court to obtain a court order for your business to complete the work under the contract.

the three elements of contract
There are three elements which are common and essential to all contracts:

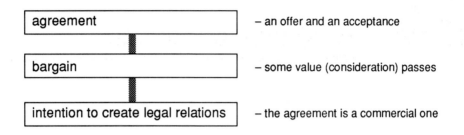

agreement	– an offer and an acceptance
bargain	– some value (consideration) passes
intention to create legal relations	– the agreement is a commercial one

We will now look at these three elements in more detail.

the agreement - offer and acceptance

the offer
A firm and clear offer must be made either to a single party, a group, or to the world at large, as in an advertisement. In a famous legal case in 1893, a manufacturer of medicines (the Carbolic Smoke Ball Company) advertised a patented smoke ball and promised to pay a £100 reward to any person who contracted a specified illness having used the ball three times a day for two weeks. A Mrs Carlill used the ball for eight weeks and still contracted 'flu. She claimed her £100, the company refused, and she had to take the matter to the court which ruled that she should be granted her £100, as the offer of £100 had been to the "whole world", and needed no communicated acceptance from Mrs Carlill. It formed part of a valid contract which the company had to honour.

Note that an offer is quite different from an *invitation to treat* which is an invitation for a person to make an offer. Goods on supermarket shelves are an invitation for a customer to take them to the checkout where that customer can *offer to purchase them* at the price indicated at the checkout, which is where the contract takes place. That is the reason why shop tills indicate the price for each item, normally on an illuminated display; it is also the reason why a shop is not obliged to sell the goods at the price shown on the shelves.

termination of an offer
An offer may only be accepted while it is still open for acceptance. An offer may be terminated in the following circumstances:

- the time limit (if there is one) expires; if there is no time limit the offer lapses after a reasonable period of time
- the offeror – the person making the offer – may revoke (cancel) the offer, as long as the revocation is communicated to the offeree(s) – the person (or persons) to whom the offer was made – and before the offer is accepted
- an offer may be rejected by the making of a counter-offer; for instance, if you offer your car for sale for £1,500 and someone offers you £1,350, that is a counter-offer
- the death of the person making the offer
- failure of a condition which is part of an offer, eg "I offer you £85,000 for your house provided that you repair the roof"; if the roof is not repaired the offer does not stand
- by unconditional acceptance
- by outright rejection

acceptance of an offer

Acceptance of an offer must be firm and unambiguous; it may be in spoken words, written form or even implied by action. Acceptance cannot be assumed from silence on the part of the person to whom the offer is made. For instance, if you say "I offer you my car for £1,500; if I have not heard from you within a week I will assume the deal is done," there is no acceptance. The offeree may go on holiday, or forget it even happened. Acceptance must also be unconditional. Any new term introduced - "I will agree to buy your car as long as the wing is resprayed" - amounts to a counter-offer (see above) and revokes the original offer.

The term "subject to contract", often seen on estate agents' boards, means that the terms of the offer to the offeree are agreeable, but have not been finally accepted. The two parties involved have agreed to draw up a formal contract for signature at a later date. There is no binding contract at this point.

communication of acceptance

The rules relating to communication of acceptance are largely dictated by what is required by the offer:

- the acceptance must normally be communicated to the person making the offer
- if the offer, as in the Carlill smokeball case, does not require notice of acceptance, communication is not necessary, acceptance is implied by the conduct of the offeree
- if the offer requires acceptance by a specific means (letter/fax/verbal message) then that means must be used

the postal rule

An acceptance by post is effective as long as the letter of acceptance is:

- correctly addressed
- correctly stamped
- actually posted

The time of acceptance is when the letter is posted (not when it is received). Given that letters may be delayed or lost in the post, this rule may seem unjust to the offeror! The postal rule only applies to an acceptance, it does *not* apply to a posted offer which *must* reach the offeree.

the bargain: consideration

definition of consideration

A valid contract involves a bargain, a passing of value, known in law as *consideration*. If a business buys goods there is a two way process involved:

- the supplier promises to deliver the goods
- the buyer agrees to pay for them

The parties involved are:

- the *promisor,* the supplier which promises to supply the goods
- the *promisee,* the buyer who has to make payment

The consideration here is the payment, the price paid for the service provided. The principle is simple in itself, but there are a number of rules which relate to consideration and which will now be discussed.

consideration must be sufficient

Consideration must by law be *sufficient*. This means that:

- *it must have value,* although the value need not be adequate in some eyes; for example, you could sell this book for 5p; many would consider the amount to be inadequate, but the 5p still has value and is therefore consideration

- *it must be sufficient,* ie it must be in return for the promise; money due for some *other* reason or obligation is not *sufficient* consideration

consideration must move from the promisee

This legal phrase means, in effect, that the person who is promised goods or a service must themselves provide payment if the promise is to be enforceable as a contract. If you buy goods, you must make the payment. If someone else pays for you (an unlikely event!) you cannot take the supplier to court if the goods do not arrive.

consideration cannot be past

This legal phrase means that the consideration should not precede the promise. If you mend someone's car without any mention of payment, and the car owner the following week promises to give you £5, and subsequently refuses to pay you, there is no contract. The promise of payment *followed* the good turn done, consideration (the repair) was past as it had taken place the previous week.

the intention to create legal relations

A contract is an agreement involving consideration which the parties *intend to be legally binding.* In other words the parties entering a contract can reasonably expect the agreement to be enforced in a court of law if the necessity arises.

The law assumes:

- commercial agreements are intended to be legally binding
- social and domestic arrangements are *not* intended to be legally binding

In short, if a man enters a contract to buy your car and then, without reason, refuses to pay for it, you can take him to court. If you ask a friend out for the evening, promising to give him or her a good time, and your friend doesn't turn up, you can hardly take court action. The sale of a car involves the intention to create legal relations, the invitation out does not.

breach of contract

terms of a contract

A contract normally contains certain terms which must be fulfilled as part of the agreement. If a person breaks one of those terms, that person is in *breach of contract.* For example, if a supplier undertakes to supply goods, it must send the goods on the due date, and in turn expects the goods to be paid for by a certain time. If the customer does not pay, he or she is in breach of contract.

Contract terms may be classified as follows:

express terms	explicitly stated terms which are binding on both parties to the contract
conditions	fundamental terms of the contract which, if broken, will enable the injured party to repudiate the contract and to seek damages
warranties	minor terms which if broken can be cause for an action for damages for loss suffered; the contract, however, remains in force
implied terms	terms which are not stated, but which are implied by trade custom or by law; for instance, goods sold should be of "satisfactory quality" in accordance with the Sale of Goods Act

In short
- express terms are physically present in the contract; implied terms are not
- conditions are important terms, warranties are less important

remedies for breach of contract

If there is a breach of contract, the liability is *strict:* the fact that the breach has occurred gives the injured party the right to apply to the court for an appropriate remedy.

Remedies available through the court include:

damages	compensation in money intended to place the person taking the case to court in the same position as he or she would have been if the contract had been performed
quantum meruit	the latin means "the amount he deserves" and refers to an award of money related to the extent that a contract has been carried out by the injured party (eg if a decorator has painted part of a house but has not been paid)
specific performance	a court order instructing one of the parties to carry out his or her obligations under the contract, eg to finish painting the house
injunction	a court order restraining someone from carrying out an action which would result in a breach of contract (a common example of an injunction is one served on a newspaper to prevent it from printing some scandal or other)

contracts of sale

When a business orders goods, the order is normally placed on a purchase order (see page 13), and the goods are sent with a delivery note followed by an invoice. It is rare for a formal written contract of sale to be drawn up, except in the case of large items of equipment or a long-term contract of supply. What normally happens is that the supplier will send a copy of its "Terms and Conditions" to the buyer at the time of intended purchase, either as a separate document, or printed on the back of the quotation. If the buyer does not object to these terms and conditions, or offer an alternative set of terms and conditions, these are then assumed to be the terms and conditions of the contract.

The following terms and conditions are typical – as you will see they are very much weighted in favour of the supplier:

specifications	the supplier can change the specifications of its products without notice
prices	prices can change without notice, they exclude VAT and carriage
orders	orders (and cancellations) must be notified in writing
damaged goods	notification of goods received damaged must reach the supplier within three days of delivery, or the supplier will accept no responsibility for damage
return of goods	goods may not be returned without the written permission of the supplier
settlement terms	strictly cash with order, credit accounts settled within 30 days of invoice date, or as otherwise agreed

risk	the risk of damage or loss to the goods while in transit will be borne by the buyer
retention of title	the goods will remain the property of the supplier until they are paid for; if the buyer goes into liquidation the supplier can enter the premises of the buyer and seize back the goods if they are not paid for

You will see from these terms and conditions that the supplier has the advantage in dictating terms. If there were a dispute, the terms and conditions would be upheld in a court of law. It would be possible for the buyer to object when the order was being placed, but it would depend on how anxious the supplier was to sell whether or not the objections were accepted!

contracts between a business and its bank

types of contract
There are many different forms of contract which exist between a business (or any customer) and its bank; the majority of these are in writing. The list below gives examples; you may be able to think of others:
- the authority to open the bank account
- loan agreements and security forms
- orders for foreign currency
- orders to buy and sell investments

types of relationship
Because of the varied duties which a bank carries out for its customers, there are a number of different relationships which exist between a bank and its customer:

debtor and creditor
If a bank accepts money from its customer, the bank is a debtor and the customer a creditor. If a bank lends money, then the bank becomes a creditor and the customer a debtor.

bailor and bailee
If a customer deposits valuables with a bank, a contract of *bailment* is entered into. The bank as bailee accepts the goods from the customer (bailor). A fee is normally charged for this service.

mortgagor and mortgagee
A mortgage is a formal document which a borrower signs stating in effect that if the loan is not repaid, the lender (bank) can sell the mortgaged items, eg a house or investments. A mortgage is itself a contract: the customer is the *mortgagor* and the bank is the *mortgagee*.

the bank as agent
An agent is a 'middleman' used by a person to enter into a contract with a third party. For example, an insurance broker as agent will set up a contract between a customer and an insurance company to insure a car. The rules of agency state that the agent has no liability on the contract; this is fair enough – you would not expect the broker to be liable if you failed to pay your car insurance! An agent is also expected to take a commission. A bank can act as an agent in setting up insurance (eg travel insurance) and for buying and selling investments. In each case it will take commission, and in each case it will not be liable on the contract.

special relationship
A bank, because it advises customers, has a 'special relationship' with them. This requires the bank to exercise a high degree of care. If it fails to do so, a contract set up with the customer may be held by a court to be invalid. This could have serious consequences for the bank if it is a contract involving security for borrowing – a bank could in fact lose its security.

CONTRACT OF EMPLOYMENT

Particulars of Terms and Conditions of Employment pursuant to the Employment
Protection (Consolidation) Act 1978

Employer.........Osborne Electronics Limited...

Employee.........Helen Cassidy...

1. **Continuous Employment**
   You are on a fixed term contract of ....2...................years
   Your continuous service dates from........21 January 19-9.................................

2. **Job Title**
   You are employed as........Computer operator...

3 **Salary**
   The rate of your salary is.........£8,400.................per annum, paid monthly

4. **Hours of Work**
   Your normal hours of work are ..35...... hours a week, worked over a five day period
   (Mondays to Fridays inclusive)

5. **Leave**
   You are entitled to....22..........days paid holiday per annum in addition to statutory
   holidays. The leave is to be taken at a time convenient to the employer.

6. **Sickness**
   Notification of absence should be made on the first day of sickness, in writing or by
   telephone.
   If you are absent for a period in excess of five working days, a doctor's certificate
   must be submitted to the employer.
   Regulations for payment during periods of sickness or injury may be inspected on
   request in the Administration Manager's Office.

7. **Notice**
   The length of notice for termination of employment required from employer or
   employee is.....4.........weeks, subject to statutory requirements.

8. **Grievance Procedure**
   In cases of dissatisfaction with disciplinary procedure you are to apply in the first
   instance to the Manager of the Sales Department. Details of the rules of the
   Company and disciplinary procedures may be obtained from the Administration
   Manager's Office.

9. **Pension Scheme**
   Details of the contributory Company Pension Scheme, for which you are eligible,
   may be obtained from the Administration Manager's Office.

   Signed this....21st.......day of...January..19...-9.....

   T J Hardy

   T J Hardy, Managing Director and Company Secretary

Fig. 24.1 Example of a Contract of Employment

contracts of employment

Employment is a form of contract – money is paid for labour. Fig 24.1 on the previous page shows a typical written contract of employment. The law does not make a written contract of employment compulsory, but it does require an employer to give to the full-time employee within thirteen weeks of the beginning of employment a written statement setting out:

- the names of the employer and employee
- the date when the employment started
- the job title
- details of pay, and when it is to be paid
- working hours
- holidays and holiday pay
- sick pay
- details of pensions
- details of grievance procedures
- length of notice required

These details will normally be written into a contract of employment. If you have signed a contract of employment, look at its terms and see if they correspond with the details set out above.

chapter summary

- ❑ A contract is a legally binding agreement enforceable in a court of law.

- ❑ A contract is made up of three elements:
  - the agreement – an offer and an acceptance
  - the bargain – involving the passing of some sort of value (consideration)
  - the intention to create legal relations

- ❑ If a contract is not carried out according to its terms, a breach of contract has taken place, and the injured party can apply to the court for redress. Contract terms can be
  - express terms
  - conditions
  - warranties
  - implied terms

- ❑ Contracts of sale are often governed by terms issued by the supplier of goods.

- ❑ The contract between a business and its bank may take many different forms. In addition, the customer/bank relationship may be that of
  - debtor and creditor
  - bailor and bailee
  - mortgagor and mortgagee
  - principle and agent
  - the special relationship

- ❑ A contract of employment does not have to be in writing, although it often is. In law an employer must give a permanent full-time employee specific details relating to the terms of employment.

Student Activities

24.1   Give two examples of a contract in writing, and two examples of an oral contract.

24.2   What are the three elements of a contract?

24.3   An order is placed over the telephone, and confirmed with a purchase order posted a day later. When was the contract of sale made?

24.4   If you buy a car for £500 from Dodgy Motors Limited, what is the consideration in the contract?

24.5   If you offer your car for sale for £500, and someone makes a counter offer of £450, does the original offer still stand?

24.6   If you post an acceptance of an offer under a contract, when is that acceptance made?

24.7   Jim does some decorating for Bill. Afterwards Bill says "I will give you £50 for the work done", but fails to do so. What are Jim's rights?

24.8   What is the meaning of the phrase "the intention to create legal relations"?

24.9   What are your rights if

(a) a holiday company sends you to a resort where the hotel is still being built, and you have to camp out in a hostel; the brochure showed a picture of a completed hotel

(b) you order and pay for a new set of kitchen units; the supplying company fail to finish the job

24.10   If you are buying goods from a supplier and he sends you a list of terms and conditions of supply, are these immediately binding?

24.11   What types of bank/customer relationship are involved in the following situations:

(a) the customer deposits a deed box for safe keeping

(b) the customer has an overdraft with the bank

(c) the customer has a savings account with the bank

(d) the customer signs a mortgage over property pledged as security to the bank

(e) the customer instructs the bank to arrange holiday insurance

State in each case the term given to both the bank and the customer.

24.12   Give three examples of a written contract between a bank and its customer.

24.13   Does a contract of employment have to be in writing?

24.14   List the details which you would expect to find in a written contract of employment.

24.15   When would you expect to receive the details normally contained in a written contract of employment?

25 Business communications

As we saw in the first chapter of this book, communicating with your colleagues and your customers is an essential part of your job, if you are in employment. If you are studying, you are likely to be required to draw up the basic forms of written communication as part of your course work.

The communication process involves a number of stages

- formulating your message
- choosing the means of sending it
- composing and sending it
- confirming that it has been received
- dealing with any queries and carrying out any follow-up actions

In business organisations there are likely to be many set procedures for communicating: for example there will be standard letters on word processor files for giving price quotations, for chasing up bad payers, and so on. There will be situations, however, when you may be required to compose one of the following forms of communication:

internal communications	*external communications*
a memorandum	a letter
a note	a fax message

In this chapter we will deal with each of these, starting with the most common style of letter – the fully-blocked letter.

the letter

If you deal with business letters you will see that the appearance and format of each letter is in a uniform 'house' style, a style which readily identifies that business, and is common to all letters that it sends. The letter will normally be on standard printed stationery showing the name, address and details of the business, and will be set out with headings, paragraphs, signatures – the 'elements' of the letter – in a uniform way.

There are a number of different ways of setting out the text of a letter. The most of common of these – the 'fully blocked' style is illustrated and explained on the next two pages.

Elements of the letter *(see page 357 for a full explanation)*	**Wyvern Electrical Services Limited** **107 High Street** **Mereford MR1 9SZ** Tel 0605 675365 Fax 0605 675576
reference	Ref DH/SB/69
date	14 December 19-9
name and address of recipient of letter	J D Smart Esq 23 Pedmore Close Sinton Green Mereford MR4 7ER
salutation	Dear Mr Smart
heading	<u>Invoice 8288 £1,589.50</u>
body of the letter	We note from our records that we have not yet received payment of our invoice 8288 dated 30 September 19-9. Our up-to-date statement of account is enclosed. Our payment terms were strictly 30 days from date of the invoice. We shall be grateful if you will settle the overdue £1,589.50 without further delay. We look forward to receiving your remittance.
complimentary close	Yours sincerely
signature	*Derek Hunt*
name and job title of sender	Derek Hunt Accounts Manager
enclosure indicator	enc

Fig 25.1 Example of a fully blocked letter

characteristics of a fully blocked letter

- the most commonly used style of letter
- all the lines start at the left margin
- the use of *open punctuation*, ie there is *no* punctuation, except in the main body of the letter, which uses normal punctuation
- paragraphs are divided by a space, and are not indented
- a fully blocked letter is easy to type as all the lines are set uniformly to the left margin

elements of the letter

The references in the panel to the left of the letter on the previous page (fig 25.1) describe the *elements of a letter*. These are explained below:

printed letterhead   This is always pre-printed, and must be up-to-date.

reference   The reference on the letter illustrated –*DH/SB/69* – is a standard format
- DH (Derek Hunt), the writer
- SB (Sally Burgess), the secretary
- 69, the number of the file where Mr Smart's correspondence is kept

If you need to quote the reference of a letter to which you are replying, the references will be quoted as follows: *Your ref TR/FG/45 Our ref DH/SB/69.*

date   The date is typed in date (number), month (word), year (number) order.

recipient   The name and address of the person to whom the letter is sent. This section of the letter may be displayed in the window of a window envelope, so it is essential that it is accurate.

salutation   *'Dear Sir. . . Dear Madam'* if you know the person's name and title (ie Mr, Miss, Mrs, Ms) use it, but check that it is correct – a misspelt name or an incorrect title will ruin an otherwise competent letter.

heading   The heading sets out the subject matter of the letter – it will concentrate the reader's mind.

body   The body of the letter is an area where communications skills can be developed. The text must be
- laid out in short precise paragraphs and short clear sentences
- start with a point of reference (eg referring to an invoice)
- set out the message in a logical sequence
- avoid jargon, eg "please send your OPP to the IM"
- avoid slang expressions
- finish with a clear indication of the next step to be taken (eg please telephone, please arrange appointment, please buy our products, please pay our invoice).

complimentary close   The complimentary close (signing off phrase) must be consistent with the salutation:
'Dear Sir/Dear Madam' followed by *'Yours faithfully'*
'Dear Mr Sutton/Dear Ms Jones' followed by *'Yours sincerely'.*

name and job title   It is essential for the reader to know the name of the person who sent the letter, and that person's job title, because a reply will need to be addressed to a specific person.

enclosures   If there are enclosures with the letter, the abbreviation 'enc' or 'encl' is used.

continuation sheets   (not shown in the illustrations)
If the text of the letter is longer than than one sheet of paper will allow for, the letter will conclude on a continuation sheet, a matching plain sheet of paper headed with the recipient's name, the page number and the date.

the memorandum

format

The *memorandum* (plural *memoranda*) is a formal written note used for internal communication within an organisation. It may be typed or handwritten, and will often be produced in a number of copies which can be circulated as necessary. It can be used for situations such as

- giving instructions
- requesting information
- making suggestions
- recording of opinions
- confirming telephone conversations

A memorandum is normally pre-printed by the organisation with all the headings in place, and can be half page or full page in size. A blank and a completed memorandum are illustrated on the next page, in figs. 25.2 and 25.3.

elements of the memorandum

Most of the headings on the pre-printed memorandum form are self-explanatory, as they are also to be found on business letters. You should, however, note the following:

heading	the name of the organisation may be printed above the word 'Memorandum', although this is not strictly necessary, as the memorandum is an internal document
'to' and 'from'	the name and job title of the sender and the recipient are entered in full, and as a consequence the salutation 'Dear......' and complimentary close 'Yours ....' are not necessary
copies to	memoranda are frequently sent (as in the example on the next page) to a large number of people; the recipients will be indicated in this section of the document
reference	as in a business letter the reference indicates the writer, the secretary, and the file number
date	as in a business letter the order is day (number), month (word), year (number)
subject	the subject matter of the memorandum must be concisely stated
text	the message of the memorandum should be clear and concise
signature	a memorandum can be signed, initialled, or even – as is often the case – left blank
enclosures	if material is circulated with the memorandum, the abbreviation 'enc' or 'encl' should be used

---

MEMORANDUM

To

From   **Ref**

Copies to   **Date**

Subject

Fig 25.2 A blank memorandum

MEMORANDUM

To Edgar Pound, Accounts Supervisor

From K Perch, Finance Director   **Ref** KP/AC

Copies to Managers and Supervisors   **Date** 7 July 19-9

Subject COMPUTERISATION OF ACCOUNTING RECORDS

Please attend a meeting on 14 July in the Conference Room. Attendance is
vital as the new system comes on line on 1 September. Summary details of
the new system are attached.

enc

Fig 25.3 A completed memorandum

the facsimile message (fax)

the technology

Fax is an abbreviation of *facsimile transmission*.   A fax machine scans a document and sends an exact (facsimile) image of the document through the telephone system. A receiving fax machine will decode the message and print out an exact copy of the document. A fax machine will therefore enable a copy of a drawing, an invoice, a handwritten message, or a letter to be sent instantaneously to the recipient. A fax can be sent within an organisation, or externally to a customer or client.

fax header sheets

It is customary for an organisation sending fax messages to precede the actual document (or documents) being scanned with a pre-printed *header sheet*, so that the recipient will know what is being transmitted. An example is illustrated below.

FACSIMILE TRANSMISSION HEADER

From
HEREWARD INSURANCE BROKERS
18 High Street
Mereford
MR3 5RJ
Telephone 0605 921222   Facsimile 0605 926311

TO..

....

....

TELEPHONE NUMBER....................................FACSIMILE NUMBER..

NUMBER OF PAGES INCLUDING THIS HEADER.............................DATE...

message

If you have any enquiries regarding this message please telephone the above number and

ask for extension.......................

elements of a fax header

sender the sender's name, telephone number and facsimile number are present so that the recipient can telephone if a reply is needed, or if there are transmission problems (an extension number is also given in case of need)

page numbers the header will indicate the number of pages being transmitted, this is so that the recipient can check that the whole document has printed out

recipient the recipient's name, address, telephone number and facsimile number are present so that the recipient can be contacted in case of problems, and also so that the message can be filed correctly after transmission

message box a box is provided for brief messages or notes relating to the pages which follow; it may also be used for the substance of a message if there are no pages to follow, for example "Confirm lunch 12.30 Friday. See you then."

The fax is a less formal document than a letter, and is often hand-written rather than typed. Its main advantages are that it is fast to draft, fast to transmit, and is very useful, particularly if diagrams or maps have to be transmitted.

written notes

One of the simplest forms of internal communication is the *written note* to a colleague.

In the example below an Accounts Manager has had to go out of the office and has set out a list of duties for Anna, a senior Accounts Assistant (the Supervisor is off sick).

Anna

22.2.19-9   12.45

Had to go out on a customer visit unexpectedly. Not back until tomorrow. Please
1. Ensure cheques are banked by 3.30
2. Post off customer statements by First Class post.
3. Sign my letters – they are in for typing.

Any problems, refer to Mr Lamont. Thanks
Justin

Note that:
- the note is brief but clear
- the note is informal – first names are used and the simple "Thanks"
- the date and time are stated – to prevent any confusion should the note reappear at a later date
- the note is signed
- a point of contact is given in case of difficulties – a very important requirement if responsibility is being given to a comparatively junior member of staff

chapter summary

❏ Effective written communication is essential to the efficient functioning of an organisation.

❏ Communication involves the stages of:
  - formulating a message
  - choosing a means of sending it
  - composing and sending it
  - confirming that it has been received
  - dealing with queries and follow-ups

❏ The most common forms of external communication are the letter and the fax.

❏ The most common and traditional forms of internal communication are the memorandum and the note, although the fax is now becoming more commonly used.

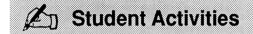 Student Activities

Note: the activities set out below are a supplement to the written communications which are required within the student activities and assignments.

situation

You work as an Accounts Assistant in the Accounts Department of Wyvern Electrical Services (see letterhead on page 356). Choose and draft the form of written communication appropriate to the situations set out below.

As part of the exercise you should design your own forms/letterhead, based on the examples shown in this chapter. Use your own name and today's date.

25.1 An apology is due to Mr Smart (see letter on page 356): his cheque was received by your department two weeks ago, but was posted to the wrong ledger account.

25.2 You need to send a copy invoice (No 8115 for £2,457.70) urgently to Tina Moore, Blackham & Blackham, Architects, 1 New Passage, Mereford, MR4 3FC, Tel 0605 827279, Fax 0605 761667. She has telephoned to say that the original invoice has not been received.

25.3 You need to circulate to all managers in the business a list of customers who may become bad debts. You wish that all dealings with these customers be referred to the Accounts Department Manager. Note: you do not need to produce the list (it has been output from your computer).

25.4 You feel extremely ill and need to tell your supervisor that you are going home. You still have the monthly statements to print out from the computer and process ready for depatch that day, and there is no way that you can finish them.

appendix 1

***

sample blank documents
- purchase order
- invoice
- credit note
- remittance advice
- statement of account
- stock record card
- payroll sheet
- cash analysis
- P11 deduction sheet
- petty cash voucher
- petty cash book
- cash book
- payslip

PURCHASE ORDER

Order No:

Quantity	Cat. No.	Description	Price £ p

INVOICE

No.

Date/Tax Point:

Order No.

Quantity	Description	Catalogue Number	Unit Price £ p	Total Amount £ p
		Total before VAT		
		VAT		
		Total due		

CREDIT NOTE

No.

Date/Tax Point:

Quantity	Description	Catalogue Number	Unit Price £ p	Total Amount £ p

	Total excluding VAT	
	VAT	
	Total credit	

Reason for credit:

REMITTANCE ADVICE

No.

Cheque reference no:

Date	Description	Reference No.	Amount Payable £ p	Balance £ p
		Total cheque enclosed		

STATEMENT OF ACCOUNT

Date	Reference	Debit £ p	Credit £ p	Balance £ p
		Amount now due		

STOCK RECORD CARD

Stock Description ....

Stock units .... Minimum ....

Stock Ref. No. .... Maximum ....

Location .... Re-order level ....

Re-order quantity ....

DATE	GOODS RECEIVED		GOODS ISSUED		BALANCE
	Reference	Quantity	Reference	Quantity	

STOCK RECORD CARD

Stock Description ....

Stock units .... Minimum ....

Stock Ref. No. .... Maximum ....

Location .... Re-order level ....

Re-order quantity ....

DATE	GOODS RECEIVED		GOODS ISSUED		BALANCE
	Reference	Quantity	Reference	Quantity	

PAYROLL
Employees paid weekly in cash

..............**Week ending**..............**Week** ....**EMPLOYER**.............................**Week** .... **no**............

Work Number	Name	Earnings				PAYE (Income Tax) £	Deductions			Employer's National Insurance Contributions £	Net Pay £
		Basic £	Overtime £	Bonus £	Total Gross Pay £		National Insurance £	Savings Scheme £	Total Deductions £		
	TOTALS										

| CASH ANALYSIS | | | | | | | | | | |
NAME	£20	£10	£5	£1	50p	20p	10p	5p	2p	1p	TOTAL (£ p)
TOTAL (£ p)											

deductions Working Sheet P11 (representation only – adapted for weekly pay)

employer _____ **employee** _____ **tax code** _____

NATIONAL INSURANCE CONTRIBUTIONS

	1a Earnings on which employee's contributions are payable	1b Total of employee's and employer's contributions payable	1c Employee's contributions payable

PAYE INCOME TAX

week no.	2 Pay in the week	3 Total pay to date	4a Total free pay to date	5 Total taxable pay to date, ie column 3 minus column 4a	6 Total tax due to date as shown by Taxable Pay Tables	7 Tax deducted (or refunded) in the week. Mark refunds 'R'
1						
2						
3						
4						
5						
6						
7						
8						

Petty Cash Voucher

No_____

Date _____

For what required

AMOUNT

£

Signature _____
Passed by _____

Petty Cash Voucher

No_____

Date _____

For what required

AMOUNT

£

Signature _____
Passed by _____

petty cash book..

Receipts	Date	Details	Voucher No.	Total Payment	Analysis columns					
					VAT					
£				£	£	£	£	£	£	£

petty cash book..

Receipts	Date	Details	Voucher No.	Total Payment	Analysis columns					
					VAT					
£				£	£	£	£	£	£	£

Dr. **Cash Book** Cr.

Date	Details	Folio	Cash	Bank	Date	Details	Folio	Cash	Bank
19			£	£	19			£	£

Dr. **Cash Book** Cr.

Date	Details	Folio	Discount allowed	Cash	Bank	Date	Details	Folio	Discount received	Cash	Bank
19			£	£	£	19			£	£	£

Pay Advice	Week		
payments	**deductions**		
	£		£
Basic pay		Income tax	
Overtime		National Insurance	
Bonus		Superannuation	
TOTAL GROSS PAY			
		TOTAL DEDUCTIONS	
Gross pay to date			
Taxable pay to date		TOTAL NET PAY	
Date	**Employee**	**Code**	Income tax to date
			National insurance to date

Pay Advice	Week		
payments	**deductions**		
	£		£
Basic pay		Income tax	
Overtime		National Insurance	
Bonus		Superannuation	
TOTAL GROSS PAY			
		TOTAL DEDUCTIONS	
Gross pay to date			
Taxable pay to date		TOTAL NET PAY	
Date	**Employee**	**Code**	Income tax to date
			National insurance to date

appendix 2

Wyvern (Office Products) Limited
Catalogue, Price List and Customer Discounts

Quality Quill
Catalogue and Price List

Pen & Ink Limited
Catalogue and Price List

Wyvern (Office Products) Limited
12 Lower Hyde Street Mereford MR1 2JF Tel (01605) 241851 Fax (01605) 241879

CATALOGUE AND PRICE LIST

WYVERN   OFFICE   FURNITURE

Own brand quality office furniture at economical prices. All items are made from textured finish high density melamine that is stain, heat and scratch resistant. All desks are 72 cm. high and all units have welded steel frames. All items available in light oak and teak melamine. (State colour choice when ordering.)

DESKS

Reference No.

Single   Pedestal   Desk with three box drawers all locking.

Large top	150 cm x 75 cm............................	F1006
Small top	120 cm x 65 cm............................	F1007

Double   Pedestal   Desk with two box drawers in each pedestal, all drawers lockable.

Medium top	135 cm x 75 cm............................	F1005

Executive   Double   Pedestal   Desk
L.H.S. is fitted with deep filing drawer and one box drawer.
R.H.S. has three drawers, all drawers lockable.

Extra large top	450 cm x 75 cm............................	F1003
Large top	150 cm x 75 cm............................	F1004

Secretarial   Unit
Large size single pedestal desk with secretarial return unit (105 cm x 48 cm), fitted complete with four stationery trays and tambour shutter.

Left hand unit	....	F1010
Right hand unit	....	F1011

TABLES

Office   Table
Eight sizes of office tables are available, all have detachable steel legs for ease of transport and storage. Can also be fitted with drawer.

Office table	75 cm x 75cm............................	F1022
Office table	120 cm x 60 cm............................	F1023
Office table	90 cm x 90 cm	F1024
Office table	120 cm x 75 cm............................	F1025
Office table	135 cm x 75 cm............................	F1026
Office table	150 cm x 75 cm............................	F1027
Office table	180 cm x 60 cm............................	F1028
Office table	180 cm x 75 cm............................	F1029

(If drawer is required, add D to reference number.)

Canteen Tables
A wide choice of these stackable steel frame tables in ten sizes.

Canteen table	60 cm x 60 cm	F1030
Canteen table	75 cm x 75 cm	F1031
Canteen table	90 cm x 60 cm	F1032
Canteen table	120 cm x 60 cm	F1033
Canteen table	90 cm x 90 cm	F1034
Canteen table	120 cm x 75 cm	F1035
Canteen table	135 cm x 75 cm	F1036
Canteen table	150 cm x 75 cm	F1037
Canteen table	180 cm x 60 cm	F1038
Canteen table	180 cm x 75 cm	F1039

Telephone Table
Useful table with bottom shelf to use in combination with any desk or by itself.

	40 cm x 70 cm	F1040

STORAGE   UNITS

Glass Front Bookcases
Glass front bookcases with glass sliding doors. Adjustable shelf height.

	90 cm x 30 cm x 160 cm high	F1060
	150 cm x 30 cm x 85 cm high	F1061

Open front bookcases

(Fixed shelves)	90 cm x 18 cm x 115 cm high	F1051
(Adjustable shelves)	90 cm x 21 cm x 120 cm high	F1052
(Adjustable shelves)	90 cm x 21 cm x 150 cm high	F1053
(Adjustable shelves)	90 cm x 21 cm x 195 cm high	F1054

Combination   Cupboards
Fitted with adjustable shelves and double lockable doors. The cupboards can be used in multiples to create a wall unit.

A 180 cm high unit with three shelves		F1055
A 100 cm high unit with one shelf...		F1056

Filing Cabinets
A matching range of filing cabinets in two, three and four drawer units
Designed to accommodate foolscap files. Lockable drawers.

4 drawer	134cm high.............................	F1070
3 drawer	103cm high.............................	F1071
2 drawer	71cm high................................	F1072

Flat Storage Units

An inexpensive way of storing Artwork, Keylines, Blueprints Plans and other oversize documents. Five reinforced drawers per unit.
Choice of 4 sizes available to take up to A1 papers.

100 cm x 41 cm x 68 cm	F1080
100 cm x 41 cm x 95 cm	F1081
45 cm x 41 cm x 60 cm	F1082
65 cm x 41 cm x 75 cm	F1083

Roll Store Units

A convenient and space saving method of filing rolled documents. Each unit has sixteen compartments and comes in three different sizes with a tambour roller door.

43 cm x 43 cm x 68 cm long	F1090
43 cm x 43 cm x 100 cm long	F1091
43 cm x 43 cm x 135 cm long	F1092

OFFICE   CHAIRS

Wood Framed Chairs

A quality hardwood framed chair, upholstered in tweed for comfort. Available in either teak or mahogany finish with peat or charcoal fabric. Ideal for reception or general office seating. (State finish choice when ordering.)

Wooden framed chair (no arms)	C1010
Wooden framed chair with arms	C1011
Wooden framed swivel armchair	C1012

Metal Framed Chairs

Welded steel frame in black with foam padded seat and back.
Available in peat or charcoal fabric finish.   (State finish choice when ordering.)

Metal frame chair (no arms)	C1020
Metal frame chair with arms	C1021

Metal Stacking Chairs

Welded steel frame with one piece polypropylene seat, available in grey, orange, charcoal or brown (State colour when ordering) C1025

Typist Posture Chair

All chairs have black enamelled steel 5 star bases fitted with heavy duty easy glide castors, manual height and back adjustment. Upholstered in either charcoal or peat.
(State colour when ordering)

Typist posture chair (no arms)	C1030
Typist posture chair with arms	C1031
Typist posture chair, gas lift	C1032
Typist posture, arms with gas lift	C1033

EXECUTIVE   CHAIRS

Quality made executive chairs which provide day long comfort. Each chair is craftsman made and upholstered in either black leather or charcoal or peat quality tweed. Chairs can either be fixed stainless steel frame based or five star chromed base with castors.

All chairs are standard 53 cm wide. (State colour of tweed when ordering.)

Low back leather, fixed base	....	C1040
High back, tweed, fixed base	....	C1041
Medium back, tweed, fixed base	....	C1042
Low back, tweed, fixed base	....	C1043
High back, leather, swivel base	....	C1044
Medium back, leather, swivel base	....	C1045
Low back, leather, swivel base	....	C1046
High back, tweed, swivel base	....	C1047
Medium back, tweed, swivel base	....	C1048
Low back, tweed, swivel base	....	C1049

THE "FISLEY" RANGE
Superior Quality Products at Competitive Prices

> *Fisley storage cabinets are excellent quality and stylish. These all steel cabinets are available in two finish colours, Coffee & Cream and Goose Grey.*
> *(State colour when ordering.)*

Filing   cabinets

All steel available with 2, 3 and 4 drawers, fitted with anti-tilt mechanism and lock.

Takes standard size foolscap suspension files.

Two Drawer	70 cm high	S1010
Three Drawer	100cmhigh...............................	S1011
Four Drawer	130cmhigh...............................	S1012

Storage   cupboards

All steel cupboards fitted with flush front doors, magnetic door catch and two point locking mechanisms.

Size	180 cm x 90 cm x 45 cm	S1020
Size	100 cm x 90 cm x 45 cm	S1021

Multidrawer   cabinets

Multidrawer cabinets provide the most versatile answer to information storage problems.

All models are mounted on black plinths except desk top cabinet.

All cabinets are 11 ins wide and 17 ins deep.

Series 12, Desk Top Five	5 cm drawers, 32 cm high	S1030
Series 29, Multidrawer Ten	5 cm drawers, 68 cm high	S1031
Series 29, Multidrawer Six	7.5 cm drawers, 68 cm high	S1032
Series 39, Multidrawer Fifteen	5 cm drawers, 95 cm high	S1033
Series 39, Multidrawer Nine	7.5 cm drawers, 95 cm high	S1034

THE WYVERN RANGE OF STATIONERY

PAPER

A great selection of quality cut products from one of the UK's leading paper manufacturers.

Sherman Paper

A symbol of elegance in this range of high quality water marked wove.
In 80 and 100 gsm weights, the perfect choice of paper to fulfill all business and promotional requirements.

The colour range offered is White, Dark blue, Amber, Light blue, Oyster, Buttermilk and Grey. (State colour when ordering.)

Paper is packed in smart black boxes with 500 sheets (1 ream) per box.

Sherman White wove	A4,80gsm	P1010
Sherman White wove	A4,100gsm	P1011
Sherman Coloured wove	A4,80gsm	P1012
Sherman Coloured wove	A4,100gsm	P1013
Sherman White, laid	A4,80gsm	P1014
Sherman White, laid	A4,100gsm	P1015
Sherman Coloured, laid	A4,80gsm	P1016
Sherman Coloured, laid	A4,100gsm	P1017

Sceptre Paper

A selection of cut paper for general office use, lightweight 45 gsm bank papers 70 and 80 gsm bond papers, 80 gsm copier bond and 70 gms duplicator paper.
In a variety of colours all packed in strong boxes of 500 sheets to protect paper
Colour range: Blue, Green, Pink and Yellow. (State colour when ordering.)

Sceptre Bank, White	A4, 45gsm	P1020
Sceptre Bank, Coloured	A4,45gsm	P1021
Sceptre Bond, White	A4,70gsm	P1022
Sceptre Bond, White	A4,85gsm	P1023
Sceptre Bond, Coloured	A4,70gsm	P1024
Sceptre Bond, Coloured	A4,85gsm	P1025
Sceptre Copier Bond, White	A4,80gsm	P1026
Sceptre Copier Bond, Coloured	A4,80gsm	P1027
Sceptre Duplicator, White	A4,70gsm	P1028
Sceptre Duplicator, Coloured	A4,70gsm	P1029

Fax Machine Rolls

We supply these high quality thermal paper rolls in two basic sizes to suit the following fourgroups:
FR1-399 A4, FR1-338 A4, FR1-316 A4, all 210 mm W x 100 m L with 25 mm core and FR1-396 A4 210
mm W x 100 m L with 50 mm core.
Check your machine against our Fax Roll. Packed in boxes of four per group.

Fax Roll	FR1-399A4	P1040
Fax Roll	FR1-338A4	P1041
Fax Roll	FR1-316A4	P1042
Fax Roll	FR1-396A4	P1043

Adding Machine Rolls

Quality wood-free paper rolls in three popular widths to suit most of today'sdesk-top adding machines.
Packed in boxes of twenty per group.

Machine Roll	57 mm x 57 mm Grade A	P1050
Machine Roll	57 mm x 86 mm Grade A	P1051
Machine Roll	57 mm x 70 mm Grade A	P1052
Machine Roll	37.5 mm x 35 mm Grade A	P1053
Machine Roll	70 mm x 70 mm GradeA	P1054

ENVELOPES

High quality envelopes to match the **Sherman** range of paper. Packed in boxes of 500.

Sherman matching self seal	wovewhite	E1010
Sherman matching self seal	wovecoloured	E1012
Sherman matching self seal	laidwhite	E1014
Sherman matching self seal	laidcoloured	E1016

Banker: Business gummed envelopes available in White and Brown Manilla, windowed and plain.
Packed in boxes of 1,000.

Brown manilla plain	90 mm x 150 mm	E1020
Brown manilla window	90 mm x 150 mm	E1021
White plain	90 mm x 150 mm	E1022
White window	90 mm x 150 mm	E1023
Brown manilla plain	110 mm x 160 mm	E1030
Brown manilla window	110 mm x 160 mm	E1031
White plain	110 mm x 160 mm	E1032
White window	110 mm x 160 mm	E1033
Brown manilla plain	100 mm x 220 mm	E1040
Brown manilla window	100 mm x 220 mm	E1041
White plain	100 mm x 220 mm	E1042
White window	100 mm x 220 mm	E1043

PENCILS

Gainsborough   'Chemi-sealed'   pencils available for both general and drawing office use. Packed in boxes of 12.

General Office	range: 4B to B, HB, H to 4H	W1010
Drawing Office	range: HB, B to 8B, H to 7H	W1011
Please quote hardness quality.		
General Office Rubber topped	HBonly......................................	W1012

Gainsborough   Automatic   pencils in both general office and professional quality; featuring fine line rapid refill cassette system. Professional, suitable for drawing office work, offers constant lead thickness range of 0.3, 0.5 & 0.9 mm.

General Office	packed in boxes of 10	W1020
Drawing Office	packedsingly..............................	W1021

ERASERS

Wipeout White Plastic Eraser	packed in boxes of 20	W1090
Suitable for paper or film.		

Felix range of Erasers

Standard white (for soft pencils)	packed in boxes of 10	W1091
Medium green (for H pencils)	packed in boxes of 20	W1092
Ink/pencil (for soft and ball pen)	packed in boxes of 20	W1093

PENS

Ball point pens available in two qualities.
Banmate 2000, long lasting tungsten carbide ball, and the famous *Rocoball*pen, the clear crystal barrel with medium point. Available in black, blue, red and green. (Packed in boxes of 12.)

Banmate 2000	finepoint...................................	W1030
Banmate 2000	mediumpoint.............................	W1031
Rocoball	....	W1032

Fibre Tip Marker Pens
Heavy duty felt tipped, ideal for display work. Available in waterproof ink and dry wipe form. Colour choice: Black, Blue, Red and Green. State colour when ordering.
(Packed in boxes of 12 except where specifically stated.)

Board Marker C61	hard wearing, chisel point, dry wipe marker	W1041
Board Marker B60	hard wearing, bullet point, permanent marker	W1042
Board Marker B61	hard wearing, bullet point, dry wipe marker	W1043
Board Marker C60	hard wearing, chisel point, permanent marker.......	W1040
Board Marker C60	hard wearing, chisel point, permanent marker........	W1040
Giant Board Marker C80	chisel point ,(packed 4 per box)	W1044
Giant Board Marker C81	chisel point dry wipe marker (4 per box)	W1045

Fibre Tip Highlighters

A superb range of board tip fluorescent ink highlighters for attracting attention to important points. Available in Yellow, Green, Orange, Pink, Blue and Red. (State colours when ordering.)

Single highlighter	packed 10 per box	W1050
Wallet of 4 different colours	Blue, Green, Orange, Red	W1051
Wallet of 6 different colours	Complete range..........................	W1052

CLEAR PLASTIC RULES

Graduated in both imperial and metric.

150 mm	clear plastic rule...........................	W1080
300 mm	clear plastic rule...........................	W1081
300 mm	clear shatterproof rule	W1082
450 mm	clear shatterproof rule	W1083

OFFICE   SUNDRIES

CORRECTION PAPER AND FLUID

Wippex Correction paper	50 strips.....................................	D1010
Wippex Correction fluid	available in white, yellow, blue, pink or green..............................	D1011
Wippex Thinner	....	D1012
Wippex Twin Set	Correction and thinner fluid	D1013

HOLE PUNCHES

Available in red or yellow. State colour when ordering.

Economy 2 hole punch	capacity 12 sheets.......................	H1010
Medium 2 hole punch	capacity 28 sheets.......................	H1012
Heavy Duty 2 and 4 hole punch	capacity 50 sheets.......................	H1013

STAPLERS

Available in Black and Red. State colour when ordering.

Mercury, pocket size	No. 25 staples.............................	M1010
Mars, standard arm	No. 56 staples.............................	M1012
Titan, long arm	No. 56 staples.............................	M1013
Hercules, heavy duty lever arm	No. 56 staples.............................	M1014
Electra 5000, electronic	240 volt power supply	M1015

STAPLES

Refill staples, 5000 per box	No25......................................	M1090
Refill staples, 5000 per box	No56......................................	M1091

PAPER   CLIPS

Full range covers three standard sizes, plain and coloured in green, red and blue.

State colour when ordering.

Small plain	packed in boxes of 1000	M1080
Medium plain	packed in boxes of 1000	M1081
Giant plain	packed in boxes of 100	M1082
Small coloured	packed in boxes of 1000	M1083
Medium coloured	packed in boxes of 1000	M1084
Giant coloured	packed in boxes of 100	M1085

Wyvern (Office Products) Limited
12 Lower Hyde Street Mereford MR1 2JF Tel (01605) 241851 Fax (01605) 241879

PRICE LIST

Catalogue Number	Pack Quantity	Price £	Catalogue Number	Pack Quantity	Price £
C1010	1	52.95	F1003	1	124.95
C1011	1	57.95	F1004	1	144.50
C1012	1	95.95	F1005	1	104.95
C1020	1	41.00	F1006	1	99.95
C1021	1	48.95	F1007	1	89.50
C1025	1	8.75	F1010	1	175.00
C1030	1	31.95	F1011	1	175.00
C1031	1	47.50	F1022	1	55.75
C1032	1	46.50	F1022D	1	64.75
C1033	1	63.25	F1023	1	58.50
C1040	1	142.50	F1023D	1	67.50
C1041	1	144.95	F1024	1	61.50
C1042	1	128.00	F1024D	1	70.50
C1043	1	122.95	F1025	1	65.50
C1044	1	169.50	F1025D	1	74.50
C1045	1	153.50	F1026	1	68.95
C1046	1	147.50	F1026D	1	77.95
C1047	1	149.95	F1027	1	76.25
C1048	1	133.00	F1027D	1	85.25
C1049	1	127.95	F1028	1	80.50
D1010	50 pack	1.20	F1028D	1	89.50
D1011	1	0.78	F1029	1	84.95
D1012	1	0.55	F1029D	1	93.95
D1013	1 set	1.20	F1030	1	29.95
E1010	500	29.95	F1031	1	34.50
E1012	500	30.95	F1032	1	36.25
E1014	500	29.95	F1033	1	42.50
E1016	500	30.95	F1034	1	47.75
E1020	1000	8.60	F1035	1	49.95
E1021	1000	10.95	F1036	1	53.95
E1022	1000	14.35	F1037	1	55.75
E1023	1000	16.50	F1038	1	55.75
E1030	1000	17.25	F1039	1	64.95
E1031	1000	21.20	F1040	1	53.95
E1032	1000	18.75	F1051	1	39.95
E1033	1000	29.15	F1052	1	49.95
E1040	1000	20.25	F1053	1	58.95
E1041	1000	24.95	F1054	1	67.95
E1042	1000	24.70	F1055	1	134.95
E1043	1000	30.95	F1056	1	104.95

Catalogue Number	Pack Quantity	Price £	Catalogue Number	Pack Quantity	Price £
F1060	1	95.95	P1029	500	6.25
F1061	1	99.95	P1040	4	33.00
F1070	1	159.95	P1041	4	40.00
F1071	1	139.95	P1042	4	33.00
F1072	1	124.50	P1043	4	36.00
F1080	1	114.95	P1050	20	4.00
F1081	1	144.95	P1051	20	10.95
F1082	1	69.95	P1052	20	7.75
F1083	1	79.95	P1053	20	4.50
F1090	1	41.95	P1054	20	10.75
F1091	1	45.95	S1010	1	89.95
F1092	1	48.95	S1011	1	94.95
H1010	1	2.80	S1012	1	99.95
H1012	1	7.95	S1020	1	99.95
H1013	1	19.45	S1021	1	89.95
M1010	1	1.35	S1030	1	29.95
M1012	1	6.25	S1031	1	49.95
M1013	1	20.65	S1032	1	39.95
M1014	1	79.99	S1033	1	72.95
M1015	1	74.95	S1034	1	72.95
M1080	1000	0.95	W1010	12	1.95
M1081	1000	1.60	W1011	12	3.95
M1082	100	0.45	W1012	12	2.25
M1083	1000	4.25	W1020	10	9.30
M1084	1000	6.40	W1021	1	1.85
M1085	100	2.25	W1030	12	0.85
M1090	5000	1.70	W1031	12	0.80
M1091	5000	0.90	W1032	12	1.25
P1010	500	10.60	W1040	12	8.25
P1011	500	12.60	W1041	12	7.85
P1012	500	11.60	W1042	12	8.25
P1013	500	13.60	W1043	12	7.85
P1014	500	10.60	W1044	4	6.60
P1015	500	12.60	W1045	4	6.10
P1016	500	11.60	W1050	10	7.75
P1017	500	13.60	W1051	4	3.10
P1020	500	4.40	W1052	6	4.65
P1021	500	3.95	W1080	1	0.18
P1022	500	6.25	W1081	1	0.35
P1023	500	7.50	W1082	1	0.40
P1024	500	5.60	W1083	1	1.20
P1025	500	7.10	W1090	20	7.95
P1026	500	3.25	W1091	10	3.75
P1027	500	4.95	W1092	20	4.15
P1028	500	6.25	W1093	20	5.30

WYVERN (OFFICE PRODUCTS) LIMITED

CUSTOMER DISCOUNT LIST

Note: this does not form part of the Catalogue but is kept in the Accounts Office

---

Wyvern (Office Products) Limited

Customer   discount   allowed

Greenhouse Supplies, London	5%
Harper & Co., Oxford	5%
J Smith & Son Ltd, Mereford	5%
S W White, Southport	5%
A Black, Blackpool	10%
P Woodhouse, Leeds	10%
Enock Ltd, Swindon	10%
S Smith Ltd, London	15%
A H Shatterford, Hirmington	15%
Carpminster College, Carpminster	15%
Mereford College, Mereford	15%
Blackheath Ltd, London W7	15%

EXTRACTS FROM STATIONERY CATALOGUE

Quality   Quill
215   West   Street
Mereford   MR2   6PQ

Catalogue No.	Item	Size	Price (£)
	OFFICE MACHINERY		
	Hole Punch		
210014	Economy two hole	12 sheet capacity	2.55
210124	Medium duty two hole	28 sheet capacity	6.40
210421	Heavy duty two/four hole	50 sheet capacity	18.10
	Staplers *(Juno range)*		
200162	Junior	No. 25 staples	1.20
200184	Standard arm	No. 56 staples	5.90
200186	Heavy duty	No. 56 staples	73.40
200201	Long arm	No. 56 staples	18.40
	STATIONERY		
	Pencils *(Mercury range, available in all standard hardness numbers)*		
100204	General office range (4B to 4H)		1.80 per box of 12
100205	Drawing office range (HB to 7H)		3.60 per box of 12

(state hardness number when ordering)

Catalogue No.	Item	Size	Price (£)
	Ball point pens *(available in black, blue, red and green)*		
100501	Vic fine point		0.80 per box of 12
100502	Vic medium point		0.75 per box of 12
100503	Roco Ball clear barrel medium point		1.15 per box of 12

(state colour when ordering)

Catalogue No.	Item	Size	Price (£)
	Paper *Leda A4 business paper*		
90012	White Bank	45 gsm	4.20 per 500
90022	White Duplicator	70 gsm	6.35 per 500
90032	White Copier Bond	80 gsm	3.20 per 500
90042	White Bond	85 gsm	7.60 per 500
90013	Coloured Bank	45 gsm	3.80 per 500
90023	Coloured Duplicator	70 gsm	6.10 per 500
90033	Coloured Copier Bond	80 gsm	4.80 per 500
90043	Coloured Bond	85 gsm	6.95 per 500

Colours: light blue, cream, orange, grey, green, (state colours when ordering)

Envelopes

80014	Brown manilla plain	220 mm x 100 mm	9.95 per 500
80015	Brown manilla window	220 mm x 110 mm	11.95 per 500
80004	Brown manilla plain	155 mm x 90 mm	4.00 per 500
80020	White plain	220 mm x 110 mm	11.85 per 500
80021	White window	220 mm x 110 mm	14.95 per 500
80028	White plain	155 mm x 90 mm	6.95 per 500

EXTRACTS FROM STATIONERY CATALOGUE

Pen & Ink Ltd 12 Haven Road Mereford MR1 85T

Catalogue No.	Item	Size	Price (£)
Enigma range of office paper (A4 size)			
A73	Bank white	45 gsm	4.60 per ream
A74	Bank coloured	45 gsm	4.05 per ream
A83	Duplicator white	70 gsm	6.45 per ream
A80	Copier Bond white	80 gsm	3.50 per ream
A81	Copier Bond coloured	80 gsm	5.15 per ream
A70	Bond white	85 gsm	7.75 per ream
A71	Bond coloured	85 gsm	7.40 per ream
Nimrod Business gummed envelopes			
E16	Brown manilla plain	220 mm x 110 mm	11.05 per 500
E16A	Brown manilla window	220 mm x 110 mm	13.25 per 500
E15	White plain	220 mm x 110 mm	13.00 per 500
E15A	White window	220 mm x 110 mm	15.25 per 500

Sabrina chemical sealed pencils

| P101 | General office | range 4B to 4H | 2.05 per box of 12 |
| P102 | Drawing office | range HB to 7H | 4.05 per box of 12 |

Eros carbide ball point pens

C31	Fine point black		0.90 per box of 12
C32	Fine point blue		0.90 per box of 12
C41	Medium point black		0.85 per box of 12
C42	Medium point blue		0.85 per box of 12
C43	Medium point red		0.85 per box of 12
C44	Medium point green		0.85 per box of 12

Paper Punchers (two hole)

A214	Hole Master	12 sheet capacity	3.10
A216	Medium duty Hole Master	30 sheet capacity	8.50
A218	Heavy duty Hole Master	60 sheet capacity	20.95

Staplers

551	Juno Junior	No. 25 staples	1.55
554	Juno Standard arm	No. 56 staples	6.55
558	Juno Heavy duty	No. 56 staples	81.50
564	Juno Long arm	No. 56 staples	21.95

notes

index